How Canadians Communicate II

How Canadians Communicate II

Media, Globalization, and Identity

Edited by David Taras, Maria Bakardjieva, and Frits Pannekoek

UNIVERSITY OF
CALGARY
PRESS

University of Calgary Press
2500 University Drive NW
Calgary, Alberta
Canada T2N 1N4
www.uofcpress.com

Library and Archives Canada Cataloguing in Publication

How Canadians communicate II : media, globalization, and identity / edited by David Taras, Maria Bakardjieva, and Frits Pannekoek.

Includes bibliographical references and index.
ISBN 978-1-55238-224-0

1. Mass media – Social aspects – Canada.   2. Information technology – Social aspects – Canada.   3. Communication and culture – Canada.   I. Taras, David, 1950–   II. Bakardjieva, Maria, 1959–   1947–   III. Pannekoek, Frits,

P92.C3H68 2007   302.230971   C2007-900608-6

The University of Calgary Press acknowledges the support of the Alberta Foundation for the Arts for this published work. We acknowledge the financial support of the Government of Canada through the Book Publishing Industry Development Program (BPIDP) for our publishing activities. We acknowledge the financial support of the Canada Council for the Arts for our publishing program.

Printed and bound in Canada by Transcontinental Printing
∞ This book is printed on Rolland Enviro 100 acid free paper

Cover design by Melina Cusano
Page design and typesetting by Garet Markvoort, zijn digital

Contents

Media, Globalization, and Identity in Canada: An Introduction

DAVID TARAS

This volume is the second in a series entitled *How Canadians Communicate*. The first volume, which was published in 2003, was for the most part an industry-by-industry assessment of the state of Canada's cultural industries. The reports on the health of Canada's cultural industries were largely gloomy and filled with dire predictions. Television drama, music, libraries and archives, and publishing, among other sectors, were described as needing emergency care, as gasping for survival. The tone was one of sadness, exasperation, and defiance. This latest volume focuses on how global forces are shaping Canadian media, culture, and identity. We have undertaken a new examination of Canada's media health, but the emphasis is on how Canada is adapting to the new cultural horizons of globalization. We also look at how new media forms such as blogs, video games, and peer-to-peer networks are changing the ways in which Canadians communicate. The architecture of Canadian cultural life has changed dramatically in the last decade. iPods, personal video recorders, personal messaging, web sites, BlackBerrys, plug and play technologies, and, of course, copyright are crucial to this new structure.

Canada is now at the vortex of global culture, the most international of countries. Cities such as Toronto, Montreal, and Vancouver have become true global cities reflecting a diversity found in few other places. Indeed, in 2005 Canada ranked as the sixth most globalized country in the world according to a globalization index created by *Foreign Policy* magazine (Kearney 2005,

52–60). The measures used were based on trade, travel, use of technology, and personal contacts, among other factors. Canada was far ahead of countries such as France, Germany, Australia, and Japan.

The Canadian experience is propelled by a unique constellation of forces – the size of our immigrant population, our acceptance and encouragement of multiple identities, the openness of our economy, and the belief in "Charter" values with their emphasis on freedom of expression and equality. In a classic essay, Northrop Frye has described Canada's long journey from being a frontier society at the periphery of world events to being the "new global Switzerland" – the great new meeting place (Frye 1982, 70).

I will argue that at least four distinct but interrelated global developments have transformed the Canadian media landscape in profound ways. These are Americanization, the emergence of powerful regional and global treaties and institutions that have taken some aspects of sovereignty away from nation-states, the new global economy created by advances in digital technologies, and corporate concentration of media industries on a global scale. These four developments, among others, have shifted the boundaries so dramatically that little of the old landscape remains.

Americanization

The first globalization that Canada has had to contend with is Americanization.

Thomas Jefferson once observed that "every man has two countries – his own and France." Of course, much has changed since the early nineteenth century when Jefferson made these remarks. Today the sentiment would be that every person has two countries – their own and the United States. American culture and American cultural products are now so pervasive, so deeply ingrained, so much an inescapable part of virtually every cultural landscape that Americanism itself is a key engine of globalization. Indeed, European commentators such as Rob Kroes view Americanization as the twentieth century's "great modernist project of trans-nationalism" (Kroes 2000, 6). With ideas about political citizenship based on an acceptance of a way of life rather than on hard religious or ethnic identities – consent rather than descent – the American project has challenged old ideas and old regimes and indeed spurred their collapse.

If American power were only economic and military then that would be one thing. But American influence is also based on a vast cultural matrix. American films, TV programs, music, literature, sports, and theme parks have been, one can argue, the principal challenge to national and local cultures across the globe. Part of the reason for this is that Hollywood entertainment conglomerates have been able to maintain a tight stranglehold over distribution, particularly with regards to films and DVDs, and they enjoy economies of scale that allow them to discount their products in foreign markets (Epstein 2005). Small wonder that an important collection of essays on European attitudes towards the United States is simply titled *Within the U.S. Orbit: Small National Cultures vis-à-vis the United States* (Kroes 1992).

No other country is as much in the American line of fire as is Canada. We share a common border, a common economic space, and, except for Quebec, a common language.

Indeed, European observers once used the term "Canadianization" to describe the degree to which one culture could be taken over and occupied by another culture. Canadianization was among the worst fates that a country could endure and had to be resisted at all costs. For those who fear that Canada is unable to fend off Americanization, the facts on the ground speak volumes; 95 per cent of the movies that we watch are American. So are 84 per cent of the retail sales of sound recordings, 85 per cent of the prime time drama that we watch on English-language television and 75 per cent on French language TV and almost 85 per cent of magazine sales at newsstands (Schultz 2003, 30).

In a seminal article, John Meisel, one of Canada's leading academic thinkers, once theorized that American cultural influence is so complete that "inside every Canadian, there is in fact an American" (Meisel 1986, 152). The degree of American-ness might vary from person to person depending on their values, education, and adherence to mass culture, but the harsh reality is that with the exception of our legendary devotion to hockey, at the level of mass culture Canadians differ very little from Americans. We watch the same TV, listen to the same music, go to the same movies, and eat at the same fast food restaurants. Canadian literature, art, music, TV productions, and films tend to attract a much smaller and more elite audience. Pessimists might argue that Canadian culture remains a minority culture in Canada, one fiercely and deeply cherished, but a minority culture nonetheless.

Meisel would later refine his original thesis, arguing that Canadian cultural institutions had spawned their own strong networks and constituencies and were more enduring and vibrant than he suggested in his first account (Meisel 1996). There was, however, still cause for worry. Although Canadians have a voracious appetite for Canadian cultural products, much depends on whether Canadians have an independent cultural sector to turn to. In the first edition of *How Canadians Communicate* almost all of our authors contended that our industries were either shrinking or evaporating. Moreover, U.S.

media conglomerates largely set the table and decided the seats that Canadians could occupy. The question was whether we had the energy, imagination, and will power to fully occupy these spaces.

A number of prominent scholars have argued, not the least being Richard Schultz and Christopher Dornan in this volume, that the torrent of American cultural products does not prevent Canadians from acting decisively in the cultural sector. "The fault is not in the global stars but in ourselves," to quote Schultz. In fact, Schultz goes as far as to argue that American media have had little effect on Canadian values. Not only do the two countries seem to have less in common than they did ten or twenty years ago but they seem to be pushing away from each other. This is essentially pollster Michael Adams' "fire and ice" hypothesis, the notion that the two countries have different trajectories and spin on different axes (Adams 2003).

On one level, there is the argument that the greater the presence of American media, the stronger the resistance by Canadians to American values. But on another level, it may be that the United States no longer exercises as strong a pull. A number of observers have noted that the United States has changed dramatically since the 1990s and has less in common with the values of other western democracies. John Micklethwait and Adrian Wooldridge of the *Economist* point out that the "centre of political gravity" in the United States has moved far to the right of what it once was and that Americans are becoming increasingly more conservative and far more religious than Canadians or Europeans (Micklethwait and Wooldridge 2004). The value divide seems to be widening.

A close reading of Adams' book, *Fire and Ice*, suggests that regional variations within the United States may offer at least part of the explanation for why the two countries seem to be moving apart. While we have much in common with "Canada's America," those parts of the United States with which we do business or travel to as tourists, Canadians have less in common with the values of the Republican heartland: states where the culture of religion, guns, private medicine, prisons, and populist morality seem to dominate. As the balance of power and population shifts to the south, Americans become less recognizable to Canadians and indeed Europeans. On one level this may make life with the Americans far more difficult, but on another level we may not have to worry nearly as much about our cultural sovereignty.

Global Governance

The second great factor that has influenced Canada's development is the emergence of international institutions that have to varying degrees subverted

the authority and sovereignty of the nation-state. The crucial point here is that
Canada has played a critical role in the development of virtually all of these
institutions. The United Nations, NATO, GATT, then its successor the WTO,
the World Bank, the IMF, and, of course, NAFTA all bear a significant Canadian imprint. The principal architect of Canada's role was Lester Pearson,
who served first as Secretary of State for External Affairs and then as Prime
Minister. His idealistic view was that Canada could be a bridge between the
United States and Europe and between the developed and underdeveloped
worlds. "Middlepowermanship" would give Canada a vital role to play – a
historic mission. Internationalism through the United Nations, and especially
through peacekeeping, would be a defining feature of Canadian identity.

The "Pearsonian internationalism" that dominated the 1950s and 1960s,
however, gave way to Pierre Trudeau's "third option" in the 1970s and early
1980s. Trudeau believed that Canada had three choices in its relations with
the United States; relations could remain the same, Canada could move
closer to the United States or Canada could move further away by developing
global relationships as a counterweight to American influence. By choosing
the third option, Canada could blunt American power by bringing the combined weight of other countries and institutions to bear against the Americans. While Trudeau chose the third option, his successor Brian Mulroney
chose the second – greater integration with the United States. Nonetheless,
aspects of the third option remain.

In the cultural sphere, the third option strategy is a double-edged sword.
The same international trade policies that can bring international power
to bear against the Americans can also be used to limit Canadian cultural
expression. For example, the WTO ruled against Canadian policies that
sought to limit the use of "split runs" by American magazine publishers. In
2005, Canada amended the copyright bill in order to comply with the World
Intellectual Property Treaty, succumbing, one can argue, to powerful international pressures at the expense of domestic considerations.

As R.H. Thomson told the House of Commons Standing Committee on
Canadian Heritage,

... public policies are increasingly at risk from the restrictions written into international trade agreements.... The political repercussions of trade liberalization ... [are]
that the power of my elected government ... [is] diminished, and my single democratic
vote is downgraded. The repercussion ... for an artist is that the cultural measures that
successive Canadian governments have put in place for the last two generations ... are
regarded by the trade liberalization lobby as either trade barriers or trade distorting
subsidies.

The critical point is that Canada has embraced institutionalized globalization to an extraordinary degree and that sovereignty in the cultural realm can
be limited in critical ways.

Digital Globalization

A third strand of globalization is the "flat world" that has been created by
advances in digital technology. While much of the globe still remains mired
in poverty and is largely shut out of and shut off from the hyper-connectivity
of the digital age, most Canadians live in a world of "manufactured magic"
(Mosco 2004, 41). We routinely traverse the great divides of time and distance
with an ease unknown and unimaginable to those who lived before us. We
can chat, play games, or do business with people who live on the other side
of the globe by a simple touch of the keyboard. According to Todd Gitlin,
technology has created a "relentless horizontal momentum" that is "irrevers-
ible" (Mosco 2004, 99). The practical reality, as the *New York Times*' Thomas
Friedman has pointed out, is that production no longer takes place in a single
city, region, or economy but can be divided up and parcelled out between
places as distant in time, space, and culture as Brampton, Beijing, and Ban-
galore (Friedman 2005). The vertical barriers erected by nation-states, the old
loyalties and trade patterns, are being challenged as never before. Our borders
are infinitely porous.

Another aspect of digital globalization is that all media are merging with
all other media. Or to put it more precisely, all media are converging on and
through the Internet. One can download music, games, photos, articles from
newspaper web sites, archives, films, and TV programs on the Internet and
even on cell phones. Whereas ten or fifteen years ago broadcast and telecommunications were distinct realms, these boundaries have long since faded.
Major media conglomerates in Canada such as Rogers and Quebecor have
merged content and hardware and operate through multiple platforms.

The federal government's reaction to the realities of convergence has been
slow at best. While countries such as Australia and the United Kingdom have
created a single communications Act that governs all aspects of communications, Canada still bears the weight of three separate Acts; the Broadcasting Act, the Telecommunications Act, and the Canadian Radio-Television
and Telecommunications Commission Act. Moreover, the federal regulator,
the CRTC, has decided that it will not regulate Internet activity despite the
fact that broadcasting on the Internet is an everyday reality. Clearly, the old

assumptions and the old institutions are crumbling whether the federal government likes it or not.

While digital globalization is now deeply embedded in many aspects of economic and social life, strong winds are also blowing in the opposite direction. The Canadian philosopher John Ralston Saul has written a devastating critique of market-driven corporate globalization. According to Saul, international trade agreements and institutions became the sharp end of the stick for expanding the definition of trade to include not only goods and investments but also services and employees. The new rules were designed to help corporations move into new markets and areas of the economy. Moreover, the discipline of the marketplace would be imposed on economies across the globe. The theory was that new global medicine, while painful at first for many countries to swallow, would usher in a new era of global prosperity. According to Saul, what has occurred instead is "the collapse of globalism" (Saul 2005).

What is remarkable and indeed shocking for Saul is that the "Globalization movement has produced myriad market-oriented international agreements at the global level and not a single binding agreement on the other areas of human intercourse – work conditions, taxation, child labour, health and so on" (Saul 2005, 25). Moreover, market-driven globalization has failed to deliver the prosperity that was to be at the end of the rainbow. Gross domestic products (GDPs), the chief barometer of economic health, have stagnated in the developed world at rates far below what they were prior to the new era of corporate-driven globalization, and the economies in much of Latin America and Africa are in decline and in some places they have imploded. The world's poorest countries are in disarray and despair.

Globalism's political edifice also seems to be cracking. Voters in France and the Netherlands recently voted to reject a constitution for the European Union that would have imposed a common social and foreign policy. The United States, still reeling from the events of 9/11, is increasingly turning in on itself. Americans have become more fiercely patriotic, more suspicious of their neighbours and trade partners, and less open to the world. Security has become the new imperative overshadowing other global considerations.

There is also evidence that despite the marvels of the Internet and the imperatives of the new digital economy, we are less aware of foreign cultures and events than was the case a generation ago. The high cost of maintaining foreign news bureaus has meant that news organizations provide less coverage of international issues and developments than was previously the case. A cynic might argue that if it were not for car bombings in Baghdad, the horror of earthquakes and tsunamis, and outbreaks of global flu epidemics, we would receive little information at all.

Corporate Concentration

A fourth aspect of globalization, one that is linked to deregulation and trade liberalization, is the emergence particularly in the cultural sphere of a handful of vast corporate conglomerates. Companies such as Disney, Time Warner, Bertelsmann, the News Corporation, Sony, Viacom, and NBC Universal together have a stranglehold over much of the world's cultural production. Although they are fierce competitors, they work together to control and coordinate the global distribution of films, music, TV programs, and DVDs. In the media world, size does matter. If one takes TV, for example, the American networks enjoy economies of scale that allow them to sell TV programs at prices far below the costs of production. As Canadian TV executives have long known, it costs far less to buy a TV show off the shelf in Hollywood than to produce a Canadian program from scratch. Small wonder, then, that our airwaves, and those of so many other countries, are dominated by shows such as *Law & Order*, *The Simpsons*, *Desperate Housewives*, *Lost*, and *Grey's Anatomy*.

The existence of giant conglomerates also means that for Canadians at least the media traffic is almost all in one direction. Attempts to sell Canadian TV programs in the United States, an essential requirement if Canadian TV programs are to be profitable, invariably come up against the high walls created by the vertical integration of American media conglomerates. Increasingly American TV networks air programs made by their own studios and have little need to look for shows produced beyond the confines of their own corporate family, let alone beyond the borders of their own country. For all of the hoopla about globalization, the American market is as tightly sealed as it ever has been. Without access to these revenues, producing TV programs for the Canadian domestic market makes little economic sense.

The American scholar Joseph Nye has described globalization as resembling a complex chess game played on a number of different levels at the same time (Nye 2002). Nation-states change their shape as they go from one level or set of issues to another. In some areas, nation-states have the power to exercise considerable authority; criminal law, education, cities, taxes, policing, health care, etc. On other levels, power is both muted and limited. International monetary and investment agreements, the dissemination and adoption of new technologies, interest rate policies set in Washington or by European bankers, the price of oil and other commodities, the cost of airline travel, etc., condition if not dictate the actions or more precisely the reactions of governments.

With regard to the mass media, Ottawa can only move some pieces on the chessboard. It can support public broadcasters, subsidize publishers, set Canadian content regulations for TV programs or radio, limit foreign ownership, and pass laws regulating copyright. But the federal government can only maintain certain key footholds. When it comes to Internet broadcasting, the grey and black markets for satellite television and radio, an international film distribution system that sidelines Canadian films, the downloading of music from offshore providers, or the unrelenting flood of American cultural products, the Canadian government seems to have little if any control.

Optimists and Pessimists

If there is a dividing line within this collection it is between optimists and pessimists. The optimists believe that Canada has all of the tools that it needs to create its own cultural space and that failures in media policy are the result of a lack of will and imagination. These contributors blame Ottawa for allowing great cultural institutions such as the CBC to languish, for not giving the CRTC the instruments that it needs to monitor and shape broadcasting and telecommunications policy and for giving too much emphasis to the industrial aspects of culture rather than to the democratic and nation-building ones. The federal government has ignored both the harsh realities and the splendid opportunities brought by the new communications era. The pessimists take a much gloomier view. They argue that Canada has few levers with which to control the onrushing tide of media change. In the new world of iPods, video games, digital television, satellite radio, and the selling of databases, the old structures on which national cultures were based simply won't work.

The lead article in the first section of the book has been written by Ken Goldstein, one of Canada's leading experts on the mass media. Goldstein describes the vast changes that have shaped the media landscape as we have gone from a regulatory regime based on a scarcity of signals to one that has to cope with an almost endless cornucopia of audience choices. Goldstein's assumption is that if we knew at the beginning of the broadcasting era what we know now, we would have created a very different media system.

Audience fragmentation, which Goldstein sees as the primary engine of media change, has smashed the old edifice in irreparable ways. For Goldstein, the effects of media and audience fragmentation permeate the culture.

Investing in high quality programming has become risky. The boundaries of taste and decency have been stretched because shock and sensationalism are needed in order to grab viewers' attention. The shared experiences that are so critical to creating a common culture are disappearing. Moreover, corporate concentration has increased as media conglomerates have had to expand in order to "re-aggregate" fragments. For Goldstein, it is now time to ask hard questions and make hard decisions about the basic rules that govern the media system.

Hard questions are also asked by Richard Schultz of McGill University. While Schultz believes that the key solutions regarding our media future rest solely in our hands, he also feels that Canadian media policy is mired in indecision, ineptitude, and hypocrisy. For all of the rhetoric about Americanization and globalization, Canadians only have themselves to blame for a media system that is failing them. Schultz gives three examples – magazines, media concentration, and Canadian drama – where tougher or more imaginative domestic policies could make a critical difference. As one example of how new and innovative policies could alter the media equation to the benefit of Canadian viewers, Schultz suggests that the "benefits" tax from the sale of television licences that is imposed by the CRTC could go to the Canadian Television Fund to boost Canadian programming.

In an equally eloquent and hard-hitting article, Christopher Dornan contends that fear of foreign control is used as an excuse by Canadian media corporations that nonetheless flood the airwaves with American programming. We need not fear foreign investors if we can be assured that they will play by rules that can benefit Canadians. Dornan gives the example of *Reader's Digest*, an American owned company that fills its magazines with made-in-Canada copy and creates high-end jobs in the country, as the model of what foreign-owned companies can do in Canada, given the right conditions and incentives.

But opponents of foreign ownership are suspicious and skeptical. They argue that large vertically integrated global media conglomerates such as NBC-Universal and Disney have little interest in producing Canadian TV programs or music and are more than a match for government regulators whom they could easily fend off with teams of lawyers and the threat of long, drawn-out court battles. They argue that inviting in the behemoths would be globalization on their terms rather than ours. Dornan is optimistic, however, that we can find the right formulas that are needed to become global in ways that will serve Canadian interests and identity.

For Bart Beaty and Rebecca Sullivan, Canadian broadcasting is not international enough. In their view, Canadians are more than capable of finding

Canadian content on the airwaves and need to be exposed to the diversity of programming that the world offers. The two University of Calgary scholars echo Dornan's concern that a handful of Canadian broadcasters use cultural protectionism as a lever to enhance their own businesses. The goal of broadcasting should be to create a truly public space, and this includes real globalization. If we are serious then we should not be "criminalizing Portuguese soccer" or preventing Italian Canadians from receiving TV channels from Italy.

The final article in this first section is by Marc Raboy and David Taras, both of whom served as expert advisors to the House of Commons Standing Committee on Canadian Heritage during its two-year-long study of the Canadian broadcasting system. Raboy and Taras contend that public broadcasting remains an essential instrument for achieving cultural goals and indeed for maintaining the public square that is so essential to a democracy. Moreover, the CBC is at once the most Canadian broadcaster, airing the most Canadian programming during its broadcast day, and at the same time, it is the most international, offering a steady diet of international news and documentaries.

Raboy and Taras argue that public broadcasting in Canada may be close to taking its last gasps. Decades of budget cutbacks, and decisions by the CRTC to keep the public broadcaster from participating in the burgeoning and lucrative world of cable TV (except for all-news channels, *Newsworld* and *RDI*), have taken a heavy toll. Two charts tell the story. The first shows that Canada is close to the bottom among developed countries in its expenditures on public broadcasting. The second points out that there is a strong link between revenues and audience share. Public broadcasters that receive substantial funding, such as those in countries like Denmark, Germany, Italy, and the United Kingdom, dominate the airwaves. Audience fragmentation does not occur to nearly the same degree when public broadcasters are well funded.

The volume's second section, entitled *The Quest for Identity*, is substantially different from the first section. Gone is the certainty that Canada's fate in the cultural sphere remains in our own hands. Articles dealing with how ordinary citizens navigate and use the Internet, the advent of blogs as a new form of life writing, the dramatic changes that have shaken the music industry, and the new place and power of video games suggest that control by Canadians is illusory at best. Canadians can adapt, resist, find niches and toeholds, and debate how children in particular can be protected from commercial exploitation and exposure to salacious sex and violence, but these are at best small Canadian islands in a vast and turbulent global sea. The room for national expres-

sion seems to be far smaller and more curtailed in the arenas dominated by
new media technologies than in the regulated worlds of the old media.

Maria Bakardjieva's contribution takes the themes of media, identity,
and globalization into the personal worlds of Canadian Internet users. She
describes the everyday practices of these users and the ways in which they
draw on global resources to continuously re-invigorate and re-negotiate their
identities. The Internet can serve as an agent of personal empowerment and
allow people to construct and share their experiences in a global context.
The story is a hopeful one. If anything, it replays Schultz's motif with a twist:
"The *hope* is not in the global stars but in ourselves." But the vital link is
between the personal and the global. National meeting places and filters are
bypassed.

While the same can largely be said for bloggers, a distinct Canadian blogosphere has emerged – one increasingly tied to Canadian media and politics. The most prominent Canadian blogs seem to be those written by leading pundits such as Paul Wells, Andrew Coyne, Warren Kinsella, Norman
Spector, and Antonia Zerbisias. These individuals already have a significant
public following and blogging has allowed them to magnify their influence
and interact more directly with readers. While big names seem to dominate
the Canadian blogosphere, there are a host of others who were previously
unknown and who have built followings from scratch. Popular political blogs
include *Small Dead Animals, Angry in the Great White North, Calgary Grit,*
and *The Tory Bloggers,* to name but a few. Beyond the political universe there
are literally thousands of Canadian bloggers who comment and post notices
on a myriad of topics. Michael Keren has drawn from this larger pool in order
to ask whether there is a Canadian way of blogging.

The blog that he examines is one written by a woman baby boomer, a child
of the 1960s, who lives a quiet life in the country tending to her cats and her
garden. She not only pays little heed to news events but has actively retreated
from them. Yet in her own way she is both an onlooker and participant in the
culture that surrounds her. Keren suggests that the boundaries that she draws
are in their own way very Canadian. The action occurs elsewhere, but its
reverberations are felt even by the endearing cat lady.

While Keren's cat lady lives far from the storms of global change, the
Canadian music industry has been jolted by a series of shock waves. Richard
Sutherland and Will Straw describe the extent to which the computer has
transformed the industry not only because of illegal downloading but because
it offers listeners many competing forms of entertainment. Instant messaging,
gaming, and surfing have taken listeners away from music as much as they

have taken viewers away from TV. The great irony, however, is that while the music industry has driven advances in computer technology (iPods and ISPs) these same technologies have weakened the industry generally and in the case of the Canadian industry have jeopardized its very existence.

The Canadian industry is caught in a pincer movement from which it seems to have no escape. On one side, a handful of corporate giants dominate global production. Their Canadian operations concentrate on marketing American sounds rather than developing Canadian talent. To make matters worse, distribution is increasingly in the hands of non-music companies such as Wal-Mart and Amazon that are so large that they can smother or co-opt any competition. On the other side, Internet-savvy consumers can get the cheapest prices by buying compilations from either legal or pirate Asian or European distributors. While there are glimmers of hope – the *Canadian Idol* phenomenon, enterprises such as *Star Academe*, and a vibrant "indie" sector – Sutherland and Straw ask whether under these conditions the music industry is capable of conveying any meaningful cultural identity.

In the last article in this section, Stephen Kline, a scholar at Simon Fraser University who has written extensively on mass media and its effects on children, charts the development of the video game industry and the debate that it has generated among concerned parents in particular. Originally a by-product of the computer "hacking" culture of the 1970s, gaming has now surpassed the film industry in annual sales. Microsoft, which released its 360 console in late 2005, has predicted that there will be a billion gamers in the next generation. Moreover, video games are no longer confined to teens but attract a large number of people over fifty. In fact, almost 20 per cent of those who are over fifty played video games in 2004 (Chapman 2005, C1).

As Kline points out, video games are multimedia extravaganzas that incorporate aspects of film, literature, music, and art. Some are wonders of technological and artistic imagination. While some scholars laud the ability of games to sharpen the cognitive skills of children, opponents warn that for some users the combination of fantasy and realism has an intoxicating quality and the games become both an addiction and an escape. Moreover, a large number of games are "gorific"; they depict battlegrounds of various kinds where killing by gangsters, snipers, or terrorists is rewarded. Their texture is dark and forbidding and death is everywhere. To the horror of many parents, these games have become the neighbourhood playground for many children and adolescents. While one might argue that parents are to blame for allowing violent video games into the lives of their children, the ability of governments to stem this particular global flood seems limited at best.

The last section of the book is entitled *The Struggle for Control*. These articles describe the clash among governments, citizens, interest groups, and global institutions to set agendas and create new legal regimes. Two articles, one by Graham Longford and the other by Sheryl Hamilton, deal with the contentious issue of copyright. Longford describes the high stakes battle over music downloading. On one side is the Canadian Recording Industry Association (CRIA), which argues that file sharing is tantamount to theft and does irreparable harm both to artists and to the music industry. The opposing view is that music is "a public resource for the common good" and not the exclusive property of mega corporations who seek to make exorbitant profits. According to Longford, the battle over the right to "rip, mix, and burn" is in essence a battle over who owns culture generally. There are important Canadian players on both sides of the question.

Sheryl Hamilton has a slightly different view. In her analysis, global forces and Canadian values clash in fundamental ways. The tension is between an emerging "global matrix of legislation and reciprocity" that serves the interests of global corporations and Canadian courts that have interpreted the law in ways that recognize and protect the rights of citizens and consumers. While the emerging global legal regime has become an increasingly important part of the communications landscape, it is not clear that the values that it espouses coincide with Canadian values. The major issue is whose values will bend to the will of the other.

For Frits Pannekoek and his colleagues, Canada's failure to construct a national digital information infrastructure to enhance knowledge creation and communicate Canadian identity is partly due to our own negligence and partly the result of powerful international forces. A main culprit is corporate concentration. Control by a handful of corporations has meant that prices for journals and digital archives have skyrocketed to the point where they have threatened the viability of libraries. They have given priority to medical and scientific journals from which they can make the most profit while neglecting humanities and social science journals. Moreover, Canadian publications and archives are at the margins in international collections.

The article also describes how the Patriot Act in the United States and the American insistence on maintaining an embargo against certain countries has the potential to both limit Canadian sovereignty and hamper the exchange of scientific information. In particular, the need for Canadians to comply with the Patriot Act in order to do business with Americans may bring a host of new problems and concerns. The issue, to again paraphrase Schultz, is that some of the fault at least is with the global stars.

The last article in this collection is by David Mitchell, who reports on an extraordinary experiment that is taking place in Alberta. The goal of the Alberta SuperNet project is to connect rural and Aboriginal communities with broadband technology. The project is noteworthy for the sheer size of the undertaking in terms of the geographic expanse that was being connected, the speed with which it was built, and the mix of government and private investment. But providing access to broadband at reasonable cost was not the only challenge, although that alone was formidable. For small communities that have only subsistence economies and are losing their young people, the bigger question is how to use the technology to create new businesses and revitalize their communities. It will take years to determine whether the SuperNet experiment has proven to be successful in human terms.

The perspectives offered by our student participants, Yvonne Poitras Pratt, Sharon Mah, Darren Blakeborough, and Gina Grosenick, are instructive and insightful. They stress the need for the media to better reflect local and ethnic communities, create opportunities for a more involved citizenship and enhance Canadian-ness. The essential question that they ask in their "Keywords in Canadian Communication" is how the public interest can best be served in the new media world. It is a question that pervades and captures the spirit of this book.

The debate between optimists and pessimists, which is at the heart of this volume, reflects a wider societal debate about media technologies, culture, and identity in the age of digital globalization. To some degree the optimists tend to be those who write about the old regulated media. They are the ones who believe that our fate is in our own hands and that the mass media can be shaped to fit and promote national needs and aspirations. The contributors, however, who have written about the effects of the largely unregulated new media tend to give much more weight to global forces. Although new media forms can provide individuals with extraordinary opportunities for expression and interaction, the nation-state is often bypassed or pushed to the margins. Global players dominate the horizon and crowd out local cultures.

Powerful arguments are presented by both sides in this debate. What is not in dispute is that much of our future will depend on how Canadians communicate.

Bibliography

Adams, Michael. 2003. *Fire and Ice: The United States, Canada and the Myth of Converging Values.* Toronto: Penguin.

Chapman, Paul. 2005. "Boomers grow attached to gaming." *Calgary Herald*, 18 June, C1.

Epstein, Edward Jay. 2005. *The Big Picture: The New Logic of Money and Power in Hollywood.* New York: Random House.

Friedman, Thomas. 2005. *The World is Flat.* New York: Farrar, Straus and Giroux.

Frye, Northrop. 1982. "Sharing the Continent." In *Divisions on a Ground: Essays on Canadian Culture.* Toronto: Anansi.

Kearney, A.T. 2005. "Measuring Globalization." *Foreign Policy* (May/June): 52–61.

Kroes, Rob. 2000. *Them & Us: Questions of Citizenship in a Globalizing World.* Chicago: University of Illinois Press.

Kroes, Rob, ed. 1991. *Within the U.S. Orbit: Small National Cultures vis-à-vis the United States.* Amsterdam: VU University Press.

Micklethwait, John, and Adrian Wooldridge. 2004. *The Right Nation: Conservative Power in America.* New York: Penguin.

Meisel, John. 1986. "Escaping Extinction: Cultural Defence of an Undefended Border." In *Southern Exposure: Canadian Perspectives on the United States,* eds. David Flaherty and William McKercher, 152–68. Toronto: McGraw-Hill Ryerson.

———. 1996. "Extinction Revisited; Culture and Class in Canada." In *Seeing Ourselves: Media Power and Policy in Canada,* eds. Helen Holmes and David Taras, 249–56. Toronto: Harcourt Brace.

Mosco, Vincent. 2004. *The Digital Sublime: Myth, Power and Cyberspace.* Cambridge, MA: MIT Press.

Nye, Joseph. 2002. *The Paradox of American Power.* New York: Oxford University Press.

Saul, John Ralston. 2005. *The Collapse of Globalism and the Reinvention of the World.* Toronto: Viking.

Schultz, Richard. 2003. "From Master to Partner to Bit Player: The Diminishing Capacity of Government Policy." In *How Canadians Communicate.* eds. David Taras, Frits Pannekoek, and Maria Bakardjieva, 27–49. Calgary. University of Calgary Press.

A: The Debate Over Policy

1: From Assumptions of Scarcity to the Facts of Fragmentation

KENNETH J. GOLDSTEIN

Introduction

"Globalization" is a long, and somewhat awkward, word. In recent years, it has also become a "loaded" word, often used as a form of political shorthand by those who disagree with various policies that have been linked to more open borders and the freer movement of ideas and goods. Indeed, there is a worldwide movement of what might be called "anti-globalization" groups. But surely a worldwide movement against globalization is a contradiction in terms – isn't the movement itself an example of globalization? The ironies abound. What medium is used to link the anti-globalization forces? The Internet, the newest medium, and the one that knows almost no borders at all as it extends the content of many other media around the world.

Regardless of the internal contradictions of the anti-globalization movement, the emergence of communications tools that know no borders is, itself, a matter that should be of interest to students of the media, and to those who make public policies that affect the media. The erosion of traditional media borders has been driven by technology, fuelled by economics, and cheered on by millions of consumers. And Canadians have been in the forefront of this evolution/revolution. Today, Canadians can receive more information and more entertainment from more sources than ever before in history. Their choices are no longer limited by what is available locally, by what a regulator approves, or by what a program scheduler predetermines.

But, and there is always a "but," the resulting fragmentation of choices and erosion of traditional borders strikes at the very core of the economic and regulatory assumptions that have governed public policies and regulatory tools for the media in Canada over eight decades. The goal of those policies – that our media should be able to tell Canadian stories – remains the same. But fragmentation of choices and more porous borders may mean that the public policies and regulatory tools will have to be questioned, and perhaps changed, in a fundamental way.

If we had known then what we know now ...

The fragmentation of media and the erosion of traditional borders are prompting a fundamental re-examination of public policies in many countries. In Australia, for example, in October 2003, the Australian Broadcasting Authority (ABA) published a discussion paper titled "Trading the Regulatory Obligations of Broadcasters" – the idea that the same overall output of mandated content could be produced if broadcasters were able to trade their content quota obligations. In inviting discussion on this concept, the ABA noted:

Australian commercial broadcast licensees are subject to obligations imposed in pursuit of public policy objectives. These include requirements to show specific types of programs which are valuable to audiences for social and cultural reasons....

Changes in the broadcasting environment such as the growth of subscription television and the introduction of digital television have prompted debate on revised approaches to content regulation....

The pace and direction of change resulting from digitalisation is unclear. There is some consensus, however, that existing mechanisms will require review and that flexible and innovative approaches need to be explored. (Australian Broadcasting Authority 2003, 5)

In the United States, in 2005, a number of media owners asked the U.S. Supreme Court to overturn the ruling the court made in 1969 in *Red Lion Broadcasting Co. v. FCC* – a ruling that validated broadcast regulation by the U.S. Federal Communications Commission on the grounds of "spectrum scarcity." However, the U.S. Supreme Court subsequently declined to hear the case. Had the court allowed the case to proceed, it could have reopened the question of whether or not "spectrum scarcity" can still be used as a rationale for broadcast regulation and, indeed, whether it is still a reality in today's technological environment (Halonen 2005a, 2005b).

In the United Kingdom, in November 2003, Ofcom, the new regulator for broadcasting, announced that it was undertaking a year-long review of public service broadcasting. In a subsequent article, posted on the Internet on December 11, 2003, a British trade publication, *Media Week*, noted:

There is little doubt that in the current world of multichannel, multi-platform TV, the existing framework makes little sense. If the Government had a clean sheet, it certainly wouldn't produce a design similar to the current set-up ("PSB" 2003).

Canada is not exempt from any of these trends or any of these debates. So it may be time to rephrase that *Media Week* comment, put it into a Canadian context, and ask these questions:

- If we had known in the 1930s and the 1950s (and even the 1970s) what we now know about the technology and economics of broadcasting, would we have created the same system we have today?
- Will the institutions and models created in the past be capable of adapting to the future?

Some History Is in Order

To help us understand how we got to this point in terms of the regulations, institutions, and models for Canadian media, some history is in order. And one observation that flows from a study of media history in Canada is that many of our current institutions and models are rooted in a time when the underlying assumption about Canadian media was that there could only be a small number of participants.

In May 1920, an experimental private radio station in Montreal, the forerunner of CFCF, broadcast what many believe to be the world's first real radio program (Godfrey 1982). It was one of a series of developments, starting after World War I and running well into the 1930s, during a time when radio was "new media." And like the more recent past, when "new media" referred to the Internet, there were questions about business models, public participation and regulation.

Because our technical ability to use the radio frequency spectrum was then more limited, the early days of radio brought with them the concept of "spectrum scarcity," and the assumption that there could only be a limited number of players using that scarce public resource. So we entered the 1920s both fascinated and unsure about radio. Some daily newspapers dismissed radio as a fad, some feared it as a potential competitor for advertising, and some began to experiment with radio stations of their own.

In January 1920, the daily newspapers in Winnipeg were unable to publish for six days because of a shortage of newsprint. The student newspaper at the University of Manitoba, the *Manitoban*, had sufficient newsprint, and published as a daily for four days until the regular dailies resumed publication. Since the *Manitoban* did not have access to news services, it monitored radio broadcasts from the U.S. and used them as a source for non-local news. The editor of the *Manitoban* was a remarkable young Canadian named Graham Spry, whose interest in radio would later have a profound influence on the development of this new medium in Canada ("News Famine in Winnipeg" 1920).

By 1922, the daily newspapers experimenting with radio included the *Tribune* and *Free Press* in Winnipeg, and the *Star* in Toronto. In Winnipeg, however, by 1923, the experiments by the two Winnipeg dailies were not going well. The business model was unclear, and they both foresaw a long period of losses. At the same time, Manitoba Government Telephones was interested in radio, in part because the provincially owned telephone system saw radio as a potential competitor.

The two daily newspapers agreed to vacate the field, and the telephone system established a new radio station in Winnipeg, CKY. To make that happen, the governments of Manitoba and Canada negotiated a deal in 1923 under which the provincial telephone system would receive 50 per cent of the radio receiver licence fees collected in Manitoba, and would have what amounted to a veto over any other radio station licences in the province (Vipond 1986). (In 1928, Manitoba Government Telephones added a second radio station, CKX, in Brandon, while exercising its veto over other attempts to establish radio stations in the province.)

And here is the interesting historical footnote – in 1923, the federal government indicated its willingness to make similar licence fee sharing arrangements with stations in other provinces, but none of them took Ottawa up on the offer (Canada 1923, 2785–2787; Peers 1969, 27–28; Allard 1979, 15–16). One can only speculate on how broadcasting in Canada might have developed differently if other stations and/or other provincial governments would have acted on the federal government's willingness to share some of its jurisdiction at that time.

While the business models may have been uncertain, public interest in radio was high. As has been the case with the Internet, teenagers were teaching the technology to adults. One of the teenagers in Winnipeg in the 1920s was a young man named Spencer Caldwell; at nineteen, he was managing the radio department in the Hudson's Bay store in downtown Winnipeg (Allard 1979; Corelli 1962). He decided to enter broadcasting as a career. Many years later, in 1961, he was awarded the licence for CTV – Canada's first private television network.

At the same Winnipeg high school Caldwell had attended, and two years younger than Caldwell, there was another young man interested in radio – in fact, he had built his own crystal set at the age of twelve (Gordon 1997, 11). His name was Marshall McLuhan. James Carey (1993) has written that McLuhan "came to communications from literary criticism" (441). While there is no reason to disagree with that assessment, Wordsworth made a useful observation when he said "the child is father of the man." So one might amend Carey's comment to suggest that McLuhan may have come to communications from literary criticism *and* from building his own crystal set.

By the late 1920s, interest in radio had grown sufficiently that the federal government set up the Aird Royal Commission, which recommended a publicly owned system. This was followed by a jurisdictional reference to the British Privy Council, which ruled that the federal government had exclusive jurisdiction over broadcasting.

To support the Aird Commission proposals, Graham Spry and Alan Plaunt established the Canadian Radio League, which lobbied successfully for the creation of a national public broadcaster in Canada. The Canadian Radio Broadcasting Commission (CRBC) was created in 1932 and was replaced by the Canadian Broadcasting Corporation (CBC) in 1936. In Spry's famous phrase, Canadians had to choose between "the State or the United States" (qtd. in Peers 1969, 91). And Spry, of course, is commonly considered to be the father of the CBC.

Framing the Debate

From 1929 to 1932, many influences contributed to the decision to adopt a public broadcasting model for Canada. Those influences ranged from hopes that the new medium of radio would be a tool for education and culture, to fears by some newspaper publishers that radio, if left in private hands, would be a competitor for advertising. The example of the BBC in the United Kingdom was referred to by those on both sides of the debate over public broadcasting. Another recurring theme in the ongoing debate was the fear that, without the proposed national public broadcaster, Canada's proximity to the United States, the difference in size between the two markets, and the nature of radio itself, would result in Canadians being overwhelmed by U.S. radio content.

In the context of what was known at that time, a publicly owned broadcast corporation was seen as the appropriate vehicle for both the production and distribution of programs and as the regulator of broadcasting. But let us remember that all of this was being played out against the guessing and assumptions by public and private interests about how many players this new field of radio could accommodate – with the guessing ranging from a monopoly to very limited numbers, and with public policy and private business decisions depending on those guesses and assumptions.

The idea that radio could only be considered in the context of very small numbers of potential participants, or, indeed, that radio was a "natural monopoly," became one of the framing propositions within which the future of radio was debated in the early 1930s.

One of the members of the Aird Commission was Charles Bowman, the editor of the *Ottawa Citizen*. In December 1929, the *Citizen* published four articles by Bowman in defence of the Aird recommendations. In dismissing the idea that the best result for radio would come from private stations in a competitive marketplace, Bowman wrote:

The number of broadcasting stations is limited, however, by nature…. Radio transmission is, in effect, a natural monopoly. The result of free competition would be chaos in the radio realm. At the same time, it is as economically unsound to promote competitive broadcasting stations in one community as it would be to promote competitive telephone exchanges. (Qtd. in Peers 1969, 55)

Indeed, the proceedings of the 1932 House of Commons Special Committee on Radio Broadcasting, which led to the legislation creating the CRBC, provide a graphic example of public policy being made in the context of that same framing proposition. As noted above, the debate over public or private ownership at the time was conducted against an underlying assumption by many participants and observers that radio could be regarded as a "natural monopoly." On April 20, 1932, the committee heard from Edward W. Beatty, the president of the Canadian Pacific Railway. Beatty argued for private ownership with government regulation. Beatty's appearance before the committee was reported in *The Globe* on April 21, 1932, in an article headlined "Private Monopoly, State Regulation, Advised For Radio." The article went on to report on an exchange between Beatty and E.J. Garland, the United Farmers of Alberta MP for Bow River, Alberta: "[Beatty] admitted to Mr. Garland that radio was a natural monopoly" (Marchington 1932, 3). While it was not the only reason the government ultimately decided in favour of public broadcasting, it is a fact that many of the decision makers of the day saw the essential policy option as a choice between public and private monopoly.

In the case of Manitoba, the changes of the early 1930s put an end to the government telephone system's veto power over competitors, and to the licence fee sharing, but it continued to operate CKY and CKX as commercial affiliates of the CRBC and then the CBC.

In Toronto, in an editorial titled "Public Ownership of Radio," in March 1930, the *Toronto Star* had referred to radio as "this most important and significant of all monopolies" ("Public Ownership" 1930, 6). But Joseph Atkinson, the publisher and owner of the *Star*, viewed the move to government involvement as negative to the *Star*'s position in radio. A new public competitor was on the horizon, and, at one point, Atkinson reportedly declared that, if he couldn't have a monopoly, he didn't want to have a radio station (Nolan 1986, 79).

On August 31, 1933, the *Star* took its radio station, CFCA, off the air, and, effectively, gave its licence back to the federal government. The *Star* reported its decision to get out of radio in a front-page story on August 29, 1933, titled "Pioneer Radio Station CFCA to Discontinue Bids Adieu Thursday." In that story, the *Star* stated:

As our readers know, we have been advocates of nationalized broadcasting and have always supposed the ultimate result must be the elimination of privately operated stations. ("Pioneer Radio" 1933, 1)

Of course, as we now know, Atkinson guessed wrong. It can be argued that the *Toronto Star* has spent the last seventy years regretting its decision to get out of broadcasting. In fact, despite the *Star*'s editorial protestations about supporting public broadcasting, Atkinson telephoned Prime Minister W.L. Mackenzie King on January 8, 1937, asking for King's support for a new radio licence for the *Star* in Toronto. King wrote in his diary that Atkinson had asked that "no one else should get ahead of the 'Star' on a licence for radio broadcasting, as their application had been in for some time" (Canada. National Archives 1937a, 2).

Prime Minister King's view of radio at that time is indicated in an entry in his diary the day before Atkinson's call, and is consistent with the prevailing view about the "monopoly" nature of the new medium. In response to a request from another Toronto publisher for a radio licence, King stated:

I thought the feeling in Canada was increasingly for both Government ownership and control of the air which was a natural monopoly. (Canada. National Archives 1937b, 3)

Assumptions for Newspapers

But the assumptions about small numbers were not made only for radio. While it was not argued that newspapers were "natural monopolies," from the 1920s on, it was also common to assume that markets could only support a small number of daily newspapers.

In 1936, a charismatic and ambitious thirty-one-year-old named George McCullagh convinced a wealthy mining magnate to provide the financial backing for his newspaper ambitions. In October 1936, he purchased *The Globe*. In November 1936, he purchased the *Mail and Empire*. He then merged the two into a single morning paper, *The Globe and Mail*. (And, in case you are wondering, McCullagh was the other Toronto publisher asking Prime Minister King about a radio licence in January 1937, the day before Atkinson's phone call to the Prime Minister.)

What did the *Toronto Star* have to say in 1936 about the reduction in the number of newspaper voices in Toronto? In an editorial titled "The Inevitable Merger is Announced," on November 19, 1936, the *Star* stated:

The merger has now come, and very few informed newspaper men will be surprised to hear of it.... There will be one morning enterprise with prospects of profitable operation instead of two without such prospects.... This is a natural and proper development. ("Inevitable Merger" 1936, 4)

At the time, McCullagh was a Liberal, and the *Star* did not seem particularly concerned about the loss of the Conservative *Mail and Empire*. Toronto's other afternoon daily, the pro-Conservative *Telegram*, did raise some concerns about the loss of another Conservative voice. (By 1938, McCullagh had become a major figure in Canadian media and politics; an article about him in the January 22, 1938 issue of the *Saturday Evening Post* was headlined "Canada's Wonder Boy" (Furnas 1938).)

After World War II – Continuing Assumptions of Scarcity

We entered the 1940s with an underlying assumption that the numbers of radio stations and daily newspapers would be limited by technology and/or economics. As we moved into the post World War II period, those assumptions of scarcity continued to influence public and private policies. After World War II ended, the governments of Alberta, Quebec, and Saskatchewan all expressed an interest in being able to operate radio stations in the same manner as Manitoba.

In fact, in early 1946, the CCF government of Saskatchewan entered into an agreement to purchase CHAB in Moose Jaw and applied to the Board of the CBC – which was then also the regulator – for permission to have the ownership of the licence transferred. In response, the federal government changed the rules and announced a new policy in May 1946 that prohibited the granting of broadcast licences to provincial governments (Peers 1969, 375–76). To support the change of policy, an internal background paper was prepared, likely by the CBC, dealing with the question of provincial ownership of stations. In part, this is what it said:

If channels for broadcasting were available in unlimited numbers it might be reasonable to license particular groups and bodies because then all opposing factions could be licensed separately.... Channels are, however, extremely limited. (Canada. National Archives 1946, 2)

So "spectrum scarcity" was one of the arguments used to deny a radio licence to the CCF government of Saskatchewan.

One of the consequences was that the Manitoba government was forced to sell its two radio stations. In 1948, CKY in Winnipeg was sold to the CBC and became CBW. (The CKY call letters were reactivated the next year for a new private station in Winnipeg.) The government's station in Brandon, CKX, was sold to an automobile dealer named John Boyd Craig.[1] (Through all of these changes, CKUA in Edmonton somehow managed to stay under the radar and remained provincially owned, probably because it was considered educational.)

In that same year, 1948, George McCullagh, by then a staunch Conservative, added another Toronto newspaper to his holdings, the *Telegram*. In 1948, the combined daily newspaper circulation in Toronto was equivalent to more than 100 per cent of the households[2]; McCullagh controlled two of the three daily newspapers. And broadcasting in Toronto consisted mainly of five AM radio stations, two owned by the CBC (CBL and CJBC), and three private stations regulated by the CBC (CFRB, CHUM, and CKEY). (McCullagh died in 1952, and the *Telegram* and *The Globe and Mail* were each subsequently sold to different owners.)

And Then Came Television

And then came television. It began with a CBC monopoly in 1952. CTV was added in 1961. In the 1960 licensing process by the Board of Broadcast Governors[3] that led to the creation of the stations that became part of CTV, the *Toronto Star*, the *Telegram*, and *The Globe and Mail* were each applicants for the first private television station licence for Toronto. On March 26, 1960, after the *Telegram* was awarded the licence (for what became CFTO-TV), the *Star* carried an editorial titled "Principles for Private TV." In that editorial, the *Star* stated: "The Star for years has maintained that broadcasting is a semi-monopoly and therefore should be treated as a public utility rather than a private commercial enterprise" ("Principles" 1960, 6). The *Star* also stated: "The linking of the earning power of a television station to that of a newspaper could radically worsen the competitive position of the two other newspapers in Toronto" ("Principles" 1960, 6). With the benefit of hindsight, we can see that the *Star* was wrong on both counts. The television market now is fragmented and highly competitive. And the fact that the TV licence was awarded to the *Telegram* did not prevent that newspaper from going out of business in 1971.

The Myth of Media "Concentration"

Despite the considerable evidence to the contrary, one of the first great myths of the twenty-first century seems to be the argument that, in Canada and the U.S., there is media "concentration." While some media companies have grown larger, the media market itself has also grown and fragmented. The degree to which markets are actually less, not more, concentrated, can be demonstrated in a number of ways. One approach is to apply tools from the field of competition law to the data on viewing of television by Canadians.

In competition law, regulators often use an index to determine whether or not a market is concentrated. The index is called the Herfindahl-Hirschman Index (HHI), and it is calculated for a given market by squaring the market shares of each owner in a market, and then adding up the results for each owner. In an atomized market with 100 competitors, each having a one per cent share, the HHI would be 100. In a monopoly, where one owner has 100 per cent, the HHI would be 10,000. In a market with 10 competitors, each with a 10 per cent share, the HHI would be 1,000. But what if those 10 competitors did not have equal shares? For example, what if the division of market shares among the 10 competitors was 50 per cent for the top firm, 10 per cent for the second firm, and 5 per cent for each of the other eight firms? The

Table 1.1   Total daily newspaper paid circulation, and circulation of largest
newspaper group (by circulation), as % of households in Canada, 1950 to 2006.

	Canada	Total daily newspaper circulation		Circulation of largest daily newspaper group (by circulation)		
	Total house-holds	Total	% of house-holds	Total circulation	% of house-holds	Largest publisher (by circulation)
1950	3,350,000	3,403,326	101.6	434,711	13.0	McCullagh
1960	4,450,000	3,984,428	89.5	608,931	13.7	Southam
1970	5,900,000	4,675,697	79.2	882,653	15.0	Southam
1980	8,119,000	5,291,914	65.2	1,455,911	17.9	Southam
1990	9,948,000	5,814,510	58.4	1,609,872	16.2	Southam
1998	11,290,000	5,134,761	45.5	2,210,311	19.6	Hollinger/ Southam
2000	11,620,000	5,164,255	44.4	1,608,194	13.8	CanWest
2002	11,970,000	5,004,619	41.8	1,533,086	12.8	CanWest
2004	12,295,000	4,911,071	39.9	1,413,508	11.5	CanWest
2006	12,631,000	4,767,357	37.7	1,351,302	10.7	CanWest

Source: Canadian Advertising and Canadian Advertising Rates and Data, selected issues; Canadian
Newspaper Association; Statistics Canada. (Circulation data are based on paid circulation – subscriptions
and single copy sales – in each of the years.)

HHI would then be 2,800; by squaring market shares, the HHI gives a sense
of market power among the competitors. Generally, an HHI under 1,000 is
considered unconcentrated, and an HHI from 1,000 to 1,800 is considered
moderately concentrated.

Using data from the ratings services (BBM and Nielsen), it is possible to
compare the ownership shares for television in Canada in 1970 and in 2005–
2006, based on the tuning to each network, station or service, and each owner.
One can then calculate the HHI based on those results. In 1970, including
the audiences of networks on stations not owned by the networks, the HHI
based on tuning to television in Canada was 1,278. Today, the comparable
HHI would be lower.[4]

There are more radio stations than ever before. And over 60 per cent of
Canadian households are connected to the Internet, which provides access to
many thousands of additional radio stations and newspapers.[5]

The advent of television in the late 1940s and early 1950s had a fragmenting
effect across media. In other words, even before the television market itself
fragmented, it was fragmenting the markets for magazines, radio, and newspapers. TV forced radio to change the nature of its programming. And the

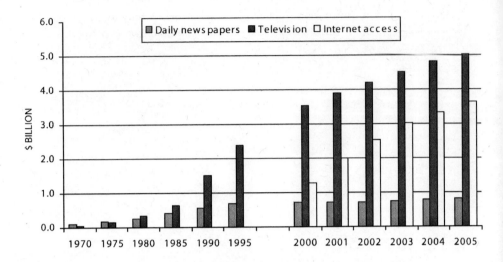

Figure 1.1　Subscription revenues for daily newspapers, television, and Internet access, Canada, 1970–2005.

Source: Statistics Canada; CRTC, Canadian Newspaper Association. For newspapers, revenues include subscriptions and single copy sales. For television, revenues include subscriptions for cable, satellite, specialty, and pay services.

time consumers spent with television began to eat away at the time they were prepared to spend with newspapers.

In 1950, the combined circulation of daily newspapers in Canada was equivalent to 101.6 per cent of the households. By 2006, that figure was 37.7 per cent. In 1950, McCullagh's two newspapers had combined circulation equivalent to 13 per cent of Canada's households. Today, the largest daily newspaper group, by circulation, is equivalent to about 11 per cent of Canada's households (Table 1.1).[6]

Perhaps the most dramatic illustration of how Canadians' media habits have changed comes from a comparison of what we paid for media in 1975 and what we pay for media today. In 1975, Canadians spent more to purchase daily newspapers than they spent on television. By 2005, for every dollar spent on daily newspapers, Canadians were spending more than six dollars on television and more than four dollars on Internet access (Figure 1.1).

It is clear that we have moved from a time of media scarcity to a time of media fragmentation. But many of the public institutions and private business models are still rooted in the old assumptions of scarcity and now are scrambling to catch up with this change.

Economic Consequences of Fragmentation

At one level, fragmentation means more choice – more channels and more opportunities to tell Canadian stories and reflect Canadian diversity. But more choice – fragmentation – also profoundly changes the underlying economic nature of the market that is being fragmented. The reason – fragmentation puts downward pressure on unit costs.

In 1950, Harold Innis made an important observation in his book, *Empire and Communications*. Referring to the economic development of the North American continent, Innis wrote:

As the costs of navigation declined, less valuable commodities emerged as staples – precious metals ... timber ... and finally wheat ... (Innis 1972, 6).

In other words, Innis saw a relationship between the cost of transportation and the value of the staples that were being transported. We moved from limited and high-cost transportation that could only be justified if the staples were also high in cost, to modern transportation carrying low-cost staples in high volumes.

There is a lesson here for the media. Technology now allows us to lower the cost of "transporting" channels. And that is already putting pressure on the staple those channels carry – programming. By simply modifying and replacing some of the words in the quote from Innis, one can see how the sheer volume of channels has an impact on content:

As the costs of *channels* declined, *less costly programs* emerged as staples – *long-form drama ... variety programs* ... and finally *reality-based shows* ...

All media are facing this pressure on unit costs, because fragmentation can be seen as a phenomenon both within and across the various media.

For television, one of the consequences of the downward pressure on unit costs is the fact that fragmentation makes it more difficult – and more risky – to invest in high-quality drama programs. In this context, it can be seen that content sharing across a number of outlets is a response to fragmentation and the resulting downward pressure on costs. Another consequence is that fragmentation also makes it more difficult to do local programming. That is further compounded when the new, fragmented channels are also specialized channels, which take audiences and revenues away from the local general services that previously offered some of the same types of programs.

And it is fragmentation, not consolidation, which is at the root of the current public concern about "indecent" or risqué content. When there were only a few outlets in the media market, profitability was more certain, so there was little incentive to stretch the boundaries of taste. Fragmentation has changed that equation. (Fragmentation has also contributed to the fulfillment of Andy Warhol's prediction that everyone would be famous for fifteen minutes, because one of the other effects of fragmented media markets is to lower the threshold for celebrity.)

And what about media consolidation? This, too, is a response to fragmentation, as media seek to maintain economies of scale by attempting to re-aggregate fragments. However, those re-aggregated combinations rarely achieve the market shares that single services had before the market was fragmented. (The Toronto radio market is a good example. In 1975, BBM reported that one station, CFRB, had a 28.5 per cent share of tuning. By 2006, the BBM data indicated that no single station had a tuning share greater than about 9 per cent, and no commonly owned group of Toronto radio stations had a combined tuning share greater than 20 per cent.)[7]

The Erosion of Borders

All of the consequences of fragmentation described to this point would represent a fundamental change even if the fragmentation were occurring entirely within a closed system. But it is not. The system is no longer closed. Borders are eroding. And that erosion of traditional borders compounds the problem.

The erosion of borders also adds one further dimension – it plays havoc with decades of copyright practice on which the media industries are based. The extension of unauthorized distribution impedes the rights of copyright users that are authorized in each market. And peer-to-peer file sharing has the potential to remove programming from the copyright industries altogether.

In fact, peer-to-peer file sharing represents another profound change in the way we relate to the media, as citizens and consumers. Here's why: For the first time in history, on a mass scale, the means of production and distribution of information and entertainment products are finding their way into the hands of the consumers.

One wonders if Spry or Caldwell or McLuhan could have imagined all of this as they were experimenting with radio in Winnipeg in the 1920s. Even in the 1960s and the 1970s, only a very few theorists could begin to glimpse the future that has become today's reality.

The Challenge to Current Institutions and Business Models

So we turn now to the question posed at the outset. Are current institutions and business models, rooted in many cases in assumptions of scarcity, structurally able to adapt to face the facts of fragmentation?

In the private sector, media companies have responded to fragmentation with a variety of approaches – indeed, such a variety of approaches that the word "convergence" now has a different definition for almost every player. Some of those approaches will succeed, some will fail, and some may grow and evolve into something else.

But what of our public institutions? Canada is a large country, but a relatively small market. So, for many years, public policy in broadcasting has been based on two major premises – regulation, and a crown corporation that would deliver programs and services that the marketplace would not allow the private sector to do. Other funding mechanisms were also used to help prime the pump for certain types of content.

Because of fragmentation, we may be approaching the point at which some of those techniques may become far less effective. When the television market was essentially an oligopoly, it was reasonable to expect most players to be profitable, and at levels of profitability that allowed them to fulfill regulatory obligations. But if fragmented markets put downward pressure on unit costs, the regulatory approach of the past may become a smaller part of the process. Because of fragmentation, it may be necessary in the future to place less reliance on regulation, and more on the expenditure of public funds by government, to achieve precisely the same goal that Spry enunciated over seventy years ago – Canadian content.

And that brings us to a key issue: In a fragmented marketplace, are the current public institutions – the CBC, Telefilm, the Canadian Television Fund – the best ways to achieve that goal? That is a difficult question to answer. And one of the reasons it is a difficult question to answer is because we seem too often to be afraid in Canada to let that question be asked. If one questions such hallowed institutions as the CBC, one is often accused of being unpatriotic, or of being against public broadcasting, or of being against public intervention at all.

But if we believe, as a society, that public intervention has a place, surely we have an obligation to craft the form of that intervention in the most efficient and effective manner. So we have to pose the following three sets of questions:

- *First:* Given the realities of today's broadcast marketplace, if those public institutions did not exist, what would be missing? Sports? News? Documentaries? Drama?
- *Second:* As a society, to what extent are we prepared to use government spending to supply what would be missing? The federal government currently spends about $1.6 billion per year on broadcasting, of which almost 60 per cent goes to the CBC.[8] Should we spend more? Should we spend less?
- *Third:* What is the best way of spending that money to achieve the goals we have set?

Unfortunately, we tend to use up too much of our debating time in this area talking about institutions, not goals. On February 24, 2004, for example, on CBC Newsworld, the *Inside Media* program devoted a whole hour to the CBC. And for the most part it was both predictable and, sadly, irrelevant. We heard that the CBC only costs so much per year per Canadian, and we heard someone else argue that those payments should be made voluntary. Too much of the debate was about the institution.

Yet it is possible that the CBC, as currently structured, may not be the best way to organize the public spending power in broadcasting in the future. So it was encouraging to hear this comment from Carole Taylor, who was then the Chair of the CBC, during the discussion on that *Inside Media* program:

I'd love to see a discussion where everyone puts aside some of their prejudices and says where are we going in the future? If we think that this idea of Canadian content is a good one, how should we fund it? If I were Prime Minister for a day, the first thing I'd do is take all of this bag of ways that we subsidize culture and Canadian content in this country, and there are many of them – from tax credits to Telefilm to CBC to the Television Fund – and I would say where are we trying to get to here? If this is a value that Canadians want, and does all of this disparate funding, sometimes with different mandates, get us there? I would say no, so let's think how we want to fund this in Canada going forward (CBC Newsworld).

Ms. Taylor is right. It is time for a fundamental review. To paraphrase the words from the United Kingdom – as Canadians, it's time to give ourselves a clean sheet, and see if we do or don't come up with a design similar to the current set-up.

The Impact on Shared Experience

In discussing the impact of fragmentation, one additional brief comment may be in order. In Canada and the United States, broadcasting may already have passed its peak as a shaper of our shared experience. While broadcasting will continue to be a major influence on our experience, the fragmentation of the medium may at the same time be reducing the amount of that experience that is common or shared.

Our common knowledge base on public affairs will be different. It will tend to focus more on major events that can cause people to move out of their customized media streams, and less on smaller events that are part of the day-to-day conduct of public affairs. For those in politics and government, the new communications challenge will be to find a way of balancing the ability to speak to narrow segments and the need to communicate broader messages to all of the participants in our democratic society. To put it even more succinctly: How will a modern democracy function if we all have less in common?

Newton Minow was the Chair of the U.S. Federal Communications Commission in the early 1960s, under President John F. Kennedy. Three decades later, in 1991, he made the following observation about the changing television environment:

We see 400- and 500-channel systems on the horizon, fragmenting viewership into smaller and smaller niches, and we need to remember that for all their presumed benefits these developments undermine the simultaneous, shared national experiences that comprise the nation's social glue (Minow 1991, 17).

As we start to ask the fundamental questions about our public institutions, we need to keep that in mind as well. We are not likely to go back to three channels of television or give up the Internet. But we must still try to find a way to continue to build shared experience in a fragmented environment.

Conclusion

Over a period of eight decades, we have moved from assumptions of scarcity to the facts of fragmentation. As fragmentation is accelerated by technology and increasingly porous borders, it adds to the economic pressure on traditional business models, regulatory policies, and public institutions. We have seen that serious questions about these issues are being raised in Australia, the United Kingdom, and the United States. Canada must face the same issues. Will our approach be based on incremental changes to established institutions? Will we be sidetracked by the mythology of media "concentration"? Or will we be prepared to ask hard questions about shared goals and the fundamental changes that may be required to achieve them?

Bibliography

Australian Broadcasting Authority. 2003. "Trading the Regulatory Obligations of Broadcasters." October. www.aba.gov.au/newspubs/radio_TV/documents_research/trading_oblig.pdf.

Allard, T.J. 1979. *Straight Up: Private Broadcasting in Canada: 1918–1958*, Canadian Communications Foundation.

Canada. House of Commons. 1923. *Debates* (Hansard), April 27, 2785–2787.

Canada. National Archives of Canada. 1946. Canadian Broadcasting Corporation fonds (RG41-Vol. 988), "Broadcasting Licences, Provincial Governments and Special Groups." April 2.

Canada. National Archives of Canada. 1937a. Diaries of W.L. Mackenzie King, 7 January.

Canada. National Archives of Canada. 1937b. Diaries of W.L. Mackenzie King, 8 January.

Carey, James W. 1993. Book review in the *Canadian Historical Review* 74(3); pp. 437–442.

CBC Newsworld. 2004. *Inside Media*, 24 February.

Corelli, Rae. 1962. "Spencer Caldwell: The Man Who Challenges CBC's TV Supremacy." *Star Weekly Magazine*, 13 January.

Furnas, J.C. 1938. "Canada's Wonder Boy." *Saturday Evening Post*, 22 January.

Godfrey, Donald G. 1982. "Canadian Marconi: CFCF, The Forgotten First." *Canadian Journal of Communication*, 8(4) (September): 56–71.

Gordon, W. Terrence. 1997. *Marshall McLuhan: Escape into Understanding*. Toronto: Stoddart.

Halonen, Doug. 2005a. "Washington Notes: Media Firms Target Red Lion." *Television Week*, 7 February, www.tvweek.com.

———. 2005b. "High Court Won't Review Deregulation Case" *Television Week*, 13 June, www.tvweek.com.

Innis, Harold A. 1972. *Empire and Communications* Toronto: University of Toronto Press (originally published in 1950).

"The Inevitable Merger is Announced." 1936. *Toronto Star*, 19 November.

Marchington, William. 1932. "Private monopoly, state regulation, advised for radio." *The Globe*, 21 April.

Minow, Newton N. 1991. "How Vast the Wasteland Now?", address to the Gannett Foundation Media Center, Columbia University, New York City, 9 May.

"News Famine in Winnipeg: Improvised College Daily Only Paper in Manitoba City." 1920. *Editor & Publisher*, 22 January.

Nolan, Michael. 1986. *Foundations: Alan Plaunt and the Early Days of CBC Radio*, CBC Enterprises.

Peers, Frank W. 1969. *The Politics of Canadian Broadcasting 1920–1951*. Toronto: University of Toronto Press.

"Pioneer Radio Station CFCA to Discontinue Bids Adieu Thursday." 1933. *Toronto Star*, 29 August.

"Principles for Private TV." 1960. *Toronto Star*, 26 March.

"PSB Must Reflect Changing Industry." 2003. *Media Week*, 11 December, www.mediaweek.co.uk.

"Public Ownership of Radio." 1930. *Toronto Star*, 22 March.

Vipond, Mary. 1986. "CKY Winnipeg in the 1920s: Canada's Only Experiment in Government Monopoly Broadcasting." *Manitoba History*, Autumn.

Notes

1   In December 2001, at a CRTC public hearing in Hamilton, Ontario, the successors to Joseph Atkinson at the *Star* (now called Torstar) and the grandsons of John Boyd Craig were among the competitors for a new television station licence for Toronto – the Craig company seeking to expand from its Western base, and the *Star* seeking, once again, to get back into broadcasting. The Craig application was approved; Torstar's was denied. Ironically, the start-up difficulties with its new Toronto station led to the sale of all of Craig's television stations in 2004.

2   Communications Management Inc., based on census data and industry sources.

3   The Board of Broadcast Governors took over the regulatory functions from the CBC in 1958; it was succeeded by the CRTC in 1968.

4   Communications Management Inc., based on data from BBM and Nielsen.

5   Communications Management Inc., based on data from Statistics Canada and industry sources.

6   Communications Management Inc., based on data from Statistics Canada and industry sources.

7   Based on data from BBM for 1975 and 2006.

8   Based on data from Statistics Canada; CBC.

2: Canadian Communications and the Spectre of Globalization: "Just another word ..."

RICHARD SCHULTZ

In my contribution to the first volume of *How Canadians Communicate*, I focused on the need/desire to control as the primary motive force in shaping Canadian communications policies, and the forces, technological, social, and international, that were challenging the capacity of Canadian governments to exercise such control (Schultz 2003). In this article, given the overarching theme of this volume, namely the interrelationships between identity, domestic tensions, and the presumed power of globalization, I want to turn my attention to the other side of what I called the "compulsion to control," specifically the underlying force that motivates, energizes, and sustains this compulsion. I want to link that force to the contemporary concentration – or is it an obsession? – with globalization and its presumed deleterious effects on domestic cultures, particularly Canadian, and the efficacy of policy instruments to shape and defend those cultures.

My central thesis is that globalization is the contemporary variant of a deeply ingrained fear on the part of some Canadians and consequently is "just another word for" Americanization. Moreover, I argue that concentrating on Americanization *qua* globalization is, as it always has been, a convenient, and, to my mind, an unfortunately effective one at that, distraction for what really ails Canadian communications: the profound inadequacy of domestic policies and institutions. If there be fault to be found in our contemporary situation, the fault is not in the global stars but in ourselves. The unwillingness to both appreciate and accept this and the consequent failure to confront this situation serves only those who benefit from both the outcomes of contemporary policies and the status of being entrenched dominant players in the domestic policy system.[1] On the other hand, it arguably ill serves Canadians in how they communicate.

I propose to develop my argument in four sections. The first section discusses the building blocks of the contemporary policy regime, namely the linkages between the presumed power of communications to shape political and social values and the consequent apparent need for governmental control over the media. In the second section, I will discuss some of the major issues or problems related to the concentration on global forces, particularly in the attempt to create a new international agreement protecting or exempting culture from trade agreements. In the next section I turn the focus to a few of the more significant problems in Canadian communications and argue, contrary to the globalization proponents, that their solution rests solely in Canadian hands. Finally, in the concluding section, lest I be accused of either a Pollyannaish approach or simply, and more seriously, of being a neo-conservative advocating a reduced role for the state, I want to discuss three specific steps the Canadian Government should take to ameliorate some of the problems in "how Canadians communicate."

On Media Power and the Threat to Canadian Identity

Almost from the introduction of modern means for mass communications, two central premises developed in Canada. The first, albeit one not unique to Canada, was the assumption that modern media, starting with radio broadcasting, constituted an immensely powerful cultural force that had to be subject to effective public, that is governmental, control. This was first articulated in Canada by the Aird Royal Commission and then by R.B. Bennett, who, when introducing legislation to create the public Canadian broadcaster, defended the need for public control so that radio broadcasting could become "a great agency for communication of matters of national concern and for the diffusion of national thought and ideals [...and] the agency by which national consciousness may be fostered and sustained and national unity still further strengthened." As a unique engine for cultural formation and transmission, it was presumed to be inconceivable that broadcasting systems should not be under public control.

What made such control imperative was the second assumption, namely, the "fear of the other," to use President Clinton's evocative phrase from his speech to the Forum on Federations.[2] Public control was necessitated by the assumption that, absent such domestic control, given the economic power and, it needs to be remembered, the Canadian domestic appeal for American media products, Canada would lose control over such an important cultural instrument. The result would be a loss of Canadian identity and culture, a loss of any shared values, a loss of any sense of community, and ultimately, to quote modern commentators, an undermining of "the viability of Canada as a national community" (Fletcher and Everett 2004, 427). Or, as the Caplan-Sauvageau Report (1986) intoned: "There can be no political sovereignty without cultural sovereignty" (9), thereby invoking a phrase, lifted incidentally by a federal Liberal government from Quebec nationalists in the 1970s to serve the ends of Canadian nationalists, that went from slogan to legislative icon and policy template without passing through understanding and definition (Caplan and Savageau 1986).

In brief, the initial compulsion to control was driven in part by the presumptive power of the media over Canadian beliefs, values, attitudes, and behaviour and the concomitant overwhelming fear of what George Grant would subsequently decry as the "universal homogenizing state," namely the United States. This is not the place to ask if the power of the media as a socializing force may not have been overstated, but we can ask, in the context of the current interest in globalization and its supposed impact on cultural and national identities, where is the evidence that American media products have ever had the presumed impact that underlay the justification for extensive and permanent Canadian public controls? Where is the evidence that Canadians have become Americanized in their popular and political cultures? Where is the evidence that the constant impact of American broadcasting and other forms of media have threatened the stability, the viability, of the Canadian polity?

Although the presumptive power of American media, and the assumed threat of Americanization of the Canadian public and our political culture, have been routinely invoked in almost every public inquiry from Aird to Massey, through Fowler I and II, and from Caplan-Sauvageau to the recent report by the House of Commons Standing Committee on Canadian Heritage (the Lincoln Report), not to mention the majority of academic and popular writing on the topic, there has been almost no attempt to document the actual power of American media over Canadians. We have instead fallen back on slogan mongering, by academics as well as government departments and agencies, to the effect that we have become Americanized because it is claimed "we are what we watch."[3] If I may be allowed an American political expression: Where's the beef? Where is the evidence that sustains this fear? Absent such evidence, such remonstrations should be seen for what they apparently are: mere ritualistic invocations.

If the preceding sentence appears to be unduly harsh, it is motivated by the fact that, contrary to the arguments of those who decry Americanization and the need for not only continuing public controls but strengthening them if possible, there is evidence that profoundly challenges the myth of Americanization and indirectly the myth of the culture-shaping power of mass media. That evidence is found in Michael Adams' (2003) provocative and, to this reader, highly persuasive book, *Fire and Ice: The United States, Canada and the Myth of Converging Values*. In this book, Adams develops what he describes as "the rarely heard, and even more rarely substantiated, thesis that Canadians and Americans are actually becoming increasingly different from one another" (Adams 2003, 4).

Adams (2003) bases his conclusions on three large social values surveys taken between 1992 and 2000 comprising over 14,000 interviews conducted among a representative sample of Canadians and Americans aged fifteen and over. His interviews probed views and beliefs on a wide range of social and political questions. Contrary to the conventional wisdom, which even he acknowledges is shared by the general public, as shown in other surveys, Adams (2003) concludes that "at the most basic level – the level of our values, the feelings and beliefs that inform our understanding of and interaction with the world around us – Canadians and Americans are markedly different, and becoming more so" (4).[4] Recent and ongoing public controversies such as on same-sex marriages as well as support for the war in Iraq would seem to lend considerable support for this conclusion.

What Adams' (2003) findings suggest is that those who assume the Americanization of Canada and Canadians through popular media, who argue that "we are what we watch" (and listen to) are guilty of what Magder (1993) labelled "hermeneutic naivety, in which audiences are assumed to accept wholesale the message of the media and to change their values and attitudes accordingly" (8). Magder goes on to argue that "the cultural effect of foreign media products on Canadian audiences … has to be investigated on its own terms; it cannot be assumed on the basis of statistics that illustrate the heavy penetration of foreign media products" (9). What Magder does not say is that, to date, until Adams, there have been no such investigations.

In addition to his overall conclusion that the values of Canadians are substantially different from American popular values, Adams directly challenges the conceptual underpinnings of current governmental communications policies and just as importantly offers important cautionary advice for policy makers and their supporters. On these points he is worth quoting at length:

It is also clear that the trajectory of social change in Canada that the policies of cultural nationalism put in place over the past seventy-five years will not have the same resonance with average Canadians in the future as they have in the past. Canadians have become much less deferential to hierarchies and their leaders over the past half-century and we are therefore less likely to allow nationalistic elites to define, regulate, and finance that uniqueness. The average Canadian wants access to all that the world has to offer, and much of that foreign content will be American. But unlike in the past, more autonomous, inner-directed Canadians wish to decide for themselves what they will consume and when (Adams 2003, 141).

Globalization and Canadian Cultural Communications

One would reasonably presume that such a fundamental assault on the contemporary communications policy regime would cause if not a paradigm shift at least a thorough-going debate on its premises and policy prescriptions. This has not happened and one can advance at least two reasons for this. One, which Adams acknowledges, is the deep-rooted belief even among Canadians, and not just their cultural and political elites, that we are becoming more like the Americans.[5] The other is that his findings have been submerged in the most recent debate over Americanization, in the new guise of globalization.

Those who propagate the Americanization of Canada thesis have in recent years added another arrow to their quiver: globalization. In 1999, for example, the government-appointed Cultural Industries Sectoral Advisory Group on International Trade, a committee dominated by executives from the cultural industries, issued a report stressing the pressures that Canadian cultural policy and its instruments now face as a result of international developments, particularly international trade agreements, and called upon the Government of Canada to lead the march for the creation of a new international instrument that would restrict the impact, if not exempt entirely, domestic cultural policies, from trade agreements.[6] The argument they make is that the threat to Canadian culture and identity, and indeed almost all national cultures, has been greatly compounded in recent years by the growing scope of globalization which, it is claimed, will radically transform the nation-state, national economies and, not surprisingly in its wake, undermine national cultures. What George Grant predicted for Canada is now presumed to be the sorry end state for every country but the United States. In the cultural and mass communications context, as Richard Collins and others noted some time ago, the world, it is claimed, is increasingly being Canadianized, that is, dominated by American media (Collins 1990).

There is no need, in the context of this chapter, to enter into the larger debates that surround globalization: What does globalization really mean? Is globalization greater today than before? Will it mean the demise, or at least the severe crippling, of the nation-state?[7] Our focus is more limited: what does globalization mean from the perspective of communications industries and will it constitute the final nail in the coffin of Canadian identity and culture, the end of our ability and opportunity "to tell our own stories"? Alternatively, is there anything really new about globalization from the perspective of affecting how Canadians communicate? Is it not little more than a repackaging of the traditional fear of the other, of Americanization?[8]

Globalization as it pertains to cultural communications is said to comprise three interrelated phenomena: first, the emergence of giant multi-media conglomerates such as AOL Time Warner, Disney, News Corporation, Viacom, and General Electric; secondly, the power of new communications technologies that will presumably undermine state capacities to control communications policies; and finally, the subjection of cultural industries to the constraints of international trade agreements and obligations. A quick review of each of these phenomena suggests that the new threat of globalization, with one important qualification, is not particularly different from that of Americanization.

In terms of giant media conglomerates, it is not clear how or if the situation has changed for Canada, which has always had to deal with large foreign corporate and lobbying entities in the communications arena, as anyone who has followed the dealings of the Motion Picture Association of America can attest. New corporate linkages and ownership patterns have not, I would argue, substantially changed that. Moreover, notwithstanding the routine invocation of the god of synergy each time a new conglomerate has been created, in the United States or in Canada, the success of the marriages has been less impressive than the rhetoric. The dismal performance of AOL Time Warner and Vivendi Universal stands as eloquent testimony to this, as does the continuing tepid commitment of BCE to its continued ownership of CTV.[9]

In any event, there is no logical argument that the enhanced size of non-Canadian conglomerates per se constitutes a new threat. One obvious example where home-grown policies, as opposed to those dictated or demanded by foreign companies, have prevailed is the maintenance of restrictions on foreign ownership of Canadian broadcasting licensees and newspapers. It should also be recalled that in the late 1960s the Canadian government was powerful enough to order what were for the time some of the largest foreign media companies to reduce their ownership of Canadian broadcasting licensees to 20 per cent or less. Moreover, even when we were negotiating, in the 1980s and early 1990s, international trade agreements such as the Canada-U.S. Free Trade Agreement, NAFTA, and then the General Agreement on Trade in Services, we were able to protect our restrictive ownership policies in the cultural and more general communications industries.

The second reason for the presumed power of globalization/Americanization comes from the development of new distribution technologies for broadcasting and other media. Cultural nationalists emphasize the importance of traditional governmental powers to control access to foreign media and are concerned that new technologies such as DTH satellites, wireless technologies, and the Internet will undermine the capacity or relevance of traditional tools such as regulatory licensing and content regulations. From the perspective of both history and contemporary developments, however, the threat may be exaggerated. Successive Canadian governments have introduced regulatory controls to dilute the foreign impact of what were in their own time new distribution technologies such as radio, television, cable television, pay television, and specialty channels.

More recently, despite the predictions of some, including this writer, that regulatory control would be undermined by DTH satellites, as a result of an effective pincer movement from the Department of Justice and industry participants such as Astral Media and Bell ExpressVu, the threat appears to have been deflected. The grey market sale of access to American DTH systems has virtually disappeared in Canada as a result of cumulative criminal charges, copyright lawsuits, and related equipment seizures. Indeed, the governmental-industry attack was so successful, DTH grey market industry participants were driven into bankruptcy and consequently were unable to pursue the court challenge they had launched for protection on the basis of Charter of Rights and Freedoms guarantees to free speech.[10]

Although cultural nationalists worry about a reduced capacity for the government to control communications media presumably because new technologies, such as the Internet, will make the communications market more complex and fragmented, it is not clear whether their real concern is with an undefined external push from globalization or the internal pull of Canadian consumers to exercise what John Meisel described as their assumption that "their basic rights give them access to any television signal that modern technology makes available" (Meisel 1989a, 193). I personally believe it to be the latter.

Contrary to those who fear the power of globalization, I have argued elsewhere that it was not neo-conservative governments, as some would have it, that compelled the Canadian governmental acceptance of reduced or removed regulatory controls. Rather it was the newly found power, and ravenous exercise of it, by consumers, from individuals to large and small businesses, to "exit," in Hirschman's terminology, various regulatory systems of command and control that sought to impose constraints on their choices, for example, in the air, rail, and trucking sectors (Hirschman 1970). Coming to a home theatre near you, particularly with the Internet, Canadian media consumers are about to enjoy the same leverage and will undoubtedly exercise it. Moreover, Canadian governments and their advisors should take heed of Michael Adams' (2003) finding cited earlier that, unlike in earlier periods, Canadians today "are less likely to allow nationalistic elites to define, regulate and finance that uniqueness ... [and] wish to decide for themselves what they will consume and when" (141).

The third pillar of the globalization thesis is stronger than the other two, although even it is not unassailable. This pillar contends that a real and present threat has recently emerged that challenges, if not undermines completely, the capacity of countries such as Canada to continue to be able to define and implement policies and to use traditional instruments such as subsidies, quotas, regulations, and restrictions that have been central to domestic public policies for cultural industries. The threat is found in recent trade agreements that significantly restrict and discipline the employment of certain governmental tools. This threat, it is argued, has emerged notwithstanding the inclusion of a so-called "cultural industries exemption" clause in trade agreements such as the Canada-U.S. Free Trade Agreement and its extension in NAFTA.

Although it was defended at the time of its first use as evidence that "culture was not on the table" in the negotiations, the fact that a related clause permitted retaliation by the affected country, it has been argued, deprived the exemption clause of any value.[11] In addition, cultural nationalists have come to fear that the prophylactic measures Canada took in subsequent trade negotiations such as in the General Agreement on Trade in Services, namely opting out of Most Favoured Nation obligations for audio-visual services, along with the European Union and thirty-three other countries, and not making any commitments in the cultural sector, will also prove to be as inadequate as the cultural exemption strategy.

The fear of trade agreements undermining not only current domestic policies but more seriously domestic policy capacity came to a head with the WTO decision in 1997 that in effect gutted Canada's protectionist magazine policy, which consisted of a mix of import restrictions, excise taxes, and postal subsidies. When the United States challenged the legislative proposals to replace the invalidated policies and threatened retaliation if Canada went ahead, Canada subsequently withdrew the package and substituted a domestic subsidy system, of which more below.[12]

More than any other incident or factor, the WTO magazine decision and the subsequent Canadian response prompted the Cultural Industries SAGIT to urge the Government of Canada to take the lead in forging an international agreement that would exempt culture from any and all trade agreements.[13] Consequently, Canada, represented by the Department of Heritage Canada, helped establish the International Network of Cultural Policy, made up of like-minded nations, whose purpose was to create a legally binding agreement to promote cultural diversity that would either exempt culture completely from trade agreements or seriously restrict the scope those agreements could play with respect to national policies to promote and protect culture. To paraphrase Graham Spry, the modern call to arms for Canadian cultural nationalists appears to be "The international community or the States."

While the principle of promoting and protecting cultural diversity is undoubtedly laudable, it is not clear for several reasons whether the pursuit of an international instrument is either the most appropriate or the most efficacious means for satisfying this objective. Ted Magder, for instance, while supportive of the principle, has developed a very persuasive critique of the draft International Instrument and finds it wanting in a number of respects. In particular he is critical of the proposed definition of culture, which is:

"Culture" is the whole complex of distinctive spiritual, material, intellectual and emotional features that characterize a society or social group. It includes creative expression (e.g. oral history, language, literature, performing arts, and crafts), community practices (e.g. traditional healing methods, traditional natural resource management, celebrations, and patterns of social interaction that contribute to group and individual welfare and identity), and material or built forms such as sites, buildings, historic city centres, landscapes, art, and objects.

He finds that the "definition is remarkable not only for its breadth, but the fact that it fails to mention the media at all." He concludes that "It is hard to see how a legally binding agreement could emerge from such a broad definition, especially given its lack of reference to the media, the one sphere of cultural expression that, more than any other, is regarded as constituting a threat to cultural diversity."[14]

The second problem with Canada's pursuit of an international instrument removing culture from the ambit of trade agreements has been raised by Christopher Maule, namely the inconsistencies in our negotiating positions and the overall lack of clarity in our objectives.[15] Maule contends that in our existing agreements, and those currently being negotiated, "Canada now presents several faces to the world," which has led to considerable uncertainty. He maintains that

The uncertainty surrounding Canada's current position is due to the different stances we have taken in different trade agreements, and our preference for the status quo in the GATS, failing negotiation of a satisfactory new instrument. Differences also arise as the preferred location of [the new instrument] with the Minister of International Trade wanting it inside, and the Minister of Canadian Heritage outside the WTO. Our several conflicting positions present opportunities for those negotiating with Canada to play off one interest against another (Maule 2002, 41).

The implication of Maule's assessment is that, regardless of what one thinks of the merits of a new instrument, Canada, as one of the early advocates for such an outcome, is making the process of negotiating a satisfactory agreement difficult.

The difficulty is compounded by the fact that the United States, the primary target for any international instrument, won an extremely significant victory in its trade dispute with Canada over the protectionist magazine policy regime. Although many commentators glide over the facts of this dispute by lumping all the trade agreements together, the magazine decision is significant for the fact that the United States did not challenge Canadian policies under the FTA, NAFTA, or the GATS but rather under the 1947 General Agreement on Trade and Tariffs. Moreover, the United States won a decision that declared that magazines are goods and not services and therefore were subject to existing, not the new, trade disciplines. Having won this conceptual victory, it is highly unlikely that the United States would acquiesce to having such goods redefined as services and put under the protective umbrella of the proposed instrument.

Canada's role in this conceptual transformation is not significantly appreciated and arguably undermines our negotiating position. Canadians, at least amongst members of the elite, have long rejected the American commoditization of the media and of culture generally. They reject the American commonplace view, for example, that broadcasting is just another commodity, "simply another appliance ... a toaster with pictures" to quote Ronald Reagan's Chair of the Federal Communications Commission, Mark Fowler (ironically born in Canada) (qtd. in Leanza and Feld 2003, 19). The traditional Canadian approach was that, contrary to the American commercial conception, broadcasting was to be "a great agency for the communication of matters of national concern and for the diffusion of national thought and ideals ... by which national consciousness may be fostered and sustained and national unity still further strengthened."

Yet for most of the last quarter century, successive Canadian governments and their advisers have employed a different rhetoric and rationale for developing and justifying various media and communications policies. Starting at least with the 1982 report of the Federal Cultural Policy Review Committee (known as Applebaum-Hébert after the co-chairs) the term "cultural industries" became part of the Ottawa lexicon.[16] This was shown in 1983 when Francis Fox, then Liberal Minister of Communications, issued a statement "Towards a New National Broadcasting Policy" in which economic considerations received as much attention as cultural.[17] Fox's paper had the usual cultural gloss but it placed great weight on the economic significance, or as he put it "the jobs and dollars at stake in this broadcasting strategy are considerable."[18] He also emphasized the export potential of the industry by including an "export thrust" for the international marketing of Canadian television programs. He also applauded the CRTC's Canadian content changes, which were designed to "ensure significant creative and *industrial* participation."[19]

Ironically, the Cultural Industries SAGIT report of 1999 cited earlier is only the most recent manifestation of this shift in emphasis. It reviews the economic characteristics of sectors of the cultural industries and emphasizes the contribution the industries make to Canada's gross domestic product, employment, the tourist industry, and technological innovation. The SAGIT claims, for example, that the entire cultural sector accounted for over $20 billion or 3 per cent of Canada's gross domestic product in 1994–95 and that its growth between 1989 and 1994 was greater than the growth in transportation, agriculture, and construction. In addition it claimed that the cultural sector provided almost 5 per cent of Canada's labour force in 1994–95 and grew over the previous four years 5.6 per cent while total employment dropped 0.5 per cent.[20]

The point is not to challenge these figures, and the conclusion that the cultural industries make a significant contribution to Canada's overall economy and economic performance is indisputable. The point, however, is that it is probable that our trading partners, particularly the United States, are asking themselves, "what is the Canadian concern – cultural or economic?" To the extent that we emphasize the economic aspects of our cultural industries, we encourage others to assume that our cultural protectionism may be little more than an attempt to mask our true or at least primary purposes, which are economic. If this is the case, notwithstanding the approval by the UNESCO General Conference of the Convention on the Protection and Promotion of the Diversity of Cultural expressions on October 20, 2005, we can hardly expect the United States to significantly change its behaviour because of any international instrument to exempt "culture" from trade disciplines.[21]

International Diversions/Domestic Problems

There is an additional problem with the concentration on globalization and the need for an effective international instrument to govern global cultural diversity. It serves as a significant diversion (and it can be argued deliberately so) that permits Canadian policymakers and the cultural industry policy community to ignore or downplay the significance of current domestic problems, problems that are not caused by international factors but could be and arguably should be addressed regardless of the progress on the international agenda. I contend that the primary public problems in Canadian communications have little to do with globalization, trade agreements, or the continuing overwhelming presence of American cultural products in Canada.

Time and space constraints do not permit me to go into too much detail so I will have to ignore such issues as the perennial underfunding, which was exacerbated in the 1990s by successive Canadian governments, regardless of political stripe, of the one policy instrument that takes its public mandate seriously, namely the CBC.[22] My primary point in what follows is simply to establish, through three specific examples, that we have sufficient domestic problems that must be addressed, far more pressing than an undue concentration on the presumed threats of globalization and a wistful search for an unlikely international treaty.

Domestic Magazine Policy Developments

The primary cause of the angst over international trade agreements and their negative impact on culture, namely the successful American challenge to Canada's magazine policy, has been mentioned. Here we can acknowledge a direct relationship between trade and cultural policies. However the most recent developments have nothing whatsoever to do with international or specifically American pressures, but flow from domestic considerations alone. After making a commitment to progressively increase the Canadian Magazine Fund from $25 million to $100 million, the Government of Canada declared victory after only three years when it announced in July 2003 that "the Canadian periodical and magazine industry is now on a solid footing and enjoying healthy growth."[23] Consequently it was cutting back its 2002–2003 grant from $32.6 million to $18 million for 2003–2004 and would impose a cap of $16 million for subsequent years.

For all the gnashing of teeth that had accompanied the original trade dispute and its impetus for the search for an international agreement, this action shows how tepid the government's commitment to its policy actually was. It also provides an excellent illustration of why regulatory instruments for governments are preferable to direct financial commitments as critics had often maintained (Posner 1971; Stanbury and Lermer 1983). For our purposes what is central about this development is that it was based solely on domestic governmental factors – the industry was both "dumbfounded" and extremely critical of the decision (Cheadle 2003). There is no evidence that the American government or the American magazine industry pressured Canada to take such an action. By implication, United States interests appear to have accepted the principle of the program that direct explicit subsidies of the type provided are not a violation of trade commitments under GATT or any other trade agreement.

Media Concentration and Cross-Ownership

There are probably not two more purely domestic issues than those of cross-ownership of different forms of media, especially broadcasting and newspapers, and concentration of ownership. Both have caused significant public debates about the appropriate policies to be adopted in recent years in several countries such as the United States, Australia, and the United Kingdom. In Canada the fact of cross-ownership has been a long-standing one with almost all of our newspaper chains owning, at one time or another, either radio or television stations within the same communities. There has also been a long-standing call for action on the part of the federal government. The 1970 Senate Special Committee on the Mass Media recommended action to limit cross-ownership. The 1981 Report of the Royal Commission on Newspapers (Kent Commission) called for rather stringent controls on ownership as well as on the behaviour of owners.

As a partial response to the Kent Commission's recommendations the Liberal government of the day issued a direction to the CRTC "to refuse to issue or renew broadcasting licenses to the proprietors of daily newspapers unless such an action would adversely affect service to the public or create exceptional or unreasonable hardship to the applicant and the level of existing competition in the area served or to be served" (qtd. in Bartley 1988). The immediate result was that the CRTC found grounds for exempting every relevant licence application that came before it. The larger result was that, according to Bartley citing David Townsend, "the direction may have served only to legitimize ownership patterns which could have been dealt with over time using other means."[24] Within three years the direction was withdrawn.

More recently the issue of cross-ownership has re-emerged, tied as it has been to a concern for concentration of ownership. The issue came alive again in 2000 as a result of the Hollinger purchase of the Southam newspapers, which resulted in a situation where one owner, Hollinger/Southam, controlled 42 per cent of the Canadian daily newspaper market.[25] The subsequent resale of the Southam newspaper component to CanWest Global Communications, even though it led to a decrease in concentration, caused considerable controversy because of CanWest's ownership of the Global Television Network, the third largest English-language network in Canada. Associated developments that reinforced the debates were the increase in media ownership by Quebecor in both newspapers and cable television systems, and the purchase by BCE, the largest telecommunications company, of both the *Globe and Mail*, the fifth largest newspaper in Canada as measured by weekly circulation, and CTV, the largest private English-language television network. Other players also extended their holdings in various forms of media.[26]

In response to these and other concerns, the House of Commons Committee on Canadian Heritage undertook an extensive study of Canadian communications and issued a mammoth report of over 870 pages. Notwithstanding the debates about the merits and problems with cross-media ownership and concentration of ownership, the best it could recommend was that "the potential problems with cross-media ownership are sufficiently severe that the time has come for the federal government to issue a clear and unequivocal policy on [the] matter" and, until it did so, the CRTC should be directed to impose a moratorium on the issuance of new licences where cross-ownership is involved.[27] Three years later, neither action has been taken. Subsequently the Senate Committee on Transport and Communications took up the issue of the "state of Canadian media" and recommended that the Competition Act be amended, that a new section be added to deal with news gathering organizations to subject them to merger review if unspecified thresholds were reached.[28] As of September 2006 no action has been taken on this recommendation.

For our purposes, the significance of this debate is that it is the result, with one qualification to be noted below, of purely domestic developments and forces. If media ownership concentration and cross-ownership are public policy problems, and it should be noted that not everyone believes them to be,[29] they are our problems, caused by Canadians and permitted to date to continue by Canadian policy makers. To the extent that these issues must be addressed, and two parliamentary committees, not to mention media observers and government ministers, believe they must be, globalization and Americanization are irrelevant to the issues.

The one qualification one should make to the last statement is that media concentration in Canada may be the perverse consequence of our fear of the other, namely the fear of Americanization. By imposing rigorous restrictions on foreign ownership of Canadian broadcasting and other forms of media such as newspapers, we have restricted the potential pool of buyers of those media. Concentration is thus a made-in-Canada policy outcome. Our own domestic policy preferences have produced the Conrad Blacks and the late Israel Asper of CanWest. In this regard, Chris Dornan raises a telling question in his contribution to this volume: Given the financial difficulties that continue to plague the *National Post*, the creation of Conrad Black and now owned by CanWest, how and why would Canada, and the goals of media and cultural diversity, be better served by letting the paper die rather than letting a foreign buyer attempt to rescue it? We may soon have to provide an answer.

The Perilous State of Canadian Programming

One of the most trenchant statements about the objectives of Canadian broadcasting that arguably has broader relevance is the opening statement of the report from the 1965 Fowler Advisory Committee on Broadcasting: "The only thing that really matters in broadcasting is programme content; all the rest is housekeeping."[30] The need or desire for Canadian content, for "Canadian stories," whether in broadcasting, film, magazines, or newspapers, is presumably the primary justification for the policy regime and the fear of being overwhelmed by American content that is the motive force for that regime.

Yet almost from the advent of television and certainly since the 1960s, Canadian programming, particularly drama, has been routinely described as being in a sorry state, if not in crisis. Almost every major inquiry has documented the problem. Three most recent public inquiries, all concluded in 2003, by the House of Commons Heritage Committee, by François Macerola for the Minister of Canadian Heritage, and by Trina McQueen for the Chair of the CRTC and Telefilm Canada, are simply the most recent iterations.[31]

Everyone, except perhaps the English-language broadcasters, acknowledges that there is not enough Canadian drama being shown, but few are in agreement on either the causes, aside from the easy availability to, and popularity amongst, Canadian viewers of resource-rich American television shows, or the solutions. For Macerola, the problem is the intermingling of cultural and industrial objectives in the Canadian content policy and an extremely confused policy infrastructure "that is fragmented, and, as a result, it lacks coherence, synergy and transparency."[32] His solution is to simplify the process and accentuate the cultural over the industrial. For others, like McQueen, the problems have been the traditional lack of funding, which was exacerbated by the recent government cut, since rescinded, in its contribution to the Canadian Television Fund, and therefore the solution is more money. For many in the industry, such as the Canadian Coalition of Audi-Visual Unions, the problem, in the words of Trina McQueen, even though she rejects the allegations, is that "the CRTC and the private broadcasters were a sort of 'Axis of Weasels' who had cozily arranged a policy regime that favoured corporate greed over the public interest." For the coalition the solution is "simple: overturn, by regulation, the licenses recently granted to the major private broadcasters and impose a stern regulatory regime, with comprehensive rules on drama hours, originals, spending, CTF (Canadian Television Fund) credits and scheduling."[33] For its part, the House of Commons Heritage Committee found itself in agreement with critics of the CRTC's self-proclaimed "success story." The critics maintained that the new policy governing priority programming and the enhanced flexibility it granted private broadcasters permitted them to schedule Canadian programs in off-peak hours and to use cheaper non-drama shows. These initiatives, it was argued, had produced a crisis for English-language television programming. Consequently, the Committee urged the Government to order the CRTC to review its 1999 television policy.[34] This it did in 2003, and it issued its report with a new set of incentives to encourage English-language Canadian content for television drama. It is too early to assess whether this approach will be any more successful than earlier attempts.[35]

What stands out in the contemporary debates, and the historical ones for that matter, is that whatever the differences in the analyses or preferred solutions, all of the commentators share one view in common: the causes of the problem, namely the inadequacy of Canadian drama, are overwhelmingly domestic in origin, not foreign. Canadians are not forced by foreign devils, American or global, to watch American programming – they simply prefer it. The dearth of Canadian programming is caused by either individual, or a mix of, domestic sources: inadequate public funding, corporate greed, confused administrative systems, regulatory lassitude. To extend Hardin's argument, in such a situation it would be a serious diversion to focus on the foreign if Canada wishes to effectively address the need for Canadians to tell their own stories.

Conclusions and Some Suggestions

For most of the past half century, Canada's communications policies, particularly in the broadcasting sectors, but with offshoots in others, have been built essentially around a regime of "command and control." Other instruments have been employed primarily in a supporting role. The ostensible rationale or justification for such a regime is that, absent such control, given the overwhelming presence of the United States and the vast Canadian appetite for its cultural products, Canadian identity, culture, and indeed its continued survival as an independent nation could not be assured. This "fear of the other," of Americanization, permeated almost every nook and cranny of the Canadian communications policy regime. More recently, the fear of the other has taken on a new guise or mask: globalization.

The central argument of this chapter is that the original premise of the regime has been highly questionable and that its repackaging would be not only highly unnecessary but diversionary. Canada has built its policy regime, especially its reliance on regulation, on premises or assumptions that are highly contestable. The central one was encapsulated in the cliché that "we are what we watch." This presumes, as Magder and others contend, that audiences are passive and simply react to and are consequently shaped by the media messages they receive. In the Canadian context, this assumption leads to the conclusion that the overwhelming presence of American media will ineluctably lead to the Americanization of Canada and Canadians. Magder suggests, supported by recent media scholarship, that the relationships between media transmitter and receiver are far more complex and interactive than the "transportation" model suggests. Supporting his argument is the evidence from Michael Adams that finds, notwithstanding the historical and contemporary omnipresence of American media products in Canada, that Canadian values are diverging from, and in very significant ways, not converging with, American values. I would suggest that this is probably even more the case since the election, and re-election, of George W. Bush as president and especially since the decision to invade Iraq.

To argue that neither Americanization nor globalization is the threat we have built our cultural/communications sectors policy edifice on is not to argue that we do not face some serious public policy problems in those sectors. Nor is it an argument that there is, consequently, no role for the state to play in these sectors. On the contrary, I would argue first that an unregulated broadcasting sector in particular cannot provide the media choices and diversity that we need and undoubtedly benefit from, and consequently, that there are some very important roles for the Canadian government to play if Canada is to help ensure cultural diversity and in particular provide an opportunity both for Canadian stories to be told and for Canadians to develop the imagination and skills necessary to tell them.

I would suggest, however, that the traditional forms of "command and control," especially those attempted primarily through regulatory instruments such as now employed by the CRTC, have outlasted their usefulness. Indeed, the longstanding and generally well-supported claim, rejected, it seems, only by the CRTC and the private broadcasters, that the CRTC has had rather limited success in commanding the private broadcasting sector and therefore attaining its primary broadcasting objective, namely ensuring high-quality

Canadian programming, especially Canadian drama, argues that new tools or instruments should be explored. Moreover, since one of the prerequisites for any successful "command and control" system is that both producers and consumers must be effectively controlled for the regime to be effective, given the increasingly opportunity for broadcasting consumers, i.e., audiences, to escape the attempted constraints on their behaviour through new, probably unregulatable delivery systems, surely makes such an exploration even more appropriate.

If program content is indeed all that really matters, and if, as all the studies appear to agree, to a greater or lesser extent, Canadian drama is severely under-provided by Canadian private broadcasters, then the Canadian state has several instruments at hand to redress the situation. One is through a well-funded public broadcaster, namely the CBC, which to date, whatever its flaws, is the only broadcaster that has traditionally and continuously taken its mandate to provide Canadian programming, especially drama, seriously. The other is to retool the regulatory regime so as to develop a funding system that can provide the resources necessary.

To date, Canadian regulation has relied primarily on Canadian content regulations for the private broadcasters, which, if not easily ignored, can be distorted and watered down so as not to impose an undue burden on them. To argue this is not to support the claim cited earlier that private broadcasters favour corporate greed over the public interest. Here I find myself in agreement with the editor of *Canadian Business* who wrote: "I don't find anything wrong with operating a TV network, even a Canadian one, as a business first and foremost" ("What made Izzy" 2003, 8). Writing of the death of Israel Asper, the editor continued "And Asper did it brilliantly – in large part by taking advantage of a win-win regulatory environment that, on the one hand, has no teeth and, on the other, was willing to grant quasi-monopolistic rights to broadcasters meeting Canadian content minimums."

The point the editor is making is not that private broadcasters are greedy but that they are simply rational economic actors. Given the weaknesses of the current Canadian content regulatory system, there is no incentive for them to spend more than they necessarily have to in order to fulfill their licence obligations. Invocations of some undefined, probably indefinable, public interest are not going to carry much weight, as the record of the past fifty years amply demonstrates.

Consequently, I would suggest that we should emphasize a system of financial incentives that will, if not encourage all private broadcasters to change their behaviour, at least result in a funding program that should be sufficient for those in the broadcasting community, public and private, who wish to produce Canadian drama that doesn't simply act as an industrial employ-ment policy but deals with Canadian themes and stories. One measure that could be employed is a variation of that proposed in the 1988 version of the Broadcasting Act, namely an incentive fund for Canadian programming.[36] This fund would be financed by a revenue tax on private broadcasters that is similar to the existing Canadian Television Fund, which is funded by the Canadian government and Canadian cable and satellite subscribers – not, incidentally, as is claimed, cable and satellite companies. Unfortunately, at the time this proposal was fought vigorously by both private broadcasters and by the Chair of the CRTC as being unnecessary and was dropped when the next version of the legislation was approved by Parliament in 1991 (Partridge 1987; Meisel 1989b). The justification for such a tax is straightforward: until broadcasting entities are no longer licensed, they are valuable commodities and should be treated as such and they should pay royalties for public pur-poses, just as occurs, for example, in the energy and lumber industries where crown lands are involved.[37]

The second measure relates to corporate sales and transfers of broadcasting licences. Although the Broadcasting Act states that the airwaves are public property, for most of the past forty years or so they have come to be treated essentially as private property. To use Marc Raboy's (1990) phrase, the public sphere has been, in effect, privately appropriated. When one leases a car or an apartment, for example, at the end of the lease, the car or apartment revert to the original owner. That has not been the case for the leasing of a temporary right to use public airwaves. When licence holders choose to leave the busi-ness, they have been free to negotiate the price for the sale of their corpora-tions, licences included, subject initially only to regulatory approval of the new owner/operator.

More recently, the CRTC has imposed a "benefits tax" on the purchaser of another licensee which amounts to 10 per cent of the overall sale price of the specific transaction.

However, while an improvement, there are serious flaws in this tax. In the first place, it is the purchaser who, subject only to regulatory ratification of the package, decides who receives the benefits of this tax. Why this should be so is unclear. Trina McQueen, in the report cited earlier, recommended that half of the proceeds of this tax should go the Canadian Television Fund. I would go further than this in two ways. In the first place, I would place all the pro-ceeds of the tax in the Canadian Television Fund. I would also substantially increase the size of the tax. I presume that the primary component of any corporate sale is the value of the broadcasting licence or licences involved. I do not understand why the seller should be the primary beneficiary of this valuable *public* resource. Consequently, the public, through the instrument of the Canadian Television Fund, should receive a share commensurate with the value of the licence as part of any sale. To determine what that share or percentage of the sale proceeds should be, the government should develop a methodology for establishing the true economic value of the public airwaves. Ensuring that those private parties who most benefit from the use of public property pay for the privilege while simultaneously developing a much expanded fund to underwrite the production of Canadian drama and other underfunded areas of Canadian content would appear to be much more useful than chasing ghosts and other ephemera such as globalization.

Bibliography

Acheson, Keith, and Christopher Maule. 1999. *Much Ado about Culture: North American Trade Disputes.* Ann Arbor: University of Michigan Press.

———. 2004. "Convention on Cultural Diversity." *Journal of Cultural Economics* 28: 243–56.

Adams, Michael. 2003. *Fire and Ice: The United States, Canada and the Myth of Converging Values.* Toronto: Penguin.

Bartley, Allan. 1988. "The Regulation of Cross-Media Ownership: The Life and Short Times of PCO 2294." *Canadian Journal of Communications* 13(2): 45–59.

Brawley, Mark R. 2003. *The Politics of Globalization.* Peterborough: Broadview Press.

Caplan, George, and Florian Sauvageau. 1986. *Report of the Task Force on Broadcasting Policy.* Ottawa: Minister of Supply and Services.

Cheadle, Bruce. 2003. "Ottawa halves magazine industry subsidy; reallocates funds to minority papers." *Canadians Press,* 8 July.

Clarkson, Stephen. 2002. *Uncle Sam and Us.* Toronto: University of Toronto Press.

Clinton, Bill. 1999. Verbatim Transcript of Speech to Forum on Federations International Conference. Mont Tremblant, Quebec, 8 October (available from CIO).

Cloutier, Rachelle. 2003. "The Cultural is Political: A Different Look at the FTAA." *Canadian Dimension* 37(2) (March–April): 37–38.

Collins, Richard. 1990. *Communications and National Identity.* Toronto: University of Toronto Press.

Fletcher, Frederick, and Robert Everett. 2004. "The Media and Canadian Politics in an Era of Globalization." In *Canadian Politics in the 21st Century,* ed. M. Whittington and G. Williams, 381–402. Toronto: Nelson.

Held, David, Anthony G. McGrew, David Goldblatt, and Jonathan Perraton. 1999. *Global Transformations*. Stanford: Stanford University Press.

Hirschman, Albert O. 1970. *Exit, Voice and Loyalty: Responses to Decline in Firms, Organizations and States*. Cambridge, MA: Harvard University Press.

King, Mike. 2004. "Restrictions lifted on foreign satellite TV systems." *Montreal Gazette*, 29 October.

Leanza, Cheryl, and Harold Feld. 2003. "More than 'a Toaster with Pictures': Defending Media Ownership Limits." *Communications Lawyer* 21(3): 19.

Magder, Ted. 1993. *Canada's Hollywood: The Canadian State and Feature Films*. Toronto: University of Toronto Press.

——. 2003. Made in Canada – An International Instrument on Cultural Diversity. Paper read at On the Edge: Is the Canadian Model Sustainable? Weatherhead Center for International Affairs.

Manera, Tony. 1996. *A Dream Betrayed: The Battle for the CBC*. Toronto: Stoddart.

Maule, Christopher. 2002. "Trade and Culture: Rhetoric and Reality." *Policy Options*, March.

Meisel, John. 1989a. "Fanning the Air: The Canadian State and Broadcasting." *Transactions of the Royal Society of Canada*, Series V, vol. IV.

——. 1989b. "Near Hit: The Parturition of a Broadcasting Policy." In *How Ottawa Spends 1989–90: The Buck Stops Where?* ed. K.A. Graham. Ottawa: Carleton University Press.

Nevitte, Neil. 1996. *The Decline of Deference*. Peterborough: Broadview Press.

Partridge, John. 1987. "CRTC Chief takes pot shot at licensing fee suggestion recently floated by minister." *Globe and Mail*, 17 November.

Posner, Richard. 1971. "Taxation by Regulation." *Bell Journal of Economics and Management Sciences* (Spring): 22–50.

Raboy, Marc. 1990. *Missed Opportunities: The Story of Canada's Broadcasting Policy*. Montreal and Kingston: McGill-Queen's University Press.

Schultz, Richard. 1995. "Paradigm Lost: Explaining the Canadian Politics of Deregulation." In *Governance in a Mature Society: Essays in Honour of John Meisel*, ed. C.E.S. Franks, 259–77. Montreal and Kingston: McGill-Queen's University Press.

——. 2003. "From Master to Partner to Bit Player: The Diminishing Capacity of Governmental Policy." In *How Canadians Communicate*, ed. D. Taras, F. Pannekoek, and M. Bakardjieva, 27–49. Calgary: University of Calgary Press.

Senate of Canada. Standing Committee on Transport and Communications. 2004. Interim Report on the Canadian News Media. April.

Stanbury, W.T., and George Lermer. 1983. "Regulation and the Redistribution of Wealth." *Canadian Public Administration* 26(3): 378–401.

Sørensen, Georg. 2004. *The Transformation of the State: Beyond the Myth of Retreat*. New York: Palgrave Macmillan.

Townshend, David. 1984. Regulation of Newspaper/Broadcasting Media Ownership in Canada. *University of New Brunswick Law Journal* 33: 261–82.

Vieira, Paul, and Kevin Restivo. 2004. "Satellite TV ruling alarms broadcasters." *National Post*, 30 October.

"What made Izzy so smart." 2003. *Canadian Business*, 26 October, 8.

Notes

1   This is a theme that has perhaps best been developed by Richard Collins (1990), in a book which has been widely read but, unfortunately, given the continuity of the arguments to be discussed later, apparently was insufficiently persuasive.

2   President Bill Clinton, Verbatim Transcript of Speech to Forum on Federations International Conference, Mont Tremblant, Quebec, 8 October 1999, available from CIO Medianet, no pagination. Ironically, the speech was widely praised by English-speaking Canadians for its presumed criticism of Quebec separatists, but they ignored or missed its relevance to larger issues in Canadian nationalism particularly, I would argue, as it pertains to Canadian broadcasting and communications issues.

3   For two such explicit instances, see Cloutier (2003), and Canada, Canadian Heritage, "Broadcasting: You are What You Watch" (1996), cited in Fletcher and Everett (2004).

4   Although less definitive, there is indirect support for Adams' argument in Neil Nevitte (1987).

5   Adams cites an Ekos poll from 2002 that 58 per cent of Canadians questioned thought that Canada was becoming more American.

6   Cultural Industries Sectoral Advisory Group on International Trade, "New Strategies for Culture and Trade in a Global World," February 1999, available from website of Department of Foreign Affairs and International Trade under head "Trade Negotiations and Agreements."

7   Three useful introductions and overviews are: David Held et al. (1999), Mark R. Brawley (2003), and Georg Sørensen (2004).

8   Perhaps the most explicit example of this is Stephen Clarkson's (2002) recent book, with a chapter on culture, which is ostensibly about globalization but is titled *Uncle Sam and Us*.

9   This is not to suggest that there are not significant implications of giant media conglomerates such as the impact of the profit motive on journalism, the apparent dumbing-down of entertainment generally, and the decline in local coverage, but these are beyond the subject of this paper.

10   Since this paper was originally written, a Quebec Provincial Court Judge has acquitted two individuals who defended themselves against charges of illegally accessing the American DirecTV system. She ruled that this prohibition was contrary to the freedom of speech provisions of the Charter and could

not be supported under Section One of the Charter. The decision is *Cour de Québec*, No. 405-73-000132-991, *Sa Majesté La Reine c. Richard Theriault et Jacques D'Argy (Oct. 28, 2004)*. For commentary, see Mike King (2004) and Vieira and Restivo (2004). This decision, however, was overturned by a Quebec superior court which argued that there was no necessity to consider freedom of speech issues.

11 For the most comprehensive survey of some of the incidents that led to this conclusion see Acheson and Maule (1999).

12 In addition to Acheson and Maule (1999), see Richard Schultz (2003).

13 Cultural Industries Sectoral Advisory Group on International Trade.

14 Ted Magder, "Made in Canada – An International Instrument on Cultural Diversity." Notes for Presentation at "On the Edge: Is the Canadian Model Sustainable?", Weatherhead Center for International Affairs, 9–10 May 2003 (unpublished but available on Magder's website at New York University), p. 9. See also Acheson and Maule (2004).

15 Christopher Maule (2002) and the articles cited therein.

16 Federal Cultural Policy Review Committee, *Report* (Ottawa: Minister of Supply and Services, 1982).

17 Minister of Communications, "Towards a New National Broadcasting Policy" (Ottawa: Department of Communications, 1983).

18 Ibid., 2.

19 Ibid., 18 (emphasis added).

20 Cultural Industries Sectoral Advisory Group on International Trade, 6.

21 The full text of the Convention can be found at http://portal.unesco.org/culture/en/ev.php-URL_ID=11281&URL_DO=DO_TOPIC&URL_SECTION=201.html (accessed March 16, 2006).

22 On this see, for example, Tony Manera (1996).

23 Department of Canadian Heritage, News Release: "Government of Canada modifies its support programs for Canadian magazines and periodicals." Ottawa, 8 July 2003, 1.

24 David Townshend (1984), as quoted in Bartley (1988).

25 Senate of Canada, Standing Committee on Transport and Communications, "Interim Report on the Canadian News Media," April 2004, 8.

26 For overviews, see the statistics provided in both the Interim Report of Senate Standing Committee on Transport and Communications cited above and the Report, entitled "Our Cultural Sovereignty," from the House of Commons Standing Committee on Canadian Heritage, June 2003.

27 Ibid., 411.

28 Senate of Canada, Standing Committee on Transport and Communications, "Final Report on the Canadian News Media," Vol. 1, p. 26. June 2006.

29 See, for example, the contribution of Ken Goldstein to this volume. Goldstein makes an impressive argument that, notwithstanding the growth in concentration, the actual effect is much diminished because of the increase

in media outlets and the corresponding fragmentation of markets and audiences.

30 Advisory Committee on Broadcasting, *Report* (Ottawa: Queen's Printer, 1965), p. 3.

31 See House of Commons Standing Committee on Canadian Heritage, op. cit.; François Macerola, "Canadian Content in the 21st Century in Film and Television Productions: A Matter of Cultural Identity," (Ottawa: Department of Canadian Heritage, June 2003); and Trina McQueen, "Dramatic Choices" (Ottawa: CRTC, May 2003).

32 Macerola, "Canadian Content,", 53.

33 McQueen, "Dramatic Choices," 14. The charge is similar to that made almost twenty years ago by Herschel Hardin in his book, *Closed Circuits* (Vancouver: Douglas & McIntyre, 1985), 44, that "The CRTC was not primarily a regulatory agency. It was a diversionary agency."

34 House of Commons Standing Committee on Canadian Heritage, 126–32 and 171–72.

35 See CRTC, "Incentives for English-language Canadian television drama," Broadcasting Public Notice CRTC 2004-93, Ottawa, 29 November 2004.

36 Minister of Communications, "Canadian Voices, Canadian Choices" (Ottawa, 23 June 1988), 28–32.

37 The current administrative fees levied by the CRTC are not comparable to the proposed revenue tax.

3: Other People's Money: The Debate over Foreign Ownership in the Media

CHRISTOPHER DORNAN

The Global and the Local

Although awash in foreign (i.e., American) media content, Canada draws the line at foreign (i.e., American) ownership of domestic media outlets. The vast apparatus of Canadian cultural policy – an ungainly contraption geared toward the protection and promotion of domestic media – has always been predicated on the insistence that, above all else, ownership must reside in Canadian hands.

Why should this be so? What nationalist imperatives or cultural priorities are advanced by such a policy? And is such a policy still tenable, or even prudent, at a time when new concourses of communication are blurring traditional demarcations between the creation, ownership, and delivery of media content, not to mention the traditional demarcations of nationalism itself? Imagine a "publication" – for lack of a better word – that exists everywhere and nowhere all at once: a pan-global ethereal amalgam of editorial content and commercial messages, as stateless as a listserve. Think of all those people all over the world with a common interest in the breeding, grooming, pedigree, and sheer love of Labradoodles. Picture a web-channel devoted to the subject, alive with contributions from Labradoodle owners in Vancouver and Melbourne and Cairo, and from people in a position to offer commercial services to Labradoodle owners: trainers, groomers, breeders. Imagine an organic, rolling, planet-wide conversation about Labradoodles. What sense does it make to talk of the "national identity" of such an undertaking?

That is what is meant by globalization. The term does not mean the wholesale imposition of American products and American values on the rest of the world. Rather, globalization refers to the capacity for trade to find and exploit market niches in countries the world over no matter the local culture. Globalization is a company's products covering the planet like a thin veneer. The Scotch whisky Glenfiddich, for example, is manufactured in a distillery that is large by local standards but still occupies grounds smaller than a mid-sized shopping mall. And yet its product can be found in bars from Singapore to Anchorage. The distillery thrives on a market that extends from Scotland to the farthest reaches of the world. The ability to do so has been healthy not only for Glenfiddich but for a number of other Scottish distilleries that would otherwise be derelict if forced to rely on a purely local market. The benefit to the Scots is not only economic but cultural, assuming one accepts that the manufacture of quality whisky is part of the Scottish cultural heritage.

It just so happens that the Americans are particularly adept at this type of international business, as anyone who has had a Pepsi in Istanbul or a Big Mac in Prague can attest, and they have a number of advantages over everyone else. They have economy of scale on their side: a domestic market large enough to support very large, intensively capitalized corporations that can use their home business bases to launch overseas expansion. They have a culture of competitive capitalism. They have a geopolitical interest in trade regimes that foster such competition, combined with the geopolitical influence to bring them about. Even more than all that, though, they have the power and the appeal of their own self-image. In the United States, Marlboro cigarettes long advertised themselves using the image of the Marlboro Man – a cowboy, a rugged individualist, a horseman in the great outdoors, resonant with the myths of the American West. When Marlboro advertised in Japan and Spain, did the brand drop the cowboy imagery in favour of local, culturally specific icons of virility? Was it the Marlboro matador in Madrid and the Marlboro sumo wrestler in Tokyo? No, it was not. People in Spain and Japan smoke Marlboro precisely because they are American cigarettes.

So, paradoxically, globalization means the promotion of national and local identity in a trade environment that obliterates national borders and pays no heed to localism. If it were not for the Scots' reputation for distilling superior whisky – which is to say, if the product were not universally acknowledged to be part of the Scottish cultural character – the Glenfiddich company would have nothing to sell worldwide. It is selling "Scottishness." Or, to put it another way, no one would buy a whisky made in Saudi Arabia.

Globalization therefore puts into play national identity and regionalism in a way that is both enticing and threatening. Living so close to the juggernaut of the United States, this country has had more experience of what globalization entails than any other. Canada has been the proving ground and the stepping stone, the test market for everywhere else. When U.S. companies from MacDonald's to Starbucks decide to expand beyond U.S. national borders they invariably begin with Canada. And what has been Canada's response to the ambitions of our largest trading partner? We have all but surrendered the large-scale manufacturing industries to American ownership, although not under conditions to our disadvantage. Canadians drive foreign cars and buy foreign kitchen appliances, but for the most part they were manufactured domestically under licence from a parent corporation.

Off Limits

Nonetheless, and despite our economic integration with the United States, we declare certain sectors off-limits to foreign control. From wheat to softwood lumber, resource extraction traditionally has been bounded by domestic policy controls. So have our national banks and financial institutions, as have our national transportation companies, from VIA Rail to Air Canada. And so have our media companies. Explicitly, and in a variety of legislative and regulatory injunctions, foreign ownership of the media in Canada is not permitted.

The reasons for prohibitions on foreign ownership of Canadian media are both political and economic.

The political rationale is that a country's culture, if it wishes to have a culture, cannot be administered by the branch-plant operations of another country's culture. Clearly, if interventions had not been taken in the early days of broadcasting, today there would be no CTV, no CanWest Global, no Alliance-Atlantis. Private-sector broadcasting in Canada would have become merely an extension of CBS, ABC, and NBC. What then for the national project?

The economic rationale is that to allow foreign ownership in the media sector would be to surrender a domestic industry to interlopers. If there are opportunities for jobs, investment, and profit, let them be ours rather than someone else's. Under U.S. ownership of the cable specialty channels, for example, why would we need the Discovery Channel (Canada) when we could as easily take the Discovery Channel (U.S.), why History (Canada) rather than History (U.S.), why the Comedy Channel (Canada) and not Comedy Central (U.S.), why Teletoon (Canada) instead of the Cartoon Network (U.S.), why YTV (Canada) over Nickelodeon (U.S.), etc.? The economic fear is that foreign ownership of Canadian media would transform Canada into the equivalent of the U.S. midwest: a vast territory that receives programming from New York and Los Angeles but generates almost no content itself.

And yet both culturally and economically the Canadian media are obviously extensions of the U.S. media. Teletoon airs *Sponge Bob Square Pants*, MuchMusic pays as much attention to Britney Spears as MTV, the Comedy Channel is happy to carry *The Daily Show*, CTV picked up *The Sopranos*, Bravo grabbed *Sex and the City*, and Showcase got *Six Feet Under*. Ownership of Canadian media outlets is not about keeping American content out. Quite the contrary. It is about channelling foreign content into the country under the most advantageous conditions.

It can certainly be argued that this arrangement has been very much to our advantage. The U.S. juggernaut has not exterminated local production. We have managed to engineer circumstances such that we get full exposure to almost everything the Americans have to offer and our own cultural content besides. In that regard, we are a richer nation than the United States. We read their novelists, but we read our own as well. We listen to their music, but we listen to our own, too. Their TV schedules and their radio airwaves are indistinguishable from ours, except that we have the CBC and they do not. We eat at Wendy's and Taco Bell and Pizza Hut, but we also have the option of Harvey's and Tim Horton's. America is just Canada with fewer choices.

Those extra choices are what make Canada distinct. Surely, then, any public policy determined to preserve a distinctive national identity should have as its singular priority the defence of that greater choice. And yet the blanket prohibition on foreign ownership of Canadian media – or, rather, the insistence on ownership as the crucial and determining factor – leads to an escalation of absurd situations in which the culturalist justification for preventing foreign control is exposed as mere camouflage for commercialist motives, or in which the logic of justification is so tortured as to be incoherent.

Citizenship

To begin with, there is the hypocrisy of a nation that outlaws majority foreign investment in its media corporations on the grounds that cultural sovereignty is at stake, but whose own nationals control media outlets in other countries without apparently compromising those nations' cultural sovereignty. Can-West Global can own television interests in New Zealand but no New Zealand company can own any media outlet in Canada. If the arrival of Can-West Global did not jeopardize national identity in New Zealand, why would

Canada be imperilled if CanWest Global were owned by a company based in Auckland?

Fixating on the citizenship of proprietors presumes that nationalist ideals course through a company as a consequence of whatever passport the boss happens to hold, as though patriotism is a trickle-down current with an on-off switch. That iconic Canadian company, Tim Horton's, is in fact owned by Wendy's, the U.S. hamburger chain. Tim Horton's did not cease to be a distinctive feature of Canadian populism when it was acquired by Wendy's in 1995, any more than the Southam newspapers overnight ceased to be Canadian the moment their then-proprietor, Conrad Black, gave up his Canadian citizenship in order to accept a seat in the British House of Lords. Nor do companies suddenly become Canadian through a quirk of birth. Edgar Bronfman Jr., CEO of the Seagram's corporation, hails from a very prominent Montreal family. When Seagram's purchased MCA, the communications colossus, that did not abruptly transform MCA into a Canadian media company, deserving of the type of tax credit support, film production subsidies, and other financial assistance measures designed to nurture homegrown companies.

Or consider the trade dispute that almost ignited between the United States and Canada in 1995 when the CRTC bumped the U.S.-owned Country Music Television channel from Canadian cable carriers. In the absence of a Canadian-owned equivalent, CMT had been a feature of upper-tier cable offerings in Canada since the mid-1980s. But in 1995 the CRTC licensed a Canadian country and western channel, what was then called the New Country Channel, based in Calgary. On the grounds that Canadian cultural interests must be protected from foreign encroachment, the CRTC removed CMT from Canadian cable.

The Americans understandably complained that this was a capricious, unfair restraint of trade. CMT had been doing business in Canada for a decade; it could legitimately argue that it had not only serviced a demand for a country and western channel in Canada, but created and expanded the market for one. Then one day it was summarily and arbitrarily deported on the pretext that Canadian culturalist imperatives trump the rules of fair trade. Even by the sinuous logic of Canadian cultural policy this was difficult to defend. Country music, after all, is a manifestly American cultural form, just as the fado is a manifestly Portugese cultural form. So, by insisting on the culturalist justification in making its ruling, the CRTC was in effect arguing for the right of Canadians to mimic a genre of U.S. cultural production while cocooned from competition from the genuine article. It was not enough to simply license a Canadian counterpart to CMT and let it fight for market share, since any domestic competitor would flounder given CMT's head start. No one would want a broadcasting licence under such conditions. CMT had to be removed from domestic cable offerings in order to provide a fail-safe commercial subscriber base for the new Canadian entrant. The loftiest arguments about cultural sovereignty were being invoked to guarantee sure-fire profits for a Canadian knock-off brand.

Rhetoric aside, the episode had very little to do with culture and almost everything to do with money – in an age when culture and money are pretty much the same thing. We have the Americans to thank for that, but there is no use crying about it now. The fact that the incident *was* about money, not culture, is revealed by how the dispute was resolved. The company that owned the U.S. Country Music Television channel was allowed to purchase 20 per cent of the new Canadian country channel. Money traded hands and the problem went away. In short, we bought them off.

Satellite Signals

Perhaps an even more telling example of the consequences of the Canadian focus on ownership of domestic media systems is the ongoing campaign to criminalize those who choose to pull their TV signals from a satellite transponder not sanctioned by the state. These are the so-called "grey area" troublemakers. They are not engaged in theft in the sense that they are not receiving a service for which they are not paying. They are not hacking into the satellite providers' systems so as to receive free TV. Rather, they are going out of their way to pay a U.S. company to deliver them television signals. Once hooked up, with their payments crossing the border monthly, they receive a panoply of channels not available through Canadian distributors: C-SPAN, HBO, Comedy Central, the Cartoon Network, etc. The signals are already in the ether, drenching urban Canada. All that is required is a satellite dish pointed in the right direction and the subscription to descramble them.

The state and the Canadian media industries – from broadcasters to cable and satellite signal distributors – are unanimous in their zeal to exterminate the grey area. They are unequivocally adamant that what the grey area amounts to is video piracy. If it is, it is a form of postmodern theft. After all, what are the grey area viewers "stealing" exactly? Presumably they are stealing customers from the domestic channels. Every Canadian who watches *Oprah* on an American network piped in from an American satellite system is a set of eyeballs lost to the Canadian network that carries *Oprah* as well as a monthly subscription payment lost to the domestic signal providers, Shaw, Rogers, Star Choice, or Bell ExpressVu. But if the grey area viewers are stealing customers, they are in effect stealing themselves. The position of the Canadian government is that Canadian viewers are the rightful property of Canadian media companies and they are not entitled to pay for the privilege of watching almost exactly the same programming on some other wavelength.

For the broadcasters, their position is that they have paid for the exclusive rights to screen their duly purchased, off-the-shelf American programming in Canada, and anyone in Canada who watches this programming via foreign signals is avoiding the tithe built into the system. For advertisers, the fear is that Canadians who do not watch television on outlets carrying Canadian advertising are a lost demographic. For the specialty channels, the danger is that they might not be able to compete if their U.S. equivalents were easily available to Canadian screens. For the cable and satellite providers, U.S. companies' competitive access to the Canadian market would mean an immediate erosion of their customer base and therefore a decline in revenue.

All this assumes that the grey area pirates choose to take their TV from U.S. providers *instead of* Canadian sources. For the moment it is more likely that they are aficionados for whom the best thing on television is more television. They are TV geeks. In which case, if a resident of Moose Jaw is purchasing services from a U.S. satellite provider *as well as* a Canadian signal provider, where is the crime?

The grey area is currently a minuscule, hounded segment of the overall viewing population. But the commercial media industries and the entire cultural-policy political apparatus are terrified of it. If the grey area were to become a legal option – if Canadians could choose between U.S. and home-grown satellite providers on the basis of the bundles of channels they offered – the elaborate cultural edifice we have built for ourselves might disintegrate. Though it never became law because Parliament dissolved, in 2004 a bill (C-2) moved into committee that would have authorized "inspectors" to enter homes and examine hardware to determine whether the household occupants might be picking up a foreign satellite signal. The penalty for being found guilty would have been up to a year in jail or a maximum fine of $25,000. Domestic ownership of media signals and systems is such a priority that our elected federal representatives barely thought twice about the suspension of fundamental rights of privacy or the conferral of extraordinary powers of search and seizure on the Television Police.

Once again, this is all about money. Canada does not block the sale or distribution of USA *Today* – or any other newspaper – anywhere within its borders, but HBO is prohibited from exhibiting itself on Canadian television screens. Why? Because being able to buy a copy of USA *Today* at a news agent in Vancouver does not compromise the customer base of the Vancouver *Sun*, much less the Canadian newspaper industry. To allow an undiluted HBO to do business in this country, however, might wreak havoc in the TV industry. And so we twist ourselves into knots trying to police our airwaves. We are worried about media convergence and concentration of ownership on the grounds that this will lessen the diversity of perspectives available to the population. At the same time, over the summer of 2004, the CRTC agonized about new program licences, eventually allowing the Arab channel Al Jazeera onto the roster (although with monitoring conditions that no distributor is equipped to enforce) but ruling against RAI, the Italian network. If "diversity" is what we are after, perhaps we might open our airwaves to any legitimate broadcasters willing to sell their wares on an open market and to any customer willing to subscribe. Certainly, the cultural policy apparatus should not be allowed to trumpet its concern for diversity without being asked to account for itself. How does the state reconcile its pride in Canada's multiculturalism, for example, with a cultural policy that prohibits Greek Canadians from watching TV from Greece, Turkish Canadians from watching TV from Turkey, and so on? When it is technically feasible for them to do so, and if they are willing to foot the bill, why is it not politically permitted?

The grey area is not a pocket of obstinate thieves of whom the state should make an example. The grey area is the future. It is already possible to tune in radio stations from all over the world on the Internet. High-quality video is only a matter of time. The walls this country has built around itself have been superceded. We can insist all we like on domestic ownership of our own media companies, but it will not prevent the tide from coming in. Whether we own the rights or the distribution networks, new types of content are on the way. The challenge is to make this work to our advantage.

Regulation

Though the insistence that Canadian media companies must remain in Canadian hands is a bedrock principle of this country's cultural policy, there is no single, blanket prohibition on foreign ownership or majority investment. Rather, different media industries are covered by a variety of different legislative and regulatory injunctions contained in a number of federal statutes. The Telecommunications Act, the Broadcasting Act, and the Radiocommunications Act all constrain ownership and control of the industries they govern. In each case, 80 per cent of company directors (and in some cases the chief executive officer) must be Canadian citizens, as must 80 per cent of voting shareholders. The Investment Canada Act also pertains to ownership of media companies and contains language defining what is meant by the cultural industries in Canada. Unlike most foreign direct investments from World Trade Organization countries, any potential foreign investment in the cultural industries is all but automatically reviewed to determine whether it passes a "net benefit" test.

As noted in a report prepared for the Department of Canadian Heritage by the Centre for Trade Policy and Law at Carleton University and the University of Ottawa:

The Investment Canada review process, as set out in the Act, remains inscrutable to all but the fully initiated and relies on satisfying bureaucratic and political judgments about what constitutes a "net benefit to Canada." The criteria set out in section 20 serve largely to provide the government with the scope to reach politically acceptable decisions. Additionally, any investment that is "related to Canada's cultural heritage or national identity" is treated more stringently than other investments and could expose any foreign investor contemplating an investment that may, indirectly, entail acquisition of Canadian assets in the cultural sector, to a forced divestiture of those assets to a Canadian buyer or the Crown. (Centre for Trade Policy and Law 2002)

In political terms, this is laying out the unwelcome mat. This is advance warning to foreign investors that the Canadian government anticipates no "net benefit" from any controlling interest in a media venture operating on Canadian soil. In 1998, when it seemed the Sun chain of newspapers might be purchased by Torstar, the company that owns the *Toronto Star*, the Sun management went looking for a white knight. Interest from American companies evaporated as soon as the U.S. properties took stock of the thicket of discouragement that stood between them and acquisition. The Sun chain is today owned by Quebecor, the Montreal-based company that is a global power in the printing industry, owns the Videotron cable company and the TVA network in Quebec, and began with the ownership of *Le Journal de Montréal*, a racy tabloid. Is the country better off because a chain of English-language urban tabloids is now the property of a debt-saddled Canadian conglomerate with next to no experience in the Sun market rather than a foreign conglomerate with next to no experience in the Sun market? Quebecor has pared employees at the Sun newspapers so as to whittle away at operating costs. The proprietor has shown no real interest or imagination for what might be done with the Sun papers. So far, they are merely chattel to be milked. As long as we are measuring what is best for the country, what is the "net benefit" of Quebecor's purchase of Sun Media?

Newspapers, books, and magazines are exempt from the statutes that regulate ownership in the media industries that rely on electricity. There is no print equivalent of the CRTC. Nonetheless, the cultural industries that rely on trees have their own set of strictures. The book publishing and retailing industries have been steadfastly protected from foreign incursion even as publishing houses disappeared and the major big-box national retailer, Chapters, began to look more and more like Air Canada: an infuriating monopoly trying to run things on the cheap. Newspapers are mainly protected by a provision of the Income Tax Act that disallows tax deductions for advertising placed in a publication that is not at least 75 per cent Canadian-owned. This means that a foreign-controlled competitor to the Montreal *Gazette* would be at a commercial disadvantage because local and national companies could not deduct the cost of advertising in its pages as a business expense. Under those conditions, advertising would never gravitate to the *Gazette's* competitor. There is nothing that outright prohibits a foreign company from publishing and selling a newspaper in Canada. It is simply that the circumstances have been rigged so as to make the prospect unprofitable.

Loophole

In the 1990s the U.S. magazine industry found and exploited a loophole in the provisions. *Sports Illustrated* produced a Canadian edition – essentially its U.S. edition with a smattering of Canadian content – and had it beamed into a printer in Canada (thereby supporting Canadian jobs). Because most of the cost of producing the magazine had already been recouped through the U.S. edition, the Canadianized version of *Sports Illustrated* (a "split-run" edition in the parlance of the industry) could afford to offer advertising rates to Canadian customers at such a low cost that businesses could do without the tax write-off. No matter that *Sports Illustrated* was proposing to fill an empty market niche – there was no indigenous Canadian sports magazine and therefore no direct competition – the appearance of the split-run edition generated near-panic in the Canadian magazine industry and the cultural policy sector. If this precedent were to stand it might only be a matter of time before publications such as *Redbook* or *National Geographic* also produced Canadian split-run editions, threatening the existence of indigenous magazines such as *Chatelaine* or *Canadian Geographic*. The incident triggered a trade dispute that was only resolved once changes were made to the regulatory regime that governed magazine publishing in Canada. The Foreign Publishers Advertising Services Act came into force on July 1, 1999, and now permits foreign publishers to sell up to 18 per cent of their advertising space to Canadian advertisers. In addition, foreign publishers whose investments in Canadian periodical publishing have been under the net benefit provisions of the Investment Canada Act are permitted unrestricted access to the Canadian advertising market. At the same time, amendments to section 19 of the Income Tax Act became effective on June 1, 2000, allowing for deductions of the cost of advertising placed in periodicals regardless of whether the publication is Canadian or foreign-owned. If the ad is placed in a magazine directed at the Canadian market and in which at least 80 per cent of the editorial content is "original," a full tax deduction is allowed. If the ad is placed in a magazine with less than 80 per cent "original" content, a 50 per cent tax deductibility is allowed (Canada 2002). These amendments pertained only to magazines; they did not apply to newspapers.

In sum, as the Centre for Trade Policy and Law has noted:

For the full panoply of cultural industries, therefore, there is a presumption that maintaining these industries in Canadian hands is critical to achieving the government's objectives regarding content. As a result, any ambitions on the part of privately-owned firms in the Canadian cultural industries to strengthen their capacity to satisfy the demands of Canadians for access to the best technologies and content are effectively constrained by the small size of the Canadian capital market and by statutes, regulations, and policies that prevent or condition access to foreign capital markets. (Canada 2002)

Industrial Tangles

Further complicating matters is the question of who, or what, precisely counts as "Canadian." As the Standing Committee on Canadian Heritage observed in its mammoth report on Canadian broadcasting, released in June 2003:

The definition of Canadian is key. This may be straightforward for individuals but can be complicated for organizations. Shareholders can own a company that itself owns other companies. The company that owns all or part of another company or companies is a holding company. Thus, the owners of the holding company indirectly own any companies owned by the parent company. (Canada 2003, 389)

In typical journalistic shorthand, the foreign ownership limit on broadcasters is often described in news reports as 47 per cent. In reality, however, this figure is arrived at via a complicated formula. As set out in a 1997 government Direction to the CRTC, foreigners may own up to 20 per cent of a broadcaster directly and up to 33.33 per cent of a holding company that owns the broadcaster. The net result is that 46.7 per cent of a broadcaster may reside in non-

Canadian hands. Nonetheless, as the Standing Committee noted, "For large corporations whose shares are widely held, a block of voting shares less than 50 per cent can still provide effective control of a corporation" (390). Accordingly, the Direction to the CRTC denies Canadian status to any company effectively controlled by foreign interests.

As tangled as the regulatory restrictions on foreign ownership may be, so is the current ownership and competitive structure of the Canadian media industries, in which newspapers are owned by broadcasters, broadcasters by telecommunication interests, cable companies compete with telephony for market share of the Internet Service Provider market, and satellite services compete with cable companies for share of the television reception market. It is the intertwining of once-distinct sectors of the media industries that brought the foreign ownership question to the fore of policy considerations in 2003 and even made it briefly an election issue in 2004, when it was suggested that the Conservatives favoured relaxing restrictions on foreign majority investment in media companies.

In the mid-1990s, with deregulation of the telephony market, a number of new ventures sprang up to compete with the two major established phone companies, Bell and Telus. In order to do so, however, they had to build their own massively expensive technical infrastructures, which left them laden with debt. When revenues failed to materialize according to projections, the upstart telcos were left floundering and in need of additional capital. Their agitations for assistance took the form of pleas to the government – principally to the Department of Industry – that the requirements for domestic corporate control be lifted, in order to allow them access to the foreign capital markets. In January 2003, a House of Commons Industry Committee began hearings to consider the issue. Almost immediately, however, other communication interests stepped forward to argue that if restrictions on foreign investment were to be lifted for the telephony companies they should also be removed for the cable TV companies and for the satellite signal providers. After all, Rogers, the cable giant, was in competition with Bell to provide high-speed Internet access. And Bell, through its subsidiary Bell ExpressVu, competed with Rogers for share of the TV distribution market, and the two of them both competed with the Star Choice satellite provider, which is in turn owned by Shaw Cable. The debate – which had begun over whether foreign investment restrictions might be relaxed for mere common carriers and signal providers – spilled over into the realm of the media content companies when the last witness to appear before the Committee offered his testimony. Leonard Asper, CEO of CanWest Global, argued that if the government were to drop foreign ownership restrictions on the telecommunication and cable companies then it should also do so for broadcasters. Mr. Asper allowed that boosting the upper limit on foreign ownership to 49 per cent would be an acceptable first step, but that any ceiling should eventually be lifted entirely (Jack 2003, FP7).

The entire drift of the Industry Committee set off shudders in the cultural-ist camp. To allow foreign ownership of the pipes, the wires, and the satellite dishes would be to open the door to foreign ownership of the newspapers, the magazines, and the television networks, because delivery and content are no longer distinguishable. The companies that own the delivery systems are implicated in the companies that provide the content, and vice versa. Mr. Asper addressed this anxiety in his remarks to the Industry Committee. He suggested that it hardly mattered who owned the media since they would still be required by the CRTC to carry original Canadian content as a condition of doing business in this country. "There is no evidence," he said, "that the nationality of the ownership is a factor at all" (Jack 2003, FP7).

Still, a majority of Canadians believes the opposite. In January 2003 a Decima Research poll found that 66 per cent were opposed to foreign owner-ship of newspapers and 54 per cent opposed foreign takeover of the private TV broadcasters (Decima Research 2003). In May 2004 an Ipsos Reid survey commissioned by the Friends of Canadian Broadcasting – a lobby group devoted to cultural nationalism – found that 70 per cent of respondents were unfavourable to foreign ownership of the media (Ipsos Reid 2004). The news media themselves sensed that this was shaping up as a little drama within government and policy circles, with the commercialist desire to liberalize trade regimes pitched against the culturalist insistence on the sanctity of the forums of public attention. It so happened that the Minister of Industry at the time, Allan Rock, was a long-shot contender for the leadership of the Liberal Party, as was Sheila Copps, the Minister of Heritage. Of such things are news stories born.

Commerce vs. Culture

The thought experiment in the business press began in earnest. What if the government actually did allow foreign controlling capital into the telecom-munication sector? Surrendering the media content companies to foreign control was politically unsaleable. Could this mean a scenario in which the carrier companies – the wires and wireless people – divested themselves of their content companies? That would mean that Bell Communication Enter-prises (BCE) would have to shed Bell Globemedia, which owns CTV and the *Globe and Mail*. Shaw would have to unload Corus Entertainment, which owns YTV and the production company Nelvana. Rogers would have to rid itself of Rogers Media, which owns *Maclean's* and *Chatelaine*. Some of these companies may well wish to sell some of their content subsidiaries, but forcing them all to do so in one fell swoop is like taking a cleaver to a Gordian knot.

The Commons Industry Committee delivered its report in April 2003. What started out as an inquiry into the telephone business controversially included in its recommendations the cable and satellite providers, even though these, as content companies, fall under the purview of the Ministry of Heritage. In a nutshell, the committee called for an end to foreign ownership limits on Canadian signal providers. As to the suggestion that this opened the door to U.S. domination of Canadian culture, the committee was convinced that "carriage and content are distinct entities, and that distribution can be separated from programming undertakings" (Canada, 2003a, Chapter 4; subsection "Canadian content and the role of the CRTC").

Meanwhile, a Commons Committee on Canadian Heritage had been conducting a two-year inquiry into Canadian broadcasting. Six weeks after the Industry Committee delivered its verdict, the Heritage Committee delivered an 872-page report (Canada, 2003) that came to utterly opposite conclusions, arguing that the Industry Committee's recommendations were the result of "an extremely simplistic approach to a complex set of issues" (421). Amid a general sentiment that somehow the brakes should be applied to galloping developments in media corporatism, the Heritage Committee explicitly recommended that the prohibitions on foreign ownership be maintained. It did so on the grounds of absolute terror. "The Committee is of the view that one wrong move could do irreparable harm to the Canadian system. Once this happens, there will be no turning back" (420). Better to do nothing at all than to muck about with what we currently have.

When a parliamentary committee delivers a report, the government is required to read a response into the record. Here, a government in the throes of a leadership transition was compelled to react to two contradictory reports from two competing constituencies without committing itself to anything. The response to the Industry Committee recommendations came in late September 2003. Signed by Allan Rock, it allowed that ownership restrictions of the telecommunication companies should be abandoned and that it would be "irresponsible" not to do the same for cable and satellite companies. Nonetheless, it conceded that the entire issue required further study by the bureaucracy, who were enjoined to report by spring 2004. Six weeks later, in November 2003, the Liberal government responded to the report of the

Heritage Committee. Signed by Sheila Copps, the response accepted that "convergence is now a core business strategy in the information era" (a nod to commercialist imperatives) but called for further study of the issues raised by cross-media ownership. It also noted that yet another government body was in the midst of inquiring into a related area – the Senate Committee on Transportation and Communications was examining the news media – and that it would be premature and presumptuous to come to conclusions until the Senate committee had rendered its findings.

Following the election of 2004, the new Minister of Heritage, Liza Frulla, declared that there would be no relaxation of the ban on foreign control of cable distributors or broadcasters (Jack, 2004, B5), while the new Minister of Industry, David Emerson, mused that the government should not stand in the way of mergers in the banking industry and should lift foreign ownership restrictions on the telecommunications industry (Tuck 2004, B1; Carmichael 2004, FP5). Since then, the minority Liberal government was defeated in the general election of 2006, to be replaced by a minority Conservative government. More than two years after the Industry and Heritage committees delivered their reports, the issue stood at the same impasse. It is unclear what latitude the government will have to arrive at a resolution, since its minority status presumably means it must attend, in some regard, to the priorities of the other parties, and only the Conservatives would be favourable to easing restrictions on foreign ownership in the media sectors. Nonetheless, at some point the issue will have to be addressed foursquare.

What If?

Obviously, no one wants the Canadian media to become mere comprador subsidiaries of U.S. giants – or, at least, no one sane who lives north of the 49th parallel. If foreign investment means the extermination of Canadian content then it is a hideous and malign idea. But what if the prospect of more foreign capital in Canadian media markets could be engineered so as to be neither a surrender of cultural sovereignty nor a threat to an indigenous industry? Consider the case of the *National Post*.

The paper may well now be on a course toward solvency, but for the first years of its existence it lost millions. Just hypothetically, suppose the paper continued to record losses that its corporate parent, CanWest Global, simply could not sustain, threatening the paper's very existence. Suppose, if it were to close, that it dragged the *Financial Post* down with it. The country would then have lost not only a competitor to the *Globe and Mail* and its *Report on*

Business, but a rare and precious opportunity. National political and business newspapers are difficult to start up. Once they are dead, they are impossible to resuscitate.

What if a foreign buyer were to step forward? What if it were the *New York Times* corporation, a company of considerable resources, multiple holdings, and an eminent reputation? What if the *Times* said, yes, we will purchase the *National Post.* We will keep it alive, we will invest in it, we can take the losses for a while, and we will do so with the intention of establishing the Canadian equivalent of the *New York Times*: a paper of record that is profitable to those who invest in it, rewarding to those who work for it, and of clear benefit to those who read it. Obviously such a property would have to be staffed and run by locals, even if they reported to a head office in New York.

Why would that be a bad idea? Why would it be better to let the *National Post* die than allow a foreign undertaking to take the risk of trying to keep it alive?

Canadian cultural policy should not be about devising ways to keep the Americans at bay. It should be about devising ways to make their money work in our interests, culturally, economically, and selfishly. There is a model of how to do so. It is the *Reader's Digest* corporation.[1]

Globalization in Reverse

It is true that the concept of *Reader's Digest* is American, that the Canadian company is an offshoot of a global company with headquarters in the United States, and that there are editions of the magazine in every developed country in the world. Still, if one compares an issue of the Australian *Reader's Digest* with the same month of the Czech edition they have almost nothing in common. The content is not homogenous. It is the formula that is consistent. Around the world, the stories *Reader's Digest* carries are of a certain type. Whether about encounters with grizzly bears or the triumph of good souls over adversity, they are intended to be uplifting. The *Reader's Digest* franchise has been built on the premise that it is possible to cheer people even as you inform them. Newspapers are mostly depressing because they specialize in bad news and trivia, day in and day out. *Reader's Digest* is like a monthly rebuttal to the local broadsheet: it is upbeat to its core.

The *Reader's Digest* operation in Canada has a good deal to do with a previous generation's attempt to finesse the foreign-ownership question. Thirty years ago the Trudeau Liberals sought to eliminate U.S. players from the domestic media market. Faced with restrictions that would otherwise have shut down the *Reader's Digest* presence in Canada, in 1976 the company instead elected to comport itself as a Canadian company, investing in its Canadian operations. The publisher of the magazines is Reader's Digest Magazines (Canada) Ltd., which is 75 per cent owned by the wholly Canadian-owned Reader's Digest Foundation. The remaining 25 per cent of the shares are owned by the Reader's Digest Association (Canada) Ltd., which is U.S.-owned. The result is that, today, the *Reader's Digest* presence in Canada is fiercely and proudly Canadian. On all manner of criteria it performs far better than most domestic media companies. To begin with, it publishes in both English and French, and its French-language edition is markedly different from its English-language sister. Does the *Globe and Mail* publish a French-language version for readers in Sudbury and St. Vital and Dollard des Ormeaux? No.

Reader's Digest does carry articles from the U.S. version, but only when it is clear that these would be of interest to Canadian readers. In relative terms, the amount of U.S. copy in its pages is small. Its Canadian content far outstrips the proportion offered by Canadian private sector broadcasters. And as the largest circulation magazine in the country it employs a full complement of advertising, marketing, circulation, and editorial staff, not to mention providing a well-paid market for Canadian freelance writers and photographers. In addition, Canadian writers and photographers receive international exposure in markets from Finland to Singapore through other *Reader's Digest* editions.

More than that, though, the company is sufficiently knowledgeable about its market that in 2004 it launched a new magazine, *Our Canada*. Edited by the staff of *Reader's Digest* in Montreal, the magazine is entirely devoted to the stories of this country and written by ordinary Canadians (e.g., the worst snowstorm I ever lived through, the best hockey game I ever saw, the most memorable Canadian I ever met). It is pure Canadian content. It is a venture launched by a company with the wherewithal and the confidence to take the risk. Where is the downside?

Reader's Digest offers a model of how globalization can work in the media. It is not the Glenfiddich model, in which one markets around the world a product that is very much the issue of a local culture, and does so on the strength of the product's local cultural attributes. Rather, *Reader's Digest* is the Glenfiddich model in reverse, in which a pan-global product is purposely adapted to the different national and regional markets it seeks to address. It is globalism inflected with local cultural identity – globalism with a distinctive face.

What is so wrong, then, with *Reader's Digest* doing business in this country under these terms? And if there is nothing wrong with it – if, in fact, there is a good deal to be said for it – then why not learn from it? There may be a way to permit an influx of foreign capital that is to everyone's advantage.

Bibliography

Canada. Department of Canadian Heritage. Centre for Trade Policy and Law. 2002. "Canadian Cultural Policy, Ownership Restrictions, and Evolving International Trade Rules." http://www.pch.gc.ca/progs/ac-ca/progs/rc-tr/progs/dpci-tipd/pubs/cdpc-ctpl/index_e.cfm

Canada. Parliament. House of Commons. Standing Committee on Canadian Heritage. 2003. *Our Cultural Sovereignty: The Second Century of Canadian Broadcasting.* Standing Committee on Canadian Heritage; Clifford Lincoln, chair.

——. Standing Committee on Industry, Science and Technology. 2003a. *Opening Canadian Communications to the World: Report of the Standing Committee on Industry, Science and Technology.* Walt Lastewka, chair.

Carmichael, Kevin. 2004. "Telco rules on owners no harm: Emerson." *National Post,* 4 September.

Decima Research. 2003. "Canadians Oppose Foreign Control: Poll." 16 January.

Ipsos Reid. 2004. "Attitudes toward Protecting Canadian Culture on TV, the CBC, Foreign Ownership and Media Concentration." 16 May.

Jack, Ian. 2003. "CanWest's Asper calls for fair rules: Foreign ownership." *National Post,* 28 February.

——. 2004. "Foreign ownership limits will stay: Cable, broadcasters must be Canadian owned: Frulla." *National Post,* 21 July.

Tuck, Simon. 2004. "Top minister calls for bank mergers; David Emerson, newly minted Industry Minister, wades into policy minefield." *Globe and Mail,* 3 September.

Notes

1   In the interests of full disclosure, the author sits on the boards of Reader's Digest Magazines (Canada) and the Reader's Digest Foundation.

4: Canadian Television and the Limits of Cultural Citizenship

BART BEATY and REBECCA SULLIVAN

In November 2002, the authors were invited to Ottawa to speak before the Standing Committee on Canadian Heritage on the issue of diversity in broadcasting. Filled with an ennobling sense of national duty, we entered the arena prepared to raise questions on how diversity is being defined and implemented in the current framework and suggest new ways of thinking through the role of television in creating a sense of cultural citizenship. We left rather chastened, with the realization that some politicians charged with the stewardship of television were not quite ready to listen. While comments on expanded markets for ethnic language programming were politely received, there was still an overarching sense that politicians and industry executives alike continue to view broadcasting as a national exercise in cultural obligation rather than a new kind of public sphere in which Canadians have an active, participatory role to play. It is specifically on this area of ethnic broadcasting that we would like to focus our arguments here. While other issues such as sexual, economic, political, and religious diversity are just as important, the example of ethnicity strikes at the heart of one of Canada's cherished nationalist ideals, multiculturalism, and can point to new strategies for television as a key site in the formation of cultural citizenship in the global mediascape. By that we mean that a Canadian public sphere can no longer be considered in the singular and that public cultures are by necessity mediated through our cultural industries like broadcasting. What it means to be Canadian and how we express, consume, debate, and imagine our identity are questions that are increasingly formed through our relationship to the mass media. That the media are less and less curtailed by national borders disrupts traditional notions of citizenship as a nationalist ideal. Rather, cultural citizenship is about reframing the national in juxtaposition with the local and the global and embracing diversity and multiplicity in a wide range of interrelated public cultures.

All these bold ideas went out the window when Bart Beaty responded to concerns about the encroachment of so-called grey market satellite providers onto the national services regulated by the CRTC. Grey market satellite systems are subscription-based television services that are not owned by Canadian companies, but whose subscriber base is from Canada. They are seen to be siphoning off revenue that could potentially go to licensed Canadian cable and satellite companies like Bell ExpressVu or Rogers digital cable, for example. Rather than straightforwardly condemn them, Bart commented that, in his opinion, a large portion of the audience for these services were recent immigrants and ethnic communities seeking programming from their home country. Thus, the expansion of this market should be seen as a call to the Canadian industry and regulatory agencies that they were not serving the needs of the nation in its current make-up and that the solution lay in more flexible, open access.

The response of the committee was near-unanimous: It's illegal, therefore they shouldn't do it, end of story. The "just say no" attitude of the committee on that day was not merely short-sighted. It speaks to the way that the Canadian television industry has positioned its audience as passive consumers marshalled in the service of a massive economic infrastructure that cunningly plays each side against the other. Under the cloak of cultural sovereignty, Canada continues to promote protectionist measures for the broadcasting industry that undermine diversity and multiculturalism. It also steadfastly refuses to acknowledge that the cultural and technological landscape has changed dramatically since the earlier and still dominant model of media scarcity and border patrol. From industry to governmental agencies, it appears that those who have been appointed the gatekeepers of Canadian broadcasting are not yet willing to consider the potential of globalization and transnational culture to transform the industry into a world leader for openness, access, and diversity. Thus, the example of Canadian television at the crossroads speaks to the limits of Canadian cultural citizenship more broadly.

Our Cultural Sovereignty: The Lincoln Committee and its Aftermath

Released in June 2003, the Heritage Committee report, *Our Cultural Sovereignty: The Second Century of Canadian Broadcasting*, offered ninety-seven recommendations pertaining to the future of the broadcasting industries.

These included suggestions for changing the way that broadcasting is governed and administered, including reforms to the structure of the Canadian Radio-television and Telecommunications Commission (CRTC), the development of a new act that would replace the Telecommunications Act, the Canadian Radio-television and Telecommunications Act, and the Broadcasting Act, and a resolution of the conflict that is derived from having two government departments – Industry and Canadian Heritage – sharing jurisdiction over broadcasting. Additionally, the committee called for a new broadcasting monitor, a revamping of support programs, and initiatives to promote community and local broadcasting. Highlighted in the report was the transition to digital technologies, and Canada's opportunity to become a world leader in the new digital age. While this has long been a priority of the Canadian cable and satellite industry, the industry players who have most benefited from the digital transition to date, the committee did not accept the cable industry's desire for greater levels of foreign ownership. This put the Heritage Committee firmly at odds with an Industry Committee suggestion from April 2003 that called for the dismantling of foreign ownership regulations, highlighting the discrepancy between the cultural and industrial dispositions towards broadcasting policy. As Chris Dornan argues elsewhere in this book, it appears that the drive towards globalization is still viewed by some as an encroachment on national culture. The committee took a dim view of cross-media ownership and called upon the government to announce a clear policy on the matter in order to ensure broad access and representation for all Canadian publics. Finally, the committee called for stable long-term funding for the CBC and the Canadian Television Fund (CTF) in order to preserve Canadian programming and for the CRTC to permit cable companies and satellite services to offer a wider range of international programming services.

While many hoped that such a major initiative would bring culture back to the front burner of Canadian political debate, the report ultimately garnered little attention. The government's response to the Heritage Committee report, under the jurisdiction of Sheila Copps, then-Minister of Heritage and a dark horse candidate for Liberal party leader, promised little other than reviews of existing frameworks. On key questions such as foreign ownership and cross-media consolidation, the government proposed to conduct further research into the questions and offered little sense of the direction that it might take. While agreeing that stable funding for the CBC and CTF were important priorities, it was also noted that these organizations had a responsibility to better manage themselves and communicate their visions and priorities to Canadians. On the issue of promoting local television, the government promised very little. They pledged to examine the existing situation, but no more. Further, they minimized any criticisms by noting that the Direct to

Home (DTH) satellite providers were required to carry local commercial stations in small markets, despite the fact that this is radically different from the vision of open-access community television proposed by the committee. The usual multicultural platitudes were present, but there were no suggestions to ensure that diversity would be an integral value in any reforms of the broadcasting system. Both Copps and the new minister, Liza Frulla, have publicly reiterated their commitment to protecting Canadian ownership of media and broadcasting outlets as a cornerstone of national culture building.

In their first response to the Lincoln report, the government rejected calls for additional leniency with respect to foreign-language broadcasters, noting that ninety-three foreign-owned channels were licensed for broadcast in Canada. The government failed to acknowledge that only ten of these were ethnic language (i.e., neither English nor French) (Canada 2003). This rather pathetic representation of channel choice for a vast number of linguistic minorities in Canada was apparently not perceived as a problem by the government, whose response frames the issue in light of Canada's relationship with the United States (the originators of the vast majority of those ninety-three channels) rather than with the rest of the world. It is this tension between old border relationships and new forms of globalization that frames our concern over the future of Canadian television and the role it can play in the formation of a distinct kind of cultural citizenship that transcends nationalist rhetoric. It reflects a longstanding dynamic between economic and technological theories of scarcity and social and cultural anxieties over identity. Now, in an era of media abundance, the technological fix is put forward to mitigate against accusations of protectionism while claims of threats to cultural sovereignty prevent an opening up of the airwaves to a truly multicultural broadcasting universe.

Canadian Programming versus Canadian Audiences

In June 2003, the Canadian Cable Television Association (CCTA) applied to the CRTC to add sixteen American English-language channels to the list of eligible channels that cable companies could offer to digital cable subscribers. These included such popular networks as ESPN, HBO, Showtime, and Nickelodeon Kids. As the main lobby organization for the cable industry, whose major players include Shaw, Rogers, Cogeco, Videotron, and Eastlink, the CCTA proposed that these channels be bundled with existing licensed Canadian digital channels, and that these bundles would increase consumer choice and diversity, maximize competition, reduce the black and grey markets, and accelerate the adoption of digital television by consumers (CCTA 2003). The Canadian Association of Broadcasters (CAB), representing

Canada's private broadcasting channel owners such as CHUM, CTV, and Global, vehemently opposed the application, arguing that it was "a cynical cash-grab" that would erode the Canadian broadcasting system (CAB 2003a). CAB argued that allowing American specialty channels directly into Canada would mean that many popular imports like HBO's *Six Feet Under* would be moved from basic cable channels like Showcase to more expensive digital cable services, to which only one-third of the country subscribed. It is important to note that this response didn't protest the influx of American programming into Canada *per se*, just how it would be delivered and who stood to profit. For cable companies, bringing popular U.S. channels into the country would mean more people would subscribe to expensive digital cable services. For broadcasters, the status quo means that they control the market for these shows and keep the advertising revenue for themselves.

The CCTA framed the issue as one of cultural rights and consumer choice, arguing that Canadians should be allowed to watch ESPN or HBO or FOX News legally if they so choose. CAB, on the other hand, suggested that the question revolved around cultural sovereignty and the integrity of the broadcasting system as a whole, generally equating the health of the Canadian broadcasting culture with the financial health of private broadcasters. CAB was correct to point out that private broadcasters contribute far greater percentages of their revenues to support Canadian programming. Thus, if producing original Canadian content is the prime motivator of broadcast policy then it makes sense to maintain the system as is, using revenue from popular U.S. shows to subsidize original Canadian programming like *Corner Gas*. Yet, cutting through the nationalist cultural rhetoric reveals a rather simple case of two wealthy industries attempting to ensure their own profitability. Licensing American channels benefits American interests and those of cable and satellite companies who will derive revenue from new subscriptions. Barring those channels, on the other hand, ensures that Canadian broadcasters can continue to maintain an inexpensive pool of popular foreign-produced programming that they can purchase in order to sell their own channels. The core question became, whose bottom line most deserved further enriching? Ultimately, the CRTC sided with CAB and denied the application, maintaining a tight lid on the number of American channels available legally to Canadian viewers.

CAB has long promoted itself as the core of the Canadian broadcasting system. A press release days after the Liberal Party leadership convention in 2003 reminded the new government of Paul Martin that more than 80 per cent of television watched in Canada was watched on Canadian private broadcasting stations (CAB 2003b). The next day, CAB released a Decima poll indicating that Canadian media was important for keeping Canadians informed of world and national events, and that seven in ten Canadians would accept a greater proportion of tax dollars being used to ensure that Canadian content is available for years to come (Decima Research 2003). A Strategic Council survey in March 2004 also indicated a preference for Canadian programming, in which 57 per cent of respondents wanted more Canadian stories on television. The same survey, however, indicated that 22 per cent of Canadians wanted more international and foreign-language programming (CCTA 2004b). While on the surface, these two studies may suggest clear support for continuing a longstanding policy of cultural protectionism, their findings must be qualified in several important ways. In the CAB poll, broadcasting was not in the top ten responses for government priorities, meaning that it failed to reach even 1 per cent in an unprompted response (Decima Research 2003, 4). Further, the poll respondents were not asked if they would support shifting funds from priority areas such as health care, education, and other social programs to bolster Canadian content on television, so the favourable response comes without any real weight or consequence. Finally, in neither case are the results borne out by actual viewing patterns in Canada.

According to the weekly ratings of Canadian television viewing compiled by BBM Canada for the 2003/04 season, only three Canadian programs regularly cracked the top twenty most watched English-language shows in the country: the CTV Evening News, Hockey Night in Canada, and the NHL Playoffs. Instead, what most Canadians watch in large numbers are American programs carried by CTV and Global, with the most popular consistently being *Survivor, C.S.I., C.S.I. Miami, Law & Order, Law & Order SVU, Law & Order: C.I., Fear Factor, Friends,* and *American Idol*. Of these, the closest to being Canadian content is the CSI franchise, which is co-produced by the Canadian company Alliance-Atlantis, although the shows are set in American cities, shot in America, and use predominantly American actors. While the 2004/05 season is still in its infancy as of this writing, there are some interesting developments for Canadian television. *Canadian Idol,* the franchise show hosted by Ben Mulroney and airing on CTV, saw its finale crack the Top 3 in September. While this can't exactly be called indigenous or unique Canadian programming, CTV has other reasons to cheer since its sitcom *Corner Gas* regularly ranks in the Top 20, with its season premiere debuting in the 14th spot. The only other Canadian show to make it to the Top 20 was the first episode of CBC's *The Greatest Canadian,* which made it to 16 but failed to keep its audience on a weekly basis.

In French-speaking Canada the situation is quite different, with no non-Canadian programs regularly cracking the Top 20 lists. Instead, indigenous programming provided overwhelmingly by SRC, and by private broadcasters

TVA and TQS, dominates the ratings. Among the consistently most popular shows for 2003/04 are *Star Académie, Les Bougon, Fortier, Km/h, Occupation Double, Loft Story, Tribu.com,* and *Arcand.* Furthermore, Quebec is a major partner in a unique global media experiment, TV5. This is a pan-francophone cable broadcaster that airs dramatic and current affairs programming with the aim of strengthening francophone culture worldwide, transcending national barriers. Thus, both by its success at nationally based programming and its ability to raise its sights beyond the borders, the example of Quebec suggests that Canadian identity can actually be strengthened through a more globalized, cross-cultural approach to television rather than through protectionist measures that limit Canadians' access to alternative perspectives and visions.

Indeed, the recent small successes of *Canadian Idol* and *Corner Gas* for English Canada nestled amidst predominantly American programming suggest that Canadians are more than capable of navigating the television landscape in order to carve out a distinct sense of national culture that is built on diversity and globalization as well as distinct identity. This leads us to question the validity of curtailing access to foreign channels in the name of preserving Canadian programming, as CAB argued. In fact, despite their poll results, it seems that Canadian audiences do not want to sacrifice choice for the good of the nation. The rise of grey market satellite, whereby Canadians subscribe to a satellite system that is not owned by a Canadian company, has touched off a storm of debate over the limits of cultural sovereignty in a globalized market. It pits Canadian viewers against a paternalistic Canadian broadcasting system that claims to be doing what's best for the country while it really seems to be just protecting its own profit margin.

The Satellite Grey Market

A major argument of the CCTA for bringing U.S. channels to Canada was that it would prevent satellite signal theft. This has been a front-burner issue for several years now, particularly with the formation of the Coalition Against Satellite Signal Theft (CASST) to lobby government for stiffer penalties and to try to convince Canadians that signal theft is not a victimless crime. In September 2002, the president of the CCTA estimated that there were as many as 700,000 illegal satellite dishes in Canada (Yale 2002). However, not all of these were actually "stolen." In most cases, Canadians had purchased the satellite service, just not from a Canadian company. This, in a nutshell, is the definition of the grey market. The distinction between grey and black markets was apparently lost on the Supreme Court of Canada when it ruled in April 2002 that the decoding of encrypted signals originating from a foreign distributor, even if you paid for the privilege, contravened the Radio-communication Act. That said, the courts left the door open as to whether that Act violated the Charter of Rights and Freedoms. A grey answer to a grey question. Unfortunately, a court challenge that the law violates the Charter's guarantee to "freedom of thought, belief, opinion, and expression, including freedom of the press and other media of communication" by Incredible Electronics was abandoned in August 2003, with the company citing "prohibitive legal costs" relating to the case (Schechter, FP 1). This left the question of the constitutionality of grey market satellite use unresolved, although the CASST, CRTC, and other industry players routinely insist that the matter is closed: "You know, stealing books in a bookstore is wrong – this is equally true when an individual steals programming using illegal satellites. It's clearly wrong and the Supreme Court of Canada has unequivocally upheld this today" (CAB 2002). However, this is not "equally true," as a Quebec court ruled in October 2004, declaring the ban on grey market satellite systems unconstitutional. In the case of grey market satellite users, they are not stealing, but paying for an unauthorized service. The apt comparison is not to stealing books from bookstores, but to buying books from Amazon.com instead of Indigo.ca. Television is, as Dornan also points out, the only medium in the country that tightly supervises Canadians' access to ensure that we only use authorized national outlets.

If the CCTA focus groups are correct, one of the prime motivators for grey market satellite use is consumer choice and cultural diversity. In the simplest terms, American satellite providers offer a greater selection of channels than do Canadian providers. This discrepancy is particularly pronounced in the case of ethnic language television channels. A 2003 CRTC report on ethnic television services in Canada trumpeted, "Canadians enjoy access to a wide variety of ethnic services," yet the regulatory agency had to be using a very narrow definition of the term "wide" to draw this conclusion (CRTC 2003; 2004d). The CRTC found that in the fourteen largest Canadian television markets, four analogue specialty services were available (Telelatino, Fairchild TV, SATV, and Odyssey), catering to the Italian/Spanish, Cantonese, South Asian, and Greek communities respectively. Further, eleven of the forty-four licensed Category 2 ethnic digital specialty services were available in at least some regions of the country, primarily in Rogers' territory of Ontario. While Rogers made available to its subscribers channels in Portuguese, Punjabi, Korean, and Urdu, ethnic television choices were severely restricted in other parts of the country.

Even where ethnic populations are sizeable, their interests are not always well represented. For example, in Toronto, no channels specifically target the more than 100,000 Jamaican Canadians or the 90,000 Polish Canadians, while in Winnipeg, the 36,000 Ukrainian Canadians had no channel to call their own. Further, even when a community was served, it was often in a rudimentary fashion. Perhaps the best example is that Toronto's 318,000 Italian Canadians, 8 per cent of the city's total population, were served by Telelatino, a channel that broadcasts only half its time in Italian, with the remainder in Spanish. Their only other resource is CFMT, a basic cable channel that only airs in Ontario, which boasts 60 per cent of its programming in fifteen non-official languages, serving eighteen distinct cultures ("About OMNI" 2004). That a significant linguistic minority in the nation's largest city was provided only half a television channel as late as 2003 speaks loudly to the way that the CRTC understood its responsibilities under the Broadcasting Act to "reflect the circumstances and aspirations, of Canadian men, women and children, including equal rights, the linguistic duality and multicultural and multiracial nature of Canadian society." While some would argue that limits to ethnic broadcasting are necessary to strengthen Canadian cultural identity as a unique and cohesive experience that binds from sea to sea to sea, we believe that what is unique and cohesive about Canada is precisely our openness to diversity and multiculturalism. We are, therefore, far better served by opening up the airwaves to express that identity than perpetuating a nationalist attitude that insists on protectionist measures and a homogenous view of Canadian cultural citizenship.

The significance of the grey market satellite industry to ongoing debates about television's role in reproducing national cultural identity can be easily understood with reference to ethnic language channel selection. While in 2003, there was only half of a channel broadcast in Spanish in Canada (with four and a half additional Spanish language channels authorized to broadcast in 2004), the American satellite leader DirecTV offered a total of thirty-one channels. For Canadians wanting television in Spanish, the choice was seemingly clear cut and has led to a significant audience for grey market satellite. Canadian broadcasters and regulatory agencies may want to present this issue as a necessary form of cultural protection from the American television behemoth, but with the wide access to U.S. cable programming on Canadian channels, the idea that the grey market is being used predominantly to get HBO does not hold up, especially since American programming is already widely available on basic and extended cable in Canada with even more on Canadian digital services.

Rather, it exposes Canada's lack of support for diversity and multicultural access in a globalizing environment, as is evident in the government's response to this growing demand. First, the CRTC authorized a small number of additional non-Canadian ethnic language channels in Canada, then the government made a tough albeit hollow stance on satellite signal theft with new legislation. Introduced in February 2004, Bill C-2 would have amended the Radiocommunication Act to significantly increase the penalties for retransmitting or decoding an unauthorized signal. This bill, which died on the table and has not yet been revived, angered a large number of ethnic groups across the country, as it was seen as a direct attack on cultural diversity and an attempt to criminalize the cultural choices of a large number of Canadians whose interests were not being served by the existing regulatory framework. The *Montreal Gazette*, for example, quoted Francisco Salvador, a Portuguese Canadian who regularly watched Portuguese soccer matches at a community centre in LaSalle: "If Bill C-2 closes that door, we would have to close. If we don't have the television, we have nothing" (Thompson 2004, A14).

In July 2004, the CRTC attempted to respond to Canadians like Salvador by authorizing nine non-Canadian third-language services. These new channels, whose authorization was ostensibly intended to help fight signal theft (CRTC 2004b), included general interest channels in German and Romanian, four Spanish channels (Canal SUR [news], CineLatino [movies], Grande Documentales de TVE [documentaries], and Utilisima [women]), a Spanish and Portuguese movie service, and two Arabic channels, ART Movies and Al Jazeera. Clearly, the new channels did little to deal with Mr. Salvador's interest in Portuguese soccer, a service that he would still need to access from a grey or black market provider. Six additional channels, including four in Spanish, one in Arabic, and one in Italian, were denied authorization. These included RAI International, the extremely popular broadcaster from Italy, and TVE, the popular Spanish channel.

The hearings pitted the economic interests of the cable industry (CCTA), who would benefit from increased channel subscriptions, against those of the Canadian broadcasters (CAB), whose members feared increased competition for viewers and escalating prices for foreign programming. Ultimately, the CRTC rejected channels in cases where they were perceived to threaten the economic interests of established or proposed Canadian channels, despite demands from cultural communities for greater viewing options. For example, three general-interest Spanish-language channels (Azteca 13 Internacional, TV Chile, and TVE Internacional) were rejected with the reasoning that Spanish-Canadians were already well served by half of Telelatino's programming time, and by two licensed, but unlaunched, channels, Telemundo Canada and TV Chile Canada. Similarly, RAI International was denied authorization despite a petition signed by more than 100,000 Italian Canadians requesting access to the popular channel. Amidst growing outrage, Minister Frulla agreed to amend this decision to allow consumers to subscribe to an international channel if they also pay for the Canadian-based channel. While the television situation for some linguistic minorities in Canada was improved in mid-2004, the partial measures taken by the CRTC cannot reasonably be seen as a significant effort to alleviate the problem of the grey market, and given the minister's public commitments to protect Canadian broadcasters, it seems more likely that the government will continue to seek ways to criminalize access to Portuguese soccer rather than to authorize it.

The extra attention to Spanish rather than Italian or Pacific Rim services also raises an important issue about the way Canada continues to view the role of broadcasting in service to a national culture. Canada, and in particular Toronto, has the highest proportional population of Italian immigrants and one of the largest Chinatowns in the western world, with expanding communities across the country from Korea, Vietnam, and Japan as well as China. Yet access varies across the country. For example, the industry leader, Rogers, offers one channel each for the four main Pacific Rim countries, while western Canada's Shaw only provides Fairfield (Cantonese) and JapanTV. In the latest round of licensing, only one Italian channel received the green light compared with four Spanish channels. Speculation suggests that this result did not arise from a desire to best serve Canada's linguistic minorities in a way that reflects our own cultural landscape, but was rather an economic initiative directly targeting U.S.-based satellite services by offering something that poorly approximates the selection available quasi-legally to Canadian subscribers through DirecTV. Rather than looking outward onto a global field in which Canada could serve as a leader in transnational, multicultural broadcasting, we continue to set our sights resentfully and jealously on America. In other words, we insist stubbornly on playing a game that we are doomed to lose rather than seek new players and transform the field on a much bigger scale. Yet, it appears that the CRTC still hopes to keep a tight lid on broadcasting while maintaining a façade at least of Canadian culture as open, accessible, and tolerant. This is evidenced in two major licensing controversies that tested the limits of tolerance and diversity; one by its authorization and the other by its censure.

Licensing Controversies: Who Speaks for Canadians?

The July 2004 authorizations of new ethnic-language television channels raised a number of issues about the direction that the CRTC was moving with regard to serving the interests of Canadians, yet no issue occupied the public's attention as much as the licensing of Al Jazeera. Indeed, so controversial was this ruling that the CRTC separated it from the announcement of the other eight channels, providing it with its own Broadcasting Public Notice (CRTC 2004c). The authorization of Al Jazeera, the Arab-language news channel based in Qatar, was supported by Canada's Arab and Muslim population, but opposed by many members of the Jewish population on the grounds that its programming was anti-Semitic. More than 1,200 comments were filed in support of Al Jazeera with the CRTC, and more than 500 were filed in opposition to the proposal. The significant issue revolved around accusations made by the Canadian Jewish Congress and others that "under the guise of a seemingly legitimate news agency, Al Jazeera has provided hatemongers and terrorists with a platform for their views" (CRTC 2004c). The CRTC rejected this characterization of the channel and also noted that it would be inappropriate for the agency to rule on the question of whether Al Jazeera violated the Canadian Broadcasting Act based on uncontextualized hearsay that may or may not accurately reflect the channel's current programming. Nonetheless, it ruled that there was credible evidence that Al Jazeera *could* include abusive comment that could be contrary to Canadian law even though it hadn't yet.

Based on this guilty-until-proven-innocent ruling, and because the CRTC's licensing power does not extend to non-Canadian networks or channels, it ruled that cable and satellite companies distributing Al Jazeera would be held responsible for its content. In a general climate of anti-Arab hysteria, such a ruling has had a decidedly chilling effect. Michael Hennessy (2004), president of the CCTA, indicated that this form of prior restraint "sets a frightening precedent and virtually ensures that no distributor will ever carry this service in Canada" (Mah 2004, A3). The requirements that distributors delete anti-Semitic or other offensive programming meant, according to Shaw Communications president Peter Bissonnette, that each cable or satellite company would have to have a twenty-four-hour monitor of the channel, fluent in Arabic and conversant in contemporary broadcasting standards (Mah 2004). The decision, therefore, paid lip service to traditional Canadian notions of tolerance, while, in practice, keeping the news station off the air and further underscoring the cultural importance of the grey market. Indeed, the day following the announcement, The *Toronto Star* ran an article reporting that a large number of Arab-speaking Canadians regularly watch Al Jazeera in cafés that are equipped with grey or black market satellite dishes.

The Al Jazeera ruling, which effectively satisfied neither side in the debate about the news channel, was further highlighted by the CRTC's decision in that same month to withdraw the broadcasting license of CHOI-FM, a popular Quebec City based radio station. The problem in that case, however, was that supporters explicitly argued in favour of allowing intolerance and bigotry on the air, so long as it was directed at the right minorities. This is underscored in a front-page article in the *National Post* entitled "Canada's Cultural Hypocrisy" that explicitly linked the two decisions, arguing against Al Jazeera and in favour of CHOI (Cosh 2004). In the weeks that followed the decision, CHOI became a *cause célèbre* in Quebec and across Canada. Seven thousand people protested the decision on Parliament Hill in August, and Quebec premier Jean Charest called on Minister Frulla to intervene to keep the station on the air (Ouellet 2004). Editorialists across the country took up CHOI's fight with the CRTC, which was depicted as a heartless, out-of-touch, and pointless government bureaucracy. What they frequently failed to point out was that, unlike Al Jazeera, which had only been accused of a vague propensity to commit hate crimes, CHOI's attacks on minorities were well documented. In the official CRTC decision not to renew their licence, CHOI was accused of, among many abuses, arguing for the extermination of the mentally handicapped, denouncing some African university students as being cannibals and the children of torturers, and making lewd comments about a female broadcaster's breasts (CRTC 2004a).

Central to the CRTC's reasoning in the decision was the fact that CHOI had been warned about their repeated violations of the Radio Regulations in 2002, had made no effort to alter their behaviour, and took no responsibility for it in 2004. Faced with clear violations of the law, and an intransigent licensee, the CRTC ruled that the use of the public airwaves must be in the public's best interest, and subsequently called for immediate applications for a new radio station to replace CHOI. Generally, editorialists ignored the reasoning behind the decision, framing the issue narrowly in terms of "freedom of speech," minus any reference to its legal context within either the Broadcasting Act or the Canadian Charter. Typical of this tendency was a letter written to the *Vancouver Sun* by Garth Evans (2004), who argued that "it is irrelevant whether others dislike what is said on the radio station. Unless the announcers promote hate or criminal activity, they must be allowed to express their views" (A7). Of course, CHOI's license was withdrawn precisely because the announcers promoted hate and criminal activity. In the CRTC's ruling, the racist, sexist, and bigoted comments received primary attention. However, also noted prominently are complaints from satellite providers about on-air host Jean-François Fillion's incitement to satellite theft. According to complaints filed by Bell ExpressVu and others, he said, "Keep on going to the store, you know, the one that supplies the stuff you need to pirate Bell ExpressVu. You're doing the right thing" (CRTC 2004a). With such industry heavy hitters pushing for action, it is not quite so surprising that the CRTC took the unprecedented step of shutting down the radio station altogether. What is disheartening is how their action was treated as Draconian and out of touch with Canadian values, without any corresponding support for Al Jazeera.

Regardless of one's position on either CHOI or Al Jazeera, the significance of these two rulings only becomes clear when they are considered in light of each other and in terms of how the debates were framed as public standards versus freedom of speech. It is interesting that criticisms of Al Jazeera stemmed from the former while the same news outlets supported CHOI based on the latter. In other words, and to take things to their logical extremes, in supporting CHOI but not Al Jazeera, the implication is that actually calling Muslim foreign students cannibals and torturers is within the standards of Canadian public discourse, but the mere possibility that Muslims might accuse others of such crimes is cause to censure that group from Canadian airwaves. This calls into question the way that we understand and promote the idea of publicly accountable broadcasting within a society based on multiculturalism and diversity. Furthermore, the inclusion of the complaint against CHOI by big industry leaders should not be overlooked. In light of the CRTC's long history of promoting the economic interests of a few over the social interests of the many, their radical action against CHOI deserves to be examined not for its trampling of our right to "freedom of speech" (which is nowhere near as cut and dried as the *National Post* might like to think) but for its protection of the industry status quo.

Canadian Publics versus the Canadian Audience

While CAB issued a press release explicitly outlining their neutrality in the CHOI affair, increasingly the struggle in Canadian television is framed as a debate between broadcasters and cable companies, with audiences constructed to serve the needs of either side but rarely treated as meaningful political actors in their own right. CCTA's effort in 2003 to license popular American channels for carriage in Canada, an effort opposed by CAB, is only the tip of the iceberg. In November 2004, the cable industry received permission to offer FOX News Channel in Canada, after they argued that the right-wing news channel would "stimulate the rollout of digital platforms" (CCTA 2004a). On the other hand, in May 2004, CAB applied to remove the American Spike TV channel from the approved list of extended cable channels, arguing that its rebranding as a men's channel diverged too greatly from its original mandate as a rural issues station (The Nashville Network) and brought it into direct competition with the Canadian Men TV, a subscription-based digital channel that is not as widely accessible in Canada as is Spike. CCTA argued that the application "suggests a growing indifference to consumer choice in the system" (CCTA 2004c). The rhetoric of choice mobilized by the cable industry stands in contrast to the nationalist rhetoric utilized by broadcasters. However, both are ultimately scarily similar in their insistence on depicting the issue in terms of Canada's historic relationship to the United States rather than our potential future as a global leader in a radically transformed mediascape.

CCTA maintains that its focus on competition is "consumer driven" and pushes for greater levels of technological convergence (telephone, cable, Internet) that could then be managed by cable companies as consumers integrate entertainment and communications technologies over digital networks. The fear, according to the cable industry, is that if the government fails to promote these forms of convergence consumers will simply use new technologies to bypass Canadian systems entirely. CAB, on the other hand, observes that the cable industry has used its near-monopoly powers to bully broadcasters and limit consumer choice. Nonetheless, while both broadcasters and the cable industry suggest that their policy priorities are what would most benefit individual consumers, it is clear that they share a common antipathy to the broadcasting model that most Canadians strongly favour, true à la carte options with an eye to pluralism and diversity. While it is true that such a model would completely undermine the Canadian broadcasting industry, and would likely bankrupt most Canadian broadcasters, the fact that the television industry – from broadcasters, to cable systems, to regulators – is so thoroughly opposed to this idea reminds us that, rhetoric aside, the issue facing the television industry remains maximizing shareholder value through captured audiences. Platitudes about Canadian cultural sovereignty are merely fodder in this regime. It protects the industry by preventing television from becoming a truly public space in which to enact cultural citizenship, and keeps it locked down in its traditional place as a debased form of consumer passivity.

Conclusion: Television's Return of the Repressed

Despite the concerns we have raised here about economic imperatives overtaking cultural opportunities, the cable industry is correct to suggest that convergence is increasingly a reality for Canadian television consumers. Ironically, their drive toward digital convergence is what may make their own business model obsolete in the long run. Technological advances have driven the current crisis in the industry related to signal theft, and will likely resolve the issue in the future, with the CRTC's approval or not. While Al Jazeera may have been effectively blocked from Canadian cable systems by the CRTC's ruling in 2004, the issue becomes increasingly irrelevant as the network is available legally for \$9.95 per month over the Internet on JumpTV.com. Given that the CCTA survey indicated that a growing percentage of Canadians have televisions connected to the Internet, this solution effectively end-runs the CRTC. Further, DirecTV claimed in April 2004 that it had eliminated black market satellite theft through a technological fix that allowed them to "zap" illegal decoding cards (Pearson 2004). Rogers Cable acted on this change by offering to exchange "dead" grey and black market satellite systems for Rogers systems, with free installation and two free digital boxes (Brent 2004). These technological changes, along with the increasing availability of television programming on DVD, through peer-to-peer sharing online through systems like Bittorrent, and the rising popularity of personal DVRs, threaten to thoroughly undermine the traditional model of the broadcasting industry as it has existed since the 1950s.

The next few years will be critical in terms of shaping the development of the Canadian television industry, and developing new models for maintaining a strong Canadian presence on television that re-imagines national identity in ways that incorporate cultural diversity and globalization rather than old models of one homogenous public sphere protecting itself from a single Goliath-like enemy. Given the early failure of the digital rollout, the governmental response to the Heritage Committee, the attempts to criminalize television consumption through Bill C-2, and the reluctance of the CRTC to license popular foreign-language broadcasters such as RAI and TVE where they might compete with theoretical but as yet unlaunched Canadian channels, the outlook for Canadian television is not very encouraging. However, with the swift rate of contemporary technological change within the television industry, it is clear that Canadians will increasingly be able to find the programming that best serves their community, whether it's Portuguese soccer or Arabic news. It is a wake-up call announcing to broadcasters and regulators that the Canadian cultural and media landscape has changed dramatically and permanently. The test now is whether we'll embrace the rupture or retreat to fight old battles from the past.

Bibliography

About OMNI Television. 2004. http://www.cfmt.com/en_about.shtml (accessed 24 August 2004).

Decima Research. 2003. Attitudes towards Canadian Media. Ottawa: Decima Publishing Inc. 11 November.

Brent, Paul. 2004. "Rogers converts DirecTV pirates." *National Post*, 22 April, FP1.

Broadcasting Act. 1991. Section 3 (1) (d)(iii).

CAB. 2003a. Cable Proposal Not about Choice but Profit. CAB press release, 19 June.

———. 2003b. CAB President and CEO Reminds New Government that Canada's Private Broadcasters are the Undisputed Core of the Broadcasting System. CAB press release, 10 November.

———. 2002. CAB Applauds Supreme Court of Canada Decision. CAB press release, 26 April.

Canada. 2003. Canadian Heritage Response to *Our Cultural Sovereignty,* http:// www.canadianheritage.gc.ca/progs/ac-ca/progs/ri-bpi/pubs/lincoln/01_e.cfm (accessed 23 August 2006).

CCTA. 2003. Application to Add U.S. Movies, Sports, Children's and News Programming Services, 18 June.

———. 2004a. Cable Industry Applies to Carry FOX News Channel. CCTA press release, 15 April.

———. 2004b. Remember Convergence? Canadian Cable Television Association Annual Report 2003/2004. Ottawa: CCTA, 2004.

———. 2004c. Proposal to Remove Spike TV Anti-Consumer. CCTA press release, 17 May.

Cosh, Colby. 2004. "Canada's Cultural Hypocrisy." *National Post,* 16 July, A1.

CRTC. 2003. CRTC releases report on ethnic services: Canadians enjoy access to a wide variety of ethnic services. CRTC press release, 30 January.

———. 2004a. Broadcasting Decision CRTC 2004-271. CHOI-FM – Non-renewal of licence, 13 July.

———. 2004b. Broadcasting Public Notice CRTC 2004-50. Requests to add non-Canadian third-language services to the lists of eligible satellite services for distribution on a digital basis, 15 July.

———. 2004c. Broadcasting Public Notice CRTC 2004-51. Requests to add Al Jazeera to the lists of eligible satellite services for distribution on a digital basis, 15 July.

———. 2004d. CRTC releases its annual report on broadcast distribution undertakings: Their profitability improves. CRTC press release, 8 April.

———. 2004e. Pay and Specialty Statistical and Financial Summaries (with Amortization), 1999–2003, 19 May.

Evans, Garth. 2004. "Revoking radio license attacks a basic right." *Vancouver Sun,* 19 July, A7.

Hennessy, Michael. 2004. Remarks by Michael Hennessy President and CEO Canadian Cable Television Association, Speech presented to the Washington Metropolitan Cable Club, 29 June.

Mah, Bill. 2004. "Cable won't run Arab news channel despite CRTC approval." *Edmonton Journal,* 16 July, A3.

Ouellet, Martin. 2004. "Keep CHOI on the air, Quebec premier says." *Montreal Gazette,* 27 July, A9.

Pearson, Craig. 2004. "DirecTV claims signal theft thing of past." *Regina Leader Post,* 28 April, C9.

Schecter, Barbara. 2003. "Satellite pirates may abandon broadcast fight; Constitutional challenge." *National Post*, 21 August, FP 1.

Star Choice Packaging Change: CAB Calls on the CRTC to Put an End to Bullying Tactics and Subscriber Abuse. 2004. CAB press release, 9 June.

Sullivan, Rebecca, and Bart Beaty. 2003. "Canadian Television: Industry, Audience and Technology in 2001." In *How Canadians Communicate*, edited by D. Taras, F. Pannekoek, and M. Bakardjieva, 143–64. Calgary: University of Calgary Press.

Thompson, Elizabeth. 2004. "Satellite crackdown angers ethnic groups." *Montreal Gazette*, 12 May, A14.

Yale, Janet. 2002. "You can't compete with free." 19 September. http://www.digitl-home.c/forum/showthread.php?pp=13646 (accessed 29 August 2006).

5: On Life Support: The CBC and the Future of Public Broadcasting in Canada

MARC RABOY and DAVID TARAS

Canadians live in one of the most globalized societies on the planet.[1] We have gone in a relatively short period from being a largely insular and narrow society to being one of the great meeting places of the world. To begin with, Canada has since the Second World War taken in more immigrants per capita than any other country. On a proportional basis there are simply more people from more places living in Canada than can be found almost anywhere else in the world. Our large cities – Toronto, Montreal, and Vancouver – have become global cities where international commerce and connections, not to mention food, music, and faces, are everywhere. Moreover, as travellers, traders, and investors Canadians can be found almost anywhere on the globe. In foreign policy terms, Canada has been one of the pillars of the international community. We helped found almost all of the world's international organizations and have played a key role in their operations. Despite the current rhetoric about how globalized the world has become, the reality is that few countries have embraced the world to the extent that Canada has.

One can also argue that Canada is among the best places in the world to watch television. One only has to compare broadcasting in Canada to the United States to realize how international our broadcasting choices are. Despite recent flaps over whether Canadian satellite and cable providers should carry Fox News, the Italian state broadcaster RAI, or the controversial

Arab news service Al Jazeera, Canadians can on any given day watch news broadcasts from Paris, London, Rome, New York, Sydney, or New Delhi. There is a separate BBC Canada, and TV5 is an international broadcasting cooperative that links Canada to francophone broadcasters around the world. Vision TV is at the forefront of multi-faith programming, globally airing programs produced by over seventy different religious organizations. Canadians have access to digital channels that broadcast in Mandarin, Tamil, Portuguese, Spanish, Hindi, Punjabi, Korean, and Cantonese, among other languages. Indeed there are multiple Portuguese and Tamil TV services.

And, of course, there is the relentless crush of American programs from all of the major U.S. broadcasters. When it comes to certain TV genres such as drama and sitcoms, Canadians watch American TV shows virtually all of the time.

One of the critical issues that Canadians are facing is how to maintain our own avenues of communication when our airwaves are filled with so many signals from so many different places. While many Canadians feel that they have almost an inalienable right to receive TV programs from wherever they wish, and indeed the Canadian broadcasting system has gone a long way towards accommodating that need, this cannot presumably be at the expense of the country's need to communicate with itself – to keep its own channels of communication open and available. In most of the world's advanced post-industrialized countries, it is the public broadcaster that serves as the vital mirror and exhibitor of national cultures. Even in Europe, where membership in the European Union has forced countries to open their airwaves to programs from other member states, public broadcasters are still essential instruments of identity and statehood.

Some analysts believe that we are entering a new era – one in which public broadcasting is more essential than ever. They argue that commercial broadcasters have largely failed to produce programs that link people to their national experience and that address their needs as citizens. While commercial broadcasting will no doubt continue to expand, governments in many countries realize that circumstances have come full circle – the future now depends on the quality of their public broadcasters. According to writer and philosopher John Ralston Saul, "Everybody who is smart in bureaucracies and governments around the Western World now knows that public broadcasting is one of the most important remaining levers that a nation state has to communicate with itself" (Cobb 2001, A9). To Saul, the failure of global media conglomerates such as Disney and Time Warner is almost complete. In his view: "What you're watching in these gigantic mergers is the last desperate steps as the dinosaurs get bigger, bigger and bigger because they can't feed themselves. In fact the bigger they get the more impossible it becomes to survive" (Cobb 2001, A9).

In this article we will describe the challenges that now face Canada's principal public broadcaster: the Canadian Broadcasting Corporation/Radio-Canada (CBC). We will situate the CBC within the Canadian media landscape, describe the financial and regulatory pressures and decisions that have weakened the CBC, examine public attitudes towards public and private broadcasters, and discuss prescriptions for change as outlined in the recommendations of the Lincoln Report – the most comprehensive review of Canadian broadcasting to have been undertaken in a generation. We will argue that financial, regulatory, and political pressures have wounded the public broadcaster to the point where its future is in jeopardy. At the very time that public broadcasting has re-emerged as a vital tool for national and democratic expression, the CBC dangles close to the edge of extinction.

Indeed the spiral of decay and desperation seems unrelenting. The corporation was battered by a year-long hockey lockout in 2004–2005 that cost it tens of millions of dollars in lost advertising revenue. CBC management also locked out its employees for an eight-week period from mid-August to early October 2005 – the fifth strike or lockout of one kind or another in seven years – and the much-sought-after rights to broadcast the 2010 Winter Olympic Games were awarded to CTV. In 2006, the English-language TV network had to jettison two of the mainstays of its dramatic schedule – *Da Vinci's City Hall* and *This is Wonderland* – because of low audience numbers.

More ominous perhaps was the election of a Conservative government led by Stephen Harper in January 2006. During the 2004 election, Harper had suggested that the CBC should focus only on program areas where there were no commercial alternatives – leaving in fact very little food on the CBC's plate. So far the Harper government has not made any dramatic moves.

The public broadcaster is caught in a series of ironies and contradictions from which it may not emerge intact. The CBC remains one of the world's venerable public broadcasting institutions; yet, according to the OECD, it is also one of the most cash-starved. Public expectations of the CBC run high, but audience figures are low. The CBC is meant to be all things to all Canadians, but it is increasingly absent in local and regional markets. The CBC is an innovator, pioneering specialized television channels and Internet programming, but its regulator, the CRTC, would like it to focus on conventional services. The CBC has both friends and enemies in high places, and a public which clamours for more and better.

The CBC and the Canadian Media Environment

The Canadian media system is complex and multidimensional. In fact, the system has so many contingent parts working on so many different levels that keeping track of its many interactions can be a dizzying experience. At the centre of this wheel is the publicly funded Canadian Broadcasting Corporation (CBC), which operates two main TV networks (in English and French), two cable all-news channels, four radio networks, a northern service that reaches into the vast expanse of the Canadian North and broadcasts in a myriad of Aboriginal languages, and an international service, Radio-Canada International. The national public broadcaster receives 60 per cent of its funding in the form of an annual grant from Parliament with the remainder coming from sales and advertising. The CBC is the largest journalistic organization in the country and is also the main showcase for original Canadian radio and television production.

But the CBC is no match for commercial broadcasters that are part of larger media conglomerates. Global factors have played a role here. Because Canadian media companies are tiny by international standards and must compete with global giants such as Time Warner and News Corporation, the government and the CRTC have allowed Canadian companies to gain the size and buying power needed have some chance of competing. Hence, the media horizon is dominated by a clutch of privately owned media conglomerates whose stables of properties include newspapers, radio and TV stations, satellite services, magazines, cable operations, and sports franchises. Taken together, they tower over the CBC in terms of both revenue and audience reach.

The largest of these corporations is Bell Global Media (BGM), now controlled by Woodbridge (owned by the Thomson Family) together with Torstar (owner of the *Toronto Star*) and the Ontario Teachers Pension Fund. BGM includes the CTV network, Canada's most prestigious newspaper, the *Globe and Mail*, a bevy of cable channels including TSN, the Discovery Channel, and Report on Business Television, as well as a stake in Maple Leaf Sports and Entertainment, which owns the Toronto Maple Leafs and the NBA Toronto Raptors. Torstar, which owns 20 per cent of BGM, in turn owns the *Toronto Star*, Canada's largest circulation newspaper, the *Hamilton Spectator*, and a host of other valuable newspaper properties in Southern Ontario, 50 per cent of *Sing Tao*, the largest Chinese language newspaper in the country, as well as Harlequin Books – the publisher of romance novels.

CanWest Global, founded by the late Israel Asper, owns Canada's third TV network, Global Television, a host of specialty channels, and the Southam newspaper chain, which includes the *National Post*, as well as a picket fence of important regional newspapers. In the large Vancouver/Victoria market, for instance, CanWest Global owns all of the major newspapers as well as the dominant TV stations.

In Quebec, the landscape is dominated by Quebecor. It controls TVA, Quebec's most-watched TV network, Videotron, which has a firm grip on the cable market in Quebec, important newspapers such as *Le Journal de Montréal*, as well as the Sun newspaper chain, which owns tabloid papers in Toronto, Ottawa, Winnipeg, Calgary, and Edmonton, among other properties. Quebecor also produces a host of magazines, owns book and music stores, and runs concert tours. It is also the largest printing company in the world. Yet another major player, Rogers Communications, owns most of the country's magazines, is Canada's largest cable provider, has a share in a number of cable and digital channels, operates dozens of radio stations, and owns the Toronto Blue Jays baseball team.

The CBC is handicapped in any competition with these media giants. First, cross-media or cross-platform media conglomerates enjoy economies of scale and can assemble their audiences through a number of different vehicles. Most importantly, perhaps, they can promote their programs through the other media outlets that they own. TVA's hit program *Star Academie*, for instance, is touted endlessly in magazines and newspapers and in music stores, as well as on Internet sites and TV stations, all of which are owned by TVA's parent company Quebecor.

Added to the dilemma faced by the CBC is that, while the Canadian media system is dominated by a handful of corporations, audiences are fragmented to a degree not found in many other countries. This is especially the case with television. There are over 250 cable and digital TV services, including ones aimed at children, the business community, Aboriginal people, older citizens, gays, and religious viewers. There is also a blizzard of news, sports, ethnic, and pay-per-view channels. As we shall explain later, with the exception of its all news channels, Newsworld and RDI, the CBC has been denied entry into the bounteous world of cable TV. Private broadcasters have been allowed to buy the prime beach-front properties in cable TV, while the CBC has been largely shut out of the action.

Canadians are also exposed to a torrent of American programming coming directly from the major U.S. networks, super-stations, and cable channels, almost all of which are readily available in Canada. One of the mainstays of the Canadian broadcasting system is a policy of simultaneous substitution that blocks out American advertising when both American and Canadian broadcasters are airing the same U.S. program. It also needs to be pointed out that a large number of Canadians, as many as 750,000, according to one estimate, receive unauthorized satellite services from U.S. providers and are for all intents part of the American rather than the Canadian broadcasting system.

Despite the disadvantages that the CBC has had to face, the Broadcasting Act of 1991, which governs the broadcasting system, has given the corporation onerous responsibilities. Section 3, which is the main lever of the Act, stipulates that Canadian broadcasting is a public service, comprised of public, private, and community elements, and that broadcasters must air programming that reflects "Canadian attitudes, opinions, ideas, values and artistic creativity." The most controversial parts of the Act are the sections that deal with Canadian unity and identity. The Act states that broadcasting must "serve the needs and interests, and reflect the circumstances and aspirations of Canadian men, women and children, including equal rights, linguistic duality, the multicultural and multiracial nature of Canadian society and the special place of aboriginal peoples." Broadcasting is also seen as being "essential to the maintenance and enhancement of national identity and cultural sovereignty." The previous 1968 Act, which had directed the CBC to "contribute to the development of national unity," had created a swirl of controversy. The 1991 Act, which was the product of years of often painful negotiations and compromises, backed away from making national unity a goal of the system. The CBC is now expected only to "contribute to shared national consciousness and identity." But the CBC must also be in effect the living embodiment of the Act: multicultural, regional, serving minority communities, operating in both national languages, and providing special services for the North.

The simple reality is that the corporation no longer has the resources or the capacity to fulfil its obligations under the Act. The CBC doesn't have enough cloth to fit the many contours and limbs of the body envisioned by the Broadcasting Act. There is now a sharp and increasingly distant mismatch between the two.

The CBC's Battle to Survive

The Canadian Broadcasting Corporation was created by an Act of Parliament in 1936. (A previous national public broadcaster, the Canadian Radio Broadcasting Commission, operated from 1932 to 1936.) From 1936 to 1958, the CBC acted not only as public broadcaster but also regulated the private radio stations, which continued to exist. The CBC also had a monopoly on television in its early years. Its fortunes shifted, however, with the introduction in the late 1950s of an independent regulator, the Board of Broadcast Governors, eventually becoming the Canadian Radio-Television and Telecommunications

Commission (CRTC) and then, in the early 1960s, private television. Nonetheless, the CBC remained the cornerstone of the system well into the 1980s.

Since that time the winds of change have eroded the CBC's position. Government policies, regulatory decisions, and a series of self-inflicted wounds have exacted a grievous toll. First, a major policy shift in 1983 signalled a change that would contribute dramatically to the CBC's long decline. Without rewriting any of the broad objectives of Canadian broadcasting policy and the cultural institutions that it supports, the government decided to redirect a significant portion of public funds towards developing private-sector "cultural industries." A funding agency, Telefilm Canada, was created to oversee public spending on television production and the CBC went, literally overnight, from being a producer to being a programmer of commissioned works by independent producers. The impact, subtle in appearance at first, has been central to the development of Canadian broadcasting, especially television, ever since.

Second, it has to be understood that the CBC is faced with a structural problem that is not faced by public broadcasters in other countries. It has always had to contend with direct competition from the United States and with the power and influence of American cultural models. Canada is not insulated from the United States by distance or language (except, importantly, in French), and Canadians are eager and enthusiastic consumers of all aspects of American culture. Over the years analysts have referred to the flood, the sea, the torrent, the avalanche, etc., to describe the massive and constant invasion of American cultural products. What is interesting and unique is that Canadians were already exposed to American television for some years before the CBC established its first stations in 1952. In other words, American TV to some extent pre-dated Canadian TV in Canada. Loyalty to American broadcasters, and the belief that Canadians have an inalienable right to all of the American culture that they can consume, runs deep.

Scholars such as John Meisel (1986) have argued that Canadian culture has become a minority culture in Canada. Much of it is contested in Quebec while in English-speaking Canada it appeals disproportionately to older, more educated, and higher income groups. Canadian authors, films, art, and music have their principal following among the burgeoning middle class. American culture, on the other hand, has mass appeal. This juxtaposition has consequences for the CBC, which many Canadians (not surprisingly, perhaps) see as distant, refined, and elitist. Meisel suggests that those who mainly consume American mass culture are also the ones who are most reluctant to support the CBC. Hence, the licence fee which is the mainstay of financial support for public broadcasting in the UK, Germany, Italy, etc., is politically unthinkable in Canada and has been so for many years. In countries where

Table 5.1   A Comparison of Public Broadcasting Systems

	Revenues per Capita (ECU) (1997)	Revenues as % of GDP (1997)	% Commercial Revenues (1998)	TV Audience Share (2000)
Denmark	104.5	0.37	34.8	69
Switzerland	103.7	0.30	15.8	39
French				32
German				32
Italian				25
United Kingdom	99.7	0.36	26.2	
Austria	88.6	0.39	49.9	57
Germany	85.5	0.38	17.2	42
Norway	72.0	0.23	0	41
Ireland	69.8	0.36	66.0	48
Finland	68.8	0.34	25.4	43
Sweden	67.4	0.30	7.3	44
Belgium	56.3			
Flemish			33.4	32
French			27.6	25
France	55.8	0.21	45.5	44
Italy	49.2	0.20	43.0	48
Netherlands	45.0	0.22	22.5	37
Spain	33.9	0.28	77.6	33
Canada	23.8	0.13	32.0	9
Greece	17.9	0.18	43.1	12
Portugal	12.5	0.15	55.5	34
United States	5.8	0.02	13.0	2

Source: Hallin and Mancini (2004, 42).

public broadcasters rely on licence fees paid annually by consumers, public broadcasters have retained their dominant positions. In countries where public broadcasters are not buttressed by these direct infusions of cash, their situation is more precarious.

Another important distinction is that the Canadian federal government, unlike most of its European counterparts, drastically cut spending in general and eliminated its deficit in the 1990s. Almost all crown corporations and institutions were downsized during this period. The cuts to the CBC, which amounted to $400 million over the last decade, were part of a wider and determined effort to create a leaner government.

Faced with deep cuts, the CBC was forced to close stations in key markets, curtail some of its most ambitious projects, retreat into low-cost programming ghettos such as sports, documentaries, and ensemble comedy, and air some

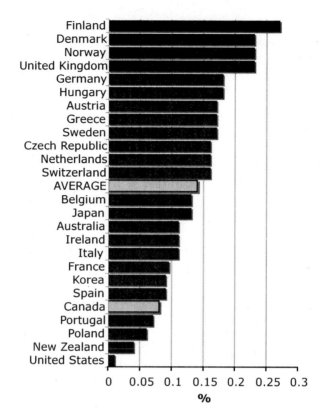

Figure 5.1
Public funding for
public broadcasters
in OECD countries
as a % of GDP,
1999[a]

[a]*Source*: Canada. House
of Commons (2003, 181).

of its programs repeatedly during a given day or a week. Talented individuals
fled the CBC amid continuing rounds of layoffs and a lack of opportunity for
advancement.

The Lincoln Committee's Report, for example, chronicled the vicious cycle
in which the CBC found itself as dwindling resources forced it to cut corners
in vital areas of its mandate such as regional programming and this in turn
eroded its ability to garner audiences. The report cites OECD figures showing
that Canada ranked twenty-second out of twenty-six countries in public funding for national public broadcasters as a percentage of GDP.[2] For instance, the
CBC's budget is one-sixth that of the BBC, even though Britain's population is
only twice that of Canada's.

In some ways decisions taken in 1990 to close a host of local TV stations
across the country proved to be a critical turning point. The strategy was to

close stations in certain markets and provide viewers with regional programming. Viewers in Calgary would be served from Edmonton, in Saskatoon from Regina, etc. The problem, of course, is that loyalties at the local level are integral to the success of national programming. Stations that are strong in local markets are able to build audiences and advertise their primetime shows throughout the day. Moreover, they have a continuing and often boisterous presence in the community through their extensive promotions of local personalities, events, and news. At the CBC this vital connection has largely been severed. One can argue that the CBC has never recovered from these deep wounds.

The Calgary situation is particularly instructive. At the time of its closing, the CBC local station had the second largest audience in what is now Canada's wealthiest and fastest growing city. The station had been making money and the prospects for fulsome profits were strong. On the day the station was shut down, tens of thousands of viewers migrated to CFCN, CTV's local flagship station. Despite numerous attempts by the CBC to re-style a local news show, viewers have never returned in appreciable numbers. Loyalties have shifted elsewhere, and the CBC is still seen by many as having "abandoned" the city.

Another blow to the corporation came with the explosion of cable and digital services. In some countries the expansion has occurred in a way that took account of the needs of the main public service broadcasters. In the UK, for instance, there is famously a BBC1 and BBC2 and there are new digital channels such as BBC4 (arts and music), CBeebies (for pre-schoolers), CBBC (for pre-teens) as well as another service for young adults. In Canada, however, the CBC has largely been denied access to the burgeoning world of cable and digital TV, and since subscription fees overtook advertising as the mainstay of Canadian television as early as 1991, this has been nothing less than a cataclysmic blow. The corporation only has two cable franchises: its English- and French-language all-news channels, *Newsworld* and *le Réseau de l'information* (RDI). Both of these services pay for themselves through pass-through charges borne by cable customers. The many lucrative sports, children's, and music channels were given to private broadcasters.

A number of formal attempts by the CBC to gain a greater foothold in the new cable universe were denied by the CRTC.[3] There is reason to believe that the public broadcaster was dissuaded from even applying for the more profitable services. No doubt much of the recent history and fortunes of the CBC would have been different if it had been awarded franchises for a sports or children's channel. Revenues from pass-through charges and the economies of scale that might have been achieved would have provided a firmer financial basis for the corporation and a much greater audience reach.

In the end, cable and digital expansion became the corporation's greatest nemesis – the largest nail in its coffin. First, it now has to compete against what in most Canadian homes is over a hundred channels and services. The market has become so fragmented that the mass audience is quickly becoming a vestige of the past. Narrow customized "boutique" television increasingly dominates the horizon. While the main private broadcasters are able to "reassemble" their audiences by owning a myriad of cable franchises, the CBC has been largely denied the ability to compete on this new and valuable terrain.

Even in the news area, where the CBC has some pride of place because of Newsworld and RDI, competition is fierce. Its news channels have to compete against a headline news service run by CTV, a regional news channel in Ontario, CNN, CNBC, a financial news channel, and of course, a torrent of local news shows. And as pointed out at the very beginning of this article, Canadians have ready access to news broadcasts from around the world. If public broadcasters in other countries were faced with the sheer amount of competition that the CBC now faces, their audiences would be bound to plummet.

Cable expansion has also meant that parts of the CBC's mandate or programming areas that were once its exclusive preserve have been parcelled out to others. Children's television, the arts, religious programming, programs that reflect ethnic diversity, and the servicing of Aboriginal communities are now provided for by other broadcasters, including other public broadcasters. Instead of expanding the role of the CBC, the CRTC allowed other public broadcasters to be created. For instance, public broadcasters such as the Aboriginal Peoples Television Network and Vision TV, the religious broadcaster, are competing against the CBC on what might still be considered its "territory."

Elihu Katz, a distinguished scholar, has criticized regulators for allowing virtually any and all broadcasters – anyone who can show that they have a reasonable business model – to be granted a licence. In his view, the endless granting of licences erodes the capacity of the major broadcasters to maintain profits and produce quality programming. As Katz has put it,

Why are governments contributing to the erosion of nation-states and national cultures? Why don't they see that more leads to less to insignificance ... to the atomization and evacuation of public space? Why don't they see that national identity and citizen participation are compromised? Why don't they realize that they are contributing directly to the erosion of the enormous potential which television has to enlighten and unite populations into the fold of national cultures? (Katz 1996)

While Katz is concerned about the capacity of a society to in effect hear itself amid the clatter of so many channels and choices, the argument for a strong public broadcaster is also based on the need to provide not just another voice but a different voice. As noted earlier, private broadcasters such as CTV, TVA, and Global are part of multi-media conglomerates that can endlessly promote and showcase programs through a wide variety of media platforms. Unlike its main competitors, the CBC does not own newspapers, cable operations, sports franchises, magazines, music stores, or phone companies. The CBC is handicapped and out-gunned in any direct competition simply because it does not have the multiple outlets that its competitors enjoy. In some markets such as Montreal and Vancouver, the media landscape is so dominated by a single corporation that the CBC is almost the only competing voice. This gives the public broadcaster a mission that is far different from the one that was envisioned fifty or even twenty years ago. Presumably, it is there to be an alternative where almost none exists.

Although the tilting of the broadcasting system toward the private sector is due to a number of factors (including the power and skill of private broadcasters and the work of industry lobbyists such as the Canadian Association of Broadcasters and public attitudes that placed particular faith in the private sector), at the end of the day, the CBC seems to have had few friends at the cabinet table and of course at the CRTC. Politicians of almost all stripes have at one time or another viewed the corporation with a mixture of animosity and suspicion and believed that they could make the corporation sing to their tune. Again, Canada seems to be a special case because of deep divisions over national unity and the disarray and turmoil that were created over Quebec's referendums on sovereignty.

The brutal reality is that the CBC has been allowed to become a political football. The media watchdog group Friends of Canadian Broadcasting has reported that, since 1936, 89 per cent of those appointed to the CBC's Board of Directors had been affiliated with the governing party. Since 1968, 87 per cent of appointees have been tied in some way to the party in power (Friends of Canadian Broadcasting 2004).

Political pressures on the CBC really began during the late 1950s and 1960s. Conservative Prime Minister John Diefenbaker (1957–62) believed that the corporation had been overrun by communists and had become a "mass propaganda agency." CBC programming would often send him into towering rages, and he attempted to have at least one radio show, *Preview Commentary*, cancelled. When the corporation resisted his efforts, Diefenbaker retaliated by freezing the salary of CBC President Alphonse Ouimet[4] and there is some evidence that he played a role in securing a TV licence for a friend and political ally. That TV licence, CFTO in Toronto, would eventually become the fulcrum and catalyst for the founding of Canada's first private network, CTV. A Liberal prime minister, Lester Pearson (1963–68), was no less thin-skinned. Stung by criticisms of his government, Pearson encouraged a parliamentary committee to hold public hearings into the popular and controversial program, *This Hour Has Seven Days*. The Prime Minister's Office then launched its own investigation into whether the program was politically biased. Not surprisingly, the program was cancelled.

The darkest days for the CBC in terms of political interference may have been during Brian Mulroney's prime ministership (1984–93). Mulroney would, according to at least one source, phone the CBC's Chair, Patrick Watson, with protestations that would range from "angry" to "subtle." He stacked the CBC board with fellow Conservatives and cut the corporation's budget. One board member, John Crispo, once suggested that cuts to the CBC's budget were made as "a down payment and a warning" following what he saw as the CBC's one-sided anti-American coverage of the Gulf War in 1991.

In 1992, *The Valour and the Horror*, a docudrama depicting the Canadian role in key battles during the Second World War, stirred a firestorm of controversy. The show stressed the incompetence of Canadian generals and the needless loss of life. The Canadian Senate held public hearings that have been variously described as a "kangaroo court," a "witch hunt," and a "Shakespearean crowd scene." Under intense political scrutiny, the corporation retreated. It issued a statement of regret, demoted senior executives, and promised not to air the program again.

The most difficult issue for the CBC has been the way in which it has reported the push for Quebec sovereignty and the politics of national unity. Journalists at Radio-Canada believe that they must accurately reflect values and opinions in Quebec or they will lose credibility with their audiences. This has meant giving airtime to Quebec nationalists and sovereigntists and criticizing federalist politicians if and when it is warranted. Federalist politicians, on the other hand, believe that during times of crisis when the country's future is at stake a broadcaster that is funded by the federal government should not undermine the federalist cause. Even Pierre Trudeau (1968–79, 1980–84) lost his composure when discussing Radio-Canada's coverage of events in Quebec. He once told a Liberal Party gathering that:

We will put a lid on the place.... we will close up the shop. Let them not think we won't do it. If need be, we can produce programs, and if not, we will show people Chinese or Japanese vases instead of the nonsense they dish out. That would be of some cultural benefit (qtd. in Nash 1994, 391).

During the close and bitterly contested Quebec referendum on sovereignty in 1995, accusations of bias reached unprecedented proportions. Prime Minister Jean Chrétien (1993–2004) openly griped about pro-separatist leanings at Radio-Canada, claiming that the network treated the sovereigntist leader Lucien Bouchard with "kid gloves" and ignored at least one of his major speeches. According to at least one report that circulated, key Liberals had vowed during the referendum to close the "separatist nest" once and for all.

It is small wonder given this history that the CBC has been at the sharp end of the stick in terms of budget cuts. What is perhaps most astonishing is the extent to which the public broadcaster has remained vulnerable to shifting political winds. Methods and procedures that could provide insulation from political pressures could easily have been adopted over the years. The corporation could have been granted multi-year funding so that it did not have to face annual scrutiny by politicians. Recommendations made by a mandate review committee in 1996 that funding come from a special tax that would replace the 7 per cent GST on certain media-related purchases was rejected almost instantly. The Lincoln Committee report suggested that the Board of Directors could be made of people representing a variety of interests in order to prevent the government from "stacking" the board with political appointees. Indeed some of the members of the Board might be drawn from the CBC itself. One interesting check would be to see the CBC president named by the board. Again, what is remarkable is that politicians have preferred to keep the corporation within easy political reach rather than provide mechanisms that would ensure its independence.

Adding to the misery may be a problem of the CBC's own making. According to some observers the public broadcaster suffers from an advanced case of bureaucratic sclerosis (Posner 2005). Senior management has been described as smug and impervious and decision making is complex and multi-layered. Moreover the corporation has undergone a seemingly endless series of re-branding exercises that have sapped energies, lowered morale, and seemed to have produced little except for ever-falling audience numbers. A small army of outside consultants seems to be ever-present.

The combination of severe budget cuts and vastly increased competition from cable and digital services has produced a dramatic drop in TV audience numbers. In 1969, for instance, CBC television had a 35 per cent audience share, while Radio-Canada attracted 40 per cent of French-language viewers (Canada. House of Commons, 2003, S8). By 1993 the audience for the CBC's main channels had sunk to 13 per cent of English-language and just 23 per cent of the French-language viewers. By 2004–2005 the combined audience for both English and French language television was 8.5 per cent (Communic@tions Management 2006). Despite the impression that CBC radio listeners remain intensely loyal, the numbers for radio listening are just as dismal. In 1975, CBC radio enjoyed close to 30 per cent of listeners in the Toronto market. By 2005 the number had plummeted to just 6.3 per cent (Communic@tions Management 2006).

The CBC responded to the decline in funding that occurred in the 1990s by concentrating on certain types of programming and not others. The corporation realized that its budget could no longer sustain a schedule that included a wide range of programs. The new diet focused on children's programs, news and current affairs, sports, especially NHL hockey, and what can be described as "event television" – large-budget one-time specials that are meant to make a splash. In 2006, on the English-language side, childrens' shows such as *Clifford the Big Red Dog* and *Rolle Polie Olie* dominated the morning schedule. The afternoon line-up featured reruns of *This Hour has 22 Minutes*, *The Royal Canadian Air Farce*, and *Da Vinci's Inquest* with two American shows – *The Simpsons* and *Frasier* – occupying key slots in the late afternoon.

In terms of event TV, the broadcasters' greatest gamble perhaps was a $25 million production entitled *Canada: A People's History*. Broadcast in both official languages on nine Sunday nights during Winter 2002, the thirty-hour production chronicled Canadian history. The production attracted sizable audiences, was sold in a CD-ROM version, and was used in history and social studies classes across the country. In 2004, it aired *The Greatest Canadian* documentary series, an idea that it borrowed from the BBC, and it spent lavishly on *Hockey: A People's History*, which was broadcast in 2006.

Another strategic decision was to Canadianize its schedule. The corporation's goal is to have 100 per cent Canadian programming throughout the broadcast day. Amid so much competition from so many other broadcasters, some of which broadcast in areas where the CBC once had pride of place, the corporation has at least one distinct feature – it can claim a mostly Canadian schedule. This may be its last and best defence. Presumably Canadians will always need a place in the broadcasting universe that they can call home. Sadly, however, the art of producing a hit dramatic series seems to have fallen from its grasp. In fact, during the period from September 2003 to August 2005, CTV aired substantially more Canadian drama than did the CBC (Friends of Canadian Broadcasting 2006).

During the period from 2004 to 2006, the corporation continued to build its schedule around programs that had a distinctive CBC quality; a dramatic mini-series on the worldwide business of sex-trafficking, another mini-series featuring a Canadian prime minister standing up to Americans who want control the country's fresh water, and a TV movie about life-and-death decisions made in an underfunded hospital. On the tenth anniversary of the 1995 Quebec Referendum on sovereignty, the broadcasters aired a gloomy multi-night documentary entitled *Breaking Point*. It also debuted a new dramatic series *Ciao Bella* about a single career women living in Montreal's little Italy. In 2004, the broadcaster experimented with its own reality programming. In this case it was *Making the Cut*, a series that put men who aspire to be hockey stars through the rigours of an NHL training camp. The audience was invited to vote for the players that it thought deserved an NHL tryout. Unfortunately, the show didn't make the cut in terms of audience ratings. In early 2007, *Little Mosque on the Prairie*, a sitcom about a small Muslim community in a small town on the Prairies, produced both controversy and large audiences.

The Public View of Public Broadcasting

Analysis of Canadian radio and television programme schedules and audience figures also demonstrate the important place of the CBC in the deep structure of Canadian broadcasting. The Lincoln Committee assembled data showing that the vast majority of Canadian programming exhibited and watched on Canadian television was broadcast by the CBC. To the extent that this is felt to be a positive value, there is no question that the CBC remains an essential cultural institution in Canada. This view is, in fact, borne out by public opinion surveys.

In mid-2004 the lobby group Friends of Canadian Broadcasting released the findings of a national public opinion survey by the independent polling firm Ipsos Reid, on attitudes of Canadians towards broadcasting.[5] One question asked respondents: "Please tell me how much confidence or trust you personally have in each (of the following) group(s) to protect Canadian culture and identity on television." The results were as follows (Ipsos Reid 2004, 1):

- CBC 76%
- TVA (French respondents only) 66%
- CTV (English only) 62%
- TQS (French only) 57%
- Specialty channels 54%
- Global TV 53%
- The CRTC 48%

- Consumer groups 43%
- The federal government 40%
- Your provincial government 40%
- Cable television companies 30%
- Telephone companies 29%
- Satellite companies 23%

When Ipsos Reid read a series of statements to survey respondents, here is the percentage of respondents who strongly or somewhat agreed with the following:

- I want to see the CBC survive and prosper – 94%
- The CBC is one of the things that helps distinguish Canada from the United States – 89%
- The CBC provides value for taxpayers' money – 77%

Regarding funding, the survey asked the following question: "Assume for a moment that your federal Member of Parliament asked for your advice on an upcoming vote in the House of Commons on what to do about CBC funding. Which of the following three options would you advise him or her to vote for ... decrease funding for the CBC from current levels ... maintain funding for the CBC at current levels or increase funding for the CBC from current levels?" The responses were as follows:

- Decrease: 9%
- Maintain: 51%
- Increase: 38%

The Ipsos Reid poll also asked Canadians, "How important is it that programming made in and about your part of the country be produced?" Seventy-eight per cent of respondents replied that it was "important" or "very important." The poll also found that 85 per cent of Canadians wanted "to see CBC strengthened in my part of Canada" and 80 per cent agreed with the statement: "we should build a new CBC capable of providing high quality Canadian programming with strong regional content throughout Canada."

These findings point to a number of key issues, indeed paradoxes, about the CBC's dilemma. First, support for the CBC and the sense of its importance among Canadians clearly surpasses by far what could be deduced from a superficial consideration of audience statistics. Second, Canadians feel a need for public broadcasting at a local and regional level that they would like to see CBC fulfil. The Friends, whose paid membership reaches into 60,000 Canadian homes, concluded that "The CBC could be mandated to play a far stronger role in citizen engagement and lifelong learning, both Canada-wide and in major communities across the land."

Despite the strong attachments that many Canadians have to the CBC, the corporation remains vulnerable. During the lead-up to the June 2004 federal election, then Opposition leader Stephen Harper suggested that the CBC's main TV networks and its two radio channels devoted to classical music be commercialized. He argued that the CBC should only operate in areas where the private broadcasters were not doing the job. Another prominent Conservative politician, the current minister of health, Tony Clement, also questioned whether the CBC should exist in its current form. Clement was quoted as saying: "Do we need the CBC in its current format, when there are so many private broadcasting channels available? When's the last time we truly looked at the CBC and its mandate and the role of the taxpayer in funding that? I think we have to do something different" (Friesen 2004). Supporters of public broadcasting worry that major changes to the CBC's role as well as further cuts may be in the offing.

As we have shown, part of the problem is that the CBC now finds itself in a Catch-22 situation. Without the resources required to meet its mandate and deliver distinctive quality programming, the case for privatizing or dismantling the CBC becomes more obvious and inviting. Having largely retreated from big budget dramatic productions and indeed from lucrative local markets, it has seen large segments of its audience disappear. What keeps CBC television afloat in English-speaking Canada at least are its broadcasts of NHL hockey, the Olympics, and a mix of mini-series, TV movies, and specials into which the corporation throws much of its resources. Even its marquee national news programs have slipped dramatically in popularity.

But even these moorings may soon be lost at sea. CTV outbid the CBC for the much-coveted right to broadcast the 2010 Vancouver Winter Olympic Games, and as we go to print the private network seems poised to win the rights to broadcast NHL hockey as well. *Hockey Night in Canada* not only gave the CBC a fabled place in the popular imagination but it also provided a substantial amount of revenue.

The question perhaps is whether a kind of tipping point has been reached where the corporation has been weakened to the point where its very weakness becomes an argument for shutting it down or privatizing it. The Canadian public would clearly like to see more Canadian programming and a stronger and more resilient CBC, especially at the local level. But political ideology and the lobbying power of the private broadcasters may alter the equation.

The last great attempt to analyze and redress each of the CBC's many problems in a systematic way was conducted by the Lincoln Committee in 2003. This was the result of a comprehensive two-year study undertaken by the House of Commons Standing Committee on Canadian Heritage. The report recommended multi-year funding, proposed mechanisms to ensure that the board of governors would not become a political instrument, and encouraged the government to find more space for the CBC in the cable and digital worlds. But the parliamentary report also sought to recast the public broadcaster by suggesting new ways in which the corporation might see its role. At the heart of its proposals was the proposition that the CBC had to find a means to re-enter local broadcasting. The parliamentarians believed that a strong national network could not be sustained without strong local roots. In recommending the creation of a Local Broadcasting Initiative Program (a fund that would bring together private, community, and governmental partners), the committee was offering the CBC a way to rebuild its local and regional presence and stature. While the LBIP would be open to all broadcasters, the CBC would clearly be a beneficiary.

It may also be time to see the public broadcaster take on an asymmetrical shape and responsibilities. The CBC does not have to have the same shape or offer the same programming everywhere in the country. There may not be a need for the CBC to maintain a local news hour in large cities where there are four or five private broadcasters that have long since filled that need. This may not be the case, however, in smaller centres or in provinces where private broadcasters have less of a presence.

The Lincoln Committee tried to set a course for re-visioning the CBC by recommending increased and stable long-term funding – in exchange for which the public broadcaster would have to submit a detailed strategic plan outlining how it proposed to fulfil its mandate with respect to local and regional broadcasting, Canadian programming, and new media initiatives. As *How Canadians Communicate* goes to press, these proposals have not been acted upon by any government. It remains to be seen whether Canada's political leaders and the public broadcaster itself have the vision and imagination that are needed to strengthen and perhaps even reinvent public broadcasting in the twenty-first century.

In the new global media environment, public broadcasters like the CBC will remain essential instruments of national cultures, civic engagement, and public life. The question perhaps is whether the Canadian government will recognize, as governments have in other countries, that in the new media age public broadcasting is as important for nation-building as it has ever been and perhaps more so.

Bibliography

Canada. Department of Canadian Heritage. 2003. *The Government of Canada's Response to the Report of the Standing Committee on Canadian Heritage, Our Cultural Sovereignty: The Second Century of Canadian Broadcasting.* Ottawa: Her Majesty the Queen in Right of Canada.

Canada. House of Commons. 2003. *Standing Committee on Canadian Heritage, Our Cultural Sovereignty. The Second Century of Canadian Broadcasting.* Ottawa: Communication Canada Publishing.

Cobb, Chris. 2001. "Saul Enters CBC Debate." *National Post*, 30 January, A9.

Communic@tions Management. 2006. "Television – past, present, and (very different) future." January, 75, 77.

Friesen, Joe. 2004. "Harper's CBC views draw fire." *Globe and Mail*, 20 May, A7.

Friends of Canadian Broadcasting. 2004. "End Patronage at CBC." 23 September, http://www.friends.ca.

Hallin, Daniel, and Paolo Mancini. 2004. *Comparing Media Systems.* Cambridge: Cambridge University Press.

Ipsos Reid. 2004. "Friends of Canadian Broadcasting Survey." 16 May, http://www.friends.ca/files/PDF/IRMay04.pdf.

Katz, Elihu. 1996. "And Deliver Us from Segmentation." *Annals of the American Academy of Political and Social Science* 546: 22–33.

Meisel, John. 1986. "Escaping Extinction: Cultural Defence of an Undefended Border." In *Southern Exposure: Canadian Perspectives on the United States*, eds. D. Flaherty and W. McKercher, 152–68. Toronto: McGraw-Hill Ryerson.

Nash, Knowlton. 1994. *The Microphone Wars: A History of Triumph and Betrayal at the CBC.* Toronto: McClelland and Stewart.

Posner, Michael. 2005. "How did it all go so wrong at the CBC?" *Globe and Mail*, 27 October.

Raboy, Marc. 1990. *Missed Opportunities: The Story of Canada's Broadcasting Policy.* Montreal and Kingston: McGill-Queen's University Press.

Taras, David. 2001. *Power and Betrayal.* Peterborough: Broadview Press.

Notes

1 An earlier version of this article was published in Gregory Lowe and Per Jauert, eds., *Cultural Dilemmas in Public Service Broadcasting* (Göteborg University, Sweden: Nordicom, 2005). For a detailed history of the evolution of Canadian broadcasting and the CBC's role therein, see Raboy (1990).

2   Table 5.1 shows Canada just above Greece and Portugal for its spending on
    national public broadcasting as a percentage of GDP in 1999. Conversely,
    Denmark, the United Kingdom, Switzerland, Austria and Germany placed
    in the top five with public expenditures that were four times greater than
    what is spent in Canada.

3   The Lincoln Committee listed eight CBC licence applications for new
    television services that had been denied by the CRTC in the 1990s and
    commented: "Given that all of these proposed services suit the mandate of a
    public broadcaster, the Committee cannot understand why the Corporation
    was denied these services by the CRTC" (Canada. Department of Canadian
    Heritage 2003, 596).

4   This section is based on Taras (2001).

5   Ipsos Reid (2004) poll conducted 4–9 May 2004.

B: The Quest for Identity

6: Dimensions of Empowerment: Identity Politics on the Internet

MARIA BAKARDJIEVA

The Objective

This chapter approaches the themes of globalization and identity from a grass-roots perspective. It is not a communal notion of Canadian identity that will be in the spotlight here, but rather concrete identity projects as they are constructed by individual Canadians in a global environment and with the help of a concrete communication medium – the Internet. The chapter sets out to find political significance in the ways in which Canadians seek answers to the question "Who am I?" drawing on resources of global scope and diversity. The study on which the chapter is based was designed to look closely at the applications people find for the Internet in their everyday lives. It employed techniques intended to elicit words of self-reflection and appraisal of the role of the medium from a wide range of users. Assessing use practices and, by implication, the social significance of the Internet with respect to its capacity to empower users and improve their quality of life is the main objective of the project. An auxiliary task is to formulate a conception of empowerment (with regard to Internet use) that would allow the leap between everyday practice and the political sphere, or in other words, to elaborate a method of crisscrossing, and possibly interweaving, the mundane and the political. As will be shown throughout the chapter, self-identity emerges as a critical site in which everyday life and pursuits and concerns of a political nature meet.

To prepare for the leap between these two levels of description and analysis, one must address the question: Does the medium increase the capacity of agents to reflexively navigate the social frameworks in which their lives unfold? In other words: Does it increase individual choice and control over the circumstances of one's own life in the face of the powerful social forces that define and delimit these circumstances? If so, what are the forms, or, to reverse Foucault, the microtechniques of empowerment, involving the Internet in everyday life? When users say that doing something desirable is now "easier" or "more convenient" thanks to the Internet, does this really mean that they have acquired more power as agents in the spheres of economic, political, and cultural life? How can we separate the empowering from the trivial? What kinds of projects, if facilitated by the Internet, will constitute empowerment? How do we recognize the instances in which Internet use leads to new functionings and capabilities enhancing self-actualization and development?

Methodology

The study took place in the period 2002–2004 and collected data from eighty Internet-connected households in Calgary through in-depth group and individual interviews and tours of respondents' domestic and computer space. Participants were recruited through calls for participation publicized in the media, local web sites, flyers, and through the personal networks of the researchers working for the project. While there was no aspiration toward statistical representativeness, care was taken to include people of different age, gender, and socio-economic status in equal proportion, as well as people representing different life experiences such as disability, immigration, single parenthood, and unemployment. The interviews were held in respondents' homes and involved all household members in a group session followed by individual interviews with the Internet users in the home. These individual interviews took place at the respondents' computers and included a show-and-tell component where respondents would show the researcher their favourite sites, bookmarks, and other electronic items of personal significance. Each respondent filled out a sheet asking about his or her most important e-mail contacts, their most visited sites, and the online groups they read or contributed to. The number of members interviewed across the participating households varied between one and five.

Examining respondents' Internet experiences, one is struck by the variety of approaches that users take to the medium and the numerous applications they have for it. Among the categories emergent from the analysis, a broad dichotomy can be discerned. Put in descriptive terms, this is the distinction between uses that extend previously existing activities and pursuits into new areas and new formats, and, on the other hand, creative applications of the medium that break new ground. Thus I would like to start with the observation that among the multitude of use practices revealed in users' narratives, some were predictable, medium- and/or market-led, while others stood out with the creativity, expressive power, and critical reflexivity that had gone into them. More concretely, while some users were simply playing chess, purchasing products, and banking online (and that was all there was to their Internet use), others were discovering new ways to be and act in the world drawing on online resources. For the former, the Internet was bringing about mere ease and convenience in accomplishing customary daily activities,[1] for the latter, the medium was acquiring a much deeper significance. For this second category of users, Internet use was closely intertwined with the advancing of the reflexive project of the self, including the development of innovative self-narratives and the invention and implementation of lifestyles anchored in new moral and political values. Global reach to resources of information, companionship, and solidarity represented an integral aspect of this process. In this chapter, I am focusing on several individual cases that I have selected as examples of this kind of creative identity work undertaken by users with the help of the Internet. What I am hoping to illustrate through these cases is the way Canadians communicate in the context of a new medium that supports the continuous re-inventing and re-defining of the self. They can be seen as examples of what 'digital globalization' (see Taras, this volume) looks and feels like at the personal level. As will be demonstrated in the ensuing analysis, both opportunities and challenges – grounds for concern and hope for individual citizens – arise in this context.

The Internet as a Vehicle of Life Politics

To frame the political quality of this type of use practices theoretically, I invoke Giddens's notions of the self as a reflexive[2] project and life politics. According to Giddens (1991), under the conditions of high modernity, the reflexive project of the self "consists in the sustaining of coherent, yet continuously revised, biographical narratives" and "takes place in the context of multiple choice as filtered through abstract systems" (5). The more daily life is constituted in a dialectical interplay between the local and the global, the more individuals are "forced to negotiate lifestyle choices among a diversity of options" (5). This imperative brings about dangers of alienation, but simultaneously, it generates chances for re-appropriation of life circumstances and for personal empowerment.[3]

In light of this conception of the self, Giddens (1991) formulates his notion of life politics as the "politics of choice" (214). It tackles the existential question: Who do I want to be? (see 216). This question, in turn, is connected to the intrinsically human desire to grow and fulfill one's potentialities as a human being (see 216–17). The stake in life-politics is self-actualization "in a reflexively ordered environment, where the reflexivity links self and body to systems of global scope" (214). By "systems of global scope" in this definition, Giddens means systems structured by formal rules such as the market, expert knowledge, and bureaucracy, but media also represent systems of global scope that contribute significantly to the formation of self narratives (see 23–27). Elaborating on their role, Thompson (1995) claims that the process of self-formation throughout modernity has been "increasingly nourished by mediated symbolic materials, greatly expanding the range of options available to individuals" (quoted in Slevin 2000, 157). A system such as the Internet is an obvious candidate for inclusion into this formula. Certainly, the way it mediates experience is substantively different from the earlier communication media characterizing modernity. Earlier media brought a stream of events and experiences from around the globe into the local setting of the subject who was compelled to accept, resist, or re-appropriate the presented content. Giddens characterizes "the *intrusion* of distant events into everyday consciousness [emphasis added]" (27) as one of the major features of mediated experience in modern times. The interactive nature of the Internet allows a movement that goes the other way round. From within her local setting, the person can reach into globally distributed resources of information and sociality. Importantly, this new feature of mediation makes the local agenda lead the interaction between local and global. It allows the *elective mobilization* of distant symbolic resources into everyday consciousness. The political ramifications of such a reversal can be far-reaching and deserve careful exploration.

Giddens also defines life politics as a *politics of life decisions*. Amid changing circumstances, individuals facing the need to shape and maintain the coherence of their self-identity narrative make decisions. Thus new identities, new biographies organized around new values emerge and acquire social currency. I argue that the circulation of these new biographies and new values with the help of the media is a crucial development that links the politics of life decisions unfolding locally to national and global discourses and strategies.

Life politics *is* politics in both the conventional and the broad sense of the term, Giddens (1991) insists. It subsumes both processes of decision-making within the governmental sphere of the state[4] and, more broadly, acts of decision-making that concern debates or conflicts "where opposing interests and values clash" (226). But if this is so, then the increased capacity of individuals to consider, make, and propagate decisions on issues concerning their life style and self identity (Who do I want to be?) represents empowerment in the political sense.

Thus, when the concept of empowerment is tied to the process of reflexive decision-making on matters of self-identity and life politics, it manifests several dimensions. The relevance of the Internet to all of them is evident:

First, access to diverse, timely, and immediately relevant information and
    knowledge concerning issues of life politics, including lifestyles, moral
    values, innovative biographies and social relationships is a precondition
    for empowerment.
Second, empowerment is connected with the possibility to narrate, that is, to
    share and propagate the creative discoveries in matters of lifestyle and
    biography performed by individuals and groups.
Third, the possibility for interactive reinforcement of the reflexive project of
    self-identity within a responsive community contains another aspect of
    empowerment in the life-political sense.
Fourth, life politics, in its mundane manifestations, includes also a process of
    active elaboration of a stance with regard to the Internet itself: What
    kind of an Internet user am I? How well does this medium serve me
    and my self-project? The answers to these questions result in the
    production of a set of rules for engagement with the medium that is
    subsequently realized in the practice of the individual user and his or
    her household members. Numerous issues addressed in larger political
    debates regarding the regulation of the Internet at the level of the state,
    and internationally, are refracted in specific ways in these domestic
    negotiations and the resultant codes of conduct.

Voices from the Grassroots: Reinventing the Self

Challenges to established self-identity occur on a regular basis in high modernity. The self is constantly provoked to revise her self-narrative in light of new developments, ideas, and mediated messages. I propose that the empowering capacity of the Internet is recognized most clearly at breakpoints in one's life course where more or less substantial revision of one's biographical narrative is called for due to changing life circumstances, sometimes including but not limited to macro-developments of various kinds.

THE CYBORG NEXT DOOR

The breakdown of the established relationship between body and self is often an instance that necessitates a radical revision of one's biographical narrative and the respective restructuring of daily life. As Giddens (1991) observes, the body, as mobilized in praxis, is immediately relevant to the identity-project the individual subscribes to (218). Whether the mobilization will occur in relation to reproduction, nutrition, fashion, sport, sexuality, etc., the body is intimately involved into the settling of the question "Who do I want to be?" As much as it can co-operate in the pursuit of a desired identity, the body can also act up and refuse to comply. These are typically the situations of assailing chronic illness or disability depriving their victims of mobility, energy, time, adequate mental functioning, expressiveness, and a whole array of other capacities anchored in the body that furnish so many socially approved and personally desirable self-identity projects. A thorough re-orientation of one's biographical narrative is inevitable under such circumstances.

My research data show that in cases of such a breakup between body and self, the Internet gets actively mobilized in the negotiation process aimed at re-establishing the cooperation between the two entities at a new level. The medium becomes a vital resource in people's struggle to resist and overturn what Parsons (1951) has called the "sick role" – the traditional expectation prescribing isolation, withdrawal from habitual activities, passivity, and submission to expert manipulation. This struggle goes far beyond the formula "searching for health information online" that appears in numerous surveys designed to capture user behaviour. Looking for information is the action observable on the surface. The underlying practice in many of these instances is the reflexive revision of one's identity project with the help of information, participation, and support that can be culled online.

All dimensions of empowerment formulated in the previous section can be discerned in the accounts of people who employ the Internet to revise their identity projects in the face of bodily adversity. An early example surfaced in the reflections of a woman (Ellen, 49) with a chronic condition whom I interviewed in 1998 (see Bakardjieva 2005). She had been an avid traveller, explorer of new cultures, biker, writer, and socialite until she started noticing that her energy level was going down, her body wouldn't carry her through a normal working day, and her mind was often uncooperative and confused. Later came severe allergic reactions that forced her to lock herself in her home sometimes in unbearable pain and solitude. The independent, adventurous, intellectual, popular woman was reduced to a helpless suffering hermit soon to be forgotten by most of her former friends – certainly not the identity project that she had cherished. Thus Ellen turned to the Internet for information and support in her struggle to make sense of her condition and to find a new self, one that could live and manage the new parameters of her existence including immobility, pain, isolation, poverty, social assistance, dependency on the health care system, etc. On the network she discovered a community of people with the same illness from which she received information, understanding, support, loyalty, and a sense of social participation that helped her work through her identity crisis. The empowering effects consisted of "a lot of confidence," "getting my life in proportion again," "getting a sense of myself," "feeling much less a failure." Learning a lot about the disease was among the benefits of group membership; however, Ellen took care to qualify the particular kind of learning that was taking place there thus:

I learned so much from these people who had had the disease for years. I had tried to get hold of some medical information. But getting online is different because there, for the first time, you get information from people who have trodden this path already! (Ellen)

The group discussions not only provided a lifeline to individual participants, but also, somewhat unconsciously, worked to articulate a kind of life politics that was characterized by an acute sense of ecological issues, passionate insistence on harmony with nature, and preference for natural remedies. The members of the group strengthened each other's resolve in upholding this stance in their relationships with doctors, pharmacists, and family.

The Internet did not give Ellen her health back. Neither did it resolve structural problems of inadequate home care, doctors' attitudes, disability insurance, and others. Ellen remained a feeble disabled person with no power to reform the institutions that were governing her existence. However, she was empowered in a generative sense through the opportunity to learn, discuss, and develop a reflexive understanding of her condition that contributed to a new sense of self and the investment in an emergent life politics.

My study conducted in the early 2000s confirmed this pattern of empowering engagement with the medium through the cases of other women and men who had faced the necessity to re-establish a body-self agreement under similar circumstances. Thus a farm housewife (Esther) suffering from a chronic condition reducing her mobility had used the Internet to start a discussion forum related to her illness. She had also developed a website promoting organic farming and offering organically grown eggs from her own farm for sale. Esther contributed to online magazines and forums outside her own. Her creative writing and publishing via the Net had replaced other creative activities such as painting and the involvement in art communities that had

become unfeasible due to her illness. A lay philosopher and voluntary thera-
pist to others, Esther explained:

... the Internet took me through all of the stages of I guess what essentially was a
grieving process for the life I had as opposed to what I could do now. Um, the groups
[the online groups she participated in] have changed and they have changed because
I evolved. And I evolved because of the things that I learned in those groups. So, it's
all interconnected. I would say that apart from a continuing interest in art, and horses,
and agriculture, and philosophy I am almost a completely different person now than
in 1996 when I first actually started this work, this project. Through my illness I've
learned how to be more patient, I've had to become patient with myself, and I've had
to learn how to be patient with other people. And the resources for learning how to do
that came from the Internet....

Answering the direct question whether she felt that the Internet had empowered her in any way, Esther engaged the theme of the self head-on:

... And so the Internet opens that door. You can feel crappy and be therapeutically
productive, you know. And so I say therapeutically productive because the fact that
you can have a purpose and even if it's saying a prayer for somebody, or, you know,
consoling them, or listening to what they have to say or complain about. You have
served a purpose in that moment. And so you feel better about yourself even though
you feel like crap [laughs]. It's very empowering.... I feel better about myself now than
I've ever felt. And I think the Internet has played a huge role in that. Every time I felt
as if a door was closing I could find a window here. In more ways than one [laughs].
[Pause] I really can't say it any better than that.... So, I think the Internet has ... gosh,
I think, in terms of personal growth I'd still be at the Neanderthal stage if it hadn't
been for the contacts and the education and the opportunity that I've encountered
online.

The pursuit of her new identity project had brought another middle-aged
woman (Marilyn, 50) very close to real politics, in the narrow sense defined
by Giddens. She had run for alderman several years after her stroke when
her ability to articulate her thoughts had been significantly impaired. All her
learning about how to run a campaign had come from online sources:

I got lots of demographics and information statistics from the different ..., our city
website and then Alberta Government you know to just check statutes and all of that
bylaw information and zoning and what's new, what studies have been done recently
and all that. So it was very helpful for somebody that had never been involved in any

political, you know. I had to start somewhere; it was a good place to start. Then I also got how to write a campaign plan. I got the whole … mostly United States. That, I tell you, they have got some excellent ideas. So, that helped me formulate my campaign so I became my own campaign manager and then there's a whole bunch of steps to follow in between … (Marilyn)

Was Marilyn successful in her campaign? "I can tell you why I didn't succeed: I didn't have any money," she relates. But nevertheless she had done something consistent with her desired self-project and had grown as a person and citizen in the process:

So, you know, I did learn a lot and it was a very valuable exercise for me. Ohm, it's one thing I can cross off my list I have done of the things that I want to do yet in my life. Ohm, and it was very educational for me. I might be able to offer assistance to somebody else because I have stored all of those websites and information and everything I did in my campaign. (Marilyn)

As one can notice, the Internet was becoming an integral part of the process of reinventing the self after the loss of bodily capacities had triggered an identity crisis. In this way, an intriguing symbiosis between humans and technology was taking place. I will take the liberty to refer to these users as cyborgs (see Haraway 1991). Indeed, a brand of modest, mundane, friendly-neighbourhood cyborgs whose practice exemplifies the empowering dimensions of Internet use.

BOLD GLIMPSES ON THE SELF
In their study of the Internet in Trinidad, Miller and Slater (2000) discuss how people engaging with the Internet get caught up in a process of identification (10). What these authors call "the dynamics of objectification" refers to the ways in which particular people "can recognize or realize themselves through a particular domain of material culture" (10) in this case, the Internet. One type of dynamics of objectification, labelled "expansive potential," leads people to envisage a novel vision of themselves – of what they can be and do in life. Miller and Slater cite examples that focus on Internet-based applications and activities such as ICQ and MP3, but they also note that often the activities and interactions taking place online merge with the activities and interactions occurring in the schoolyard or business office.

My studies of Canadian users over the past two years allow me to confirm that there is indeed an expressed "expansive potential" effect in users' dealings with the Internet. In my observations, it does not always consist of "objectifying" new visions of the self online, but rather lies in the formation and active pursuit, in one's real life, of identity projects conceived on and through the Internet.

Janice, a thirty-one-year-old former truck driver for a scrap yard and mother of two young children, was ardent in her insistence on how much the Internet had contributed to her personal growth in terms of what she saw as "finding direction." At the time of the interview, Janice was working on finishing her high school, with an eye toward becoming a respiratory technician. Importantly, as her account reveals, the empowering effect had been produced through the combination of various mediated and direct experiences for which the Internet had served as an integrator and catalyst. This was Janice's view on empowerment as it referred to her own newly revised life story:

Empowered me ... wow! Big time! My course that I was taking in [college name] was an adult employment course. And we used the government ALICE website. I was in a really go-nowhere job. And the Internet, and places to go to discover yourself, and to do Internet aptitude skills tests, and compile all your information, and go and look up job descriptions and stuff. For me, it was probably what really started my road to a better future, got me going on my career. Yeah, I have a whole different perspective now. I have direction. I figured out what I want to be when I grow up. That's pretty cool. And the Internet had a major role in that. (Janice)

The role of the Internet was clearly gauged in the context of Janice's ongoing biographical narrative and impossible to understand out of its creative formation:

Yeah, when I am older, and I look back on my life, I will be able to say that the Internet had a major impact on my life. (Janice)

As Miller and Slater (2000) have noticed in their Trinidadian study, the Internet was becoming a mode of imagining the future – Janice's personal future, but by extrapolation, the future of other people in similar situations and of the medium as such:

Now, my future, it's opened a whole bunch of doors for my future, and I hope that other people learn that. I think there's a lot of people out there too that need a computer in their house. Or that need to use their computer in their house! (Janice)

Janice had decided to volunteer for my study (she had responded to a call for participation published on a local web site) because she though that could be her personal contribution toward the social understanding of the Internet as a medium capable of helping people grow.

When I said, we can't donate financially to charities, and stuff like that, but we think that this could help the Internet ... people understanding the Internet and having access to the Internet getting the word out that it's really worth it, to investigate it and find out about it. That could be my contribution, instead of donating cash to some organization, I could be a part of this, of helping other people get into it.

Thus, I think, Janice's participation in the study was a small act of life politics that was closely related to the politics of the Internet. Janice wanted her vision of the medium to acquire social currency and legitimacy particularly with a view to the needs of other categories of people living at the margins of the mainstream economy and society – stay-home mothers, working class women, seniors. She enthusiastically described the empowering role that the Internet could play in the life of these groups and proposed ideas about how they could be supplied with computers and encouraged to go online.

One member of such a group, a single mother and recent immigrant to Canada, Amy (24-year-old) would have subscribed easily to Janice's position. Amy described herself as a student and volunteer for a woman's rights organization in Calgary. She had moved to Canada from Lebanon about four years prior to the interview and had had her Internet connection for three years already. Amy was taking a college program and was finding the Internet very helpful with her school work, especially because it allowed her to search information for her papers and communicate with teachers from home while looking after her two-year-old daughter. Asked whether the Internet had helped her solve any personal problems, Amy responded:

Yes. For me going through all this stuff of being here away from all my family and I was in school in Lebanon and taking history ... I had to get back on track.... But it is a different society and culture [in Canada], and I have had to become myself again. So, with all of these problems, I can't really relate to anyone here, so people on the Internet from my country or who are my people really understand and have helped me. And I don't have to know them.... For me having people of my own culture is very good because in my own country it is not approved to be divorced or separated, so here I can talk to people that I don't know and they don't know me, so it is good. I can vent and they understand. But, I am getting to know some people pretty good and I know their names and they know mine and I have some friends' phone numbers so we actually talk on the phone instead of just the Internet. I have about 11 or 12 Arab friends on the Internet.

Apparently, for Amy the Internet had become the means of performing a complex balancing act with regard to her identity. She was caught in the tension between two cultures: one supportive of women's rights, career development, and independence, but having little appreciation of Arabic language, feeling, music, and poetry; and another – warm and spiritually nurturing, but intolerant to marital separation and many of the values that Amy had embraced. Amy's identity project was to reconcile and integrate the valued features of both these cultural systems despite their conflicts. That is where the Internet was being drawn in order to screen and reveal in various degrees, to be an instrument for accomplishing practical tasks and an environment for sociability. As much as it may sound politically extraneous to look over the shoulder of an immigrant single mother glued to her computer screen in search for news, company, friendship, and entertainment, I argue that by dialling up every evening Amy was performing a politics of choice.

THE WAR OF KEYWORDS

Esther: Because I'm telling you right now, if you put horses into an Internet searcher, you'll get some pretty appalling responses. Appalling. I mean that's something that we can't protect children from.

Melvin: I know. There's no place in our society for those types of things. We don't need it. We have enough violence within our world right now. We don't need that. We have enough problems, we don't need to create more. I mean, let's stand up as a race, as human beings, and say no. We do not want that. This is not a part of who we are. And just say no.

Esther: You're such an idealist.

Politics fills the living rooms, the studies or basements where networked computers are located. There are clashes of principles and proclamations, covert surveillance, and open protest. Households put up a last-ditch defence against the torrent of distant events that threatens to engulf their fragile order of moral values and life-political choices. Challenges to that order abound. It is either that the mother of the family suddenly starts dividing her time disproportionately between her computer, on the one hand, and her kids and husband, on the other:

Kevin: ... I used to tell my friends I'd lost my wife to a computer, you know. Oh yeah, she got into it so much, you know, she'd play word-search, or word racer, and then your emails and everything else. She'd be on it 2 or 3 hours every night. It's like I never saw her any more ... [laughs]. Saw the back of her head [everybody laughs].

Or it is the unknown guy that the daughter is chatting with:

Nathan: Just the one, you know, just you have to be more cautious. You are exposing your family to the world. Most of the kids seem to be, they have good heads on their shoulders so I don't really worry about it but there was one time when ICQ was really big, everybody had ICQ and we checked Ana's logs occasionally and there was one guy on there where, this is wrong, and we ultimately ended up blocking this guy from participating. Ana didn't know. She's very sociable with everybody. This guy was getting intense.

Or it comes from the "dark side" that the son is visiting like Satanism and "violence and gore" sites. Or his obsession with e-Bay. Or, more prosaically, all the junk mail that is polluting one's box:

Neil: I think that they should limit that now.... Even though they do have 'unsubscribe', it doesn't work. You can unsubscribe, but the next week you got it back again. I've unsubscribed to you already! What is it you don't understand?

So, a conversation starts about where the protective barrier should be erected. Whose responsibility should it be to regulate content providers? What protection should exist for personal information? Should the government be involved? In what way? Or does the solution lie in the hands of hypothetical "world Internet organizations," presumably, professional or civic bodies that set policies for the Internet? The living rooms connected to the Internet buzz with debates around such questions. But, of course, as in the case of macro-political debates regarding regulation, the insurmountable problem stems from the fact that, as one respondent put it: "the Internet depends on who you are." Regulation expectations, consequently, will depend on what you value. And it is impossible to agree upon universal values in a global context.

Thus, an important dimension of empowerment would involve letting these voices from everyday life enter the political debate surrounding the Internet at the levels of the state and the globe. Many of the users I interviewed were looking for outlets for their opinions regarding Internet regulation. Like Janice (quoted above), some of them saw their participation in the study as one such opportunity to be heard. They wanted to put their own version and vision of the Internet in wider circulation by contributing their perspective to an Internet study that could be expected to eventually reach the ear of content providers and policy makers.

I mean we provided ourselves to you today as a helpful thing for what you do, which in turn is going to help somebody else to come to a conclusion of what the Internet's all about. (Melvin)

These positively affected or, as I insist, empowered users wanted to deliver a message through me, a message about the tremendous value of the Internet that had helped them expand and enrich their identity projects in desired directions, but simultaneously, a message against rampant consumerism, garbage mail, uninvited porno assaults, and also against giving up the struggle for a medium responsive and accountable to citizens.

Thus, I anticipate an intermediate level of Internet regulation to emerge between the micro and the macro that reflects lifestyles and alliances around values and moral principles. Both the politics of search engines (see Introna and Nissenbaum 2000) and the politics of web portals and service provision should gradually become attuned to the diverse life-political projects pursued by people worldwide. Research, I believe, has a major contribution to make toward that end.

DID THEY LIVE HAPPILY EVER AFTER?

I don't know if the users who felt empowered by the Internet lived happily ever after. I may never find out if Janice managed to receive a Respiratory Technician qualification; whether Esther's virtual forum continued to help people and to give her a sense of fulfillment; and if Amy succeeded in striking the right balance between the independent woman she wanted to be and her Muslim Arabic roots.

What I feel prepared to predict is that the Internet will continue to be the object and vehicle of life politics and that the microtechniques of empowerment people devise around it will proliferate.

With that said, I notice that in working through users' experiences I have taken the notion of life politics to a place where it probably wasn't intended to go. Was it meant to cover living room debates, immigrant self-help, and housewives' web forums? It looks like I couldn't avoid the trivialization of the concept that I feared from the very beginning. Yet at the same time, shouldn't everyday-life politics implicating the Internet be recognized for what it is: politics in the general sense of the word – "modes of decision-making that concern debates or conflicts where opposing interests and values clash" (Giddens 1991, 226). Any political project in the sphere of government, then, should take into account the everyday-life politics of the potentially affected.

Finally, I want to go back to my initial distinction between those users who employed the Internet in predictable and medium- or market-led ways and those who had come up with creative appropriations (on this concept, see Feenberg 1999) of their own. I think Giddens' (1991) work, namely his "dilemmas of the self" provides a good framework for understanding the difference. The dilemmas of the self are the axes along which Giddens proposes that the major tensions of living in the late modern world can be mapped. The unimaginative versus creative Internet use mode correspond roughly to the dilemma between "personalized" versus "commodified" experience (198). The Internet as a conduit of late capitalism reinforces a variety of standardized and commodified lifestyles. One of my respondents' comments fleshes out this state of affairs: "And I find that the vanity industry is just overwhelming. I mean the ads that you see when you're just trying to check your email are an example of that. Lose 10 pounds, win this, travel here, you know" (Esther). Thus numerous, enticing and rewarding "projects of the self" are on offer via a combination of market and network mechanisms. Clients for these lifestyles abound and the Internet is heavily implicated in the deal through interactive "calculate your ideal weight" sort of applets. However, as my encounters have shown, Giddens is right to claim that "commodification does not carry the day unopposed" (199). And interestingly enough, it is quite often the marginalized individuals who react the most creatively by redefining and re-appropriating the medium in the name of alternative sets of values and life projects.

Bibliography

Bakardjieva, Maria. 2005. *Internet Society: The Internet in Everyday Life.* London: Sage.

Feenberg, Andrew. 1999. *Questioning Technology.* London: Routledge.

Giddens, Anthony. 1984. *The constitution of society.* Berkeley and Los Angeles: University of California Press.

——. 1991. *Modernity and Self-Identity: Self and Society in the Late Modern Age.* Stanford, CA: Stanford University Press.

Haraway, Donna. 1991. "A Cyborg Manifesto: Science, Technology, and Socialist-Feminism in the Late Twentieth Century." In Haraway, *Simians, Cyborgs and Women: The Reinvention of Nature,* 149–81. New York: Routledge.

Introna, Lucas, and Helen Nissenbaum. 2000. "Shaping the Web: Why the Politics of Search Engines Matters." *Information Society Journal* 16(3): 169–85.

Miller, Daniel, and Don Slater. 2000. *The Internet: An Ethnographic Approach.* Oxford, NY: Berg.

Parsons, Talcott. 1951. *The Social System.* New York: Free Press.

Slevin, James. 2000. *The Internet and Society.* Cambridge: Polity Press.

Thompson, John. 1995. *The Media and Modernity: A Social Theory of the Media.* Cambridge: Polity Press.

Notes

1   Certainly, all these mundane activities can have high importance to people and the possibility to conduct them online could be life-transforming to users with disabilities or otherwise obstructed access.

2   Here and throughout this chapter, I am working with the notion of reflexivity defined by Giddens (1984) as "the monitored character of the ongoing flow of social life." Reflexivity is grounded "in the continuous monitoring of action which human beings display and expect others to display" (3). In the post-traditional order of modernity, Giddens (1991) claims, "self-identity becomes a reflexively organized endeavour" (5).

3   Here and in what follows, I use the notion of empowerment as a shorthand for a relative increase in individual choice and control over the circum-stances of one's own life in the face of the powerful social forces that define and delimit these circumstances.

4   Think about the hot issues of gay marriage, gender equity, disability rights, etc.

7: How Canadians Blog

MICHAEL KEREN

Canada and the Sixties

The increase in the birth rate in the United States and other Western countries after World War II, accompanied by high growth rates in Western economies of the 1950s and 1960s, had a significant economic impact, especially
because the postwar generation became a major target for marketers. The
emphasis on this slice of the market has also given rise to conceptions about
the cultural uniqueness and impact of the "baby boomers," especially during
the 1960s when many of them became university students (MacLeod 1996).
Since the "roaring twenties" no decade has been mythologized like "the
sixties," when a baby boomers' revolution was allegedly taking place in the
West. This mythology has been one of the first expressions of "globalization,"
namely, the assumption (prevailing mainly in academic circles) that certain
economic, political, and cultural processes mythologized in the United States
would ultimately be adopted everywhere with the same degree of enthusiasm.

The mythology of the sixties is understandable in light of the fact that
many writers, academics, and producers of popular culture whose university
life was marked by a sense of protest would look back to those years with nos-
talgia: "The sixties resound in our historical memory as do few other eras. It
was a time when events went into overdrive, and the postwar social trajectory

was deflected off line.... Few who reached adulthood between 1961 and 1971 remained unmarked by the events of those years" (Unger and Unger 1998, 1). And since roughly until September 11, 2001, such statements could be made without much consideration for processes occurring outside the boundaries of the United States, a global culture, carried by "baby boomers," was expected to emerge worldwide.

To be sure, the myth of the sixties was inaccurate even as regards the United States itself. Most people who reached adulthood in America during those years remained relatively unmarked by the events led, as always, by an elite, which also dominated the historiography of the era. Even if they led a hippie lifestyle for a couple of years, participated in campus sit-ins and anti-Vietnam demonstrations, and used swear words against LBJ and the CIA, most baby boomers were no Abbie Hoffmans, Bob Dylans, or Jane Fondas. The "New Left," whose principles were extensively taught in American universities by its veterans, had little impact beyond campus walls, while the more significant social changes of the decade – the civil rights movement, the Great Society programs, and feminism – were not necessarily the creations of baby boomers. The great writings of the era, such as *One Dimensional Man* by Herbert Marcuse and *The Feminine Mystique* by Betty Friedan, were often written by incumbents of their grandparents' generation, and most baby boomers followed the psychedelic counterculture, the 1968 Chicago demonstrations, and probably also the "sexual revolution" mainly on television.

The gap between the myth of the sixties and reality was particularly wide in Canada where, as in other instances, a unique national identity has been in the making while its makers were willing to adopt the American myth of the era and the false assumption that like every American myth it applies globally. The sixties were an important decade in modern Canadian history, marking a transition to modernization both in French and English Canada. This was the era of the rise of Quebec separatism, inspired by similar movements around the world, and the era of Pierre Elliott Trudeau, under whose leadership policies were advanced that distinguished Canada from the United States both as a welfare state and in pursuing an independent foreign policy. The Canadian transition in the sixties was no less profound than anything the counterculture in the United States has ever achieved. Moreover, Canada did not lack its own counterculture, embodied, for example, in Trudeau's personality and behaviour (e.g., his marriage to a twenty-two-year-old "flower child"), and coming to bear in the absorption of draft dodgers, the activities of the Canadian Union of Students, the siege at Sir George Williams University, the riots that broke out when Toronto police tried to clear hippies off the streets of the Yorkville coffeehouse district, etc.

Yet, Canadians related to "the sixties" mainly in terms of processes and events occurring south of the border. For example, Tom Fennell (1995), discussing the combination of "hippies, rock music and Trudeaumania," analyzed this experience mainly in relation to the American space program, the assassinations of John Kennedy and Martin Luther King, the American civil rights movement, the Vietnam war, and the Cuban missile crisis. And in her book *Long Way from Home: The Story of the Sixties Generation in Canada*, Myrna Kostash reported on three Canadian films made during the sixties, which portrayed, however, almost exclusively images of non-Canadian figures, such as Allen Ginsberg, Jerry Rubin, Abbie Hoffman, The Beach Boys, Adlai Stevenson, Martin Luther King, etc. "My question was: what did Canada look and feel like in the Sixties?" she asks. Her answer: "It didn't look like anything. The Sixties took place in the United States of America" (Kostash 1980, xi).

Only recently have Canadian baby boomers begun to question the global reach of the American myth of the sixties and venture to redefine their own Canadian identity in that context. A major theme in that process of redefinition has been the realization that the overall dream of the sixties has been shattered. As claimed in an *Alberta Report* piece titled "Perished is the dream of the sixties set, dissolved in the harsh light of reality," the baby boomers' vision of a society animating a sense of community, national purpose, and moral obligation to others did not take hold. This, we are reminded, is not unique. The "Forties people," who won World War II and created a prosperous, church-going society, says the *Report*, have also seen their dream of Canada disintegrate (Byfield 1994).

It seems that every generation goes through a phase in which at least some of its self-conscious members realize that the dreams of their youth have been illusory, which explains the disenchantment found among them. "American boomers," wrote Barbara Wickens (2003), "elected their first president, Bill Clinton, only in 1992. In Canada, we've yet to have a boomer prime minister – and likely never will" (79). Calling herself "just one more aging boomer," Wickens claimed in 2003 that the nine million Canadians born between 1946 and 1965 were now somewhat risible. "Yoga, plastic surgery, Viagra? Pathetic attempts at trying to maintain our illusory youth" (Wickens 2003, 79).

Whether pathetic or not, Canadian baby boomers engage in negotiation of their identity, attempting to navigate between the myths of their youth and the reality of their lives. This negotiation process, begun when Leonard Cohen called upon them to "take Manhattan" while many of them were apparently more concerned with the success of Expo 67 in Montreal, can be observed in a variety of intellectual and artistic forums: coffee house conversations, book clubs, film festivals, etc. Here, I would like to take advantage of a new medium allowing us to learn about this process from a unique perspective. I refer to online diaries known as "weblogs" or "blogs." This new medium, introduced in the mid-1990s, consists of computer software that allows individuals to express thoughts and feelings, and be exposed to thoughts and feelings by others, without having to wait for the release of a new novel, play, or film. Millions of individuals all over the world, including thousands of Canadians, publish online diaries on a daily, even hourly, basis.

This medium is a researcher's paradise in that it allows us to follow what large numbers of individuals say about a wide variety of subjects on an ongoing basis, without the mediation of publishers, editors, pollsters, etc. At the same time, it is also a researcher's hell because of the difficulty of applying traditional methods of communication research to this medium. Standard attempts to generalize about blogs on the basis of random sampling have failed in the absence of a clear, stable, finite universe of blogs to be sampled; online diaries come and go and, despite websites like Diaryland or Blogs-Canada bringing many of them together, many others float freely in cyberspace. It is also impossible to make general statements about the gender or socio-economic composure of blogs in light of the fact that the phenomenon studied is located in virtual reality. While research on such media as newspapers deals with individuals and institutions whose identity can in principle be traced, here we know little about the producers of these online diaries besides their nicknames. The person presented in the diary may be in part or in full a fictional character and for all practical purposes ought to be treated as such.

However, blogs can serve us well if we consider them as part of life-writing research, which derives theoretical and historical statements from autobiographical works whose unique character is acknowledged, and whose range incorporates both real and fictional writings. It is assumed that a systematic analysis of Winston Churchill's autobiography, for instance, may generate important insights on the political world even though it does not constitute a sample of leaders' autobiographies. It is similarly assumed that a systematic analysis of George and Weedon Grossmith's novel *The Diary of a Nobody* may generate important hypotheses on political life in Victorian England despite the fictional nature of this diary. Applying life-writing methods to blogs is quite natural because they constitute a form of life writing. Tristine Rainer has assigned life-writing genres into any number of divisions including autobiographies, memoirs, confessions, spiritual quests, meditations, personal essays, travelogues, autobiographical short stories and novels, portraits, complaints, conceptual writings, works of humour, and family histories (Rainer

1998). As blogs involve all these genres, we can view this new medium within the long tradition of life writing.

This is my point of departure; this chapter does not attempt to general-ize about the baby boom generation, nor to provide an overview of Canada's growing "blogosphere" (containing blogs written by Canadians and address-ing Canadian themes of varying importance from the Harper government, health care, and Western alienation through Generation X turning forty to the bingo game posted by the NDP on its website).[1] As any attempt to general-ize about the millions of words written about these themes every day would be misleading, I chose to follow the life-writing tradition and focus on one online diary, "Marn's Big Adventure," which caught my attention because of its good writing style, its recognition by other diarists, its longevity, and its frequent reference to Canadian themes.

As I began to read this "Life and times of a woman who makes Emily Dickinson look like a party animal,"[2] as one weblog directory describes it, I realized that this diary provides a rare glimpse into an instance in which Canadian identity is being negotiated. The lengthy recording of a life in a southern Quebec log cabin, whose most exciting feature is an occasional mouse hunted by Zubby the cat, may be read as a response to the disen-chantment over "the sixties," and the reconstruction of a new/old Canadian identity that is more consistent with the tale of Anne of Green Gables than with the myths of Che Guevara, the Students for Democratic Society, or the Black Panthers. Although by no means "representative," as no life is, Marn's life writing reflects the thoughts of a woman who came of age in the sixties, and realizes forty years later that the past adventures attributed to her, largely by herself, were mostly invented on American television. Following one aging baby boomer's life story as it unfolds in hundreds of diary entries, then, may not satisfy the aspiration to learn about society by grand generalizations, but may be as inspiring to the student of Canadian society as it is to the hundreds of Internet surfers visiting this blog on a regular basis.

Cat Lady

As mentioned before, the analysis of blogs does not refer to real individuals but merely to the diary keepers as they represent themselves in their blogs. Even if a diarist does not intentionally invent a false identity, it cannot be assumed that any representation of life in a diary depicts a complete life story. At the same time, blogs allow for an analysis of the norms, attitudes, and char-acteristics of the figure emerging in the text, whether that figure is invented or real. Now, the figure emerging in "Marn's Big Adventure" can be safely characterized as anything but an adventurer. According to the autobiographical note accompanying this blog, "Marn" was born in 1951 in southern Ontario and has been married since 1974 to Paul because he also likes cats. The autobiographical note is dominated by descriptions of the family's cats because, as Marn claims, "Some of us include our kitties as family members." This is an appropriate introduction to an online diary by a person who, while aware of the world around her and engaged in important philanthropic activity, seems to attribute no less importance to the well-being of her cats than to any issue, be it political, economic, social, cultural, geophysical, metaphysical, theological, historical, anthropological, or mystical. It is not uncommon for a gifted writer to compose cat stories, even in diary form, but the emphasis found here on the pettiest elements of life becomes worth noting when written by a baby boomer in an era of great political turmoil. With every entry in the diary, Pete Seeger's question comes to mind: "Where have all the flowers gone?"

Marn has apparently never been a "flower child" but she is very much a product of the baby boom generation. Born in 1951, she was no champion of the sexual revolution in her teens, but she belonged to the generation that announced it. "S-e-x was never talked about when I was growing up, never. As far as I can tell, my generation invented sex sometime in the 1960's" (3.4.2000). The expression "as far as I can tell" hints at some skepticism about the truism that the sixties were an era of large-scale sexual promiscuity. Before the 1960s, she writes, nobody knew anything about it. "They sure as heck didn't talk about it like we do, eh, so I have to assume we invented it. We sure talk about it enough" (3.4.2000). Her wedding, she writes, was "one of those hippie dippy, rollin' in granola kinds of weddings" (7.4.2000). She made her own dress and wore Earth Shoes that made her stroll up the church aisle with a seductive, clod-hopping farmer walk that made brides feel less stuffy at the time. She also followed other traditions of the era, such as living together with her future husband before the wedding, refraining from changing her last name to his, etc. And when describing an older friend, she considers him "a generation and a gender away from me, right wing, red white and blue, tough as nails and still has his military posture and hair cut to match," while she belongs to the baby boom generation: "I'm a flaming liberal, had a knee jerk antipathy to the U.S. military because of Vietnam, a feminista – I kept my maiden name when I married, which ain't unusual now but created a stink when I did it 25 years ago" (25.5.2000).

Looking back, however, she realizes the gap between the images of the sixties and reality. Consider the tattoo culture adopted at the time by college students as part of their identification with cons, carnies, bikers, and other representatives of "low culture." Marn treats the possibility she could have ever been part of that trend with irony:

My tattoo dates back to my prison days. Me and my bitch we.... Oh, alright, that's not completely true. Let me start again.
I ran away and joined the circus when I was in my teens, my tattoo is a souvenir of....
Stop it. Stop looking at me that way. Alright, alright, it was like this:
I woke up after a three day crack and liquor soaked binge with 50 of my closest friends from the local Hell's Angels chapter. All I was wearing was my tattoo....
OH, ALRIGHT. (10.4.2000)

The bare truth is that Marn got her tattoo at a much older age with no romantic or revolutionary flavour accompanying the experience. In a confessional mood ("I'm now spilling my guts") she admits she could not even find the tattoo parlour in Montreal on her own for lack of a sense of direction, and that she took many precautions before allowing the tattoo artist to touch her, making sure the place was licensed by all the necessary health boards and professional organizations, that a new tattoo needle was used for each client, and that the building was immaculately clean. "Getting a tattoo wasn't a spontaneous thingie where free spirit Marn waltzes into any old place. Oh no, I'm too ummm Marn for that.... As you can see, I am not a wild and crazy girl" (10.4.2000).

What is she then? Marn is explicit: "I am one of those cat people. I adore cats and I'm a bit afraid that when I get even older and even more eccentric than I am now that I might end up one of those old ladies with, like, 89 cats or something" (30.3.2000). Marn believes that "being one of those cat people" is not a matter of age, as she does not feel her life has changed much. Her identity as a cat lady is related to the revelation that the hopes and aspirations of earlier years have not given any other meaning to her life. This is what her frequent reference to her not having a life implies. The grand ideologies embraced by the sixties generation have not provided her with guidance on how to live her life. "Philosophers," she writes, "call it the leap of faith and truly that's what it is, a leap. It's not something you can will yourself to do, it's just something you do. Me, I lost my religion a long time ago. The closest I can come to believing is my daffodils" (1.5.2000).

Not only does the diary express disbelief in the philosophies, ideologies, and religions of the age, but even when preoccupied with daffodils, Marn does not trust their pictures in garden supply stores, which are as deceiving as systems of ideas. She finds meaning in an activity no system of ideas prevailing in the sixties ever promoted: "I take my new bulbs, a bag of powdered bonemeal and my trusty yellow handled shovel out to the meadows and start digging. My cat Zoe, who follows me everywhere with dog-like devotion, is particularly fascinated by this ritual. She loves the smell and taste of the flour like bone meal.... I open a hole, toss in a couple of handfuls of the white powder and bat Zoe's black nose out of the hole so I can settle in some bulbs. Cover the bulbs with soil and repeat oh, about 35 times. She never gives up" (1.5.2000).

As we follow the description of the annual bulb-planting ritual by the lady and her cat, we are led through an all-but-religious ritual. "That moment when I nestle those ugly brown lumps into the ground, believing that they will survive the winter, that buried in their core is beauty, that we will meet in the spring ... that moment is as close to faith as I come" (1.5.2000). This scene includes mythological elements – burial, belief, survival, beauty, hope, meeting – that were incorporated in every modern ideology striving to replace religious mythology by a secular set of meanings. Marxism in particular mythologized the course of human life from birth to death, making it a redemptive journey. Marn, covering her daffodil bulbs with soil in rural Quebec of the early twenty-first century, finds an alternate meaning to her life. Her writing, however, is not devoid of a subtle wish for redemption, or at least for the motive of commemoration after death sought by the ideologies and religions she has given up: "Did you know that daffodils can easily last 50, even 75 years without care? Mine will keep our spring pact long after I break it, long after I am done composting in the cemetery across the valley from my home. I like the idea that someday someone will take a walk in the woods, stumble on my daffodil meadow, and perhaps wonder ..." (1.5.2000).

It is not easy to derive such ideas from a blog written in a light-hearted manner and including every cliché in the book. Underneath many meaningless phrases filling the diary ("A woman's gotta do what a woman's gotta do, eh") (7.4.2000), a serious search for the meaning of life can however be found. "Some women, when they're blue" writes Marn, "will buy themselves new clothes. Some will splurge on spiffy shoes, whilst others come home with new bits of make-up. Silly, deluded women. They've got it all wrong. The only place you can buy everlasting joy and happiness is a garden center. It is The One True Path. Can I hear you say, 'Amen?' Yes, brothers and sisters, emotional salvation can be yours if you visit a garden center" (12.8.2000). This church preacher's style is not incidental, for Marn attributes her pious gardening to a tradition of eight generations of Methodists in her family, which survived the modern revolutionary age. "I shed the faith but one of the hymns seems to have stuck ... something about how one person's actions matter, something about 'you in your small corner and I in mine'" (12.8.2000).

The principle that one can find and sustain a meaningful life while hidden in a small corner is hard to adhere to in the early twenty-first century. Marn does not fail to realize that revolutionary events are occurring while she is in hiding. On September 11, 2001, for example, she knows she cannot simply continue to compose cat stories, although she hints she would have preferred to: "Oh, Lordy, there shouldn't be any New York voices in my head. I live in another country, in a tiny log cabin nestled in the woods. And yet ... I hear New York voices" (11.9.2001). When she hears of the attacks on the Twin Towers and the Pentagon, Marn recalls traumatic moments she did undergo in the past. She recalls, for instance, sitting at a small wooden desk at her public school on the day in which a tearful principal announced over the school intercom that John Kennedy had been shot, or being a student in Ottawa when the War Measures Act was announced. "Welcome to the new millennium, folks," she writes on September 11, "You might want to fasten your seatbelts, it looks to be a bumpy ride" (11.9.2001).

Yet this is a rather exceptional entry, for mostly Marn remains aloof from the bumpy rides of the age, while being aware that the distance she takes may mean she is lacking a life at all. She often refers to the possibility that her readers would consider her life as one not lived, but her choice to maintain her seclusion from the world with the "spousal unit" and two cats can be seen as stemming from the realization that the model of the world as spelled out for the baby boom generation by popular culture, one of "sex, drugs and rock and roll," was nothing but a set of fantasies. In one entry, for instance, devoted to her cleaning the house with a "Mr. Clean" detergent, Marn revisits these fantasies: "For a while it was just me and the guy with the shaved head, earrings, and oh so muscular torso barely wrapped in that skin tight white tee shirt. Whooo yeah, I had that guy on the floor before he knew what hit him. Then Paul joined us and we were a threesome ... Marn, Paul and ... Mr. Clean" (16.7.2000). The rest of the text reflects on the demise of the wild illusions of the past: "Oh yeah. Any time YOU'RE feeling depressed, feeling that YOU have no life, just mosey right over here. I guarantee that once you compare your life to mine you will feel much, much better. So while the rest of you spent Saturday wallowing in sex, drugs and rock and roll, the spousal unit and I just finished Day One of our quest to create the illusion of order and cleanliness at our place" (16.7.2000).

It is easier for the diarist to reflect on the shuttering of the sixties' dreams when she talks about her husband: "Sometimes I regret paths not taken. I feel guilty about the domesticity, the harness of wife, child, home. I remember the beautiful long hands, the tapped fingers he had as a man-child, fingers always caressing a guitar, a paintbrush.... Now those hands are calloused, some of the fingers scarred, the nails damaged by the work he does. I can't remember the last time he took his guitar out of its case.... Husband, child, home have been a generous place for me, the microclimate I needed. I set aside some of my dreams for this but don't regret it. I hope he feels the same" (2.8.2000).

It is hard to tell how happy the diarist is about her extreme domesticity. At times it seems that behind the irony with which she treats the "sex, drugs and rock and roll" illusions, she regrets they are gone. At one point, for example, she comes across a "Spark Slut Test" on the web and finds to her dismay that she is only 43 per cent slutty, 2 per cent below the norm. Her response: "It's not that I want to be in the top percentile or anything, but I WOULD like to be well, you know, as slutty as the girl next door. Is that too much to ask? Is it? Is it? ... Or maybe ... maybe I'm just going to have to accept who I am and deal with the fact that I've never been one to walk the well beaten path, even in matters of sex. Oh dear" (12.7.2000). The little glory accompanying her life seems to bother her more than her ironic style reveals. In a particularly ironic entry she imagines a twelve-man Greek chorus, resplendent in togas and laurel wreaths, accompanying her anywhere, but soon she realizes that the chorus would find itself in very unexciting locations like the village's bank machine. And even then, she would not be able to avoid such worries as how all twelve men could be put in the tiny bedrooms of the log cabin. "You can imagine my distress about this.... I mean, one moment I thought I had come to a major life change, the next all my dreams are dashed on the rocks of practicality" (29.8.2000).

NEGOTIATING CANADIAN IDENTITY

Whether or not "Marn's Big Adventure" represents the thoughts and feelings of others, I would like to suggest that what we are witnessing here is a negotiation process over Canadian identity. This process can be studied thanks to the new medium of weblogs, a medium allowing an observation of the ongoing life story of a Canadian baby boomer whose construction of an identity is, for once, not done in response to social scientists' questionnaires (e.g., "how do you assess on a scale from 1 to 5 your generation's political impact on Canadian society?"). In what follows, I would like to demonstrate this negotiation process in reference to the medium that enables it. My argument is that the redefinition of the Canadian baby boomer's identity is strongly related to the technical capacity she gained to speak to the world not as spokesperson for a generation but as a common individual. As the individual life story unfolds on the Web, many of the truisms attributed to baby boomers come up, but so does the search for a safe corner in which life becomes a meaningful personal experience rather than a generational declaration.

Marn is aware of the liberating nature of her blog. She sees this new medium as a way to learn about one's own feelings by observing the feelings of others. "I like to mosey the diaries here, even though most folks are plenty young enough to be my kid. They talk about love, lust, loneliness. Fear of being dorky, all that stuff and I still feel those things" (5.4.2000). This process of learning about oneself is facilitated by the Internet, for Marn admits that her capacity to express feelings offline is limited. Although having many acquaintances, the number of people outside her family she ever loved can be numbered on one hand, she writes. "Believe me, that statistic doesn't give me any happiness, it's something of a reminder that I have a dried up raisin of a heart in many ways" (25.5.2000). Friendship is a form of storytelling – friends tell each other about their hopes, fears, and desires – but despite Marn's storytelling skills and her professional experience as a writer, she always had difficulty sharing stories: "it had been many years since I'd made the effort to form a new friendship because I couldn't muster the courage or energy to share the stories you have to share to build a friendship. It all just seemed like too much of an effort" (25.5.2000). She even found it hard to meditate in the "real world": "I can't imagine how someone can have the courage to look hard and deep inside themselves for a week. Me, I'm going the passing acquaintanceship route. What I don't know can't hurt me" (13.4.2000).

Like many online diarists, Marn is ambivalent about the exposure of her personal life. On the one hand, she realizes that her grandparents, who did not have a similar opportunity to record their lives, have been forgotten, and nobody remembers anymore who the people in the family's old picture albums are, while she found a medium of self-commemoration. On the other hand, the knowledge that some of her family members and friends may read the diary makes her uncomfortable; she prefers to expose her life to strangers, as in a conversation on a night bus:

Have you ever been on a long bus trip at night, knowing that you're going to be hours on that bus, knowing that you won't sleep? I've done that, sat there in the dark beside a stranger, and begun a casual conversation to pass the time. Sometimes it evolves into something else and an incredibly personal story is told. The bus becomes a cocoon for a soft voice murmuring in the dark, features illuminated for a split second by an odd flash of light from passing traffic, a sliver of a spirit in transit. When the trip is done you part ways, each to slip back into a life the other will never know, again a stranger without a name. That's how Diaryland feels to me. (15.5.2000)

Blogs are indeed the appropriate medium for individuals who are restrained, shy, or otherwise incapable of communicating in the real world, and Marn,

whose mother committed suicide when she was nine and who had consequently withdrawn into herself, finds lots of satisfaction in the opportunity to record
her present happiness in a humoristic manner. She realizes the revolutionary potential of the Internet in this regard. "Isn't it interesting," she wonders,

... how many people we know are becoming so highly textual? Me, I'm betting that's
what the web will be remembered for ... not for the glitz, but for the fact that for the
first time ever ordinary people had a simple, inexpensive way to get their words out.
Welcome to the revolution, folks. Bet you didn't realize that when you were putting
up a web page extolling the wonders of your cat, Fluffy, or your passion for the old tin
façades they used to put on Victorian houses to make them seem posh ... well, I'll bet
you didn't realize that you were a revolutionary, eh. After all it's only words and maybe
a few pictures, right? (19.5.2000).

In the past, words have been controlled by money and power. "You won't
see hieroglyphs telling the story of some guy who made pots for a living, and
Homer wrote about gods and heroes, not about some guy who worked at a job
he didn't like" (19.5.2000). Even Gutenberg, she writes, did not set words free
because a professional writing class had been established as part of the print
culture, a whole business based on controlling tastes and selling words, that
has to be mainstream. But blogs brought about a revolution in that words are
no longer homogenized by mainstream forces but ordinary folks can express
themselves, as long as the expression remains online: "Here, in this little anar-
chist world of glowing dots on screens, as long as you can afford a computer
and an Internet connection, you can control words. You can publish yourself"
(19.5.2000). This is not only an emancipation of individuals formerly subdued
to the tastes of publishers but a way for ordinary people to be remembered:
"The lives, interests and best of all the words of all we ordinary folks are being
preserved. Oh my" (19.5.2000).
     Marn makes the best of this revolution; once she has been given the oppor-
tunity to communicate with total strangers online, she not only meditates at
great length about every intimate aspect of her life, but becomes the focal
point of an online community of devoted readers who share in "Marn's Big
Adventure" in which Canadian identity is being redefined. The new Canadian, emerging from this blog, resembles the imaginary mansion owner
familiar from the literature of the *ancien régime* preceding the bumpy rides
of the twentieth century. Marn is explicit about the role of her blog in providing a redefinition of Canadian identity: "It strikes me that perhaps one or two
non-Canadians stumble upon this diary, and so in the spirit of international
understanding I will occasionally share little nuggets about what it means to

be Canadian" (28.6.2000). It is not incidental that this declaration is made in an entry about laundry day in which the family's underwear changing habits are shared in great detail with the world, as is the presence of plaid sheets in the family's laundry. Marn finds it appropriate to engage in such petty matters because she has given up on the glory and magic attributed to her generation: "Some diaries talk about seething sexual orgies, or unspeakably hot couplings featuring offbeat sexual paraphernalia. Me, I share the magic that is laundry day" (28.6.2000). The diarist apparently feels that the triviality of her present life applies to other Canadians, for how else could one otherwise explain the rest of the entry: "Our Canadian constitution promises peace, order, good government and plaid. Even the titans of multi-national big business have had to bow to the Canadian reality, and this is the typical dress code for men on casual Fridays in my country. (The fiddle is optional of course, but ALL the stylin' guys accessorize with a fiddle.) ... we are an unusual people, eh" (28.6.2000).

National identity is defined in this blog less in terms of what is said about Canada than in terms of what is not said. Except for occasional references to political matters, such as the claim by a nationalist French-speaking parent in a school meeting that the English language is given preferential status, Canada is pictured as if it were a secluded log cabin in rural Quebec. Consider, for instance, the way in which international terrorism is treated; in this blog, Canada is immune from anything going on in the world. One morning, while having her breakfast toast and tea, Marn came across an article about travel safety in the *New York Times* magazine. The article included warnings by anti-terrorism experts on how to behave on a trip to Europe, suggesting, for example, not to wear khaki. Her conclusion was that she was safe for neither she nor the "spousal unit" had plans to go to Europe anyway, and none of them owned a khaki uniform. This conclusion was then applied to her compatriots: "Woo Hoo, we Are Canadian! We've been implementing anti-terrorist travel measures and didn't know it!" (9.11.2000). At a time in which the world was concerned with the grave phenomenon of terrorism, and many people all over the globe made desperate efforts to try and understand where human civilization is heading at the outset of the twenty-first century, one baby boomer in her log cabin felt perfectly safe and could apply her usual good humour to those who did not: "And here I thought my tiny little life – the fact that I don't go anywhere, that I live in a country almost nobody knows about, and that I am almost terminally fashion-challenged – here I thought these things might all just be further confirmation of my general dorkiness. I didn't know I was simply practicing cunning anti-terrorist moves, eh" (9.11.2000).

At one point, Marn makes an explicit reference to the *ancien régime* by comparing herself to Marie Antoinette, the guillotined French queen who shared her passion for roses. However funny the comparison, it is easy to picture Marn as an eighteenth-century mansion owner looking at the flowers blooming in her garden. It is equally possible to imagine entries such as the following to have been taken from a diary of the romantic era: "The pond water is finally warming up; the waterlilies have awakened and are sending out their first leaves. Me, I can hardly wait until they start to flower, beautiful pale yellow blossoms with the most wonderful spicy perfume. My goldfish are also big waterlily fans, just love hiding in them, but they also like to bask in the sun...." (5.7.2000), etc.

This appreciation of nature becomes a major component of what it means to be Canadian. Based on "Marn's Big Adventure," Canadian identity is defined as if the turmoil of the last century – the world wars, the communist revolution, the rise of fascism and totalitarianism, the Holocaust, the atomic bomb, colonization and de-colonization, the Cold War or, for that matter, the sixties – left no marks on what the diarist calls "my little corner of the planet" (30.6.2000). She is very concerned with genealogical research and tells fascinating and moving stories about her family members who were part of the great sacrifices Canadians paid in recent history, but these tales often seem like old family portraits on the mansion's heavy walls. The important lessons that could be derived from Canada's participation in the world wars, for example, are lost in the pettiness of this online journal.

Let me illustrate it by one diary entry written on Canada Day. Every year, Marn and Paul, accompanied by a group of friends (and of course by the devoted readers of "Marn's Big Adventure") join in a celebration of Canada's birthday in the mountains with a potluck, bonfire, and fireworks. Here is the description:

Oh Canada. Car windows down late in a summer afternoon, air around us full of the sweet smell of freshly mown hay, the soft spatter of gravel hitting the wheel wells, the grumbles of the engine as we climb some wicked hills. Oh July, a heady gift for a country that spends far too long under the icy boot of winter.... Canada, a country with a constitution that promises peace, order and good government, a country that eased into independence. (2.7.2000)

This pastoral description is of course contrasted right away to the United States, a country created through a revolution, but Marn has no objection to living in the shadow of the mighty neighbour to the south. "We Canadians live in the shadow of this world power, and often define ourselves by what makes us different from the 'Mericans, which amuses them no end, I'm sure" (2.7.2000). The peaceful border between the two countries is assumed to remain peaceful forever, and no thought is given to such issues as the need to form an independent Canadian foreign policy, defence structure, or cultural identity. All these issues are treated with the same disinterest Marie Antoinette treated the problems facing eighteenth-century France.

On Canada Day 2000, then, a group of Canadians are proud to celebrate the independence of a nation that lacks a political and cultural vision for the future. The model of the Canadian emerging in this blog is that of the rose that blossoms against all odds in Marn's garden. As she puts it in October, when the rosebush luckily survives the first frost of winter, "I want to be like this plant, still trying, still creating, long after the calendar tells me I shouldn't be" (17.10.2000). It is this non-national, apolitical form of living that is celebrated by Marn and her friends on Canada Day: "When Richard lifted his flute to his lips and wove the notes to Oh Canada through a starry summer's night, joined by the voices of my almost invisible friends and neighbors, it was strangely haunting. Sometimes it's good to remember who we are" (2.7.2000).

COMMUNITY AND RESPONSIBILITY

On August 4, 2003, the American coalition was deeply involved in battles in Iraq, North Korea warned that discussion of its suspected nuclear weapons program at the UN would be a grave criminal act little short of a prelude to war, the Palestinian-Israeli conflict seemed as unsolvable as ever, the SARS epidemic was spreading in Asia and Canada, famine, AIDS, and war killed hundreds of thousands in Africa, and Marn's cat Zoe was put to sleep. By then, the cat was twenty years old, suffered from cataracts, deafness, and stiffening joints, was vomiting, and had blood in her stool. Marn was understandably sad when the vet informed her there was no other choice but to terminate Zoe's life. She wrote that when her father was in palliative care, he felt that he did not have much to look forward to and chose to die, while Zoe, that tiny black creature, trusted her for almost all her life and now her life was taken away from her. The trauma also brought up memories of the day in which nine-year-old Marn walked into the room when her mother was committing suicide.

Apparently nothing could have sparked more emotional reaction among Marn's readers than Zoe's death. Having followed the cat lady's tales for three years, many readers were now deeply touched. Each entry of the blog begins with the traditional "Dear diary" and ends with the diarist's signature "Marn." Then, under a label stating the essence of the blog ("Going nowhere and proud of it"), readers can post their comments. On that day, no fewer than seventy-nine comments were posted in what became a steam bath of emo-tions. Here are some of them:

"Oh, my poor Marn, I'm so so sorry. I wish I could offer you something to comfort you."

"I'm so sorry. She was a beautiful cat, and you obviously meant a lot to each other. I wish there was more I could say."

"Oh, Marn."

"I'm so sorry, darlin'. Love to you."

"Hugs to you from us and our four footed friends."

"Oh Marn, I'm so sorry. I have so many hugs for you."

"Oh goodness, I am so terribly sorry. No words can do this justice, but know all your readers love and support you ::big hugs::"

"Marn, No words to make it better. Thinking good thoughts for you, the spousal unit and Zubby..."

"Rest in Peace sweet Zoe... Big Hugs Marn"

"I'm so sorry for your loss. You did give Zoe a safe and warm and loving home, with all the petting and lovins a kitty could ever want. I'm sure she's watching over you right now – and purring ..."

"{{{Marn}}}"

Gestures like these are common in North American cultures and are not much different from sympathy cards found in drug stores. These expressions of sorrow are also probably mostly genuine. However, this outburst of emotions online is no trivial matter for it hints at the formation of an "imagined com-munity." In the famous book carrying this title, Benedict Anderson discussed the formation of nations as a result of individuals imagining themselves to be part of a community by nature of their exposure to the same media, such as the novel and the newspapers (Anderson 1991). Here, the national frame-work is missing but not the imagination. Dozens of people set in separate geo-graphical locations, knowing each other only by nickname, and having noth-ing in common besides their reading of "Marn's Big Adventure," engage in an emotional exchange that can hardly be witnessed in any real life situation. This could be seen as a positive sign: individuals who are shying away from their next-door neighbours or exchanging e-mails in the workplace in order to avoid face-to-face contact with their fellow workers are given an electronic tool to express deep emotions. The problem, however, lies in the illusion that a community is being formed.

Internet researchers have stressed the formation of online communities. Online diarists (or "bloggers"), in particular, are seen as forming communities, in that they are aware of each other, exchange information, develop a degree of stratification, and follow power and status hierarchies. As Cindy Curling puts it,

People who write blogs tend to think of themselves as a community, and within that community there are neighborhoods of people with common interests. These neighbors keep in close touch, and spend time showing each other their best new information. If the neighborhood where you grew up was like mine, there were a few houses where all the kids gravitated because those folks had the swing set, the wading pool, the popcorn, and got the new Atari games first. Weblogs work in similar ways. (2003, 5)

Some researchers have tied the sense of community found among bloggers to the nature of the World Wide Web. Madeleine Sorapure (2003), for example, wrote that the Web's interactivity and the immediacy of its publishing enhance that aspect of diary writing concerned not with solitary and private reflection, but with communication and community. To her, "the online diary is anything but private, especially since many diarists use the medium to make connections with others" (Sorapure 2003, 10). Andreas Kitzmann (2003) shows how many of the popular Web diary portals encourage the formation of communities. While certain mechanisms allow Web diaries or Webcams to be completely private or restricted to only a few readers or viewers, very few diarists seem to use them. In fact, such constraints run counter to the logic of the Web diary community, Kitzmann writes, which considers public access to personal thoughts and personal space as a form of agency – a way to make one's life significant through the feedback and support of readers.

What I take issue with is the concept of "community." The diarists who visit "Marn's Big Adventure," post this blog in their list of favourites, or read it on an ongoing basis, do not satisfy one major criterion of "community": commitment. This criterion should not be forgotten as we follow the online exchange of emotional statements. The diarist who screams "{{{Marn}}}" following a description of a cat's death may feel strongly about the event at one moment and disappear into cyberspace at the next. Online contacts may lead to satisfying offline relations but cannot replace them. Ad hoc meetings of nicknames in Marn's blog may make her feel, as she says she does, that she is surrounded by friendship and support but she is not. For friendship involves more than verbal expression; it is tested in hard and challenging real-life situations. Online diarists are not there for each other; they are individuals who spell out real or fake portions of their lives, but this does not turn them into a civil group. The trust we may develop toward a blogger with whom we become familiar does not differ from that we often feel toward virtual figures like doctors or presidents played by actors on television. Living in societies in which access to our own family doctor or parliamentary representative becomes quite limited, it is not surprising that we are attracted to these actors. Similarly, living in societies in which we hardly know our next-door neighbours, it is not surprising we are fascinated by life writing on the Internet. Let us not forget, however, that another person's "big adventure" is not ours, unless we engage in communal interaction that not only stimulates our emotions but leads us to responsible civil action.

Bibliography

Anderson, Benedict. 1991. *Imagined Communities: Reflections on the Origin and Spread of Nationalism*. Revised ed. London: Verso.

Byfield, Ted. 1994. "Perished is the Dream of the Sixties Set, Dissolved in the Harsh Light of Reality." *Alberta Report* 21 (10 March).

Curling, Cindy. 2003. "A Closer Look at Weblogs." *LLRX.Com* (4 May): 5, www.llrx.com/columns/notes46.htm.

Fennell, Tom. 1995. "Maclean's and the 20th Century." *Maclean's* (11 June).

Kitzmann, Andreas. 2003. "That Different Place: Documenting the Self Within Online Environments." *Biography* 26(1): 48–65.

Kostash, Myrna. 1980. *Long Way from Home: The Story of the Sixties Generation in Canada*. Toronto: Lorimer.

MacLeod, Stewart. 1996. "The Curse of the Baby Boom Generation." *Maclean's* (24 June).

Rainer, Tristine. 1998. *Your Life as Story: Discovering the 'New Autobiography' and Writing Memoir as Literature*. New York: Putnam.

Sorapure, Madeleine. 2003. "Screening Moments, Scrolling Lives: Diary Writing on the Web." *Biography* 26(1): 1–23.

Unger, Irwin, and Debi Unger, eds. 1998. *The Times Were A-Changin'*. New York: Three Rivers.

Wickens, Barbara. 2003. "Boomers Have It Tough, Too." *Maclean's* (27 October).

Notes

1   For a list of Canadian blogs, see BlogsCanada: http://www.blogscanada.ca/egroup/default.aspx.

2   Eatonweb Portal: http://portal.eatonweb.com/weblog.php?weblog_id=6517.

8: The Canadian Music Industry at a Crossroads

RICHARD SUTHERLAND and WILL STRAW

Over the past several years, the state of Canada's sound recording industry has been usually described in pessimistic terms. We should remember, from the outset, that there are several industries involved in music – live concert promotion, music publishing, composing for film or television, and so on. The health of each of these has fluctuated significantly in recent years. It is the sound recording industry, however, which has struggled most desperately to remain afloat over the last half decade. As it grapples with a decline in the sales of compact discs, and continued uncertainty over the impact of the Internet, the recording industry has been slow to grasp the transformations it will require in order to survive. A Canadian record company executive, who did not wish to be identified, told us recently that the record industry as we knew it was dead. The successful music companies, he argued, would no longer be those which, like the firms of the last half-century, sought out artists, built careers, and recorded musical works. Rather, the only certain money to be made in music was through the repackaging of older musical recordings into thematic compact disc compilations, to be sold for $4.99 at Wal-Mart or Zeller's stores. The industry, he suggested, was now a commodity-based industry like those for eggs or sugar, making small profit margins on large numbers of almost indistinguishable products.

Music has long been a commodity in the broader sense of the term, of course. What is changing are the means by which its value is realized in the marketplace. The recording industry developed largely as a means to sell physical objects – vinyl records, cassettes, and, for the last two decades, compact discs. CDs remain the largest source of revenue from recordings, but other modes of consumption are becoming more prominent. Downloads of cellphone ringtones, subscription-based satellite radio services, and online sales of music tracks all represent new ways of packaging music and selling it to consumers. As these forms of distribution grow in popularity, the boundaries between the recording industry and other kinds of business are shifting and difficult to draw with precision. Key aspects of the music industry, such as talent development and the distribution of recorded music, are being undertaken by the broadcast industry, retailers, and electronics manufacturers, often in novel and surprising ways.

As the boundaries between industries weaken or disappear, so, too, do those which separate the Canadian market from others in the world. Unsurprisingly, perhaps, Canada's music industry has become just as integrated within a global market as have other industries, such as those producing clothing or consumer electronics. Developments and decisions made in other countries have important effects on the structure and prosperity of the industry here. These changes have imposed considerable stress upon the Canadian music industries at several levels. In the first volume of *How Canadians Communicate*, we described the year 2001 as an *annus horribilis* for the Canadian music industries (Straw 2003). That was the year which saw the closing of Canada's last publicly available industry trade magazine (*The Record*), its most-established music retailer (the Sam the Record Man chain) and the most-ambitious attempt in Canadian history to produce a fully integrated, "mini-major" music company (Song Corporation). That was also the year in which sales figures for musical recordings confirmed a significant downturn for the industry. While that downturn was by no means limited to Canada, the fragility of the music industry's infrastructures here made its effects more devastating.[1]

The despair loudly expressed by key players within the music industries in recent years has not been shared by all those involved in producing or consuming music. The revenues of major recording companies may have declined over the last five years, but no one has complained about a shortage of music. The Internet has made access to the innovative and the obscure easier for music fans than at any time in history. Important industry events, like the College Music Journal festival in New York City, continue to attract hundreds of aspiring and inventive new bands (such as Montreal's Arcade Fire, popular favourites at the 2004 CMJ event). Those who bemoaned the continued dominance of sales charts by pop-artists in 2004 still had the option of going to see Mission of Burma, the Pixies, or several dozen other credible punk, pre-punk, and post-punk bands who had reformed to satisfy or test continued public interest in their music. In 2006, popular musical fans in Great Britain once again felt a sense of energetic generational turnover, as a host of young rock bands, like the Arctic Monkeys or Kaiser Chiefs, rode waves of hype and genuine enthusiasm to the top of sales charts.

The critical acclaim accorded Canadian rock music since 2004 has been without precedent. In 2004 and 2005, a seemingly endless series of media reports hailed and strained to describe Montreal's rock music scene, now consecrated as the coolest and most productive in the world. The U.S. magazine *Spin* (2005) kicked this off in its February 2005 issue, with a long article on Montreal bands like Arcade Fire, the Dears, and godspeed you! black emperor. That same month, the *New York Times* (Carr 2005) published a lengthy piece that grappled awkwardly with the complexities of Montreal's language politics but was left breathless by the range of musical phenomena to be discovered in the city. On November 28, 2005, BBC's Radio One broadcast a documentary entitled "Is Montreal the new Seattle? Find out with the Arcade Fire." This treatment of the Montreal scene likewise floundered in its attempts to situate music within the linguistic and cultural complexities of the city but adequately captured the scene's musical effervescence. Only in early 2006 could one find signs that Montreal's status as hipster mecca might be fading. Increasingly, the North American musical press was turning to Portland, Oregon, as the continent's liveliest incubator for independent rock music, calling it the "new Montreal" (just as Montreal had been designated the "next Seattle," in reference to the birthplace of grunge in the early 1990s). More ominously, for Montrealers, the *New York Times* magazine's February 26, 2006, issue contained a long article on the Toronto band Broken Social Scene and the "Arts & Crafts" label, offering up the observation that "Toronto has become a nicer but less aesthetically coherent version of Seattle in the early days of grunge" (Quart 2006).

In the United States, the largest market for Canadian music, these successes register just below the level of mainstream popularity. Shania Twain, Simple Plan, Nickelback, and Avril Lavigne were the best-selling Canadian acts in the United States in 2005, each registering one album within *Billboard*'s list of the Top 100 selling albums of the year. Their success confirms the long-standing popularity of Canadian solo female performers within the U.S. (and international) markets, and the more recent ascendancy of Canadian hard rock bands. In 2005, *Shania Twain's Greatest Hits* was the best-selling country music album in the United States, perpetuating her extraordinary success as, by some measures, the best-selling vocalist in the world. Less predictable, perhaps, were the variety of ways in which Canadians figured on the U.S. jazz charts, a terrain which has been hospitable to Canadian acts only recently. Diana Krall is the latest in a series of Canadian female singers of popular standards to find success in the U.S. jazz market (following on from Holly Cole and kd lang), and she did so with both a conventional album and a CD package entitled *Christmas Songs*. Elsewhere amidst the best-selling jazz albums of 2005, Paul Anka (born in Canada) made the Top 10 with his *Rock Swings* CD, and the Montreal-based compilation label Madacy ranked at 17 for the year with a package entitled *20 Best of Jazz*.

Summing up the year 2003, *Billboard* magazine's Canadian correspondent, Larry LeBlanc (2003a) had spoken of an "anxious year for the Canadian music business." In 2004, it seemed clear that, while the music industry's condition remained anxious, it might no longer be disastrous. Since then, continued uncertainty over the industry's future shape and direction has been tempered by scattered signs of stabilization and by fresh thinking in different corners of the industry. For parts of the music industry, the most hope-inspiring developments of the last two or three years have come from different extremes of the technological spectrum. The enormous success of *Pop Idol* competitions around the world made the mainstream television variety show, an almost extinct form in North America, newly influential within popular musical culture. At the same time, the massive popularity of Apple's iPod music playback device, and of the iTunes website with which it is associated, brought some clarity and promise to the otherwise unsettled world of commercial musical downloading.

Declining Sales: Piracy or Competition?

The Canadian Recording Industry Association claims that sales of recorded music in Canada continued a multi-year decline in 2005, dropping 4 per cent and $23 million over the previous year (CRIA 2006). Early statistics for 2006 have shown a significant increase in music sales over the previous year, with growth in the CD market now outstripping that in the sales of DVD's, whose spectacular rise over the last five years is now slowing. Despite the slight optimism these figures might suggest, there is a sense that the last five years have been lost ones for the music industry (CRIA 2005b). The Canadian Recording Industry Association, which represents major multinationals operating in Canada, has claimed in press releases that music retail losses between 1999 and 2004 totalled $465 million (CRIA 2004c). This decline is blamed principally on the illegal downloading of music, but statistics on this behaviour and its effects are notoriously difficult to produce with accuracy. Computer possession and high-speed Internet access are tools for downloading music, but they also present people with competing forms of entertainment. Like the DVD, the computer and the Internet may simply be making music less central within people's lives. In the retail sector, it has become easy to distinguish between those stores – mostly independent – which concentrate on music and therefore suffer continued losses, and the multinational chains (like HMV or the now American-owned Future Shop) which have hurriedly moved DVD's into the prominent display space once occupied by compact discs.

The boom in DVD sales has much to do with the format's continued novelty, but it, too, may indicate a shift in consumer interest – away from music, and towards the viewing and collecting of films or other audiovisual forms. The recording industry relishes statistics that claim to measure the impact of Internet access and downloading on music sales, but it has done little to measure shifts in consumer behaviour between different kinds of pre-packaged entertainment commodities. When lovingly restored and feature-packed DVDs of classic or cult films can be purchased for $9.99, it is easy to grasp why consumers prefer them to risky new CDs that retail for five dollars more. Universal's 2003 announcement that it was significantly lowering the retail price of new compact discs was viewed as a necessary step in the compact disc's commercial recovery, but the impact of this move is not yet clear (*Globe and Mail* 2003).

Majors and Independents: Both Local and Global

Since the 1960s, levels of concentration within the worldwide music industries have grown steadily. In large measure, this has come through major companies' domination of the distribution process, and their subsequent acquisition of smaller companies so as to maximize use of their costly distribution channels. In 1998, Seagram's – then the owner of Universal Music – bought the PolyGram family of music companies from the Dutch Philips Electronics firm. This reduced the number of multinational music companies in the world to five. Together, these multinational majors account for 80 to 90 per cent of all recorded music sales in Canada, a percentage which has remained stable over many years.

Further consolidation of the international industry has been underway since 2003. In that year, the Bertelsmann Music Group and Sony announced their intention, subject to regulatory approval, to merge their music operations, creating the world's second largest music company (right behind Universal Music). This merger was approved by the European Union and U.S. Federal Trade Commission in 2004, then blocked, in a surprise decision by the European Court of First Instance in August of 2006. Sony's attempt to join with BMG came on the heels of a debt-ridden Time Warner's sale of its music division for $2.6 billion to a group of investors led by Canadian Edgar Bronfman. Bronfman had presided over the Seagram company's acquisition of Universal Music, its takeover of the European company Polygram, and the subsequent sale of both to French company Vivendi. His purchase of Time Warner's assets marks the end of Warner Brothers' life as a major record company player, which began in 1958. Earlier in 2004, Time Warner sold off its disc manufacturing and distribution facilities to another Canadian company – Cinram, of Markham, Ontario, a world leader in the disc duplication industry, and now the leading disc manufacturer in North America. In a further attempt to save itself, Warner Brothers Records had attempted a union with the British-based EMI, but this had been blocked by European regulators. Pending the final outcome of the BMG-Sony agreement, there will certainly be heightened pressure towards a union between EMI (home to the Beatles' catalogue, among many other assets) and the entity Bronfman has created with his purchase of Time Warner's musical assets. One result of all this activity may be a multinational recording industry dominated by three large players (Sony-BMG, Universal, and Warner-EMI). This consolidation continues in the music publishing sector (controlled largely by divisions of the major labels) with the sale of BMG Music Publishing to Universal-Vivendi in September 2006 for US$2.09 billion.

These changes in ownership have coincided with a gradual shift in the role of the major labels in Canada. As Larry LeBlanc has noted, major labels operating in Canada have faced pressure in recent years to reduce their signing of Canadian artists so as to save money (LeBlanc 2003a, 3). Instead, operations of major labels concentrate increasingly on marketing international repertoire. The route to international success is less likely to run through the Canadian branch of a major label; rather, success on a major label in Canada for Canadians is more likely to come through having sufficient international, particularly U.S., success.

One result of this is that more and more Canadian artists touted for success – such as Nickelback or Avril Lavigne – have signed directly to labels located outside Canada. Artist development activity on the part of major companies has therefore moved outside the country, and with it has gone the investment of money and personnel that activity requires. This is unfortunate, but it also opens up opportunities for Canadian-owned independent music companies. For much of the past thirty years Canadian independents have had to compete with multinationals for Canadian artists; the competition was especially acute at various points in the 1990s. As major labels in Canada sign fewer artists, Canadian independent labels have come to play a greater role in the

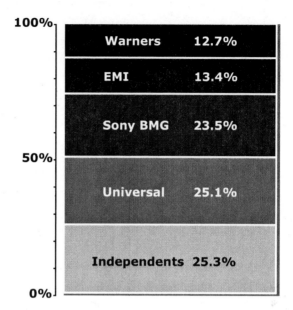

Figure 8.1
Global Market Shares of
Record Companies after
Sony-BMG Merger

development of Canadian artists, building their success within Canada and
marketing them outside the country as well (Flohil 2004b). In 2004, when
roughly a quarter of albums on Nielsen Soundscan's sales charts for Canada
were by Canadian artists – an extraordinarily high percentage in historical
terms – there were certainly grounds for feeling optimistic about the open-
ings available to Canadian artists. By early 2006, the resurgence of British
rock, popularity of U.S.-based soundtrack albums, and unstoppable success
of American hip-hop had led to much lower percentages of Canadian acts on
our domestic sales charts.

The novel structure and recent successes of Toronto-based company Maple-
Music provide an excellent example of an independent company adapting to recent changes in industry structure and working with major labels
to their mutual benefit. It also stands in contrast to the total service model
of the ambitiously conceived Song Corporation. MapleMusic has attracted
considerable attention over its relatively brief life, with significant success
both within and beyond Canada's borders (Flohil 2004a). MapleMusic
had begun as an electronic commerce website, offering compact discs and
a variety of music-related products. Following investment by multinational

Universal Music, it launched the label MapleMusic Recordings, which has found success with albums by such artists as the Skydiggers, Sam Roberts, and the Dears. In many respects, MapleMusic is like many of the great Canadian independent labels of the 1970s or 1980s (such as Aquarius or Attic), devoted to finding talent and leaving manufacturing and other functions to a multinational major (in this case, part-owner Universal, which increasingly uses MapleMusic as its means of remaining involved in the national music scene). At the same time, however, MapleMusic serves as a clearing house for independent Canadian musicians, giving them a single Internet portal through which to promote and sell their music without "signing" to a music label in the traditional sense.

Vancouver-based Nettwerk Records has a much longer history, but its recent transformations have been widely noted as evidence of a label's capacity to adapt to an industry undergoing major restructuring. Nettwerk is probably best known as the management and label for Sarah McLachlan. The company began in the manner of many independent labels, serving a particular musical genre within a distinct geographical region (it grew out of the post-punk synthesizer music scene in Vancouver). Much of its recent success, in fact, has come in the field of artist management, often involving artists who are not signed to the label itself. Nettwerk manages Avril Lavigne, the Barenaked Ladies, and Chantal Kreviazuk, as well as some of the best-known acts in the United Kingdom (such as Dido and Coldplay). Nettwerk's demonstrated skills in the management area have put them at the forefront of artist management worldwide and their success in marketing and breaking new artists has brought them into a joint venture with EMI's American operations as Nettwerk America. This is an example of a Canadian company operating at a high level internationally, building on its successes in Canada to expand its scope of operations.

A very different model of international success is offered by the Montreal-based Madacy Entertainment group, by some accounts the largest Canadian-based distributor of recorded music. Madacy, with branches servicing markets for Latin music, karaoke CD's, children's recordings, and a host of other products, functions principally as a producer of budget-line CDs and DVDs. Its ongoing relationships with the Wal-Mart and Best Buy retail chains drive Madacy's production of low-end CD packages and public-domain films on DVD – packages which include the Instant Mp3 Library series of discs, each of which offers some 200 MP3s of classic, ballroom, and other musical styles for those uncertain how to download music over the Internet. In a variety of ways, Madacy is the exemplary contemporary music company, purchasing and repackaging recordings that have fallen into the public domain and deriving revenues from the exploitation of small niches which, at a global level, form markets of significant scale.

Digital Distribution: Signs of Hope for a Legitimate Online Market

In Canada, as elsewhere, perhaps the biggest change in the music industry has been the adjustment to digital technologies, a process which has been far from easy. After years of ludicrous false starts (such as those services offering downloaded albums at the same price as those available in stores), events in 2003–2004 brought signs that some sort of order might slowly emerge in the online distribution of music to consumers. The success of Apple's iTunes website has been simultaneously a unique commercial achievement and a major spark for similar initiatives by other firms. Apple, working with the cooperation of all five major labels, demonstrated that it was possible to sell music online in significant amounts. In the United States alone, Apple's iTunes sold 30 million music tracks in its first year, principally to Mac computer users. Its expansion into the market of Windows computer users, who have had access to compatible iPod playback devices for several years now, and its introduction to Europe and Canada late in 2004, have certainly magnified this success. In early 2006, iTunes sold its billionth download.

Apple's success demonstrates that one can sell MP3 files online in large numbers, yet the total sales for legal downloads are still only a small fraction of overall revenues for the industry. In the six-month period ending June 30, 2005, the total value of CD albums and singles shipped by manufacturers in the United States reached \$4,493.6 million, while total shipments of digital albums and singles was some \$198 million, or roughly 4 per cent of the former total (RIAA 2005). The enormous growth in legitimate downloads over 2004, "more than ten-fold to over \$200 million in the US, UK and Germany combined" (IFPI 2005, 3), still leaves revenues for downloaded music as a small percentage of the overall market. Moreover, despite the supposed decline in illegal downloading activity, some estimates suggest that as many as 2.6 billion tracks are downloaded illegally for free every month (Holloway 2003). Given the level of this activity, French economist Jacques Attali may appear to be prophetic when he describes recordings as stockpiled time in an economy of repetition that may be doomed to expire from "an excess of life, from excessive, uncontrolled, carcinogenic replication" (1985, 130). His image of a post-commodity future for music is certainly suggestive. For the moment, however, as the industry continues to wage legal battles against companies such as Kazaa on three continents, with slow but steady progress, music remains well within the commodity framework in a variety of ways.[2] Not only are CDs still sold in considerable quantities but music is also economically significant as a driver of sales of goods (such as iPods) and services (principally Internet service providers), whether individual copies are authorized or not.

What has changed are the kinds of businesses involved in selling music to consumers. A distribution network dominated by the major record labels (and involving a complicated system of wholesalers, rack jobbers, and music retailers) is giving way to a supply chain that involves new media and technology companies from outside the industry. In October 2003, following lengthy negotiations with Canadian music publishers and the recording industry, Canada's first industry-approved downloading site, PureTracks, launched its operations. PureTracks was conceived by the Toronto-based company Moontaxi Media (*Globe and Mail* 2004a). It quickly moved to develop formal links with Bell Sympatico and Telus, two of Canada's largest Internet service providers. Downloading services in the United States, such as Apple's iTunes or Real Networks' RealRhapsody, have taken shape as adjunct operations of hardware or software companies, for whom music downloads are not the original or primary source of revenues. In Europe, a hazy patchwork of download providers, which ranges from Coca Cola's "mycokemusic" to Dutch music retailer "Free Record Shop," has rendered the situation somewhat more anarchic. It remains to be seen whether downloading services in Canada will be dominated by Internet service providers, as recent developments suggest. PureTracks – which sold over one million downloaded music tracks in its first five months of operation – faces competition from the French-language entertainment superstore chain Archambault, which launched its own site in January 2004. The Archambault chain is owned by Quebecor, whose other subsidiary Videotron is a major Internet service provider within Quebec. As yet, Quebecor has made only tentative moves towards using its status as ISP to push its music downloading service (in the way that PureTracks partners Telus or Sympatico have). The entry of other services such as Apple's iTunes and the revamped Napster promise to make this a volatile and competitive sector for some time to come.

This has been exacerbated by the entry of mobile phone providers into offering music downloads for customers, an expansion from their already lucrative market in ringtones. As handsets capable of playing music files came on the market over 2001–2002, mobile phone service providers began to offer a selection of downloadable ringtones. At a cost of between $1 and $3.50 in Canada, these have proved very productive for phone companies and for rightsholders (primarily record companies). In 2003 this was already a US$3 billion industry worldwide (Openwave 2004). Its significance as a market was such that, in November 2004, *Billboard* magazine initiated a chart of the Top

Table 8.1 Some of Canada's online music services

Name of Service	Ownership	Date of Launch	Initial Sel of Son	
PureTracks	Moontaxi Media Inc.	October, 2003	700,0	
				and up
archambaultzik.ca	Archambault Group (Quebecor Media Inc.)	January, 2004	300,000	99¢/track and up
Napster	Roxio Inc.	May, 2004	500,000	$9.95/month (subscription); $1.19/track; $9.25/album
iTunes	Apple Computers Inc.	December, 2004	700,000	99¢/track

Sources: Apple (2004); Napster (2004); Quebecor (2004); Telus (2006).

20 ringtone downloads. The range of available songs for download becomes a selling point (albeit a minor one) for these providers, which builds another opportunity for alliances between telecommunications and music companies or their representatives. Again, music becomes an auxiliary feature of electronic devices and services, a way of adding value.

Digital Globalization

The slow expansion of commercial downloading offers sharp lessons in the barriers that constrain globalization, even in an age of digital information and international data networks. Legitimate downloading services in Canada, over the Internet or mobile phone networks, must grapple with the intricacies of GST payments, royalties to artists and music publishers, and differences in territorial rights for the exploitation of artists and recordings. Services that aspire to be genuinely international will have to contend with all these factors, and then with differences in currencies and credit card payment systems. All of these factors have made moves towards commercial downloading very distinct, from one country to another.

Broader questions about the future structure of the music industry persist, as well. When companies like Apple Computers, Wal-Mart, Hewlett-Packard, Videotron, and Amazon all run their own download sites, they have assumed the role of distributor, which was once the province of the recording company. Having withdrawn from so many other stages in the recording process – leaving the signing of artists to boutique subsidiaries, and the actual recording process to artists themselves and their producers – major music companies may find themselves left with the one function most threatened by new technologies – that of distribution. As the success of Amazon and similar ventures has shown, however, entertainment products may be distributed by any company able to build warehouses and a website. Over time, it seems, the value of large music companies will reside less in what they are able to do (which is increasingly uncertain) than in what they own. What they own is commonly referred to as "intellectual property," the rights to millions and millions of musical compositions and performances.

Major record companies may be frightened by the challenge of illegal downloading, but they are more profoundly alarmed by provisions in copyright legislation that would allow their ownership of music to expire. As commercially active recordings (such as those of Elvis Presley) celebrate their fiftieth year since release, they enter the public domain throughout European markets, as well as in Canada. As a result, they may be released by anyone with the means to manufacture them and be sold at prices driven down by competition and the absence of royalties. While their importation into countries operating under different copyright regimes – such as the United States, which protects recordings for much longer periods – may be illegal, an international grey market in low-priced reissues of public-domain recordings has already developed. (On the Internet, Canadians may already buy European compilations of 1950s jazz or rhythm and blues music at prices far below those charged for similar collections in the United States.) Moves to harmonize copyright regimes across the world are clearly driven by the music industry's desire to standardize its operations. They are sparked, as well, by companies' fears that the collapse of their assets' value in any single territory will start a chain-reaction, as consumers seek out, on a global basis, the cheapest versions of any given recording.

Despite attempts to create a global copyright regime which is consistent across borders, through international treaties and organizations such as the World Intellectual Property Organization (WIPO), the administration of copyright is still a national affair. It is enforced by the courts of national or sub-national territories. The collectives that collect and administer funds are themselves the product of each nation's history and their relationship to governments varies widely from one country to another. (In some countries, such as the United States, the groups that collect royalties are run as private companies. In many European countries, they are public services.) For the time being, the global free flow of information is a reality only within the worlds of unauthorized downloading and uploading.

Yet harmonization of copyright remains a key issue for governments concerned with developing an information economy and international trade. It appears that the Canadian government's cultural policy is becoming increasingly trade-oriented. This does not mean that trade was not previously an issue in the cultural field. However, whereas cultural policy was, in the past, designed principally to ameliorate the effects of international trade on Canadian culture, policies are more and more oriented towards allowing Canadian producers to take advantage of international trade in cultural products. Relatively recent developments include the creation of an initiative jointly administered by External Trade and Canadian Heritage, the three-year $23 million Trade Routes program, announced late in 2001 (Canada 2003). The aim of this program is to provide assistance for Canadian cultural producers seeking to exploit external markets. It does so by providing direct funding to companies, collecting and distributing information on international markets, and providing advice from expert consultants. While a concern with trade has long marked cultural policy in Canada, the creation of a distinct new program for culture, which is located, at least in part, within the bureaucracy overseeing External Trade, is a significant development.

Canadian music industry policy has been affected in perceptible ways by these developments. In fact, the recording industry is seen as somewhat exemplary because of the considerable and sustained international success of Canadian artists, from Rush to Avril Lavigne. Despite such successes, Canada's balance of trade in terms of music is negative – $507.1 million in exports, as opposed to $1279.8 million in imports (Towse 2002, 14). However, these figures represent a situation that is far more equitable than is typical for Canadian products, and better than the traditionally anemic sales of Canadian music product in Canada (usually about 15 per cent, at best) would suggest. This balance of trade, it seems, might be a better indicator of Canada's economic strength in this sector. Keith Acheson further suggests that, were Canadian music to achieve a 5 per cent share of the English-speaking market for music in other countries, this "would generate as much or more of an inflow as the outflow from importing 95% of the same type of music in the relatively small Canadian market" (ibid.). Small market shares for Canadian music in several countries with large populations might produce a high level of prosperity for our domestic music industries.[3] Analyses of this kind represent a remarkable shift in the ways in which Canadian cultural policy is conceived. We seem to be moving from a model that sought to protect Canadian culture at home to one more oriented towards promoting and exporting it on the global stage.

Other policy concerns, such as funding programs and Canadian content broadcasting quotas, continue to be important issues for the independent sector of the Canadian recording industry. Generally, the past five years have seen funding for the Sound Recording Sector in Canada increase substantially. With the creation of its *Tomorrow Starts Today* policy in 2001, which integrated most of the Department of Canadian Heritage's existing cultural industries funding, and the introduction of a new policy for the sound recording industry, *From Creators to Audiences,* in the same year, the federal government both enhanced and integrated its programs for the sector. All funding was subsumed under a new program, the Canadian Music Fund. A number of the fund's components are a reconfigured version of the Sound Recording Development Program (in place since 1986) and continue to be administered by the private foundations FACTOR and MusicAction.

The most notable new component of the CMF was the Music Entrepreneur Fund (MEP), launched with a budget of $23 million over three years. It was initially administered by Telefilm Canada (the federal government's agency for funding film and television programming) from 2002 to March 31, 2005, when Canadian Heritage assumed control of the fund directly. With a budget of $8.5 million per year, the Canadian Entrepreneur Component receives more contributions from the federal government than does FACTOR (at approximately $7 million per year). More importantly, companies that access this fund cannot access FACTOR funds, essentially setting up an entirely different stream of funding and eligibility criteria (for instance, it is not project-based) for Canada's more-established independent labels, and one more directly under government oversight.

While this might represent a weakening of FACTOR's and MusicAction's influence over the independent recording sector, and particularly over its more established labels, it does mean that established and fledgling labels are no longer competing for the same funds. The fact that there is a substantial number of independent companies sufficiently prosperous and viable to meet the MEC's requirements of five years of continuous operation and unit sales of over 200,000 in the previous year may be taken as an indication of the Canadian industry's growing stability and maturation.

Arguably, however, the issue of greatest importance to Canada's music industry (and the issue on which the industry has been most united and has carried on the greatest amount of sustained lobbying) has been copyright. The Canadian government itself has clearly come to see copyright as the key issue for the music industry in this country. In part, this is due to music industry pressures, but it is also the case that copyright fits particularly well with the Canadian government's increasing orientation towards external trade as the principal engine of the country's economic prosperity.

The last major round of copyright revision occurred in 1997 and brought the music industry two long-sought objectives. One of these was the levy on those "media" (blank cassettes, computer discs, etc.) that might be used to make copies of copyrighted materials. The other – little known by the public, but of crucial significance for musicians and the music industries – was the adoption of a so-called performing right in sound recordings, or what is known as "neighbouring rights." Previously, Canadian broadcasters using music within their programming paid monies only to those who had composed the music (and to the publishing companies that administered their compositions). Under "neighbouring rights" legislation, broadcasters pay a portion of their revenues to recording artists (those who perform the music) and to the record companies who own those performances. The implications of this for musicians and record companies are enormous. Both stand to make significant amounts of money from the use of their music in other media (and not merely from the sale of compact disc recordings). In a sense, the legislation installing "neighbouring rights" updated the Copyright Act to allow it to deal with the technologies of broadcasting and magnetic tape. However, it did not deal in any substantial way with issues arising from the rapid development of the Internet. These issues are dealt with at length in the contributions by Sheryl Hamilton and Graham Longford in this volume.

Again, this is perhaps why copyright has emerged as the central policy issue for the sound recording industry in Canada. Both the government and industry have moved from a concern with cultural protection to an emphasis on cultural trade. The shift is evident in the issue of digital, satellite-based radio and its introduction into Canada. In July 2005, the CRTC approved all three applications to provide satellite radio service in Canada, which offers listeners a wide range of specialty radio channels, available across the country, free of advertising but requiring a monthly subscription fee of about ten dollars and the purchase of a special receiver. The applications in the hearings held the previous autumn had come from two firms in partnership with the major American satellite radio services, Sirius Canada Inc. (for Sirius Satellite Radio Inc.) and Canadian Satellite Radio Inc. (for XM Satellite Radio Inc.), as well as a stand-alone Canadian bid from CHUM/Astral Media. Sirius Satellite Radio's Canadian partners are Standard Broadcasting Ltd., one of Canada's major radio ownership groups, as well as the state-owned Canadian Broadcasting Corporation. XM Satellite Radio is partnered with Toronto businessman John Bitove Jr.

Not surprisingly, the CRTC's initial decision was appealed to Cabinet by a number of parties, including the Friends of Canadian Broadcasting and a number of music industry associations, as well as CHUM/Astral, who claimed that, given their own substantially higher commitment to Canadian content (and, it must be said, far more modest choice of programming and more limited area of coverage), the licensing of Sirius and CSR rendered their own service unworkable. Cabinet agreed to hear the appeal, but in September 2005 they ultimately upheld the original decision, despite some difficulties in reaching consensus.

Both CSR and Sirius launched their services in early December 2005, and although subscription numbers are so far fairly low (CSR recently announced that they had only 44,000 subscribers; Robertson 2006) satellite radio represents a potential shakeup in the radio broadcasting industry in Canada, offering listeners a tremendously enhanced range of choice in terms of radio listening. While many of the services are sports or information oriented, the programming remains predominantly music, much of it in channels even more tightly formatted than conventional commercial radio.

In terms of music industry policy, satellite radio represents a more immediate shift. The CRTC approved the services with a much lower overall level of Canadian (and French) content than that required of conventional radio broadcasters, and although applicants raised their commitments while awaiting the results of the appeal to Cabinet, these levels remain well below those for conventional radio. The new services offer eight Canadian channels alongside seventy-two American channels. These Canadian music channels must play at least 85 per cent Canadian content. Two interesting requirements are that 25 per cent of programming must be "new" Canadian (that is, produced by artists within the last six months) and that a further 25 per cent must be the work of artists who have not had any hits.

The requirements for the Canadian stations go well beyond what is required of their conventional broadcast counterparts; however, the overall level of Canadian content in the system is much lower, perhaps 10 per cent of the overall music programming. While there is no sign that the CRTC intends to lower Canadian content levels for conventional radio broadcasters, it is significant in the most important recent development in radio broadcasting technology that the requirement for Canadian content, which has often been characterized as the cornerstone of Canadian music industry policy, has been drastically curtailed, with the approval, not only of the CRTC but of the federal cabinet as well. In this case, as in other recent policy shifts, the Canadian government seems willing to relax protectionist measures (Cancon requirements) in exchange for commitments by companies to invest in the production and promotion of Canadian music, here and abroad.

It is highly debatable whether most internationally successful Canadian musical acts convey any meaningful Canadian cultural identity to those outside Canada; and this does not seem to be the goal – certainly not for the industry, which is by and large indifferent to such concerns. We would argue that this shift towards trade is not simply a matter of directing our national successes outwards to the rest of the world. By positing cultural goods as, fundamentally, objects of exchange, we render them economic commodities like any other. Scholars and critics have long grappled with the question of how Canadian music expresses Canadian values and sentiments. Their failure to answer that question in succinct and consensual ways does not mean that music does not fulfill that function, or that it is merely a commodity. Music remains, particularly for young people, an important tool by which identities are given shape and meaning, or through which people develop a relationship to the times and places in which they live. Policies that loosen or sever the links between music and the contexts in which it is made may weaken music's longstanding role in the shaping of identity.

Idols and Academies at Home and around the World

The recent and spectacular success of televised talent competitions – the *Idol* phenomena – in various countries is full of multiple lessons concerning the status of popular music in today's global culture. While the concept on which it is based is imported, *Canadian Idol* forcefully showed us that the success of local music is tightly bound to the media infrastructure through which it is made popular – and this infrastructure has been carefully built and controlled by Canadian companies and governments. In 2000, the *Pop Idols* television program (based on a concept developed by Bertelsmann Media's Fremantle Entertainment) made its debut in the United Kingdom. Since then, the format has been exported successfully to a number of markets, including the United States, Canada, and several European countries. *Canadian Idol*, like its counterparts elsewhere, demonstrated convincingly that there was still money to be made from music in an age of file sharing. In a music market that regularly mourns the fragmentation of tastes, the *Pop Idols* programs attracted audiences that crossed demographic groups and sustained public attention over the several weeks of each competition's duration.

The success of these programs exemplifies the complex forms of globalization that characterize the music industries today. On the one hand, as a genuinely multinational phenomena, the various national *Idols* competitions testify to the triumph of global strategies for revenue maximization within the music industries. The success of these competitions in each country has enhanced their appeal in other countries, as public familiarity with the overall concept has spread across national boundaries. *Canadian Idol*, quite clearly, benefited from the enormous audience within Canada for its U.S.

predecessor, which helped to make Canadians familiar with the format. On the other hand, few musical phenomena in recent years have so solidified the boundaries around and between national (and even regional cultures). As television systems continue to be shaped by distinctly national regulatory and industrial structures, each nation's *Idol* programs has fit into (and drawn upon) national star systems and media cross-over patterns. Contestants in these programs are covered within national and local media, strengthening audience members' loyalties to particular contestants and deepening their links to region and community. The winners move from local news shows to national talk shows and, in so doing, draw lines of continuity between the various components of each country's media system.

Both *American Idol* and *Canadian Idol* were among the highest-rated television shows of recent years in their respective markets. The first *Canadian Idol* winner, Ryan Malcolm, debuted at no. 4 on Canada's Nielsen SoundScan charts with his album *Home*, which then moved downwards over its eleven-week stay on the charts. In January of 2004, *Home* was certified "platinum" by the Canadian Recording Industry Association, indicating that Malcolm had sold at least 100,000 copies. *Home* was released on Vik Records, the Canadian imprint of the Bertelsmann Music Group. Vik is the home, as well, of musician-songwriters like Bobby Cameron, who contributed songs both to Ryan Malcolm's album and to the debut by the 2004 *Canadian Idol*, Kalan Porter. Porter's debut single "Awake in a Dream" sat atop the Canadian singles charts for at least four weeks in the Fall of 2004, as the artist went about the mall tours, CBC interviews, and other milestones that are now part of the promotion of *Canadian Idol* competition winners. His debut album *219 Days* has been the most successful of the *Canadian Idol* albums going double platinum early in 2005. Collectively, *Canadian Idol* winners and runners-up have sold more than half a million records in Canada. While *Canadian Idol* has generated fewer CD sales than the Quebec-based *Star Académie*, it stands, nevertheless, as a useful example of a media conglomerate successfully exploiting its horizontal integration and multinational reach. Bertelsmann makes significant revenues licensing the show's concept, then expects to build upon these revenues with profits from recordings featuring the contest winners.

Even more than the *Pop Idol* programs, Quebec's *Star Académie* illustrates the considerable advantages that vertical integration and cross-promotion can bring. *Star Académie* is a cross between *Pop Idols* and *Big Brother*, a talent competition during which the competitors live together as they are groomed for stardom. The concept for the program was developed by Netherlands production company Endemol and licensed by Productions J, a company owned by Quebec media personality Julie Snyder, for production in Quebec's francophone market.

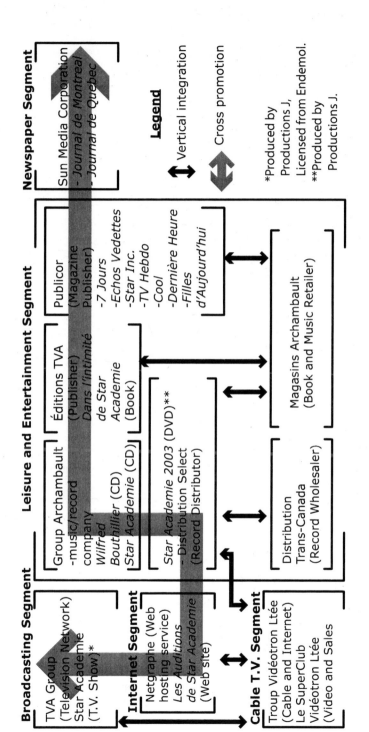

Figure 8.2   Vertical Integration and Cross-Promotion of Star Académie at Quebecor.

In its first season, *Star Académie* became one of the most successful programs in the history of Quebec television, with 3.2 million viewers (in a market of only about 7 million) tuning in to watch New Brunswick lobster fisherman Wilfred Le Bouthillier win the competition (Olive 2003). The show was broadcast on TVA, the most popular television network in Quebec. TVA is controlled by Quebecor Inc. (whose CEO Pierre Karl Péladeau is, coincidentally, Snyder's romantic partner). TVA is only one of the media interests owned by Quebecor's media division. In addition, the company controls Groupe Vidéotron Ltée, the dominant cable television and Internet provider in Quebec, and the owner of the province's largest chain of video rental stores (Le SuperClub Vidéotron Ltée.). As well, Netgraphe, a web-hosting service owned by Quebecor, developed and hosted the official website for the show – accessed largely via Vidéotron hookups.

Nor is that the extent of Quebecor's involvement in the show. Quebecor also owns Groupe Archambault, which includes a record label (Musicor), Canada's largest independent record distributor (Distribution Select), a record wholesaler (Distribution Trans-Canada), and the largest retailer of books and music in Quebec, Magasins Archambault. The first season of *Star Académie* led to two compact discs released on Musicor (Le Bouthillier's debut and a compilation from the entire first season) with sales of over 700,000 discs (CRIA 2004c), and while sales of discs from subsequent seasons have not reached these heights, these recordings remain among the best-selling albums in Canada. Additionally, Select Distribution distributed a DVD compilation of highlights from the first season, which sold over 100,000 copies (ibid.). Éditions TVA, part of Quebecor's books division, also published *Dans l'intimité de Star Académie* by Michele Lemieux, a book about the show's first season. The vertical integration within these various divisions allows Quebecor to collect revenues at most, if not all the points in the supply chain between producer and consumer.

The cross-ownership of various media and cultural industries is one way in which Quebecor maximizes its profits from the show. Clearly the large sales were a result of the television show's enormous popularity, but they also obviously greatly enhanced the revenues generated by the show. Finally, Quebecor's ownership of Quebec's two most popular daily tabloid newspapers *Journal de Montréal* and *Journal de Québec*, and the considerable number of entertainment-oriented magazines such as *Echos Vedettes* and *Star Inc.*, issued through its Publicor magazines division, allow it to both promote the show in print and to sell copies of these publications to fans eager for more coverage of the show, its stars, and competitors. Overall, the show had considerable impact on Quebecor's revenues, as noted in the company's report on its earnings for the third quarter of 2003 (Quebecor). As a number of journalists have noted, this is a rare case of a strategy of media convergence working seamlessly (Boshra 2003; Olive 2003).

Star Académie and the *Idol* programs represent another challenge to our notion of the music industry. Although music performance is at the heart of the competition, the focus of the broadcasts is on the drama of the selection process and the public's own participation in it. The competition is, in a sense, a simulation of the longstanding process whereby record companies select a number of hopefuls who then vie for public approval, with only a very limited number winning out. It is common practice in the music industry to extract every possible source of revenue from a recording following its release: through music publishing, performing rights, licensing, and so on. Now, we would argue, it has become possible to start profiting from a recording prior to its release. What were previously backstage practices of talent acquisition and development are now turned into large-scale spectacles and profitable forms of programming through television. Popular success is achieved prior to recordings, which now become almost secondary, responsible for only one portion of overall revenues. Viewed cynically, this might be seen as a system that allows entertainment corporations to profit from the failure of artists as well as from their successes.

With even more cynicism, we might see the music industries as relying more and more on others for their core functions. When television audiences and celebrity judges are called upon to make talent acquisition decisions, music companies are abdicating one of their traditional roles. When fan website and file-sharing Internet sites carry out much of the promotion and distribution of music, entertainment companies need only find ways of deriving revenue from elaborate cultural labour that is now being done for them by others.

Conclusion

"The Government will continue its leadership in the creation of a new international instrument on cultural diversity, participate actively in La Francophonie and disseminate our cultural products and works around the world." – February 2, 2004, Speech from the Throne.

If the borders between nations have become more porous, those between industries have lost their solidity as well. More and more activities that were once the preserve of the music industry, such as distribution and artist development, are being done by other industries, and on different terms. Apple

Computers is in the music industry; so, in its own way, is the CTV Network, through its production of *Canadian Idol*. Long ago, when musical programs for radio were produced by toothpaste companies, the music industry was no more distinct than it is now. Over the past forty years, nevertheless, we have expected the music industry to be unique and imposing, just as music itself had come to be an enormously powerful cultural force. If the music industry is now losing its definition, this may be because music itself has moved from the centre of cultural life, at least for the younger listeners who had once kept it there. It is unfortunate that this move coincides with our government's own transformation of culture, from collective resource into exportable commodity.

Bibliography

Apple. 2004. Apple Launches iTunes Music Store in Canada. Apple Canada press release, 2 December, http://www.apple.com/ca/press/2004/12/itunes_canada.html

Attali, Jacques. 1985. *Noise: The Political Economy of Music*. Trans. Brian Massumi. Minneapolis: University of Minnesota Press.

BMG Canada et al. v. John Doe, Jane Doe and All Those Persons Who Are Infringing Copyright in the Plaintiff's Sound Recordings. Federal Court of Canada. 2004 FCC 488. 31 March.

Boshra, Basem. 2003. "Reality comes to Quebec: Academie a smash show drawing more than 3 million viewers." *Montreal Gazette*, 19 April, D1.

Canada. Canadian Heritage. 2003. *Trade Routes: Opening Doors for Canadian Arts & Cultural Exports*. Ottawa: Minister of Public Works and Government Services Canada, http://www.canadianheritage.gc.ca/progs/ac-ca/progs/rc-tr/progs/pcrc-trcp/index_e.cfm.

———. 2004. Quoted excerpts from the February 2nd, 2004, Speech from the Throne. Ottawa: Canadian Heritage, http://www.canadianheritage.gc.ca/progs/ac-ca/progs/rc-tr/progs/ecccttcc/sft_e.cfm.

Canadian Association of Internet Providers, et al. v. Society of Composers Authors and Music Publishers of Canada. Supreme Court of Canada. 2004 SCC 45. 30 June.

Carr, David. 2005. "Cold Fusion: Montreal's Explosive Music Scene." *New York Times*, 6 February, online edition, http://www.nytimes.com/2005/02/06/arts/music/06carr.html?ex=1158897600&en=a358d4de2c5d7cba&ei=5070

CRIA (Canadian Recording Industry Association). 2000. The WIPO Treaties: Bringing Copyright into the New Millennium, http://www.cria.ca (accessed 26 August).

——. 2004a. Record industry praises Supreme Court decision preventing Internet piracy havens. Canadian Recording Industry Association press release, July 1, 2004, http://www.cria.ca/news/cria_01jul04.htm (accessed 26 August).

——. 2004b. New industry study shows downloading and burning discourages music sales. Canadian Recording Industry Association press release, July 6, 2004, http://www.cria.ca/news/cria_06jul04.htm (accessed 15 August).

——. 2004c. Industry Statistics, http://www.cria.ca/stats/1204_s.php (accessed 18 February).

——. 2005a. 2004 music shipment figures: first gain in six years. Canadian Recording Industry Association press release, January 18, 2005, http://www.cria.ca/news/180105_n.php (accessed 18 February).

——. 2005b. Legal downloading on the rise in Canada, but file-swapping still a problem. Canadian Recording Industry Association press release, January 19, 2005, http://www.cria.ca/news/190105_n.php (accessed 18 February).

——. 2006. News, http://www.cria.ca/news/020306a_n.php (accessed 8 March 2006).

Flohil, Richard. 2004a. "MapleMusic goes online to build a successful international company." *Applaud* 1(8) (January): 1.

——. 2004b. "Taking control: Canada's independent labels hustle to market their music in the U.S." *Applaud* 2(10) (June): 1.

Globe and Mail. 2003. "Music giant chops prices to combat downloads." *Globe and Mail*. September 4. Online edition.

——. 2004a. "Sympatico, Puretracks harmonize on music downloads." *Globe and Mail*. March 4. Online edition.

——. 2004b. "Digital radio hopefuls sweeten the pot at CRTC." *Globe and Mail*, November, B4.

Holloway, Andy. 2003. "A Slice of Apple's Pie" *Canadian Business* 76(18): 31. Toronto, 29 September.

Hollywood Reporter. 2004. More sour notes for music sales. 8 April, http://www.hollywoodreporter.com/thr/article_display.jsp?vnu_content_id=1000483069 (accessed 15 August 2004).

IFPI. 2004. IFPI welcomes Canadian Supreme Court decision on cross-border Internet transmissions. International Federation of Phonographic Industries press release, June 30, http://www.ifpi.org/site-content/press/20040630a.html (accessed 26 August 2004).

——. 2005. IFPI: 05 Digital Music Report. London: International Federation of Phonographic Industries.

Krasilovsky, M. William, and Sidney Shemel, with contributions by John M. Gross. 2000. *This Business of Music: The Definitive Guide to the Music Industry*, 8th ed. New York: Billboard Books.

LeBlanc, Larry. 2003a. "Anxious year for Canadian music business." *Billboard* 115(52): 66.

——. 2003b. Music Distribution in Canada. Report prepared for Department of Canadian Heritage. April.

——. 2004. "Politicians rally behind Canadian music biz." *Billboard* 116(18): 58–59.

Napster. 2004. Napster Launches in Canada. Napster Canada press release, 26 May, http://www.napster.ca/press_releases/pr_040526.html (accessed 8 November 2004).

Olive, David. 2003. "Convergence gets personal at Quebecor." *Toronto Star*, 12 September.

Openwave. 2004. Inside the Wave. September, http://www.openwave.com/us/open-wave_iq/inside_the_wave/2004/september/invogue (accessed 18 February 2005).

Quart, Alissa. 2006. "Guided by (Many, Many) Voices." *New York Times Magazine*, 26 February.

Quebecor. 2004. Archambault Group launches archambaultzik.ca – the first French-language music download site in Canada. Quebecor Media press release, 16 January, http://www.quebecor.com/htmen/0_0/7_0_1.asp?NewsID=539 (accessed 8 November 2004).

——. 2003 Quebecor Media Reports Net Income of $2.8 million. Quebecor Media press release, 30 October, http://www.quebecor.com/htmen/0_0/7_0_1.asp?NewsID=519 (accessed 21 October 2004).

RIAA (Recording Industry Association of America). 2005. 2005 RIAA Mid-Year Statistic quote, http://www.riaa.com/news/newsletter/pdf/2005midYrStats.pdf (accessed 9 March 2006).

Robertson, Grant. 2006. "CSR Expects to hit 75,000-customer target." *Globe and Mail*, 7 March, http://www.theglobeandmail.com/servlet/story/LAC.20060307.RTICKER07-1/TPStory/ (accessed 10 March 2006).

Spin. 2005. "The Next Big Scene." February.

Standing Committee on Canadian Heritage, 2004. *Interim Report on Copyright Reform*. Ottawa: House of Commons Canada.

Straw, Will. 2003. "No Future? The Canadian Music Industries." In *How Canadians Communicate*, ed. David Taras, Frits Pannekoek, and Maria Bakardjieva. Calgary: University of Calgary Press.

Telus. 2006 MyTelus. Music, http://www.mytelus.com/music/puretracks.vm (accessed 6 September 2006)

Towse, Ruth. 2004. Assessing the Economic Impacts of Copyright Reform on Performers and Producers of Sound Recordings in Canada. Report Commissioned by Industry Canada. Ottawa: Industry Canada, http://strategis.ic.gc.ca/epic/internet/inippd-dppi.nsf/en/h_ip01072e.html (accessed 9 August 2004).

Notes

1   Applaud, a new trade-oriented magazine, appeared in late 2002. Published by Al Mair, former owner of Attic Records, the new publication is issued six times a year. Its focus is on promoting and profiling the international success of Canadian musical acts.

2   On July 27, 2006, Kazaa's parent, Sharman Networks, made an out of court settlement with the four major record companies in a suit carried on in both American and Australian courts. Sharman agreed to pay US$100 million in penalties to the record companies, to build copyright protection into its software.

3   One should be cautious about these claims. In sound recording, the copyright is commonly held not by the artist but by the recording company. With an increasing number of Canada's most successful recording artists signed to U.S. labels, more of the revenue they generate (within Canada, as well) will flow to these labels. While this does not invalidate their reasoning, it should temper predictions about how achievable a trade surplus is for the Canadian sound recording industry.

9: Digital Disturbances: On the Promotion, Panic, and Politics of Video Game Violence

STEPHEN KLINE

Introduction

It is often said that Canadians have a unique appreciation of the complex place of communication media in the forging of the modern state. Indeed, as Harold Innis foresaw, innovations in communication media cause profound "disturbances" in the economics, politics, and cultural life of our nation. To understand them our analysis must be both cultural and historical. The expansive distances that separate our communities, the ethnic and linguistic diversity that Balkanizes the country, and the challenges of nation building caught between the waning colonial power of the UK and the restless commercial expansionism of the American Empire seem to have accentuated the fragility of our cultural industries. Hardly surprising, then, that each technological invention from the railway to the Internet has become a site of political and ideological struggle over our national values and sensibilities. Our obsession with cultural values and multi-cultural identities is not only reflected in our academic debates about media and social change, but in the unique institutional mandates through which the Canadian state regulates these communications technologies – from the phone to the CBC, from CanCon to Broadcast Standards rulings on Howard Stern.

Perhaps the most lively and protracted of these debates about our cultural industries concerns the representation of violence in children's media. After the Second World War, reports of a spoiled "baby boom" generation provoked considerable apprehension about the waning cultural values, which in the past at least, had maintained social control – the work ethic, respect for authority, and self-restraint (Riesman et al. 1961). The rising youth crime rates unleashed a lively debate about the widening "generational gap" rending mass-mediated society. Primed by journalistic accounts of rampant juvenile delinquency, the breakdown of the family, aimless high school dropouts, and the rising tide of youthful rebellion, the first TV cohort was surveilled with both optimism and horror (Spigel 1998). Optimism, in the belief that "television's illuminating light will go far, we hope, to drive out the ghosts that haunt the dark corners of our minds – ignorance, bigotry, fear" (Minow and LaMay 1995, 83). And horror at the prospect of a generation of anti-social couch potatoes spending all their leisure time in front of the screen.

Marshall McLuhan helped put the anxieties of the electronic age in an historical perspective: The generational conflicts that emerged in the post-war period were a sign that mass media were contributing to profound disjunctures in human experience and perceptions (1964, 33). As Neil Postman (1982) later explained, growing up within the electronic embrace of the mass-mediated domesticity, children would come to have very different values and lifestyles than their parents who were raised in a word-oriented print culture. Fearing their premature exposure to sexualization and violence, Postman worried that the protective *cordon sanitaire* of literate schooling was being eroded by children's engagement with mass media.

Stanley Cohen's (1972) book *Folk Devils and Moral Panics* set out to explain these public concerns about youth violence. Panic is the term Cohen used to characterize a "sudden and overwhelming fear or anxiety" permeating public reactions to youth violence. Cohen's case study of the Mods and Rockers in Britain during the mid-1960s led him to suggest that youth aggression was often mis-apprehended as an exaggerated moral threat to public order. With blame at the forefront, he also noted how quickly this demonization of youth became politicized in the press. He described the cycle of "panic amplification," which ensued from the labelling of deviance:

A condition, episode, person or group of persons emerges to become defined as a threat to societal values and interests; its nature is presented in a stylized and stereotypical fashion ... ; the moral barricades are manned ... ; socially accredited experts pronounce their diagnoses and solutions; ways of coping are evolved or (more often) resorted to; the condition then disappears, submerges or deteriorates and becomes more visible. (Cohen 1972, 9)

Cohen concluded that the media attention devoted to violence derived from the fact that youth culture symbolized "much of the social change taking place in Britain over the last twenty years" (Cohen 1972, 11). Scholars have since used the term "media panic" to characterize the angst-ridden dynamics underwriting public furore over violence and sex in children's mediated culture – books, comics, television, video nasties, and now video games (Cumberbatch 2001).

Panic and the Politics of Youth Culture

But rather than deteriorating, the concerns about the television generation intensified through the 1960s and 1970s. Shocked by the brutality of Vietnam soldiers abroad and the Manson slayings at home, North Americans began to question in earnest what violent entertainment was doing to our kids. As Kirsten Drotner explained, children became the focus of media panics "not merely because they are often media pioneers; not merely because they challenge social and cultural power relations, nor because they symbolize ideological rifts. They are panic targets just as much because they inevitably represent experiences and emotions that are irrevocably lost to adults" (1992, 59). To most parents, it was obvious that boys who watch cartoons filled with senseless mayhem and grow up identifying with warrior heroes become anti-social. Were not the rising crime rates, disobedient children, and falling grades at schools also linked to the endless symbolic killings in the vast wasteland that television had become?

With public condemnation of the vast wasteland of television reverberating around the world, the Federal Communication Commission in the United States began hearings focused on tightening the regulation of violence on TV (Minow and LaMay 1996; Murray 2001). Although effects were small and difficult to specify, the evidence was sufficient for the Surgeon General to tentatively conclude that media violence could be a public health concern (Surgeon General 1972; NIMH 1982). In Canada, too, the La Marsh Commission came to a similar conclusion. North American broadcasters were chastened for failing to respect children's limited ability to distinguish the imaginary from the real. As a result, children's culture became an increasingly contested zone of "social regulation" as young peoples' enthusiasm for violent entertainment increased.

This growing body of scientific research on media effects, although welcomed in Canada, was of little consequence in the aftermath of Ronald Reagan's deregulation of children's media industries in the 1980s. The reason was that cable, satellite, and Internet technology had begun to make it harder for the Canadian state to manage children's place in a globalized media marketplace. In *Out of the Garden*, I have described the sweeping implications of deregulation of children's media, as synergistic children's marketing changed the cartoon smiley face of children's TV into a perpetual war-play battlefield (Kline 1993). Without a policy for controlling the cross-border signals, ads, and cable retransmission, and in spite of Prime Minister Mulroney's promises that Canadian culture was a "sacred trust," media industries rallied against any regulation of children's television. If culture was a product, then its trade would have to treat cultural commodities as part of the "free market" in goods and services. And if American children wanted to watch and play with G.I. Joe and Ninja Turtle toys, then so too would Canadians. In Canada, where Mister Rogers' Neighbourhood personified Canadians' ideological core, the war-torn fabric of American children's programming seemed out of whack with constitutional values of peace, order, and good government. Surveys showed that up to 90 per cent of Canadian parents were opposed to the endless violence on children's television. Moreover, many of these programs and most of the advertising was in violation of Canadian Broadcast Standards guidelines. Why were we teaching children to be sharing and responsible in Canadian schools, while American media culture was teaching the ruthless exercise of force as the means of solving problems?

It took a massacre of students at Université de Montréal in 1989 to remind Canadians of the porous nature of our information borders. Virginie La-Rivière, the thirteen-year-old sister of one of the young female engineers who were killed, gathered over one million signatures to her petition, reminding government of the consequences of deregulated children's media industries. Public outrage grew louder with every Ninja Turtle and Power Ranger fan who decided to practice their moves in the nursery. The Standing Committee on Communications and Culture published a report called *Television Violence: Fraying our Social Fabric*, which stated "We have clearly found that the violence portrayed on television reflects and shapes unhealthy social attitudes.... The committee has concluded that although the risk may be small ... it cannot be ignored" (Canada 1993, 7). Keith Spicer, head of the CRTC, confessed it was no longer necessary to study the issue of media violence: it was time to act. He announced a five-point plan, which proposed a nine-o'clock violence watershed, as well as promising to negotiate a crossborder detente with the United States. But Canada's much-celebrated *cordon sanitaire* of regulation did little to reduce the drip drip of the American culture of violence across the border. Mandated by President Clinton, the v-chip became the much-trumpeted "self-regulatory" America-friendly way of protecting children while leaving the transborder communication flows unregulated. Most Canadians don't even know what the v-chip is now, let alone how to use it.

Digital Disturbance

It was a typical, if not ordinary, evening at the ProGamer Internet Cafe in the suburban Vancouver community of Coquitlam. At 7:30 on January 17, 2003, there were about forty or so patrons, mostly young and male, gazing at their screens intently engaged in their game play or messaging. But these are cafes in name only, for there is very little friendly banter taking place among the young men assembled at their combat stations. Combat stations, because at the ProGamer Café, Counterstrike (the online multiplayer video game that pits terrorists teams against anti-terrorists) is what many of the patrons are playing. Not only are these gamers playing with others here in Vancouver, but in cafes around the world they are hunting down and eliminating the enemy. The room is poorly lit, Spartan in décor, and functionally arranged, for all the users are intent on their task at hand. In gamer lingo they are intent on "player killing" – that is claiming territory and eradicating other players' characters. Arming themselves and forming into clans, they are on a mission to hunt out and kill as many enemies as possible, to gain experience points, fame, and more powerful weapons.

Most players were so intensely involved in their gaming that they were startled when the pall of silence that envelopes Internet arcades was broken by a group of young men who got up and began shouting and arguing with Christian Kwee, a seventeen-year-old regular. Mr. Kwee apparently had been playing Counterstrike too, but rather more successfully than his opponents. Three of his virtual victims were now grabbing Christian Kwee by his collar and threatening to punch his lights out. When Kwee's friends intervened, the threesome rushed out of the door, returning in a few minutes with a gun with which they blew him away with one deadly shot. The manager of the ProGamer Cafe, Harry Law, was quoted by reporters as saying that the games were not behind the slaying. However, the RCMP investigating officer, Cpl. Le Maitre, stated that, after interviews with friends and witnesses, the police had eliminated other explanations of the murder such as gang rivalries and drugs. But it looks suspiciously like a case of "real player killing." To date, the Kwee murder remains unsolved and forgotten. And the virtual battleground that provoked this act of virtual vengeance lies beyond the horizon of Canadian media regulation.

This murder indicates the other escalating reason that Canadian children would continue to encounter entertainment at odds with Canadian's cultural values. Television was no longer the primary source of violent entertainment. In the early 1990s violent video games began to rival TV and movies for both young peoples' eyeballs and their parents' dollars. But witnessing the blood moves of Mortal Kombat, the public became alarmed that the video game industry was escalating the North American culture of media violence. Called before Congress and threatened with regulation in 1992, Sega helped found the Electronic Software Ratings Board (ESRB) as a self-regulatory buffer for the industry. Like cigarettes, video games would now have warning labels that informed customers of the age-appropriate level and indemnified the industry against lawsuits. According to the Interactive Digital Software Association – the industry's lobby group – video gaming was a matter of consumer choice in the marketplace. They could be no more regulated than the press. Ironically, 1993 was also the year that Sega was granted a dispensation for distributing violent video games to children on a cable network in Canada by the CRTC. Both initiatives were compounded by the fact that "wired" content fell under the regulatory ambit of "distribution" rather than public ownership of broadcasting. For this reason the production of "digital entertainment" commodities appeared to lie outside the established frameworks of media content regulation.

By the millennium, gaming had become the fastest growing and most lucrative entertainment industry, leapfrogging films and children's television in the quest for recycling entertainment dollars (Kline et al. 2003). So too, over the last quarter century, the dramatic expansion of the digital entertainment industries has refocused the debates about violent entertainment on digital media. The industry's rhetoric of youthful empowerment (Rushkoff 1997) has echoed the optimistic promotional ideology of "cyber-culture" industries such as video gaming as defenders of free speech. They have opposed all regulation of digital content on the grounds that it was both technically impossible and legally repugnant: digital culture was a "liberated zone" where individuals voluntarily access knowledge, share opinions, chat with family, meet people and even galvanize resistive self-regulating virtual communities (ISDA website). Since Canadian cultural policy is often made in the ideological shadow of the U.S.A., it remains likely that Canadians will see control over children's culture disappear. The following discussion examines the development and extraordinary popularity of the interactive entertainment industries.

Origin of the Specious

According to geek legend, the *ur*-videogame "Space Wars" was programmed on a multi-million-dollar, cupboard-sized PDP-1 computer given to and lodged in the basement of the Massachusetts Institute of Technology. It was an appropriate birthplace for the early progeny of the "military-entertainment" complex (Herz 1997). The midwives of gamer culture were the graduate students working on space and military cybernetics research. And as computer historian Leslie Haddon noted, there was something playful about these young engineers drawn to computers where "the set of values operating in this male culture led them to develop their own terminology, the key concept in which was the 'hack.'" This term came specifically to refer to a "stylish technological innovation undertaken for the intrinsic pleasure of experimenting – not necessarily to fulfil some more constructive goal" (Haddon 1999,55). Space Wars exemplified the "true spirit of hacking" – a daring leap of technological bricolage thought to be the core mindset of the information revolution. It is revered because it demonstrated that a user could interact with a computer in a very playful (non-instrumental) way.

The programming for Space Wars was initiated by Steve Russell and fellow "hackers" who satirically styled themselves the Hingham Group for Space Research. This coterie of graduate students assembled frequently to discuss science fiction and invent new uses of the research computers they had at their disposal. Roseanne Stone comments on the continued importance of playfulness within these early hacker circles arguing that: "instead of carrying on an established work ethic, the beliefs and practices of the cultures I observe incorporate a play ethic – not to displace the corporate agendas that produce their pay checks, but ... to make space for play in the very belly of the monster that is the communication industry." By today's standards Space Wars "interactivity" was not sophisticated. The display was an oscilloscope screen. It had no sound track, no colour, no levels, and no back story. The objective of this game was for a player to manoeuvre a blip against a backdrop of moving stars until it could shoot a missile at another blip. The space ship could be controlled by toggles on the computer console that altered the ship's trajectory.

However primitive as play, Space Wars not only augured one of the American military's most enduring defence strategies, but also inaugurated what has become the defining genre of militarized masculinity – the shooter. So, long before computers could communicate with each other via Arpanet (another offspring of the military cybernetics imagination), there was an emerging hacker community gathering in the computer research labs around the world. DEC sold many PDP-1s to other universities too, and with them Space Wars spread through the underground computer culture like a "bush telegraph." Space Wars was soon followed by Star Trek, Adventure, Wumpus, and Net-Hack, each of which was uploaded onto main frames and shared in the

off-peak hours by successive generations of trainee programmers and electronics engineers.

In the early 1960s, Ralph Baer an engineer at Sanders Associates (a military
electronics consulting firm) approached interactive entertainment from the
other direction – as a novel use for surplus television sets. Baer had seen a
computer game called Tennis for Two demo-ed in the military research lab
at Brookhaven National Laboratory. He decided to prototype this game as a
military training device. He has said of this invention that he thought that
"you should be able to do something else with television besides just watch it"
(Stern and Schoenhaus 1990 99). By linking the screen display of a TV set to
some electronic control devices he created a simulator that required eye-hand
coordination – thought to be a crucial factor in military training. It had two
knobs that can control the movement of paddles moving up and down on
the screen. Although it wasn't computerized, it could simulate a very simple
tennis game where two flat sticks bounced a square ball back and forth on the
screen. He showed it to a Pentagon review board as a "secret" military training
technology. After a year's deliberation they decided they had no use for it.

Baer's importance rivals that of Steve Russell, however, because he was the
first individual to actually conceive of an interactive entertainment system as
a "hybrid" electronics technology. As McLuhan noted, "The hybrid or the
meeting of two media is a moment of truth and revelation from which new
form is born" (McLuhan 1964, 63). Pong was based on a conceptual marriage
of convenience between the TV screen and the circuit board. But the back-
blast from this fusion derived from the merger of television's mass audience
spectatorship with the cybernetic *play control* afforded by computer chips.
Released from its secret status, Baer was now free to sell his prototype in the
market. This was good timing. By the end of the 1960s, a variety of micro-
processors were readily available. Baer cleverly used them to enhance the Pong
game considerably. Now each player could twist knobs on the console to give
the ball spin. Precise movements produced immediately visualized effects on
the screen like acceleration of the ball and sound effects. Baer sold Pong to
the electronics firm Magnavox, who placed them in bars, bus stations, and
arcades. Within a few years it was a fad on a par with the hula-hoop.

Yet the final blossoming of the "gamer culture" also depended on the likes
of Owen Bushnell – an important variant of the hacker breed. As an engineering graduate student at the University of Utah, he had played Space Wars. But
his interest was in selling it. Bushnell is remembered as the prototype "hacker
entrepreneur" – a shrewd businessman who helped bring gaming out of the
lab and into the mass market. In 1972, Bushnell started a company called
Syzgy to sell a stand-alone version of Space Wars dubbed Computer Space.

Without a mainframe computer, however, he had to assemble his prototype in his daughter's bedroom from a variety of available electronics parts. He sold his prototype to Nutting Associates, which later regrouped as Atari. Soon Computer Space, Pong, Space Invaders, and Pac-Man vied in bars, arcades, roadside cafes, and airports as a welcome alternative to pool and pin-ball. Bushnell is thus celebrated not only as the godfather of this $30-billion inter-active entertainment industry, but also as the model electronic impresario with one foot on the rolling log of technological innovation and the other in the murky waters of the entertainment marketplace. In the rise and fall of Atari, we witness the tensions that bedevilled the entertainment empires of the waning twentieth century.

Quick to realize the advantages of new microprocessor technology, the arcade gaming industry leapt to the forefront of game design and develop-ment. Building on the early financial success of Space Wars and Pac-Man, Atari began to think of themselves as entertainment moguls. Because micro-technologies were evolving so quickly, they found this to be a high-risk ven-ture, foreshadowing the urgency of perpetual innovation, which came to per-meate the digital industries. The core problem for the gaming industry was boredom. Competition grew for game designs that could provide the mega-hit. Atari began to license games from the Japanese while Cinematronics supplemented its Space Wars game with Tail Gunner, Star Castle, Armour Attack, or Solar Quest. Bally/Midway launched games as diverse as Tron (launched in tandem with a Disney film) and NFL football. The list of games available rose quickly and so did their loyal following. Arcade players were soon landing jet fighters on carriers, manoeuvring futuristic tanks through mined battlefields, and protecting the galaxy from asteroids and alien attack-ers as literally hundreds of new game concepts were tested in the arcades with their most avid fans.

No longer "hacked" in computer labs, video games were increasingly designed for their marketability, defined by their quick acceptance by youth-ful enthusiasts. One of the most influential of the new professional game designers was Chris Crawford, the programmer of Tanktactics and "Eastern Front," who worked at Atari's Research Lab in the 1970s. Tanktactics was one of the first battle simulation games, and it caught the attention not only of young males but of the generals at the Pentagon who were prototyping simu-lation trainers for their tank crews. Crawford became the leading exponent of professional game design (Myers 1989).

Originally developed as a number-cruncher, the computer assumed a new personal-ity when it was given graphics and sound capabilities. These capabilities made the computer more powerful: it could now communicate with human beings, not just in the cold and distant language of digits, but in the emotionally immediate and compelling language of images and sounds. With this ability came a new, previously undreamed of possibility: the possibility of using the computer artistically as a medium for emotional communication. The computer game has emerged as the prime vehicle for this communication. (xii)

His credo privileged the notion of simulation as the foundation of digital communication. Gaming after all was a "state of mind." Players "caught up" by the emotional intensity of the games became immersed in a state of suspended disbelief. To help with game design he described the basic genres of gaming: Action games, where players landed imaginary planes on carriers, engaged in clearing minefields from Asteroid belts, or navigated a Battle Tank in a futuristic battlefield; Sports games, where players tried their hand at professional football, basketball, or wrestling; Racing games, where players could race their friends at Monaco or on futuristic motor-bikes, proved perennial winners; Role Play games, where players took on characters and explored an imaginary world; and Puzzle games that demanded players solve a virtual problem. Challenge, conflict, curiosity, and fantasy were key psychological features of all the most intense gaming experiences.

An obvious advantage of the arcade environment from the industry's point of view was how quickly you could discover which games were popular. And if the coins didn't flow, then new game boards could be inserted into the machine without replacing the whole cabinet. A programmable game was less risky, then, than the previous generation of electronic entertainments, which had populated the bars and fairgrounds, arcades, and corner stores. In this respect, the arcade businesses enjoyed a key advantage in relationship to the home market. It all depended on knowing what made a game immersive. Yet it was precisely these aspects of play that first ignited a media panic about video games. As the fad grew, the crowds of young males who seemed mesmerized by the task of manoeuvring through dungeons and shooting at virtual enemies began to disturb the public anxieties about youth. Politicians fretted about the arcade craze devouring the next generation. Worried parents rallied behind municipal legislation that restricted the age of children admitted.

But psychological studies of arcade gaming failed to confirm the public worries about violent games. Mehrabian and Wixen (1983) reported a study in *Psychology Today* noting that there is a basic confusion in our understanding of the video game medium's effects on aggression and delinquency – the difficulty of distinguishing between the agonic (playful) and aggressive elements in video game play. When students in their research first played twenty-two

commonly available arcade games, they reported emotional reactions of dis-
pleasure, arousal, and dominance, which the researchers first interpreted
as signs of hostility and aggressiveness produced by playing violent games.
But in subsequent research on different students they found that the most-
preferred arcade games were rated higher for producing feelings of control,
mastery, and competence. They concluded therefore by noting that overall
"within the limited emotional realm tapped by current video games, our findings show that both dominance and arousal responses are most important."
These are the emotions of players – not killers. And young people can tell the
difference.

As often happens, media panic can alert corporations to their vulnerability
in the market. The digital industry learned how important it was to remind
parents that gaming was a harmless form of entertainment that helped young
people to take control of their lives and to prepare themselves for a future in
which computers would reign supreme. So rather than disappear, the arcades
were transformed into the launch pad of gamer culture. With the din of
public anxiety fading in the background, the game arcades either closed or
began their long march to respectability during the 1980s by cleaning and
lighting up. Game machines were introduced into Bushnell's Chucky Cheese
restaurants and airport lounges. Nintendo opened its Powerzone arcades
nationwide and later Sega launched Playdium as the Mecca of gamer culture.
With revenues of $8 billion, they remained the place where the most fanati-
cal young fans could hang out, chat with their friends, and try out new game
concepts before buying them.

Digital Promise: The Domestication of Interactive Entertainment

With their initial fears waylaid, many educators found it difficult to ignore the
promise of new learning technology that was engaging, exciting, and dynamic.
According to Patricia Greenfield (1984), computer games were not simply fun
to play with, but multisensorial learning environments comparable to science
museums and field trips, which got children "personally involved" in exploration and discovery (101). Extolling games like Lunar Lander, she explains that
all games require the player to discover the rules that operate in the program
(110), demanding very complex problem-solving, subtle strategies, and visual
thinking. The complexity of thought required in a game like Pac-Man was
remarkable: Kids were solving maze puzzles, visually tracking four monsters
at the same time, while developing strategies for maximizing energy pellets.
Fantasy games were particularly engaging to children, she explained, because
"there is more character development than in conventional games" (119). Yet

some of parents' concerns about video game violence were misplaced. Video games are better teachers than television because they are interactive: Even violent games require analytic and strategic visual thinking, very different from mindless receptivity in front of a TV screen. Moreover, as Greenfield explains, children can take control of the events and narrative. It was the "action not violence" which drew so many young people to the screen (114). She even challenged educational gamemakers to create video games that are as compelling to play as the "shoot 'em up space games that predominate in the arcade" because the intensity of involvement is an indication of the active learning that is taking place (124).

Edna Mitchell (1985) was one of the first academics to actually document the impact of video game systems on family life. She asked the families to keep a record of their media use for one week a month over a six-month period. She found that some families enjoyed a blossoming of togetherness that Mitchell compares to playing monopoly for a previous era. Parents, she reports, retained control over the time devoted to video games, and families found that playing brought them together socially on many occasions to play together competitively. Boys often claimed privileged access to the games and played alone almost half the time. Girls played less, and mostly with their siblings or parents. Only children were also more likely to play alone (63 per cent). Her analysis concluded that computer gaming did not turn children into "gaming junkies," but she did find strong gender differences in children's use and attitudes, which persisted in other studies. Boys were mesmerized while girls were bored by computers.

The issue of the gender divide was beginning to cast a shadow upon the burgeoning video game culture. Why did boys like them so much and so few girls choose to play them? To most, the answer was pretty obvious: the subject position of most games was identified with the conflicted action and combat situations. Games were clearly designed for male fantasies of power and self-mastery; pleasures that females mostly found unpleasureably aggressive: The "gender valuence" of video games therefore afforded a means of "understanding the social patterning of the use of that technology" (Skirrow 1986, 142). Skirrow uses Melanie Klein's psychoanalytic theory to identify the "masculine position" of these games constituted as an Oedipal threat in which "the preferred male solution seems to be to bury themselves in the mother's body with their fantasy weapons and forget about the very real dangers in the world outside" (141). In short, playing video games is about "mastering a specifically male anxiety in a specifically male way" (138). In designing games for the testosterone-driven fantasy life of male teens, the video game industry was

becoming ever more deeply entrenched in the circuitry of militarized masculinity and its narratives of "action heroics."

PLAYING WITH POWER

Realizing that the taint of arcade was rapidly fading behind the promotional
smokescreen of edutainment, Nintendo parlayed their success in Japan by
launching the Famicom into the American home market in 1985 (Sheff 1993).
Their marketing strategy was the same as that of the toy industry – video
gaming was the future of home entertainment technologies. The Famicom
was designed as an alternative to watching TV. Their eight-bit console was
clearly superior to competitors', with colour graphics and sound chips, ample
memory on the cartridge, and easy-to-use interfaces, at a lower price. Learning from other children's cultural industries like Disney, Hasbro, and Mattel,
they relied heavily on advertising campaigns, investing $5 million in ads
featuring the most popular characters from their games (Donkey Kong and
Mario).

The promotional investment was worth it. In 1986 Nintendo spent $30 mil-
lion on advertising, becoming the leading spender in the whole playthings
sector. But they sold 1.1 million of the 1.4 million video game systems, rising
to 3 of 4 million units the next year – far outselling remaining console rivals
like Atari and Sega's Master system. Outpacing their competition, they then
launched a spin-off Mario Brothers TV cartoon as well as a live action movie
to maintain momentum in their sales (Kinder 1991, 97). Soon after, they
launched a fanzine, which remains the most-read magazine for young males.
By 1988 Nintendo rivalled Hasbro, the leading toy seller, with $1.3 billion in
U.S. sales. The following year sales doubled again to $2.3 billion. You could
now find a Nintendo console in one-quarter of American households. Building on their core strategy, they also launched a coast-to-coast arcade chain
called the Power Zone that featured experimental interfaces and soon-to-be-
released games to bolster the crossover between arcade and console gaming.

In 1989, a TV ad for the Nintendo Entertainment System conveyed the
renewed excitement about gaming. Opening with a swooping aerial shot of a
normal subdivision, the viewer is introduced to the suburban world – where
normalcy and tedium define the everyday life of the teen. The narrator asks:
"What's it like to play the Nintendo Entertainment System?" as the camera
enters the living room to reveal a scene of excitement as two boys – perhaps
brothers or friends, point excitedly to the video game screen. For this is no
ordinary living room scene. The sound of thunder emanates as a strange electrical energy emanates from the screen. The family dog retreats in horror, but

the boy's faces are alight with excitement, not fear. The TV set is now gyrating wildly as this Nintendo-powered house blasts off like a rocket into the night sky (perhaps to join Alex on Centauri) as the narrator intones, "Now you're playing with power!"

Of course all ads are puffery. Yet the Nintendo marketers clearly understood what their male market wanted. Sold to parents as educational, video games were really about fantasies of empowerment – the freeing of teen boys' desperate urges to overcome the boring routines of daily insignificance. Recognizing video games as a "powerful social and cultural force," Eugene Provenzo's book *Video Kids* offered a more sanguine view of the action play of the "Nintendo Generation." Noting that the video game industry has developed "games whose social content has been overwhelmingly violent, sexist, and even racist," he wonders if this medium is really breaking with the commercialized TV culture of the past (Provenzo 1991). His study indicated that "an instrumental logic of individualistic aggressiveness" pervades the storyline of most video games. "The message communicated by the rules of this video game is that violence is not only acceptable, it is necessary to win" (124). Commenting on the violence embedded in a hockey game, for example, Provenzo notes that "fused with this violence we find messages about masculinity, about power and its exercise, about winning in a highly competitive society, and thus what it means to be a man and how to survive constant threats to one's masculinity" (137).

To cultural critics like Provenzo, "interactive play technologies" have a paradoxical quality: the same qualities that make "interactive multimedia" engaging are being betrayed by the persistence of violent and sexist content. Provenzo worried that, rather than forging a brave new world of healthy interactive edutainment, the video game industry was simply extending the troubled masculinity of mass media. He warns "if the video game industry is going to provide the foundation for the development of interactive television, then concerned parents and educators have cause for considerable alarm" (138).

MORAL KOMBAT

The 1990s saw this prediction come to pass. Noting the remarkable success of Nintendo in their colonization of domestic play, arcade rival Sega decided to crash the party in 1989. Sega knew that the Nintendo brand was deeply embedded in the culture of the eight- to fourteen-year-old males. Yet as this Nintendo generation grew to adolescence, they would be looking for more exciting and challenging games. It was perhaps Sega's 1992 decision to circumvent Nintendo's hold on its core market that resulted in renewed moral panic. Sega's marketing team realized that Nintendo was vulnerable because it targeted the eight- to fourteen-year-old males. Having grown up with games, and conquered most, they were looking for something cool. Sega launched the sixteen-bit Saturn to win a hold on the older teen and young adult market. This up-age strategy did not alienate teens, however. It just opened up a different market. If Nintendo's Mario was a bumbling and goofy preteen, Sega's Sonic was a plucky and aggressive renegade with an ironic sense of humour and a compulsive attitude to gaming. Soon the TV screens were filled with ads full of testosterone-swaggering attitude and endless contests of technical power.

Intense graphic realism was clearly what Midway's lead designer John Tobias was aiming at when he conceived of the arcade version of Mortal Kombat. Adapting a theme popularized from the action film Enter the Dragon, mortal kombatants get to fight to the death in the annual Shaolin Tournament, held by the evil master Shang Tsung. The innovation was that Tobias used digitized footage of real actors as a basis for its seven distinctive warrior characters, which included a metal-faced mercenary Kano, ice-wielding ninja Sub-Zero, U.S. special forces soldier Sonya Blade, and White Lotus Society warrior, Liu Kang. A bout consisted of winning two of the three rounds before moving on to the next opponent. Each round was a matter of pummelling their foes into submission with kicks, punches, combos, and special moves until they could not get up. Once an opponent had been beaten twice, an on-screen message urged you to "Finish Him!" With a series of button and joystick moves, your kombatant would do just that by using their "fatality moves," such as ripping a foe's head off his body, breaking the spine, causing his head to explode, or ripping out his beating heart. Although tame when compared with Soldier of Fortune, GTA, or Red Neck Rampage, Midway's Mortal Kombat seemed then like one of the bloodiest, goriest, most gruesomely brutal games to hit the market. Once word of the graphic violence spread, players flocked to the machines to learn and practice, or just to gawk.

Who could blame console players for wanting the same intensity of play in their bedrooms? Sega's version of Mortal Kombat II, released in 1993, took the kombatants into the "Outworld" for another death match. Like any good sequel, MKII took everything that made the first game a success, then made it bigger, louder, bloodier, and faster. New characters were introduced and each was given multiple fatality moves, some of which required knowing the "secret" code or combo. Nintendo, still positioned in the family entertainment market, was at first reluctant to tread this path. Their early version of Mortal Kombat II had fatality moves but they made the red blood into white sweat. Not surprisingly, the Sega Genesis game which contained the gore clobbered the SNES version in sales. The blood-and-gore hungry masses had spoken and game designers were listening. From now on video games had to be gorific.

Celia Pearce, one of the rare breed of female game designers, exposes what she calls the "dirty family secret" of the industry, noting that "in the computer gaming industry, the term market is a euphemism." She accuses the industry of becoming fixated on the easiest to sell part of it – the "world's most innocent and maligned victim of demographic opportunism: the ever vulnerable, ever receptive, ever predictable adolescent male" (Pearce 1997, 210). As she explains:

What the market wants is a self fulfilling prophecy. We the industry decide what goes to market, we watch how it sells and if it sells well we just make more of the same. Like drug pushers the marketing people recognize that once you get someone hooked you have a customer for life, until of course they die. Or in the case of video games, grow up. (213)

Pearce berates the marketers for targeting the "cult of masculinity," claiming game designers take pleasure from squeezing "lunch money away from 14 year old boys" by taking advantage of their "agitated vulnerability and insecurity" (211).

Not a bad description of what happened next. Realizing that advertising was required to prime the pumps, Sega launched its thirty-two-bit system with a $45 million advertising blitz featuring thirty-five TV spots. Their strategy was textbook marketing. These ads dripped with high-energy, testosterone-packed teen humour (Kline and de Peuter 2002). The Sega system rocketed to the head of the pack based on its fantastically popular games: Mortal Kombat sold 3 million cartridges within two months of its release and Streetfighter II sold 8 million copies worldwide in one year. The following year, a James Bond derivative game Golden Eye, in which attacking enemy characters crumpled to the ground, contorting in pain differently, depending on where 007 hit them, was the top-selling game. Total shipments rose from $1.8 billion in 1989 to over $4.3 billion in 1994: Consoles were found in 45 per cent of all U.S. households, 60 per cent of households with kids, and 80 per cent of households with male children (Battelle and Johnstone 1993). And many of these games were extremely violent.

In the early 1990s, a gradual increase in youth crime in the United States was capped with a number of brutal child murders. Psychologists argued that the violent acts represented in Mortal Kombat were as graphic as those in slasher and war films. Congress began to contemplate regulation of this new source of violent imagery. The U.S.-led video game industry quickly rallied against this threat to their "freedom of expression." Spearheaded by Sega, they formed the ESRB (Electronic Software Ratings Board) to function as a self-regulatory alternative to regulation. The solution they argued was that an age-based ratings system (General, 13+, mature) would help parents choose the most suitable games for their children. Reluctant to put a legislative damper on the rapidly expanding digital market, the Clinton government decided to bully from the pulpit, but not to back Joseph Leiberman's regulatory initiatives to bring gaming in line with television.

KIDS GET IT

In 1994 the U.S. government also commercialized the Internet, creating a deregulated market which was intended to foster the expanding information economy. Media Lab guru Nicholas Negroponte sanctified this policy as a bold liberation of digital culture, declaring that "the information superhighway may be mostly hype today, but it is an understatement about tomorrow" (1995). Noting that children are already embracing multimedia while their parents hesitate, he sees "the control bits of that digital future are more than ever before in the hands of the young. Nothing could make me happier." His optimism is derived from his belief that as "children appropriate this global information resource … we are bound to find new hope and dignity in places where very little existed before" (231). Douglas Rushkoff similarly cites Timothy Leary's extolling the fast track to the information age, stating: "The importance of the Nintendo phenomenon is about equal to that of the Gutenberg printing press" (Rushkoff 1994, 30). He goes on to contrast the top-down passivity fostered by TV entertainment with the self-defining take-control culture promoted by interactive games, concluding that "while their parents may condemn Nintendo as mindless and masturbatory, kids who have mastered video gaming early on stand a better change of exploiting the real but mediated interactivity that will make itself available to them by the time they hit techno-puberty" (1994, 31).

The software designers had realized that computer gaming was the real market driver in the digital era. So the dowdy PC had to undergo a make-over, emerging as a zippy "multimedia" system, which included CD-ROMs, fast RAM, sound and game ports, and built-in modems. PC gamers no longer were confined to playing Tetris and Math Blaster. Sales of PCs more than doubled in four years in the mid-1990s, rising to 50 per cent of U.S. households, including 30 per cent that had Internet access. And by 1998, 40 per cent of consumer PC software sales were for games; yet few of these could be classified as educational and most had elements of violent conflict (Wardly 1999).

And in this respect, the PC had one advantage dramatically revealed at the release of the hit game Doom – the prototype multiplayer dungeon shooter. MORPGs (Multiplayer Online Role Play Games) are rule-bound agonic quests structured equally around exploration and strategic combat. Although not the first online game, Doom exploited better than other games the growing intersection of the Internet and simulation. Players of Doom had an option: to play in the usual first-person shooter mode against the machine-controlled avatars, or alternatively they could play against a friend on another computer linked by telephone lines and a modem. In the latter case, the remote players could see (and shoot each other) on their own screen. Moreover, they could send verbal messages, which would appear on the other player's screen by means of texting – a nifty thing to do when you are about to kill your opponent from behind. The buzz around this game was phenomenal. When made available by file transfer, the requests for access brought the University of Wisconsin computer to its knees by eager gamers clamouring for a shareware version of Doom. Eventually 15 million versions of the game code were downloaded from the server.

On August 18, 1999, the U.S. Army awarded a five-year contract to the University of Southern California in order to create the Institute for Creative Technologies (ICT). The ICT's mandate was to enlist the talents of the entertainment and game development industries and work collaboratively with computer scientists to advance the state of immersive training simulation for the military. The American military is not only currently actively involved in developing simulation video games, investing 1.1 billion a year using them for training soldiers in tactics and operations, but also in holding online gaming contests for recruiting young soldiers and actually profiting from commercial spin-offs of their simulation technologies (Prensky 2003).

So, despite the growing outcry from parents and teachers, the game developers continued to push the boundaries of militaristic fantasy ever outward to sell their games. With each upgrade of Duke Nukem, Grand Theft Auto, and Halo, designers incorporated more extreme weapons and brutally realistic graphics. And, despite industry protestations, they have been caught test marketing mature games to children under twelve in the focus groups (FTC 2000). As former U.S. senator Fritz Hollings stated: "Violence sells, and money talks, and no amount of self-regulation and no amount of antitrust exemptions is going to change the profit incentive" (2001). Elements of combat, fighting, and weapons could now be found in 80 per cent of the top twenty games in 2003. More than half of the 3,368 games listed on the ESRB website suitable for those above thirteen have some form of violence in them.

Of the 1,005 games proscribed for teens, 848 had a violence warning – some of it rather gory.

Since the release of Doom, the social encounters found in multiplayer on-line role-play games have matured considerably. Players gain power through fighting, surviving attacks, by trading and accumulating experience points, and by strategically forging social relations – forming alliances, building their forces, pooling and trading resources and weaponry, and sometimes when necessary by betraying friends and followers. The most popular online games like Counterstrike and EverQuest are best described as virtual combat zones in which ranging clans conspire in imperial conflicts over personal power, wealth, and fame. Players who wish their character to survive, need to negotiate their way into, through, and around warring factions in perpetually conflicted landscapes of struggle. Clans face off against opponents in battles to the virtual death. But at stake is the real investment of time spent online building the wealth and power of the virtual warrior character. The loyalty to their clans and guilds, and the sheer amount of time they devote to playing, have led many to mockingly call this game "EverCrack" (Kline 2003). And this time it was the console makers' turn to play catch-up. Microsoft, Sony, and Nintendo have all scrambled to interface their latest consoles with the Internet.

No wonder so many North American parents were becoming confused about their children's embrace of gaming. A national survey of parents in computerized households at the turn of the millennium suggested that American parents were deeply fearful about the Internet's influence on their children. The study shows 78 per cent are concerned that their children might view sexually explicit material, play violent games, or be cyberstalked. Nearly two-thirds of parents (64 per cent) believe computers make their children more isolated, 49 per cent claim that the medium interferes with parents' ability to teach values and beliefs, and 42 per cent believe too much Internet use can cause children to develop anti-social behaviour. At the same time, parents also believe that computers are an essential part of their lives: 59 per cent feel without computer knowledge children are at a disadvantage compared to their peers; 75 per cent say the Internet is a place for children to discover fascinating, useful things; and 72 per cent say the Internet helps their children with their schoolwork (Turow 1999).

PANIC REVISITED

Hardly surprising, then, that panic grew after a bout of schoolyard massacres, notably at Jonesboro and Littleton, which re-agitated this long political struggle over children's access to violent entertainment. Perhaps not coincidentally, Jonesboro was also the place where Dr. Dave Grossman, author of *On Killing* (1995) and a leading critic of media violence, had retired. Grossman had been a lieutenant colonel who had built a career figuring out how to train soldiers to kill. As a retired U.S. army officer, Grossman (1998) seems well positioned to comment on the similarity between the tactics used in the army to train soldiers and the use of violent video games among children today: "children don't naturally kill; they learn it from violence in the home and ... from violence as entertainment in television, movies and interactive video games." The U.S. military has long used simulation training games for its soldiers, he pointed out, because the "repetition and desensitization" of simulated killing affects kill rates (the actual percentage of soldiers that will pull the trigger in real life combat). Like the training of these soldiers, Grossman believes that violent video games may have a similar effect on young people who play them because repeated simulated killings help break down the psychological barriers that prevent killing. Grossman became an advocate for legislation of the video game industries, arguing that "the main concern is that these violent video games are providing military quality training to children." He concludes therefore that America "must reverse the tragic effects of media violence in our culture by taking on its producers and purveyors and passing laws that ban violent video games for children" (Grossman 1998).

In Canada, the last decade saw a steady rise in youth violence and widespread bullying in schools. Shocked by Reena Virk's brutal murder and the school shooting at Taber, the vast majority of Canadian parents favoured passing laws preventing children's access to video and Internet violence. Research that assessed what young Canadians experienced in the digital world have confirmed parents' concerns: Kids spend more time online stealing music than shopping, playing games than doing their homework, and surfing popular fansites than exchanging creative writing or forging political action committees (Media Awareness Network 2001). Of course some kids do use their computers for homework and e-mail – a few even organize global resistance to genetic engineering or Coke. But for the vast majority, digital culture is all about the expansion of entertainment – much of it simulating some form of combat. And that means the gender and class issues that were evident in the early days of gaming have continued to transect gamer culture. While girls chat about boy bands, the lads are busy in racing, sports, and fighting games because they have fast action, cool graphics, and all the latest weapons (Canadian Teachers Federation 2003).

Predictably, British Columbia's social democratic government took the first steps in this direction when a shocked Canadian ex-Vietnam vet asked why his eight-year-old nephew was able to download the gory war imagery of a Soldier of Fortune video game, when the same images would be restricted for sale to children under eighteen, according to the Film Classification Act. Finding no reason to disagree, the film classification board reviewed the game, noting that users assume the identity of John Mullins, an anti-terrorist mercenary who kills and maims animals and humans during a series of escalating missions. The ministry gave the game an X-rating because its depictions of violence against persons and animals are brutal and portrayed realistically and explicitly (Bailey 2000; Bohn 2000; Bronskill 2000; *Prince George Citizen* 2001). Since it was now rated X, the government would have to prosecute any merchants who sold similar games to minors as was proscribed under the Film Classification Act.

To help clarify the uncertain status of this new medium, the B.C. Attorney General drafted specific video game legislation. It was passed into law in 2000, making it illegal for merchants to rent or sell age-inappropriate games. Fearing that this legislation would set a precedent, the ISDA immediately began to lobby the B.C. government, threatening to take the province to court over their right to legislate video games at all. So too, game developer Acclaim launched an appeal of the initial Soldier of Fortune ruling on behalf of the industry. After hearing evidence from both sides, the tribunal decided that their "interactivity" did not exempt this medium from legislation intended to control violent content. What mattered in law was that games were experienced as a stream of violent representations on the screen. And since other forms of screen violence could be regulated under Canadian law, the panel found no reason to exempt video games (or the Internet?) from reasonable standards established for cultural representations that are deemed unsuitable for children. Unfortunately, this act was the last legislation of a government before an election in which it was soundly defeated. Under continual pressure from the gaming industry, especially the retail sector who were most affected by this legislation, the newly elected premier of British Columbia, Gordon Campbell, refused to enforce the Video Game Act, preferring to let the industry regulate itself.

Closing the Circuit

On June 25, 2003, Aaron Hamel was killed and Kimberly Bede wounded when two stepbrothers William and Joshua Buckner shot at their car from an overpass with a .22 rifle. Not so surprising in a country that deals with thousands of slayings every year. But in this case, the boys told investigators they got the rifles from a locked room in their home and decided to randomly shoot at tractor-trailer rigs, *just like in the video game Grand Theft Auto III*. The families of the victims filed a $246-million lawsuit, seeking remedy under Tennessee's consumer protection act, which makes producers liable for the risks associated with their products.

The furor over GTA is only the latest skirmish in the growing debate about violent entertainment industries that seems to pit concerned parents against the video game industry. Pointing out the inappropriateness of the brutal and anti-social content of games like GTA III (where players get to work their way through ghetto crime syndicates), advocacy groups such as the National Institute on Media and the Family called for further regulation of the "graphic depiction of brutal violence" on both moral and psychological grounds (Gamespot 2006). Rallying around this case, lawyers for the ISDA games makers (Rockstar Games) and Sony Computer Entertainment argue again that a video game's content is protected by the First Amendment's free-speech clause of the U.S. Bill of Rights. Given the conservatism of American courts, there appears to be little chance that these cultural standards established for film and television broadcasts will be upheld in America in the near future (Kline 2003).

But what about Canada where the rights of corporate speech must be balanced against constitutional guarantees of peace, order, and good government? On Friday, March 12, 2004, the Liberal Ontario government slapped an "R" rating on the murderous video game Manhunt, which had recently been banned in New Zealand. In April, the Manitoba culture minister Bruce Robinson threatened fines of up to $5,000 to punish retailers who would rent or sell games classified under its proposed legislation to underage customers (Lambert 2005). Round four in this political game of Moral Kombat has begun: Finish him! Most Canadians say. But no one seems to know the "secret" combination of moves.

Bibliography

Battelle, J., and B. Johnstone. 1993. "Seizing the Next Level: Sega's Plans for World Domination." *Wired* (December): 1.6.

Canada. Standing Committee on Communications and Culture. 1993. *Television Violence: Fraying our Social Fabric*. Ottawa: House of Commons. http://www.media-awareness.ca/english/resources/research_documents/ reports/violence/upload/Television-Violence-Fraying-Our-Social-Fabric-Report-pdf.pdf

Canadian Teachers Federation. 2003. Kids Take on the Media. http://www.ctf-fce. ca/en/press/2003/pr03-26.htm

Bailey, Nicole. 2000. Video game distributor launches appeal: The B.C. government says violent games like Soldier of Fortune are equal to porn. *Vancouver Sun.* 11 August, B.5.

Bohn, Glenn. 2000. Senior Mountie warns of video-game peril: The 30-year veteran is asking parents not to give their children violent games this Christmas. *Vancouver Sun,* B.5.

Bronskill, Jim. 2000. Classification; Ministers take aim at videos games. *Windsor Star.* 12 September, A.1.FRO.

Cohen, Stanley. 1972. *Folk Devils and Moral Panics: The Creation of the Mods and Rockers.* London: MacGibbon & Kee.

Cumberbatch, G. 2001. Video Violence: Villain or Victim? Video Standards Council Web site, UK (accessed 2003).

Drotner, Kirsten. 1992. "Modernity and Media Panics." In *Media Cultures: Reappraising Transnational Media,* ed. Michael Skovmand and Kim Christian Schroder, 42–62. London: Routledge.

FTC. 2000. Marketing Violent Entertainment to Children: http://www.ftc.gov/os/2000/09/violencerpttest.htm

Gamespot. 2006. http://uk.gamespot.com/news/6118699.html?sid=6118699

Greenfield, Patricia. 1984. *Mind and Media: The Effects of Television, Video Games and Computers.* Cambridge, MA: Harvard University Press.

Grossman, David. 1995. *On Killing: The Psychological Cost of Learning to Kill in War and Society.* Boston: Back Bay Books.

——. 1998. "Trained to Kill." *Christianity Today,* 10 August.

——. 1999. "We are training our kids to kill." *Saturday Evening Post* 271(5): 54–59.

Haddon, L. 1999. "The Development of Interactive Games." In *The Media Reader: Continuity and Transformation,* ed. Hugh Mackay and Tim O'Sullivan. London: Sage.

Herz, J.C. 1997. *Joystick Nation.* New York: Little Brown & Co.

Hollings, Fritz. 2001. Available: http://www.senate.gov/~hollings, (accessed 21 November 2001).

Jenkins, H. 1999. Professor Jenkins Goes to Washington. 2003, http://web.mit.edu/cms/People/henry3/profjenkins.html

Kent, Stephen. 2001. *The Ultimate History of Video Games.* Roseville, California: Prima Publishing.

Kinder, Marsha. 1991. *Playing with Power in Movies, Television and Video Games.* Berkeley: University of California Press.

Kline, Stephen. 1993. *Out of the Garden: Toys, TV and Children's Culture in the Age of Marketing.* Toronto: Garamond.

——. 2003. Real Fictional Sociality: Agonic relations in on-line gaming communities. http://www2.sfu.ca/media-lab/risk/docs/media-lab/real_fictional_society_kline.pdf

——. 2003. "Media Effects: Redux or Reductive?" *Particip@tions* 1(1): http://www.participations.org/volume%201/issue%201/1_01_kline_reply.htm

Kline, Stephen, and Greig de Peuter. 2002. "Ghosts in the Machine: Video Game Culture." In *Symbolic Childhood,* ed. Daniel Cook, 256–78. New York: Peter Lang.

Kline, Stephen, Nick Dyer-Witheford, and Greig de Peuter. 2003. *Digital Play.* Montreal and Kingston: McGill-Queen's University Press.

Lambert, Lisa. 2005. "Manitoba video game legislation remains in limbo." *Globe and Mail,* 6 January, A9.

Lowenstein, Doug. 2002. "Opening Remarks." Computer and Video Games Come of Age: A national conference to explore the current state of an emerging entertainment medium, at the Program in Comparative Media Studies, Massachusetts Institute of Technology, Cambridge, MA, 10–11 February 2000. http://web.mit.edu/cms/games/opening.html (accessed 21 March 2002).

McLuhan, Marshall. 1995 [1964]. *Understanding Media: The Extensions of Man.* Cambridge, MA: MIT Press.

Media Awareness Network. 2001. http://www.mediawareness.ca/english/resources/special_initiatives/survey_resources/parents_survey/cciaww_parents_k_findings.cfm

Mehrabian, Albert, and Warren Wixen. 1983. "Lights out at the Arcade." *Psychology Today* 17(12): 72–73.

Minow, N.N., and C.L. LaMay. 1995. *Abandoned in the Wasteland: Children, Television, and the First Amendment.* New York: Hill and Wang.

Mitchell, Edna. 1985. The dynamics of family interaction around home video games. *Marriage and Family Review* 8(1–2): 121–35.

Murray, J.P. 2001. "TV violence and children's brains: More reasons for advocacy and policy reform." *The Child, Youth, and Family Services Advocate* 24(2): 1–4.

Myers, D. 1989. "Computer Game Genres." *Play and Culture* 3: 286–301.

NIMH [National Institute of Mental Health]. 1982. *Television and Behavior: Ten Years of Scientific Progress and Implications for the Eighties*: Vol. 1. *Summary Report* (DHHS Publication No. ADM 82-1195). Washington: U.S. Government Printing Office.

Pearce, C. 1997. "Beyond Shoot Your Friends: A Call to Arms in the Battle against Violence." In *Digital Illusion: Entertaining the Future with High Technology,* ed C. Dodsworth, Jr., 209–28. New York: ACM Press.

Postman, Neil. 1982. *The Disappearance of Childhood.* New York: Dell.

Prince George Citizen. 2001. Liberals have authority to restrict video game access: movie board. 22 November, 5.

Prensky, Mark. 2003. Video Games in the US Military. DiaGraLevel Up Conference. Utrecht, Nov. 2003.

Provenzo, Eugene F. Jr. 1991. *Video Kids: Making Sense of Nintendo.* Cambridge, MA: Harvard University Press.

Riesman, David with Nathan Glazer and Reuel Denney. 1961. *The Lonely Crowd.* New Haven, CT: Yale University Press.

Rushkoff, D. 1994. *Media Virus!: Hidden Agendas in Popular Culture*. New York: Ballantine Books.

———. 1997. *Playing the Future: What We Can Learn from Digitalkids*. New York: Riverheadbooks.

Sheff, David. 1993. *Game Over: How Nintendo Zapped an American Industry, Captured Your Dollars, and Enslaved Your Children*. New York: Random House.

Skirrow, Gillian. 1986. "Hellivision: An Analysis of Video Games." In *High Theory/Low Culture*, ed. C. McCabe, 115–42. Manchester, UK: Manchester University Press.

Spigel, Lynn. 1998. "Seducing the Innocent: Childhood and Television in Postwar America." In *The Children's Culture Reader*, ed. H. Jenkins, 110–35. New York: New York University Press.

Stern, Sydney, and Ted Schoenhaus. 1990. *Toyland: The High-Stakes Game of the Toy Industry*. Chicago: Contemporary Books.

Surgeon General's Scientific Advisory Committee on Television and Social Behavior. 1972. *Television and Growing Up: The Impact of Televised Violence* (DHEW Publication No. HSM 72–9086). Washington, DC.

Turow, Joseph. 1999. The Internet and the Family: A View from the Parents and a View from the Press, http://www.annenbergpublicpolicycenter.org/04_info_society/family/

Wardly, Mary. 2001. International Data Corp, "Consumer Software 1999: Worldwide markets and Trends." http://www.idcresearch.com/Press/default.

C: The Struggle for Control

10: Download This! Contesting Digital Rights in a Global Era: The Case of Music Downloading in Canada

GRAHAM LONGFORD

Introduction

On February 10, 2004, the member companies of the Canadian Recording Industry Association (CRIA) filed "John/Jane Doe" lawsuits against twenty-nine Canadians, alleging that the as-yet-unnamed defendants – enthusiastic music file sharers on the Kazaa and iMesh peer-to-peer (P2P) networks – were violating their rights by trading files of copyrighted music over the Internet. Among the plaintiffs in the case were all of the major multinational recording companies operating in Canada, including BMG, EMI, Sony, Universal, Warner, and Virgin. In practical terms, the success of the suits rested on CRIA's ability to obtain the identities of the twenty-nine file sharers from the customer records of their Internet service providers (ISPs), who were unable or unwilling to do so. Decisions by both the Federal Court (April 2004) and the Court of Appeal (May 2005) rejected CRIA's attempts to compel the ISPs to reveal their identities, on the grounds that the evidence presented by CRIA was insufficient to warrant infringement of the defendants' privacy rights in order to allow the suit to proceed. Had the courts found in CRIA's favour, the twenty-nine defendants would have faced damage claims for copyright violation totalling millions of dollars. While a CRIA appeal to the Supreme Court of Canada is unlikely, given the weakness of the evidence in this case, in light of the stakes involved, there is little doubt that it will be back in court as soon as it builds a new and more solid one.

Armed with better evidence, however, CRIA is still far from assured a legal victory against music downloaders. Contrary to popular belief, downloading music for free from the Internet has yet to be declared illegal in Canada. The use of the term "illegal downloading" in common parlance, media reports, and even academic analysis represents a public relations victory for the music industry, but it distorts the unstable and fluid nature of the current legal landscape surrounding the practice. Under current Canadian law, the practice of downloading free music off of the Internet appears to be legal, or at least not illegal. In its April 2004 decision on the CRIA lawsuits, the federal court found, in fact, that the practice was not in violation of Canada's copyright law. While the subsequent Court of Appeal ruling called the lower court's interpretation of copyright law into question, it ruled only on the issue of the defendants' privacy rights and the quality of CRIA's evidence. In addition to the federal court decisions on the CRIA case, a number of recent Supreme Court decisions on copyright have recognized and strengthened the rights of the users of copyrighted material. For example, the Supreme Court of Canada recently ruled unanimously that ISPs are not responsible for paying royalties on copyrighted works shared over their networks and are not bound by federal copyright legislation.

CRIA's members are more likely to find relief in a series of recently proposed amendments to Canada's copyright legislation, which pay special attention to music downloading. Legislative amendments introduced into Parliament in 2005 by the Liberal minority government (Bill C-60), including a new and exclusive "making available" right, would have exposed ISPs and the millions of Canadians who download music to liability for copyright infringement. Had Bill C-60 not died with the defeat of the minority Liberal government in January 2006, it would have opened the floodgates for CRIA to pursue lawsuits against thousands more individuals, similar to a campaign of lawsuits waged against over 16,000 American downloaders, thus far, by the Recording Industry Association of America (RIAA). The ongoing instability of consecutive minority governments has likely only postponed such legislative changes, however. Mounting pressure from the oligopoly of multinational corporate copyright holders in the media and entertainment industries, along with Canada's commitment to align its domestic copyright legislation with the terms of the World Intellectual Property Organization's (WIPO) international copyright treaties (according to which unauthorized downloading is an infringement of copyright), make the criminalization of music file sharing and downloading via any means other than those authorized and/or owned by the music industry itself almost inevitable.

The legal controversy over music downloading in Canada is noteworthy in part because it weaves together all four thematic strands running through this second volume of *How Canadians Communicate*: Americanization, global governance, digital globalization, and corporate concentration. In the hands of users and consumers, new digital technologies like MP3 data compression, the Internet, and P2P networks have endowed music enthusiasts with unprecedented power to access, copy, manipulate, share, and distribute musical works on a global and instantaneous basis, opening up new possibilities for the democratization of musical culture. With popular P2P networks like Kazaa and BitTorrent registering hundreds of millions of users worldwide, it is clear that music fans have embraced such possibilities. Aligned firmly against and dedicated to neutralizing them, however, is an American-led global cartel of increasingly concentrated media and entertainment conglomerates who, backed by national legislatures and institutions of global governance like the WIPO, control the rights to vast swaths of popular music and will stop at nothing in their efforts to wring as much profit from their cultural assets as possible, including sabotaging P2P networks, spying on Internet users, and taking music fans to court. Considering the extent of the practice of downloading and file sharing by Internet users and the aggressive response on the part of media companies and legislators, one can discern the makings of a major struggle over the framework for musical culture. The battle over music downloading and file sharing represents a key skirmish in an even wider struggle over how Canadians communicate in the era of digital globalization, one being played out simultaneously in Canada and abroad, and in other branches of cultural production as well, including publishing, broadcasting, and film.

Contesting Digital Rights

At stake in the music downloading controversy, according to the industry, are the rights of artists and copyright holders to just compensation for their creative works and intellectual property, and the very survival of music itself. Failure to protect copyright, so the argument goes, removes the incentive for artists to innovate and create new works, depriving the rest of society of the fruits of their efforts. Music file sharing and downloading, the industry argues, embody a malignant disregard for ownership and property rights and are tantamount to committing theft. According to past CRIA president Brian Robertson, the file sharers targeted by its lawsuits are "blatant exploiters of artists' careers and their music" whose activities are "killing the music they profess to love" (CRIA 2004a). Figures from the International Federation of the Phonographic Industry (IFPI) suggest that retail sales of CD and cassette sound recordings in Canada have decreased by almost 30 per cent since the late 1990s, representing losses of more than $425 million for the industry thus far (IFPI 2004). IFPI estimates the global damage to the industry inflicted by downloading and other forms of "piracy" to be in the billions of dollars. CRIA also points out that 45,000 people in Canada depend on the industry for their livelihood, either directly or indirectly, and that member companies have been forced to layoff 20 to 25 per cent of their workforces in recent years. Finally, CRIA warns that Canada faces mounting competitive pressures, and the threat of trade sanctions, if it does not bring its copyright laws in line with global and, in particular, U.S. standards for copyright protection. In the face of mounting losses the industry maintains that it has little choice but to act aggressively by using all possible means to discourage and halt the spread of music downloading and other forms of "digital piracy."

Others have suggested, however, that declining sales and financial losses in the industry due to digital "piracy" have been exaggerated. A number of recent studies, including Sutherland and Straw's survey of the Canadian music industry in this volume, cast doubt on the link between music downloading and declining CD sales (FAD Research 2004; Oberholzer, Felix and Koleman Strumpf 2004; and Straw 2003). Other causes seldom acknowledged by the industry include competition from other media forms, including Canadians' growing use of the Internet for entertainment and the rising popularity of DVDs and home theatre systems. A recent and rather illuminating study submitted to the Canadian Radio-Television and Telecommunications Commission (CRTC) by none other than CRIA itself, on an unrelated matter, also undermines the link that the industry has tried to make between free downloading and declining CD sales. Survey data provided to the CRTC by CRIA show that less than one-third of all music on Canadians' computer hard drives originates from P2P networks, that the most prolific downloaders are also the most prolific CD purchasers, and that the three most common reasons offered by consumers for reduced CD purchases were high cost, lack of interest in new releases, and lack of time. The availability of music downloads was cited by a mere 10 per cent of survey respondents as a reason for purchasing fewer CDs (Geist 2006a).

Many commentators have suggested that a more tolerant and balanced approach to the downloading phenomenon is in order, one that respects and accommodates the historically acknowledged rights of users and consumers of cultural artifacts in Canada. As Sheryl Hamilton points out elsewhere in this collection, Canada's copyright regime has long recognized user rights, at least implicitly, and has recently undergone changes to strengthen and enhance them. A number of recent court decisions have attempted to further protect these in the context of new technologies. In the landmark copyright case of 2004, *Law Society of Upper Canada v. CCH Canadian Limited*, the Supreme Court ruled that the Law Society was not liable for copyright infringement merely on the basis that it provided its members with access to photocopy machines in its law library. In the case of music downloading, the Canadian Copyright Board ruled in December 2003 that the practice is protected under Canada's "private copying" regime, which permits individuals to copy protected works for personal use. A levy on the sale of blank media such as CDs, cassette tapes, and, now, MP3 players, is used to compensate copyright holders and artists in exchange for exempting private copying from liability. By emulating the RIAA's legal campaign against downloaders, CRIA's lawsuit violates the spirit of compromise between the rights of creators and users enshrined in this regime. Critics of stronger digital copyright protection argue that, far from defensive actions, industry tactics like the CRIA lawsuits are part of a global campaign being waged by corporate media and entertainment giants to limit legitimate uses of copyrighted works more strictly than they have been under previous regimes of "fair use" and "fair dealing" (which exempt specified uses like private copying from constituting infringement) by narrowing the scope for "non-infringing uses" in order to maximize profits (Lessig 2004; Young 2002).

Critical media and communication scholars, meanwhile, argue that the explosion of downloading and file sharing represents not a threat to music *per se* but, rather, to simply one framework for musical culture – one in which music is treated as a mass-produced and mass-consumed commodity to be bought and sold. The fact that over six million Canadians have already downloaded music for free over the Internet speaks to widespread consumer dissatisfaction with the current framework, which includes forcing consumers to purchase music in "album" formats for $20 per CD, even if they are only interested in one song. Downloading and sharing music files over P2P networks enables new, more participatory practices of consumption and distribution to emerge (Uricchio 2002), along with new forms of identity, communication, and community within online networks of music fans (Ebare 2004; Poblocki 2001). Aggressive industry tactics aimed at preserving the old model by using copyright to bludgeon consumers into compliance threaten to stifle the development of alternative, more collaborative and participatory forms of musical production, distribution, and consumption enabled by technologies like P2P networks, along with the new social networks and communities that emerge as a result of them (Uricchio 2002). Finally, some go so far as to suggest that the real threat to innovation and creativity in music comes not from the "pirating" of copyrighted works but from the privileging of copyright itself, which is about maximizing the rate of return on intellectual property, at the expense of a shared creative and intellectual commons to which all have access (Downes 2002; Lessig 2004).

Recent lawsuits targeting music downloaders and file sharers in Canada and elsewhere are among the latest and most visible in an ongoing battle between music copyright holders and the wider Internet public, which began with the RIAA's high-profile lawsuit against the Napster network in 1999, and which together constitute but one front in a broader global struggle pitting the rights of copyright holders against those of the users and consumers of digital media. At issue in these disputes, among other things, is what additional protection, if any, is necessary for copyright holders in light of new digital technologies? Within the span of a decade, new digital technologies have emerged that furnish millions of consumers with the ability to digitize, reproduce, and distribute a wide range of cultural artifacts with no loss of fidelity in relation to the originals, all at the click of a mouse, thus profoundly altering some of the basic terms and practices of cultural consumption. The increasingly global media and entertainment industries, backed by national legislatures, international law, and institutions of global media governance like the World Intellectual Property Organization (WIPO), argue that digital technologies, such as the Internet, P2P file-sharing networks, and MP3 data compression, pose imminent threats to the ability of copyright holders to control the reproduction and distribution of their works and to receive due compensation from users and consumers of digital content. In addition to suing P2P networks and their users, media conglomerates have responded to this perceived challenge by lobbying for legislation to strengthen and extend the terms of copyright protection and by mounting "public education" campaigns in the media and in schools to stigmatize and discourage practices like downloading and P2P networking among youth.

More is at stake here than the rights of producers and copyright holders to extract profits from their works, however. A balanced approach to copyright recognizes the rights of users and consumers of cultural works to engage in non-infringing practices like private copying. Yet, recent technological as well legal developments harbour the potential to strengthen the hand of copyright holders in relation to the average consumer of digital products. New technologies such as Digital Rights Management (DRM) software, which allows copyrighted works to be kept under digital lock and key, enable producers to exercise tighter control over consumers' access to, and reproduction and distribution of, cultural products than they have done in the past. When embedded in products such as CDs or commercially downloaded music files, DRM software enables copyright holders to strictly limit access to and reproduction of the content. DRM and similar technologies challenge historic rights of access to and use of such artifacts on the part of users and consumers and raise the spectre of a corporate enclosure of the "digital commons."

Historically, legislative protection of copyright in Canada has endeavoured to strike a balance between the rights of producers and consumers, on the grounds that society benefits as much from enabling widespread access to our collective intellectual and creative commons as it does from preventing infringement of copyright. In the current context of globalization and media convergence, the debate over music downloading reflects a tension between competing visions of digital and cultural rights: a commercial one, in which culture is treated as a global commodity the rights to which lie almost exclusively with producers and copyright holders; and another one, in which culture is understood as a public resource for the common good, necessitating robust rights of access to and use thereof on the part of everyone, regardless of ability to pay. The following chapter offers a detailed examination of the conflict over music downloading and file sharing in Canada in light of these competing visions.

Digital Copyright in Canadian, U.S., and International Context

The debate over music downloading can be situated within the context of recent developments in copyright law in Canada, the United States, and internationally. Copyright, which grants creators the exclusive right to reproduce, distribute, perform and display their works for a specified term, has been recognized in domestic Canadian law since 1924, with the enactment of the *Copyright Act*. Despite a host of technological advances affecting cultural production over the course of the twentieth century, significant reforms to Canada's copyright law have only recently been introduced, largely in response to pressure from the U.S. government and media conglomerates to harmonize continental copyright laws, and in order to align Canadian legislation with international law, such as the WIPO copyright treaties. Important legislative changes took effect in 1988, in order to bring Canadian practices in line with the Canada-U.S. Free Trade Agreement. Further amendments were made in the early 1990s to align Canadian law with the North American Free Trade Agreement (NAFTA) and the World Trade Organization (WTO)

Agreement on Trade-Related Aspects of Intellectual Property Rights (TRIPS), but neither dealt explicitly with digital copyright, with the exception of granting copyright protection to computer programs.

A second phase of copyright reform was completed in 1997 with the passage of Bill C-32, which included amendments to establish the compensation system for private copying of recorded music, and new exceptions for educational institutions and libraries to reproduce copyrighted material. The 1997 amendments also included a commitment (s. 92) to review the legal framework for copyright in Canada within five years in light of the new digital technologies beginning to emerge at the time. It was also in 1997 that the government of Canada signed the WIPO treaties, which specifically addressed issues of digital copyright. By signing the treaties, the government committed itself to ensuring that Canadian law does not derogate from their provisions, which include an exclusive right of copyright owners to make works available online, and measures to prevent the circumvention of or tampering with DRM software intended to limit access to digital works. While Canada is a signatory to the WIPO treaties, it has yet to ratify them in Parliament.

Other important developments in copyright law began to unfold in the 1990s, particularly in the United States, as the cultural industries launched an aggressive campaign to assert tighter control over copyrighted material in digital format. Corporate copyright holders convinced the U.S. Congress to extend the duration of copyright from the life-of-the-author-plus-fifty-years to as much as ninety-five years under the *Sonny Bono Copyright Term Extension Act* of 1998. In addition, media and entertainment companies began to develop and embed in their products DRM technologies like encryption and copy protection. Under the leadership of Jack Valenti and the Motion Picture Association of America (MPAA), the film industry introduced its Content Scramble System (CSS) encryption software in 1994, which it encoded onto DVD movie releases thereafter. CSS prevents DVD movies from being played back on any device other than one licensed to decrypt CSS. Within a few years, meanwhile, a consortium of over two hundred music recording and technology companies launched the Secure Digital Music Initiative (SDMI) to develop encryption code to protect copyrighted music in digital form.

Hackers succeeded rapidly in circumventing a number of these DRM tools. The U.S. Congress responded by enacting the *Digital Millennium Copyright Act* (DMCA) in 1998, which, among other things, forbid the creation and distribution of software code designed to circumvent DRM code, thus tipping the balance of power decisively in favour of digital copyright holders. Furthermore, under the DMCA, ISPs are exempt from liability for infringing uses of their networks only so long as they implement "notice and takedown" policies, under which they pledge to remove infringing material and/or suspend the accounts of users engaged in infringing activities upon being notified by the copyright owner. These "intermediary" provisions of the DMCA provided the legal basis for the RIAA's campaigns against P2P networks like Napster and MP3.com. More recently, P2P networks like Kazaa, Grokster, and Morpheus have also come under legal fire. In June 2005, for example, the United States Supreme Court ruled on the *MGM v Grokster* case, finding that P2P networks Grokster and Streamcast were liable for infringing uses of their file-sharing networks. In July of 2006, Kazaa announced a settlement with the music industry in which it agreed to pay $115 million in damages. Meanwhile, state and federal legislatures in the U.S. are considering enacting laws to criminalize anonymous file sharers and the P2P networks that "induce" copyright infringement.

It was within this context of international and U.S. copyright law reform, which has strengthened the hand of copyright holders at the expense of users' rights, and of the proliferation of new digital technologies, that the government of Canada embarked on a third phase of copyright reform in 2001 specifically aimed at addressing digital copyright issues. After releasing both a consultation paper and the mandatory s. 92 report, the government solicited public input, receiving submissions from over seven hundred groups and individuals. Responsibility for crafting proposals for digital copyright reform fell to Parliament's Standing Committee on Canadian Heritage. After a series of committee hearings and consultations, the Committee released its *Interim Report on Copyright Reform* in May 2004 (Canada 2004). The controversial report, issued in the immediate aftermath of the Federal Court's decision on the CRIA lawsuit, clearly reflected the views of copyright holders and content producers who appeared before the Committee, (including CRIA), and called upon the government to ratify the WIPO copyright treaties immediately, review the private copying regime, and enact new copyright legislation emulating the DMCA, complete with provisions for ISP liability for infringing uses of their networks (Canada 2004). The Heritage Committee's recommendations received the blessing of the Heritage Minister at the time, Hélène Scherrer, who singled out music downloading in her remarks about the copyright reform process: "we are going to make sure that downloading stays illegal [*sic*]," the Minister declared in April 2004, "[w]e will make it a priority so it is done as quickly as possible" (CBC News Online 2004). But the industry and the government are up against more than a few hackers, P2P enthusiasts, and hardcore music fans; efforts to combat downloading and file sharing fly in the face of these increasingly widespread practices in which millions of Internet users now engage on a routine basis. To appreciate the scale of the shift in popular habits and practices of cultural consumption that digital and network technologies have enabled, let us look at the growth of music file sharing in Canada and elsewhere in recent years.

Rip, Mix, Burn: We're All "Pirates" Now

If, to paraphrase McLuhan, the printing press made us all readers, then the Internet has made us all "pirates." The music industry's campaign to vilify, marginalize, and criminalize "music piracy" flies in the face of common practices widespread among Internet users in Canada and abroad. According to one Ipsos survey, 47 per cent of adult Internet users in Canada downloaded at least one music file in 2002 (Ipsos 2004). This translates into six million Canadians! In a poll released by CRIA in April of 2004, 26 per cent of respondents admitted to using the file-sharing software Kazaa alone (CRIA 2004c). According to CRIA estimates, Canadian Kazaa users download as many as 180 million files per month. Sales figures for commercial download sites pale by comparison, with sites like *Puretracks* reporting 2.5 million downloads per month. File sharing is a particularly widespread and popular practice among Canadian youth, over 60 per cent of whom download MP3s and 30 per cent of whom download movies. 57 per cent of Canadian youth identify playing and downloading music over the Internet as their favourite online activity (Media Awareness Network 2004).

Recent figures reveal a similar pattern of widespread downloading and file sharing by American Internet users, and a high degree of acceptance of the practice as a legitimate one. The Pew Internet and American Life Project reports that by the spring of 2003, an estimated 35 million American adults had downloaded music from the Internet, while 26 million of these also shared files online (Pew Internet and American Life Project 2003). Two-thirds of this group said they did not care whether the files contained copyrighted works or not. Finally, an indication of the global dimensions of downloading and file sharing is provided by the fact that Kazaa, one of the world's most popular file-sharing software products, has been downloaded over 390 million times (Kazaa.com).

In light of such figures, one is struck by the gap between what the corporate media and many legislators deem acceptable, responsible, and legal uses of digital media versus the everyday habits and practices of Internet users. The industry-led war on "music piracy" is not a battle against some marginal group of Internet users but, rather, constitutes a war on popular, everyday practices and attitudes embraced by hundreds of millions of Internet users worldwide, and which speak to a popular urge to appropriate the new media in ways which challenge the traditional commercial model of producing, distributing and consuming cultural material.

Kazaa Nation? Culture and Community in the Era of P2P Networks

While dismissed by industry as the product of moral laxity and a growing disregard for ownership, intellectual property, and the value of music, critical media scholars have read the popular embrace of downloading and P2P networking quite differently – as indicative of a significant evolution of culture, consumption, and community in the digital age. Viewed in historical context, such activities can be seen as the most recent iteration of the turn to a more "participatory culture" (Jenkins 1992) rooted in the nineteenth century, one in which new technologies in the hands of consumers, ranging from the camera and the radio to the audio tape recorder and digital video camera, have blurred the distinction between producers and consumers of cultural content (Uricchio 2002, 5–6; Ebare 2004). Just as previous technologies have done, digital technologies have helped to diffuse, decentralize, and de-hierarchize the means of cultural production, distribution, and consumption by, for example, increasing access to studio-quality recording technology or enabling downloaders to assemble their own customized MP3 playlists of favourite artists and songs. From this perspective, downloading and file sharing (of images, movies, text, and software, as well as music) constitute the typical activities and practices of an emerging digital culture, which can itself be contextualized within a broader participatory turn in culture stemming back many decades. It goes without saying, however, that these participatory moments have appeared simultaneously with countervailing developments in the political economy of media and communications – globalization, privatization, and convergence – in which efforts to centralize control over and further commodify culture have been intensified (McChesney 1999; Mosco and Schiller 2001).

Music downloading and file sharing have also been the focus of sociological studies of online music communities. Without romanticizing the nature of online music communities, many studies have attributed at least some significance to them as new virtual places where music fans gather, produce, and exchange cultural goods, communicate with and educate one another, and express and affirm their identities (Ebare 2004; Poblocki 2001; Uricchio 2002).

Viewed in such light, the battle over downloading and file sharing is much larger than that between CRIA and a handful of downloaders. It constitutes but one skirmish in a broader struggle between what Uricchio describes as two very different conceptions and enactments of cultural citizenship: on the one hand, the traditional capitalist model in which culture is defined as a commodity; and on the other hand, an emerging paradigm of cultural participation in which musical culture is produced and enjoyed in a more collaborative, decentralized, and dehierarchized fashion "outside the framework of commodification" (Uricchio 2002, 19). Now, given that the phenomenon of music downloading and file sharing is predicated on the purchase and use of new consumer technologies like personal computers and iPods, it appears that those who participate in the new paradigm Uricchio describes do so with one foot still planted in the old commodity paradigm.

Download This! Configuring the User as Consumer

The music recording industry has sensed the implications of the tectonic shift in consumer habits and attitudes for some time, and has adopted a variety of strategies and tactics aimed at inducing, disciplining and, if necessary, coercing music audiences into compliance with its own interpretation of its members' rights. The industry strategy has involved a variety of technological, ideological, legislative, and legal measures designed to defend and inculcate a code of "responsible" digital and cultural citizenship aligned with its commercial interests.

Prior to launching its legal campaign against file sharers, the recording industry initiated a number of programs designed to dampen Canadians' enthusiasm for downloading. Initially, the industry adopted a number of technological measures to prevent or reduce the incidence of CD copying and uploading by embedding copy protection software in its products. DRM technologies impose control over the use and distribution of digital music by restricting the making of copies or limiting the kinds of devices on which CDs can be played. Tens of millions of copy-protected CDs have been sold in Canada and the U.S. since the major labels adopted the technology (Iverson 2002). In addition to severely restricting the use that consumers can make of their purchases, DRM software can be designed to spy on consumers by examining the contents of their computer hard drives for unauthorized versions of the copyright-holder's music. Copy protection software can also damage computers and render them vulnerable to viruses and other malicious software. In the most notorious case thus far, Sony-BMG released millions of CDs in 2005 encoded with its new Extended Copy Protection (XCP) DRM software, which was designed to prevent CDs from being copied into MP3 format for playback on iPods (Geist 2006b). XCP was subsequently shown to open up security holes in Windows-based PCs that rendered them vulnerable to viruses and worms. Sony-BMG has since recalled the CDs, which were distributed in over one hundred countries, and has offered to compensate affected consumers. The XCP fiasco has prompted class-action lawsuits in the U.S. and Canada, and earned Sony-BMG rebukes from politicians.

The recording industry has also used more clandestine technological measures in its battle with downloaders and file sharers. CRIA and its members have used the services of Internet security firms, such as U.S.-based Media-Sentry, to monitor Canadian users of popular file-sharing networks and to identify the most enthusiastic file sharers. MediaSentry advertises a number of "anti-piracy solutions" on its web site, including MediaSentry and Media-Decoy. MediaSentry software patrols over twenty-five popular peer-to-peer networks for copyright infringements and captures information on users such as usernames and IP addresses, while Media Decoy attempts to deter file sharing and downloading by, in the company's own words, "overwhelming file trading communities with non-working versions of [...] copyrighted material" (MediaSentry 2004). While CRIA has not admitted to deploying the latter technology, a MediaSentry witness in the CRIA case testified that inoperative decoy files of the plaintiffs' songs may have been downloaded by the defendants. In any event, use of such Internet vigilante services has been endorsed by major players in the industry (MTV News 2003).

CRIA also launched a number of "education programs" designed to inculcate certain attitudes and habits of digital citizenship within music consumers, in particular to normalize the commodity form in digital music consumption and stigmatize emerging practices like file sharing. A 'Value of Music' campaign explaining the economics of the music industry was launched in early 2003, consisting of public service announcements, point of sale materials, and CD inserts aimed primarily at the youth market. CRIA also shipped 10,000 videos, complete with curriculum materials and lesson plans, for use in music education programs in schools across the country. The 'Keep Music Coming' campaign was launched later in 2003 and was targeted specifically at parents. The campaign featured a web site and television ads "designed to inform parents of what their children might be unwittingly exposed to on illegal file-sharing sites" (CRIA 2003a). A 30-second TV ad called "Virus" highlighted the alleged dangers and consequences of downloading viruses, porn, and spyware from P2P networks. The ads were timed to coincide with the launch of the industry's first "legitimate" paid download service, *PureTracks*. *PureTracks* advertises itself as being free of the nuisances, such as viruses and corrupted files, allegedly typical of the popular P2P networks (which in many instances the industry itself was responsible for introducing!). CRIA also took advantage of other features of P2P networks such as Instant Messaging, which it used to scold and threaten network users via targeted messages (CRIA 2003b).

CRIA in the Courtroom

CRIA began to take a harder line against music file sharing and downloading when it contracted the services of MediaSentry in the fall of 2004 to conduct surveillance and research on users of Kazaa and iMesh, in preparation for potential lawsuits against individual file sharers. On December 4, 2004, CRIA fired a warning shot across the bow of Canadian file sharers with the following statement:

CRIA has invested in excess of one million dollars to date in an effort to educate young people on the issues of internet piracy and we will continue to do so. For the hardcore group, however, it appears that education has and will not make any impression. They are killing the music they profess to love. They should be aware that they may face legal consequences for their actions. (CRIA 2003c)

Two months later, CRIA and its member companies made good on this threat by initiating legal action against twenty-nine file sharers identified by usernames and IP address collected by MediaSentry. The Statement of Claim filed in court by the plaintiffs alleged that the defendants infringed their copyrights by possessing and distributing copies of sound recordings in a manner prejudicial to the plaintiffs' rights and interests as the copyright holders. The claim went on to allege that the defendants had shared over a thousand copyrighted songs each over P2P networks, and that the plaintiffs had suffered "extensive damages" valued at up to $750,000 per defendant as a result. CRIA claimed to be taking action in order to recover damages and, more importantly, "to deter other infringements" (CRIA 2004b).

A subsequent motion was also filed calling on the court to order the ISPs to produce the names and contact information of the unnamed defendants, so that the lawsuit could proceed. The ISPs involved included the following (number of affected customers in brackets): Bell Sympatico (7); Rogers (9); Shaw (8); Telus (3); and Videotron (2). With the exception of Videotron, all of the ISPs resisted CRIA's motion, citing both technical obstacles to matching MediaSentry's data to their own records, and concerns over infringing on the privacy rights of their customers.

A public interest advocacy group, the Canadian Internet Policy and Public Interest Clinic (CIPPIC), was also granted intervener status by the court.

Citing the December 2003 Canadian Copyright Board ruling on downloading, CIPPIC argued that the defendants' activities were protected under Canada's private copying regime, which has already accumulated over $120 million in levies to be distributed to artists and copyright holders. In addition, CIPPIC argued that CRIA's evidence was not sufficiently compelling to warrant abridging the privacy rights of the ISP subscribers (who, CIPPIC also pointed out, could not be assumed to be identical to the actual file sharers, since any one computer may have multiple users) (CIPPIC 2004).

The presiding judge, Justice von Finckenstein, issued a decision on March 31, 2004. The court rejected CRIA's claims, largely due to lack of evidence. According to the Justice's decision, the evidence provided by CRIA was insufficient to establish that the copyrighted songs in question had been downloaded and knowingly distributed to others by the defendants, pointing out that many P2P programs are set to share files by default unbeknownst to unsophisticated users, thus undermining claims of wilful infringement and financial damage. Ironically, the possibility that the defendants might have shared bogus files planted by MediaSentry at CRIA's request, as opposed to the genuine copyrighted versions, weakened CRIA's case. In addition, the court ruled that CRIA failed to convincingly link the identities of the P2P usernames to the IP addresses attached to them. The court went on to rule that downloading and P2P networking in and of themselves did not constitute infringement:

The mere fact of placing a copy on a shared directory in a computer where that copy can be accessed via a P2P service does not amount to distribution. Before it constitutes distribution, there must be a positive act by the owner of the shared directory, such as sending out the copies or advertising that they are available for copying. No such evidence was presented by the plaintiffs in this case. (Federal Court of Canada 2004, 15)

Finckenstein's controversial decision sent shockwaves through the copyright community both in Canada and abroad, and earned Canada special mention on the U.S. Trade Representative's 2005 "Watch List" of jurisdictions deemed insufficiently vigilant about protecting intellectual property rights.

CRIA's lawsuit strategy suffered another blow when its appeal of Finckenstein's decision was rejected by the Federal Court of Appeal in May 2005. The appellate court concurred with the lower court's finding that CRIA's evidence was too weak to justify a court order for the ISPs to release their customer records. While the higher court questioned Finckenstein's interpretation of copyright law, it also made no findings on the issue of the alleged infringements (Federal Court of Appeal 2005, 27). However, by laying out in detail what tests would need to be met in order for the CRIA lawsuits to proceed, the Court of Appeal left the door open to future legal action (Dixon and Blackwell 2005).

While CRIA has failed to garner much support for its claims in the Canadian judicial system, it has received a much more sympathetic hearing among federal legislators, who have been reviewing Canada's copyright legislation since 2002, with particular attention being paid to the impact of new technologies. In its May 2004 *Interim Report on Copyright Reform* the federal Standing Committee on Canadian Heritage, chaired by Liberal MP Sarmite Bulte, recommended a series of legislative amendments that may as well have been written by CRIA, including ratification of the WIPO copyright treaties, ISP liability for infringing uses of their services, and DMCA-like sanctions against the manufacture, sale, and use of DRM circumvention software. Many of the *Interim Report's* recommendations found their way into Bill C-60, *An Act to Amend the Copyright Act*, introduced into the Liberal minority parliament in June 2005. Bill C-60 also proposed a new right of "making available," by which copyright holders would enjoy exclusive rights to distribute and make their works available over the Internet, thus transforming the act of having music files available to others on one's hard drive into an act of copyright infringement. In the dying days of the Liberal minority government, Bulte's hard work on behalf of what critics have labelled the "copyright cartel" was rewarded with a $250 per plate fundraising dinner hosted by none other than CRIA President, Graham Henderson (CBC News 2006). While Bill C-60 died on the order paper with the collapse of the Liberal government, many of its provisions will most likely be revived by Stephen Harper's Conservative government, should it decide to act in this area.

In truth, whether CRIA is ultimately victorious in the courts is really beside the point. The true objective of the lawsuits was not so much to recover alleged damages as it was to dampen Internet users' enthusiasm for file sharing in general, and to discipline them into using commercial download services like *PureTracks*. As CRIA lawyer Richard Pfohl puts it: "Our hope is that people in Canada will get the message and that we won't have to engage in litigation" (Dixon and Blackwell 2005). In this respect, CRIA's campaign appears to have had at least a moderate impact. A recent survey found that the number of Canadian adults downloading music for free had dropped from 47 per cent in 2002 to 32 per cent in May 2004 (Ipsos 2004). Industry efforts to domesticate the downloading phenomenon are paying off, as more and more consumers are also turning to paid download sites. Canada's *PureTracks*, which was launched in October 2003, now reports over 2 million downloads per month. A similar story is unfolding globally. IFPI recently reported that more than 200 million tracks were downloaded from commercial sites in 2004, up from just 20 million in 2003, and that the number of such sites had risen to 230 from 50 the previous year (CRIA 2005). In the U.S., the percentage of Internet users downloading music dropped by half, from 29 to 14 per cent, between April 2003 and January 2004. The percentage of those who shared files of any kind declined from 28 to 20 in the same period. At the same time, the percentage of Internet users running P2P applications like Kazaa and Grokster on their computers dropped anywhere between 15 and 59 per cent depending on the service used (Pew Internet and American Life Project 2004). There is controversy, however, over whether file-sharing activities have declined overall, or simply migrated to more clandestine, underground sites.

If reflective of a genuine consumer withdrawal from practices like downloading and file sharing, such figures give pause for reflection on what may be lost in the process. Aggressive legal and ideological campaigns aimed at stigmatizing and penalizing P2P networks and file sharers risks stifling the innovative, more participatory and collaborative forms of musical culture they enable, and that music audiences clearly demand. Also at risk are the aforementioned online forms of expression and community that have accompanied them.

Future Directions

Despite CRIA's recent defeats in the courts, it is unlikely that the status quo will remain in place much longer. With clear guidance from the Court of Appeal on how to proceed with future lawsuits, CRIA is likely to launch a new round of legal action against music file sharers soon. The number of suits launched by RIAA, after all, recently topped 16,000. Should Parliament ratify the WIPO treaties and follow through with promised changes to the *Copyright Act*, including the creation of an exclusive "making available" right for copyright holders, the field for non-infringing uses of digital music content will be dramatically narrowed for users and consumers. Other scenarios more tolerant and respectful of users rights are possible, if somewhat unlikely. One option would be to adjust Canada's relatively permissive private copying regime and system of levies on blank media to better reflect and offset consumer practices, through such mechanisms as the levy on MP3 players introduced in 2003. Another potential solution would be for ISPs to collect a small levy for broadband service that would then be distributed amongst the recording companies and copyright holders, along the lines of the private copying regime. Such schemes have their drawbacks, as critics have pointed out, including the effect of imposing blanket fees on all consumers of blank media and broadband service regardless of whether they engage in downloading, copying, and file-sharing activities or not. CIPPIC has suggested a form of voluntary collective licensing, whereby recording companies would form collecting societies to which P2P users would pay a reasonable subscription fee in exchange for unrestricted access to online song collections. In the current climate of intolerance on the part of copyright holders and legislators here and abroad, however, odds are against such reasonable compromises.

Conclusion

The recent lawsuits launched against music file sharers and downloaders in Canada and the U.S. represent a major shift in industry tactics from just a few years ago, since they target individual consumers of digital music content, where previous industry efforts had been focused primarily on the file-sharing networks which facilitate the downloading and trading of files. Targeting individual consumers in this way carries a certain degree of risk, since it may alienate music audiences. But the industry sees itself as fighting for survival, for the sustainability of its own business model for the commercial music industry. The future of that model depends, among other things, on cultivating disciplined *consumers* of digital music habituated to paying for commercial music online. The industry's effort to cultivate willing online consumers of music involves a multifaceted program designed to adjust the habits, practices, and attitudes of the millions of Internet users who currently download and share music files for free. It is within the context of this broader, global campaign led by RIAA and IFPI that the lawsuits by CRIA are best understood, one involving measures of both persuasion and coercion. The legal battle over downloading and file sharing is an important one. When one considers the extent to which the practices of downloading and file sharing have been adopted by Internet users, the potential cultural importance of these new forms of consumption and distribution, and the aggressive response to them on the part of media companies and legislators, one can discern a major societal and cultural struggle over the framework for musical culture. Indeed, the battle over music downloading and file sharing represents an important skirmish in a broader struggle to determine how Canadians communicate in the context of digital globalization, one being played out on an international scale and in all other branches of cultural production, such as publishing, broadcasting, and film.

Acknowledgments

Generous financial assistance and a collegial atmosphere in which to research and write portions of this paper were provided by a Canada Research Chair Postdoctoral Research Fellowship in 2003–2004, made possible by Dr. Engin Isin, Canada Research Chair in Citizenship Studies, York University. Additional support was also provided in 2004–2006 through a Postdoctoral Research Fellowship in Community Informatics at the University of Toronto, attached to the Canadian Research Alliance for Community Innovation and Networking (CRACIN) and funded through a Social Sciences and Humanities Research Council Initiative on the New Economy (INE) grant. I am grateful to Dr. Andrew Clement of the University of Toronto's Faculty of Information Studies for this support.

Bibliography

Canada. 2004. *Interim Report on Copyright Reform.* Report of the Standing Committee on Canadian Heritage, House of Commons, May, http://www.parl.gc.ca/InfocomDoc/Documents/37/3/parlbus/commbus/house/reports/herirp01-e.htm (accessed 2 September 2004).

CIPPIC. 2004. *Memorandum of Argument of the Intervener Canadian Internet Policy and Public Interest Clinic (CIPPIC),* in the matter of BMG *Canada Inc. et al. v. John Doe et al.* Federal Court – Trial Division, Court File No. T-292-04, March 15.

CBC News. 2006. "Liberal MP takes flak for fundraiser by copyright lobbyists." 6 January, http://www.cbc.ca/story/canadavotes2006/national/2006/01/06/elxn-bulte-fundraiser.html.

CBC News Online. 2004. "Scherrer vows to crack down on file sharers." 13 April, http://www.cbc.ca/arts/stories/scherrer20040413 (accessed 2 September 2004).

CRIA. 2003a. "Background: Chronology of Canadian recording industry's educational campaign." http://www.cria.ca/news/cria2_13feb04.htm (accessed 9 September 2004).

———. 2003b. "Canadian record industry initiates second phase of education program with users of file-sharing services." 14 August, http://www.cria.ca/news/140803_n.php.

———. 2003c. "The Canadian recording industry supports industry action in the US." CRIA press release, 4 December, http://www.cria.ca/news/041203a_n.php (accessed 25 May 2005).

———. 2004a. "Canadian recording industry takes next step in lawsuits against music pirates." CRIA press release, 13 February, http://www.cria.ca/news/130204_n.php (accessed 25 May 2005).

——. 2004b. Statement of Claim, BMG *et al. v. John Doe et al.*, Federal Court of Canada, 10 February, Court File No. T-292-04.

——. 2004c. "New industry study shows downloading and burning discourages music sales." CRIA press release, July 6, http://www.cria.ca/news/ cria_06jul04.htm (accessed 3 September 2004).

——. 2005. "Legal downloading on the rise in Canada, but file-swapping still a problem." CRIA press release, 19 January, http://www.cria.ca/news/ 190105_n.php (accessed 25 May 2005).

Dixon, Guy, and Richard Blackwell. 2005. "Federal court allows file-sharing, for now." *Globe and Mail*, 20 May.

Downes, Daniel M. 2002. "Intellectual Property and Copyright Issues in the Global Economy." In *Mediascapes: New Patterns in Canadian Communication*, eds. Paul Attallah and Leslie Regan Shade, 343–59. Toronto: Thomson Nelson.

Ebare, Sean. 2004. "Digital music and subculture: Sharing files, sharing styles." *First Monday* 9(2), http://firstmonday.org/issues/issue9_2/ebare/index.html (accessed 15 June 2004).

FAD Research. 2004. "The Changing Face of Music Delivery: The Effects of Digital technologies on the Music Industry." Prepared for the Department of Canadian Heritage, Sound Recording Policy and Programs Secretariat, 31 March, 16–19, http://www.pch.gc.ca/pc-ch/pubs/effects/music_delivery_e.pdf (accessed 19 September 2004).

Federal Court of Appeal. 2005. BMG *et al. v. John Doe et al.*, Ruling, 19 May 2005.

Federal Court of Canada. 2004. BMG *et al. v. John Doe et al.*, Reasons for Order and Order, Justice Finckenstein, 31 March, Court File No. T-292-04.

Geist, Michael. 2006a. "CRIA's Own Study Counters P2P Claims." http://michaelgeist.ca/index.php?option=com_content&task=view&id=1168 &Itemid=85.

——. 2006b. "Rootkit fiasco shows sterner laws needed." *Toronto Star*, 2 January, http://www.thestar.com/NASApp/cs/ContentServer?pagename=thestar/ Layout/Article_Type1&c=Article&cid=1136155809237&call_pageid=9683500 72197&col=969048863851.

IFPI. 2004. "Fact Sheet – Statistics On Internet Piracy Canada." 30 March, http://www.ifpi.org/site-content/press/20040330d.html (accessed 8 September 2004).

——. 2004. "Global music sales fall by 7.6% in 2003 – some positive signs in 2004." 7 April, http://www.ifpi.org/site-content/statistics/worldsales.html (accessed 9 September 2004).

Ipsos. 2004. "MP3 Downloading by Canadians on the Decrease: Fear of Legal Actions Curbing Download Enthusiasm." Ipsos press release, 11 May, http://www.ipsos-na.com/news/pressrelease.cfm?id=2229 (accessed 2 September 2004).

Iverson, Jon. 2002. "A Universal CD Problem?" 10 February, http://www.stereo-phile.com/news/11261/index.html (accessed 8 September 2004).

Jenkins, Henry. 1992. *Textual Poachers: Television Fans and Participatory Culture.*
New York: Routledge.

Lessig, Lawrence. 2004. *Free Culture: How Big Media Uses Technology and the Law
to Lock Down Culture and Control Creativity.* New York: Penguin.

McChesney, Robert W. 1999. *Rich Media, Poor Democracy: Communication Politics
in Dubious Times.* New York: New Press.

Media Awareness Network. 2004. "Statistics on Canadian Youth and File-Sharing."
http://www.media-awareness.ca/english/resources/special_initiatives/
wa_resources/wa_shared/backgrounders/statistics_youth_filesharing.cfm
(accessed 3 September 2004).

MediaSentry. 2004. "Solutions Overview." http://www.mediasentry.com/services/
(accessed 8 September 2004).

Mosco, Vincent, and Dan Schiller, eds. 2001. *Continental Order?: Integrating
North America for Cybercapitalism.* Lanham, MD: Rowman and Littlefield,
2001.

MTV News. 2003. "Digital Decoys Are Making Frustrated Pirates Say 'Arrr,'"
http://www.mtv.com/news/articles/1470464/20030310/
linkin_park.jhtml?headlines (accessed 9 September 2003).

Oberholzer, Felix, and Koleman Strumpf. 2004. "The Effect of File Sharing on
Record Sales: An Empirical Analysis." March, http://www.unc.edu/~cigar/
papers/FileSharing_March2004.pdf (accessed: 12 September 2004).

Office of the U.S. Trade Representative. 2005. *2005 Special 301 Report,*
http://www.ustr.gov/Document_Library/Reports_Publications/2005/
2005_Special_301/Section_Index.html.

Pew Internet and American Life Project. 2003. "Data Memo: Music Downloading,
File-sharing and Copyright." http://www.pewinternet.org/pdfs/
PIP_Copyright_Memo.pdf (accessed September 3, 2004).

———. 2004. "The impact of recording industry suits against music file-swappers."
Data Memo, January, http://www.pewinternet.org/pdfs/
PIP_File_Swapping_Memo_0104.pdf (accessed 19 September 2004).

Poblocki, Kacper. 2001. "The Napster Network Community." *First Monday* 6(11),
http://firstmonday.org/issues/issue6_11/poblocki/index.html (accessed
15 June 2001).

RIAA. 2003. "Issues: Anti-Piracy." http://www.riaa.com/issues/piracy/default.asp
(accessed 2 September 2001).

Reddick, Andrew, and Vanda Rideout. 2001. "Multimedia Policy for Canada and the
United States: Industrial Development as Public Interest." In *Continental
Order?: Integrating North America for Cybercapitalism,* ed. V. Mosco and
D. Schiller. Lanham, MD: Rowman and Littlefield.

Straw, Will. 2003. "No Future?: The Canadian Music Industries." In *How
Canadians Communicate,* ed. D. Taras, F. Pannekoek, and M. Bakardjieva,
203–21. Calgary: University of Calgary Press.

Uricchio, William. 2002. "Cultural Citizenship in the Age of P2P Networks." Paper presented to Modinet: Inaugural Conference, University of Copenhagen, Copenhagen, Denmark, 6 September, http://www.hum.ku.dk/modinet/ (accessed 6 September 2002).

Young, Jason. 2002. *Digital Copyright Reform in Canada: Reflections on WIPO and the DMCA*, http://www.lexinformatica.org/dox/digitalcopyright.pdf (accessed 31 August 2002).

11: Now It's Personal: Copyright Issues in Canada

SHERYL N. HAMILTON

In a simultaneously local and global cultural economy where information technologies are reinventing both our practices and products of communication, intellectual property in general, and copyrights in particular, have emerged as a key site of cultural contestation. In other words, how Canadians communicate is increasingly structured, regulated, managed, and shaped by our myriad encounters with copyright law. Further, while since its inception in Canada copyright has always been a matter of simultaneously national jurisdiction and international relations, changes in the global communications arena in the last decade are pressuring Canada to change as never before. Once an area of law primarily of concern to cultural producers and distributors only, copyright has emerged in Canada and around the world as a locus for debates about digital technologies, creators' rights, theft and piracy, the public interest, global information economies, access to information, and privacy rights. Yet, at the same time, in many ways, none of these issues is new to the Internet era. Each emergent medium of reproduction is accompanied by a flurry of conflict, negotiation, and adjustments. What is new, however, is the range and scope of players interested in participating in the debate and the global nature of that conversation.

On March 27, 1919, the Honourable George G. Foster noted in the Canadian Senate, "I want to impress upon honourable gentlemen who are not lawyers the fact that the question of copyright is of importance not only to lawyers, but to many people in this country" (in Harris 1995, 1). In the intervening years between Canada's first *Copyright Act* in 1924 and the 1990s, one might have quibbled with Foster's comments; however, in recent years, as legal scholar Michael Geist aptly argues,

This new reality is spearheading a profound change in the world of copyright as the widespread realization that copyright matters grows. No longer an issue best left to lawyers, individuals are taking an interest in copyright policy as never before. This leaves policy makers with the challenge of balancing competing stakeholder interests in an environment where everyone believes that they too are stakeholders. (Geist 2003, D02)

Indeed, intellectual property issues, particularly those around copyright, form a part of our communicative consciousness more than perhaps at any other point in our history.

This increased interest on the part of ordinary Canadians became painfully clear to the federal government during the "Lucy Maud Montgomery affair." In May 2003, the federal government proposed the seemingly innocuous Bill C-36, legislation to combine the National Library and Archives. However, included in the legislation was a proposed amendment to the *Copyright Act* to provide a copyright term extension of fourteen years for Canadian authors who had died between 1930 and 1950 with unpublished work of commercial interest. This amendment was dubbed "the Lucy Maud Montgomery Copyright Amendment Act," given that it appeared to have been suggested solely in order to provide the heirs of the author of the Anne of Green Gables books with the ability to exploit some previously unpublished, and potentially valuable, diaries and letters.[1] The copyright in these materials was about to expire on January 1, 2004. The amendment bore a striking resemblance to its broader American counterpart, affectionately dubbed the "Sonny Bono Copyright Extension Act," which extended copyright protection in the United States from fifty to seventy years after the life of the author. The amendment, while championed by Bono, was lobbied for heavily by Disney Corporation, which, not coincidentally, was about to lose some of its rights in its very valuable commodity rodent, Mickey Mouse.

In the Canadian extension, other dead persons of note whose works would have been affected included R.B. Bennett, Sir Robert Borden, Sir Wilfrid Laurier, Stephen Leacock, and Archibald Stansfeld Belany, better known as Grey Owl. The Canadian government clearly did not anticipate the public furor that would result from its actions. Historians, archivists, copyright activists, and outraged members of the public spoke up. Critics feared the

Americanization that David Taras outlines in the Introduction to this volume, accusing the government of trying to slip in, through the back door, American-style copyright extensions, without public consultation or proper debate. The parliamentary committee reviewing the Bill agreed to remove the offending provisions just prior to the summer recess. The provisions were then re-inserted for debate in September. Given the public outcry, the extension was eventually shortened to two years in the final bill, but did not ultimately pass Senate before Parliament was prorogued. Bill C-8 was subsequently passed, but without any mention of copyright extension. By that point, there was no longer any need for the extension; Montgomery's letters and diaries had entered into the public domain. While not resulting in legislative change, the events were an interesting gauge of the public interest in, and temperament for, contesting copyright issues.

Ironically, this new engagement by segments of the Canadian public and the overall increase in awareness of copyright issues, an element in the participatory culture that Graham Longford addresses in the previous chapter, comes at a time when the Copyright Policy Branch has suggested that there is a problem with "declining respect for and awareness of copyright in the current environment" (Canadian Heritage, 2004). To address this perceived deficiency, the Branch has commissioned a feasibility study for an awareness campaign and has met with stakeholders about how to better educate Canadians on copyright issues. Arguably the government's concern is not that individuals are unaware of copyright and copyright issues, but rather that they are acting from the perspective of their own personal interests, not from that advocated by the Canadian state. From Anne of Green Gables, to music downloading across borders, markets, and jurisdictions, to the domestic copyright reform process following international pressure, Canadians are in fact becoming interested in, and mobilized around, copyright issues as never before. And it is the courts in Canada, in particular, which are defining and defending the cultural space for that engagement. As mere consumers morph into users and creators through the heady combination of computers, networks, software, knowledge, and increased awareness, copyright is now relevant to how we communicate as never before. Now it's personal.

A Field in Flux

This reinvigorated energy around, and interest in, copyright emerges at the intersection of a number of competing sociocultural forces that combine to render intellectual property a field of uncertainty and fluidity. First, we see an increasing reconfiguration of elements of the cultural commons into personal property, or their "propertization" (Rose 2003). Characters become property through trademarks; animals and plants become property through patents, as do human genetic sequences and gene pools; distinctive gestures, body parts, mannerisms, phrases, and voices become property through publicity law; databases of our personal data become the property of the compiler through copyright; stars pursue cyber-squatters through property rights in their names; the colours of the spectrum are being trademarked. Increasingly what used to be thought of as shared cultural resources, or at least as un-ownable – words, names, scientific facts, elements of nature, shared myths, and so on – is being accepted as personal property that can be owned, bought, sold, and licensed in a global cultural marketplace.

Hand in hand with the processes of propertization comes a strengthened regime through which to legitimize and authorize these expanded notions of intellectual property. Intellectual property law has been both expanded in scope and extended in time in order to accommodate new forms of property, increased terms of protection, and support for new techniques to prevent infringement. This is evident in many places from the Sonny Bono copyright extension in the United States noted above, to the American Digital Millennium Copyright Act's prohibitions against tampering with digital protection technology (see also Longford in this volume; Hamilton 2005), to a Canadian parliamentary committee's recommendation to charge licence fees to schools for information already available for free on the World Wide Web. A stronger and implicitly more effective copyright framework (from the perspective of copyright owners) has seemingly been embraced as a shared value at the global level through the institutional auspices of the World Intellectual Property Organization (of which Canada is a member). Copyright is arguably increasingly being seen as a model in the global governance of culture that Taras maps in the Introduction to this volume. And indeed, the ongoing reform process in Canada is a direct response to our participation in this global matrix of legislation and reciprocity of enforcement attempting to control the unruly and (legal) boundary-breaking nature of digital communication.

The third sociocultural process in which this new personal copyright energy is caught up is the continued development of digital technology. The rendering of cultural products as information, widespread broadband communication, and networked communities enable the unprecedented technological and social capacity for copying and transmission of cultural works of all sorts. Further, it implants them firmly within the global digital economy (see Taras in this volume). The national location of production and consumption, key to the operation of traditional legal and regulatory mechanisms, becomes difficult to ascertain and almost impossible to police. The originating medium becomes irrelevant; the quality of the work does not decline from repeated copying; and transmission is global and virtually instantaneous. Add to this the difficulties traditional legal mechanisms face in regulating online activities, for example, the legal status of Internet service providers, and you have a social force that is troubling the move towards personal property and the expansion of intellectual property. At the same time, technological means are being continuously developed and deployed to stifle this unruly digital activity through technological protection measures and digital rights management techniques, increasingly endorsed and bolstered through strong legislative mechanisms and criminal sanctions.

The fourth contextual process – the result of the previous three – is the current scramble by individuals, media industry players, regulators, governments, and courts to sort it all out. The traditional arbiters of cultural reproduction and the various industries affected are engaged in crisis management. This is visible in lawsuits and ineffective public relations campaigns on the part of the motion picture and recording industries in North America. We see it in the public divisions among various scientific communities on the foundational ideas of experimental science, in the policy shifts in national and global intellectual property arenas, and in the resulting reform processes hastily undertaken by Western nations, Canada among them.

It is this burst of energy in the regulatory arena that I want to explore here. After a brief review of some of the basic principles of copyright law in Canada, I will examine the state of re-formed copyright in Canada. I argue that the terrain is being defined by two forces pushing in opposite directions: first, the copyright reform process in Canada moving towards a system privileging owners, in line with the World Intellectual Property Organization and the United States and second, a series of recent court decisions that combine to reassert a balance between creators/owners and the public interest, going so far as to recognize users as having rights in the copyright system. And all of us as consumers and creators are caught somewhere in the middle.

Copyright Law in Canada

Copyright forms one of five areas of intellectual property protected by statute in Canada, in addition to patents, trademarks, industrial designs, and integrated circuit topographies. Copyright means literally the right to copy and is governed by the Copyright Act. The Act grants to copyright owners the sole and exclusive right to reproduce, perform, or publish a work. Industry Canada administers the Act and both it and Canadian Heritage are responsible for developing copyright policy.

A key distinction in copyright law is between the ideas involved in creation and their expression. Only the latter are protected; ideas are seen to be part of the public domain. A second important distinction is between author and owner. The author and owner of copyright are not necessarily, and indeed often are not, the same individual. The author is the person who first expresses the work in a tangible form and copyright accrues immediately upon that creation. Usually the author is the first holder of a copyright (outside of an employment situation); however, she or he can contract away elements or all of her or his ownership to another person or corporation. The author remains important, however, because, regardless of who owns the copyright, the term lasts for the author's life plus fifty years.[2]

The legislation provides protection for "works," which are determined by three criteria: originality, fixation, and nationality of creator/place of publication. Originality is not originality in the layperson's sense of the term and historically in Canada, the threshold has been quite low: merely that the work not be copied from another, that it originate with the author, and that it reflect some labour. However, I will revisit the standard of originality in my discussion of one of the recent Supreme Court of Canada decisions. Second, works must be fixed, namely expressed in some material form, capable of identification, and having a more or less permanent endurance. Types of work noted specifically in the legislation for protection include: literary, dramatical, musical, and artistic works as well as sound recordings, broadcasts, computer programs, and live performances. Finally, all Canadians get copyright protection automatically in Canada and, given Canada's international agreements and commitments, copyright protection in Canada protects a work in more than 140 countries around the world (Harris 1995, 6).

Two kinds of rights are protected by copyright: economic and moral. Economic rights include the right of reproduction, of public performance, of publication, of adaptation, translation, and telecommunication, and the right to authorize anyone to do any of those. These rights are held by the owner, regardless of whether or not she or he is also the author. Moral rights accrue only to the author and are directed towards the protection of her or his honour and reputation. Moral rights include: rights of paternity, integrity, and association. Paternity rights protect the right to have one's name appear, the right to be anonymous, or to use a pseudonym when the work is in public. Rights of integrity protect the work against changes, damages, and so on. Finally, rights of association prohibit the owner from using the work in association with a product, service, cause, or institution without the consent of the author.

One violates copyrights by doing anything that the copyright owner has the sole and exclusive right to do. Typical remedies for breach of copyright are injunctions (to stop the further violation) and damages (to compensate for lost revenue). There are a small number of legitimate uses one can make of copyrighted material where permission does not have to be sought, nor royalties paid. The most common of these is fair dealing, where one is permitted to use copyrighted materials for the purposes of study, research, criticism, review, or newspaper summary. Historically, this exemption has been narrowly defined in Canadian law, but again has come under recent re-vision by the Supreme Court of Canada. Perhaps the most well-known exception to copyright infringement is the ability of Canadians to make one copy of a sound recording for personal use. This is because all Canadians pay a levy on recording media such as cassette tapes, CD-R's, and videotapes, which is used to compensate artists.

The Copyright Act was revised for the first time in 1988 and then went through a number of changes throughout the 1980s and 1990s, primarily to take account of technological changes and international commitments arising out of the Free Trade Agreements.[3] However, as Longford also notes in this volume, the entire copyright regime is presently undergoing a lengthy and complex review process as policy makers struggle to adapt the principles and provisions of the legislation to the current global reality. It is this process that forms the first element in delimiting the process of re-forming copyright in Canada.

Pushing for Owners: Copyright Reform Process

The Canadian government has been involved in a protracted, multi-year copyright reform process with international and national dimensions. In late 1996, the World Intellectual Property Organization (WIPO) adopted two treaties – the WIPO Copyright Treaty and the WIPO Performances and Phonograms Treaty. Canada signed these treaties in December 1997, and, as of mid-2006, has not yet ratified them. While the exact reasons for Canada's past seeming reticence or ambivalence in activating these treaties are unknown, the delays have been lamented by certain policy makers at the same time that they have been lauded by critics of the American Digital Millennium Copyright Act (DMCA) as affording Canadians an opportunity to better reflect on the implications of these treaties for the end users of copyrighted material.

Several provisions under the WIPO treaties have been in dispute in Canada. The first is the 'making available' right. This gives to copyright holders the sole and exclusive right to make their material available (on the Internet or otherwise) and would resolve once and for all the grey zone of MP3 uploading. Technological protection measures are also at issue; these include the various technologies that enable one to control or eliminate digital copying. For example, some compact discs cannot be played on computers, and American TV producers can now include a "broadcast flag" in digital television streams to prevent unauthorized copying by digital players. These measures protect copyright but also quash legitimate copying. Amendments under consideration as a result of WIPO would make it illegal to tamper with information embedded in a copyrighted work. Another issue is the criminalization of cracking copy-protection programs or technology on websites, CDs, or DVDs. As well, the status of Canada's private use copying exception and our recording media levy is uncertain in light of the WIPO requirements. Finally, the overall ethic in the WIPO treaties is one of international harmonization, and the fear of some critics was that Canada will follow the path of the more draconian American approach embodied in their much-critiqued DMCA.

In June 2001, the federal government launched this reform process with the document, A *Framework for Copyright Reform*. At the same time, it released two consultation papers on issues specific to the Internet: *Consultation Paper on the Application of the Copyright Act's Compulsory Retransmission License to the Internet* and *Consultation Paper on Digital Copyright Issues*. The call for submissions was answered with over seven hundred responses and fifty reply comments from interested individuals and organizations. The retransmission issues were addressed by Bill C-11, which came into force on March 21, 2003. However, the digital copyright issues were much more contentious and further consultations were held in meetings in six cities across the country in early 2002.

In October 2002, the Government tabled to Parliament, *Supporting Culture and Innovation: Report on the Provisions and Operations of the Copyright Act*. This document was the outcome of a five-year review required in the legislation from the revisions made to the Act in 1997. For this reason, it is often referred to as the "Section 92 Report." It reiterates the Canadian government's commitment to bringing our legislation into conformity with the WIPO treaties, provided the issues are analyzed and appropriate consultations take place. The Section 92 Report identifies a series of long-, medium-, and short-term issues that need to be addressed through copyright reform. These issues range from liability for Internet service providers for the content transmitted on their equipment to traditional and Aboriginal forms of knowledge. The short-term issues, namely those to be addressed within two years of the tabling of the Section 92 Report, have been of most urgent concern in the reform process. These include: the making available right, legal protection of technological measures, legal protection of rights management information, the distribution right, photographic works, various performing rights, the implications for private copying, the liability of Internet service providers, and access issues (various educational uses of the Internet). Some of these issues have not proved to be particularly contentious, such as those improving the rights of photographers and performers to bring them into line with other copyright holders; however, many of the others – ISP liability, the education issues, the making available right, and so on – have been highly contested.

Further to the Section 92 review, in October 2003, the Standing Committee on Canadian Heritage began its review of the Copyright Act, and that committee adopted a resolution recommending that the ministers of Canadian Heritage and Industry prepare legislation to implement the WIPO treaties by February 2004. This did not take place. Instead, the committee began its hearings on the short-term issues in February. The two departments then prepared a *Status Report on Copyright Reform*, which was presented to the committee on March 25, 2004, focusing on the short-term issues. Following this, the committee held further hearings over the month of April on the issues of: private copying and WIPO ratification, photographic works, ISP liability, use of Internet material for educational purposes, technology-enhanced learning, and interlibrary loans. On May 12, 2004, it tabled its *Interim Report on Copyright Reform*. The report made nine recommendations, including: that the government ratify the WIPO treaties immediately, that photographers receive the same authorship rights as other creators, that ISPs be made potentially subject to liability for copyrighted material being circulated on their facilities, that a licensing regime be implemented to charge fees for Internet material used for educational purposes (and that publicly available material that might be an exception to this regime be interpreted restrictively), that interlibrary loan material be subjected to licensing as well, and that the government move ahead on these issues very quickly.

The *Interim Report on Copyright Reform* was released to fairly strident criticism in the Canadian press, particularly with respect to the licensing of educational materials that were already publicly available for free. The *Toronto Star* noted in its business section that

... [u]nfortunately our low point [in Canadian Internet policy development] may have occurred earlier this month when a Canadian Heritage parliamentary committee ... presented a vision of copyright that would transform the Internet from the incredible open source of information that it is into a predominantly commercial medium available primarily to those willing to open up their cheque books. (*Toronto Star*, 2004, D01)

Commentators noted that the nine recommendations were generated quickly after limited hearings by the committee, which favoured advocates of a more effective regime of enforcement for copyright owners. Provincial ministers of education were also very critical of the educational recommendations.

However, before the recommendations could be acted upon, a federal election was called on May 22. In late November 2004, the federal government announced it would propose amendments to the Copyright Act before the end of 2004, to be finalized by February 2005. While that did not happen, in March 2005, the departments of Industry and Canadian Heritage finally made a joint statement announcing their intentions with respect to copyright reform. The announcement mapped a series of intended reforms to the Copyright Act. This was followed up by Bill C-60 – An Act to Amend the Copyright Act – which received first reading on June 20, 2005. The draft bill provided additional rights to performers for their sound recordings, bringing them into line with other creators; it brought photographers into line with other creators; it provided copyright holders with the ability to control the first distribution of their work; and tried to ensure that technological protections measures are not circumvented. It retained the exemption for ISPs, and created new rules for how libraries and educational institutions should deal with digital copies of works. Most significantly for the average Canadian, however, the proposed legislation provided that making a copyrighted work available on the Internet (i.e., uploading it for others to download), would be an infringement of copyright. The government backed off of some of its more controversial educational proposals and left the private copying exception untouched, preferring further consultation on that issue (for an evaluation of all provisions of Bill C-60, see Geist 2005).

Bill C-60 was the clearest expression to date that Canadians have had of parliamentary intention. It died with the government on November 28, 2005. It is unclear when, and even if, the minority Conservative government will take up copyright reform. However, we can see that, at every turn, the direction of the reform process and Canada's international commitments has been to move towards an enhanced regime of rights generated in the name of *content creators*, but which is fundamentally about creating a system for the management and protection of rights for *copyright owners* in the digital context. While it is clear that, whether by intention or incompetence, Canada is taking a much more tempered and long-term approach to the issues than

the United States, it is also evident that Canada is on the international band-
wagon and will eventually culminate a slow and contested reform process
that ultimately is serving to discipline the potentially unruly nature of digital
communication.

Pushing for Users: The Courts

While the public interest and need to protect the balance of rights at the heart
of intellectual property are present as discourses in the reform process, they
have been progressively muted in favour of bringing Canada into line with
its global trading partners. Interestingly, and surprising to some, where the
public interest has received its most rousing support has been in Canada's
courts. Offering a counterbalance to the Standing Committee's recommendations and to the proposed legislation, three landmark decisions over the
course of 2004 and 2005 give legal endorsement to the ethos that individuals
are at the heart of the activities of copyright and that they have rights that
need to be respected and protected.

LAW SOCIETY OF UPPER CANADA V. CCH CANADIAN LIMITED

Interestingly, a case that turned on the use of the lowly technology of the
photocopier has broken new ground in Canadian copyright law and has gone
a significant way towards restoring the balance inherent in the intellectual
property bargain. On March 4, 2004, the Supreme Court of Canada released
its decision in a dispute between the Law Society of Upper Canada, which
maintains and operates the Great Library at Osgoode Hall in Toronto, one of
the largest law libraries in Canada, and CCH Canadian Limited, a publisher
of legal materials. CCH argued that three practices by the library constituted
breach of its copyright: first, the library provided a custom photocopy service to in-library researchers; second, it offered a photocopy machine on the
premises for clients to make their own photocopies; and third, it offered a fax
service to send materials to clients who could not come to the library.

The high court concluded that the works were original and therefore covered by copyright; that the Law Society's activities were "fair dealing" within
the Copyright Act and were therefore excepted from liability; and finally,
that the presence of the photocopy machine alone (including the standard
sign denying liability for any material copied in breach of copyright by the
patron) did not constitute authorization of breach of copyright. So, in short,
the library was doing nothing wrong.

However, both the legal findings themselves and the larger themes reflected in the rhetoric of the court are significant for outlining how the courts are thinking about all of us and our copying practices. The court began by reiterating its position on balance in copyright:[4]

The *Copyright Act* is usually presented as a balance between promoting the public interest in the encouragement and dissemination of works of the arts and intellect and obtaining a just reward for the creator.... The proper balance among these and other public policy objectives lies not only in recognizing the creator's rights *but in giving due weight to their limited nature.* In interpreting the *Copyright Act*, courts should strive to maintain an appropriate balance between these two goals. (emphasis added, in para. 10, CCH)

The court then went on to give a clear articulation of what constitutes originality for the purposes of the Act. As noted above, Canada had a notoriously low threshold for originality, which favoured the finding of copyrights in a very broad potential array of material. The court itself recognized, "[w]hen courts adopt a standard of originality requiring only that something be more than a mere copy or that someone simply show industriousness to ground copyright in a work, they tip the scale in favour of the author's or creator's rights, at the loss of society's interest in maintaining a robust public domain that could help foster future creative innovation" (para. 23). Instead, the court required a standard that something not be copied and that it does not have to be novel or unique, but that it must be the outcome of the exercise of skill and judgment (which cannot be characterized as a purely mechanical exercise). Skill will involve the use of knowledge, developed aptitude, or practised ability, whereas judgment involves "one's capacity for discernment or ability to form an opinion or evaluation by comparing different possible options in producing the work" (para. 16). The court justified its test:

... [b]y way of contrast, when an author must exercise skill and judgment to ground originality in a work, there is a safeguard against the author being overcompensated.... This helps ensure that there is room for the public domain to flourish as others are able to produce new works by building on the ideas and information contained in the work of others. (para. 23)

In other words, the court upped the ante on originality, meaning it is a bit tougher to get copyright unless the author has really put some skill and judgment into the work. Thus, the court redefined originality in such a way as to re-inject the public interest into copyright law, tempering the swing towards the rights of creators/owners.

On the issue of the self-service photocopiers, the court had to define what constitutes authorization and confirmed that merely providing the means to copy is not considered authorization. In the Act, it is an infringement of copyright to do anything that only owners are entitled to do, including authorizing any of those actions. Authorize was defined as to "sanction, approve and countenance" (para. 38). The court suggested that this should be interpreted in the strictest manner and that "a person does not authorize infringement by authorizing the mere use of equipment that could be used to infringe copyright. Courts should presume that a person who authorizes an activity does so only so far as it is in accordance with the law" (para. 38). The court found that the library is entitled to assume its patrons are using the copiers legally and that they do not have control, or have to take responsibility for the actions of, the patrons.

A third key issue the court addressed was that of fair dealing. The Copyright Act provides that "[f]air dealing for the purpose of research or private study does not infringe copyright." Again, in Canada in the past, the fair dealing exception had been treated quite narrowly. The court in *CCH* not only expanded it, but went further to redefine fair dealing as a "user's right," rather than as a mere defence to copyright infringement.

[T]he fair dealing exception is perhaps more properly understood as an integral part of the *Copyright Act* than simply a defence. Any act falling within the fair dealing exception will not be an infringement of copyright. The fair dealing exception, like other exceptions in the *Copyright Act*, is a user's right. In order to maintain the proper balance between the rights of a copyright owner and users' interests, it must not be interpreted strictly. As Professor Vaver, *supra*, has explained, at p. 171: "User rights are not just loopholes. Both owner rights and user rights should therefore be given the fair and balanced reading that befits remedial legislation." (para. 48)

The characterization of the exception in a language of user's rights is a very significant endorsement of the individual in relation to copyrighted material. We, as users, have rights to access copyrighted materials for activities like research and these should be respected.

Thus, the publisher lost on all grounds and those who used the copyrighted materials won. Even more significantly, Canada's highest court unanimously endorsed the idea of not just public interest within the legislation, but also of express rights on the part of individual users. According to the Supreme

Court of Canada, copyright is personal, and although the case involved photocopy machines, it was soon to have much greater impact in a different technological arena.

BMG CANADA INC. ET AL. V. JOHN DOE ET AL.

As Longford also discusses in this volume, on February 11, 2004, the Canadian Recording Industry Association (CRIA), mimicking its American counterpart, the Recording Industry Association of America, brought legal action for copyright infringement against twenty-nine unknown individual Internet users who allegedly had swapped more than a thousand digital music files each using peer-to-peer file-sharing programs Kazaa and iMesh. CRIA could not identify the individual defendants, but had determined their Internet protocol addresses (IP addresses). It therefore brought an action to force the Internet service providers (ISPs) to reveal the identity of the Internet account holders associated with those IP addresses.

However, in an interesting twist, Shaw Cable, one of the ISPs, refused to provide the requisite information on its clients so that they could be properly identified. The individuals operated under pseudonyms associated with their software of choice. Thus, the privacy rights of the individual clients of the ISPs were pitted against the copyrights held by artists and the recording industry. The Copyright Board had previously held that, given that all Canadians pay a small levy on each blank audio-recording technology purchased (audiotapes and CD-Rs), downloading music for personal use is not illegal. CRIA, to avoid this, brought its suit specifically against individuals that were said to be *uploading* files to the Internet.

On March 31, 2004, Mr. Justice von Finckenstein of the federal court found that the ISPs could not be required to provide the identities of their clients, and therefore, the action for copyright infringement was stalled in its tracks by the privacy rights of those labelled as "pirates" by the music industry. The judge went further, however, commenting that the uploading of music was not a breach of copyright. The decision turns on more technical grounds concerning the affidavit evidence provided and so all comments with respect to the infringement of copyright can be considered extraneous to the binding aspect of the decision, or as *obiter dicta*. However, this was the first judicial pronouncement on the issue of peer-to-peer file sharing and so was being watched by all actors in the drama in Canada and around the world.

Mr. Justice von Finckenstein confirmed that downloading a song for personal use is not an infringement because of section 80(1) of the Copyright Act, which deems a recording made for private use of the person who makes the copy not a breach of copyright. CRIA was arguing that the downloading and uploading of music files constituted reproduction, authorization, distribution, or possession for the purpose of distribution. The judge stated, however, "[n]o evidence was presented that the alleged infringers either distributed or authorized the reproduction of sound recordings. They merely placed personal copies into their shared directories which were accessible by other computer user [*sic*] via a P2P service" (para. 26). Following the Supreme Court in the CCH case, the judge held,

Setting up facilities that allow copying does not amount to authorizing infringement. I cannot see a real difference between a library that places a photocopy machine in a room full of copyright material and a computer user that places a personal copy on a shared directory linked to a P2P service. In either case the preconditions to copying and infringement are set up but the element of authorization is missing. (para. 27)

Finally, the judge stated that merely placing a copy on a shared directory was not distribution either. "Before it constitutes distribution, there must be a positive act by the owner of the shared directory, such as sending out the copies or advertising that they are available for copying" (para. 28). In one fell swoop, uploading music files was legal in Canada.

The court was also very sympathetic to the position of the ISPs. The judge recognized that it would be potentially very difficult for the ISPs to identify the IP addresses of the individual account holders. Further, they would not be able to confirm the actual users of the account, only the holder of the account. The court also weighed the public interest of forcing the ISPs to reveal this information against the privacy interests of the individual account holders. The court referred to the Personal Information Protection and Electronic Documents Act, legislation enacted to assist in the protection of an individual's right to control the collection, use, and disclosure of personal information by private organizations. However, no one can hide behind such legislation to escape criminal or civil liability, and the court has the power to require those documents, if the public interest would be served. This required the judge to balance the relative interests of the individual users in retaining their privacy against the interests of the recording industry in being able to pursue potential copyright violators. Justice von Finckenstein noted that in the past, third parties, such as ISPs, have been required to disclose documents to identify a person only identified through an IP address and that privacy concerns have never before been held to outweigh the interest in disclosure (para. 41). However, "given the age of the data, its unreliability and the serious possibility of an innocent account holder being identified, this Court is of the view that the privacy concerns outweigh the public interest concerns in favour of disclosure" (para. 42).

The decision was described as a "humiliating blow" to the recording industry by one journalist (Doyle 2004, A3). Bruce Stockfish, the Director of Copyright Policy at Canadian Heritage, remarked that von Finckenstein's decision proves Canada's copyright laws need to be updated. "Right now, with radio communication, for example, it's transmitted and received at the same time. You listen or you don't. That's not the case with the Internet. The concern is that there's a possible void which needs to be filled with a special new right, called the making available right" (in Doyle 2004, A3). File sharers and those analysts concerned with user's rights and ISP liability issues were obviously jubilant. The decision flew in the face of other jurisdictions and received international press coverage. Not surprisingly, the CRIA members appealed to the Federal Court of Appeal, arguing that the judge erred in both his interpretation of the evidence and the legislation.

On May 19, 2005, the Federal Court of Appeal released its decision in the BMG case. It took a much less user-friendly approach to the issue than the Supreme Court had. The court suggested:

[t]his technology [the Internet] must not be allowed to obliterate those personal property rights which society has deemed important. Although privacy concerns must also be considered, it seems to me that they must yield to public concerns for the protection of intellectual property rights in situations where infringement threatens to erode those rights (BMG, FCA, para. 41).

Ultimately the court decided the issues on the same technical grounds also, but went further to rebuke the original judge. The Federal Court of Appeal suggested that von Finkenstein should not have made any conclusions with respect to whether or not file sharing breaches copyright in his decision and that doing so might have prejudiced the parties at trial. Given the problems with the evidence, this particular motion was not being appealed to the Supreme Court of Canada and so the case ended there. Arguably, however, Finckenstein's decision was a key catalyst in the federal government finally signalling its reform intentions to Canadians in Bill C-60. But the Supreme Court of Canada was not yet done with copyright.

CANADIAN ASSOCIATION OF INTERNET PROVIDERS ET AL. V. SOCIETY OF COMPOSERS, AUTHORS AND MUSIC PUBLISHERS OF CANADA

In late June of 2004, the Supreme Court of Canada finally resolved a nine-year-old dispute that had come to be known as the Tariff 22 case. The Society of Composers, Authors, and Publishers of Music in Canada (SOCAN), Canada's leading music collective, was seeking to have ISPs required to collect royalties for downloaded music. This possibility arose because, in 1989, Parliament added a section to the Copyright Act to provide copyright holders with the exclusive right to communicate a work to the public through telecommunication, thus recognizing satellite, Internet, and other related communications. With this new section, collective societies wanted to be able to receive royalties for Internet downloading and to have those royalties collected and owed by the ISPs because that would be the only viable way of collecting the fees. The history of the case goes back to 1995, when SOCAN applied to the Copyright Board of Canada for the tariff. Four years of hearings followed and in 1999 the Copyright Board found ISPs did not have to collect the tariff. SOCAN appealed to the Federal Court of Canada and that court held in 2002 that ISPs might be required to pay some royalties on the grounds of their practices of caching content.

However, this was overturned by the 8 to 1 decision of the Supreme Court of Canada in *Canadian Association of Internet Providers et al. v. SOCAN*. Once again, the court began by asserting the need for balance in the interpretation of the Copyright Act, situating that position explicitly in relation to the Internet. "The capacity of the Internet to disseminate 'works of the arts and intellect' is one of the great innovations of the information age. Its use should be facilitated rather than discouraged, but this should not be done unfairly at the expense of those who created the works of art and intellect in the first place" (para. 40). The court also recognized the challenge of applying legislation designed to address issues in the late 1800s and early 1900s to technologies the drafters could not have imagined (para. 43). In the absence of the ratification of the WIPO treaties, however, the court signalled that it does not intend to read into current legislation provisions that have only been proposed in the reform process. The courts wait, with other Canadians, for Parliament to speak. However, the courts continue to signal the spirit in which they will interpret any eventual legislation.

The Supreme Court found that the Copyright Act applies to international communications that have a substantial connection to Canada rather than having to be located in Canada. The jurisdictional issue was in fact the only one that divided the court. Dissenting, Justice Lebel held that the originating server had to be located in Canada for Canadian law to apply.

The entire court, however, provided clear endorsement of the protection offered to ISPs. The court suggested that the legislation clearly defines ISPs as service providers, not content providers. Paralleling its endorsement of fair dealing in the CCH decision, the court held that intermediaries engaged in the communication of copyrighted content, such as ISPs, do not enjoy merely immunity from copyright infringement, but rather they are deemed not to have communicated the work to the public at all. "[The ISP exemption] is not a loophole but an important element of the balance struck by the statutory copyright regime" (para. 89). As long as the ISP does not meddle in the content, it is not communicating work to the public for the purposes of copyright, as a matter of legislative policy. Thus, ISPs cannot be found liable for content that violates copyright if they are acting as a mere conduit.

The issue of the caching of content became important and required the court to get into the intricacies of Internet transmission. SOCAN had argued that, in caching some of the content – namely making a temporary copy on the ISP server so that the data can be transmitted more quickly – the ISPs had acted as more than mere conduits for the information. The court held, consistent with its previous position, that "Parliament has decided that there is a public interest in encouraging intermediaries who make telecommunications possible to expand and improve their operations without the threat of copyright infringement. To impose copyright liability on intermediaries would obviously chill that expansion and development" (para. 113). The court found that the creation of a cache copy was a "serendipitous consequence of improvements in Internet technology" and was content neutral. Thus, ISPs are empowered to use caching technology to improve service to their clients without concern as to liability.

Authorization came up in this case as well, with SOCAN arguing that the ISPs knew very well that people were using their facilities for file sharing. The court, following its own more stringent definition in CCH, held that "the knowledge that someone *might* be using neutral technology to violate copyright ... is not necessarily sufficient to constitute authorization" (para. 127). If the ISP were notified of the offending content and refused to take steps to take it down, this might constitute authorization. The court concluded,

By enacting s. 2.4(1)(b) ... Parliament made a policy distinction between those who abuse the Internet to obtain 'cheap music' and those who are part of the infrastructure of the Internet itself. It is clear that Parliament did not want copyright disputes between creators and users to be visited on the heads of the Internet intermediaries, whose continued expansion and development is considered vital to national economic growth. (para. 131)

Thus, until such time as that section is repealed, it would seem that ISPs are quite well protected.

The dissent in the Tariff 22 decision is also of particular interest, given Justice Lebel's comments on privacy rights in the Internet age. These comments do not have binding status, given that they are not addressed by the majority court and it is impossible to know if the other judges agree with him or not, but they certainly are consistent with the seeming trend to strengthen the status and rights of the individual in digital copyright disputes. He suggested that the legislation should be interpreted in such a way as to respect "end users' privacy interests, and should eschew an interpretation that would encourage the monitoring or collection of personal data gleaned from Internet-related activity within the home" (para. 153). Mr. Justice Lebel seems particularly concerned about the potentially invasive nature of Internet retrieval practices to identify end users, suggesting that the next step is then the monitoring of Internet accounts and activities. Because those activities tend to reveal "core biographical information" about a person, important privacy interests arise and must be protected (para. 155).

Thus, in this interesting trio of copyright cases, Canada's highest courts have radically altered the Canadian copyright terrain much more quickly and effectively than the reform process to date, despite the Herculean efforts of industry, as Longford details (in this volume). The courts are actively shaping the context of interpretation of any eventual legislation. The need to seek a balance between owners' interests and the public interest has been reinstated. The bar has been raised on the test for originality so that we have some discernment and limits in what attracts copyright. Authorization has been confirmed as something that should be strictly interpreted. Further, providing the technology for reproduction, alone, is not sufficient to garner liability, nor is suspecting that someone might be doing something illegal. ISPs are fully protected from any liability provided they provide a conduit only and technical arguments such as that made around caching will not be seen to undermine the policy directive from Parliament. Most importantly, the court has begun to speak of users as a recognized group, as a group with rights – both to access copyrighted material and to the respect of their privacy. The Copyright Act has been framed as a piece of legislation that can and should protect the rights of users. Therefore, through its courts, Canada is empowering users to share cultural products, clearly going against the global consensus.

Conclusion

It seems clear that as Canadian copyright becomes personal, as all of us begin to feel implicated in this regime so intimately connected with how we communicate, we should look to the courts, rather than to Parliament for support. The strongly pro-copyright owner position of both Liberal and Conservative governments' positions will, if eventually mobilized, move Canada considerably closer to the United States in favouring an approach to copyright that sees legislation as a regime of rights for owners to be deployed in delimiting the activities of users and punishing them for unauthorized use. Further, it will shape the understanding of the Internet in Canada as a site almost exclusively of commerce, rather than many other forms of exchange. Finally, it will put a price on all knowledge. What will be interesting to see, when a Canadian government inevitably ratifies the WIPO treaties and brings in its amendments to the Copyright Act, is not only how users will fare in the legislation, but how individuals will respond to it and act within it, and how the courts, led by a strong users-rights Supreme Court, will interpret it. To date, Canada's response to the global copyright agenda has been somewhat ambivalent and certainly cautious, opening up the door to a much richer discussion of the rights of individual Canadians than has been the case elsewhere in the world. As a result, we have seen some more creative developments in Canada (see Hamilton 2005). Finally, with the failure of the most recent legislative effort, perhaps we will even see a renewed consultation process where the dialogue between users, owners, creators, the legislatures, and the courts can continue.

Bibliography

Doyle, Simon. 2004. "Canada's laws need amending: government official." *Regina Leader-Post*, 5 April, A3.

Canadian Heritage. 2004. "Copyright Awareness." http://www.pch.gc.ca/progs/ac-ca/ progs/pda-cpb/archives/index_e.cfm.

Geist, Michael. 2003. "Reforming copyright is a concern for everyone." *Toronto Star*, 23 June, D02.

Geist, Michael, ed. 2005. *The Public Interest: The Future of Canadian Copyright Law*, Toronto: Irwin Law.

Hamilton, Sheryl. 2005. "Made in Canada: A Unique Approach to Internet Service Provider Liability and Copyright Infringement." In *The Public Interest: The Future of Canadian Copyright Law*, ed. M. Geist, 285–308. Toronto: Irwin Law.

Harris, Leslie Ellen. 1995. *Canadian Copyright Law*, 2nd ed. Toronto: McGraw-Hill Ryerson.

Rose, Carol M. 2003. "Romans, Roads, and Romantic Creators: Traditions of Public Property in the Information Age." *Law & Contemporary Problems* 66(1–2): 89–110.

Toronto Star. 2004. "Will Copyright Reform Chill Free Use of Web?" *Toronto Star*, 31 May, D01.

STATUTES CITED

Copyright Act, R.S., c. C-30.
Personal Information Protection and Electronic Documents Act, R.S., 2000, c. 5.

CASES CITED

BMG Canada, et al. v. John Doe, et al., 2004 F.C. 488.
BMG Canada, et al. v. John Doe, et al., 39 C.P.R. (4th) 97, 252 D.L.R. (4th) 342 (Fed. C.A.).
CCH Canadian Ltd. v. Law Society of Upper Canada [2004] 1 S.C.R. 339 (S.C.C.).
Society of Composers, Authors and Music Publishers of Canada v. Canadian Association of Internet Providers, 2004 SCC 45 (S.C.C.).
Théberge v. Galerie d'Art du Petit Champlain Inc. [2002] 2 S.C.R. 336 (S.C.C.).

Notes

1   Interestingly, the litigious heirs of Ms. Montgomery had been in court previously defending their interests. In *Anne of Green Gables Licensing Authority Inc. v. Avonlea Traditions Inc.* (2000), 4 C.P.R. (4th), 289 (Ont. S.C.J.), they claimed a reversionary copyright interest in the Anne of Green Gables books in the mid-1980s and were in conflict with an organization to whom they had granted licensing rights. The heirs were determined to have a valid reversionary interest, which had come to them in 1967, twenty-five years after the author's death on April 24, 1942.

2   The term of copyright varies for different media (see the Act). The life-plus-fifty-years term is the maximum and is derived from literary works.

3   The Act was not substantially modernized until 1988, where amendments included: exhibition rights for artistic works, express protection of computer programs, enhanced moral rights, the creation of a new Copyright Board, increased criminal sanctions, measures to improve the collective administration of copyright, and the abolition of compulsory licenses for the recording of a musical work. After the signing of the Canada-U.S. Free Trade Agreement, the Act was again amended in 1989 to require cable and satellite companies to pay for the retransmission of works in broadcast signals. Telecommunications was also added to broadcasting as a modality of communicating to the public.

More amendments followed in 1993, when Bill C-88 clarified the definition of musical work and held that all transmitters (whether broadcasters, specialty or pay services, or cable systems) had to pay royalties. With the coming into force of the North American Free Trade Implementation Act in 1994, additional amendments were added to provide for a rental right for sound recordings and computer programs and increased protection for pirated works, which were being imported. Canada's role in the World Trade Organization led to its amending the Act in 1996 to extend copyright protection to all WTO countries and provided performers with protection against bootleg audio recordings and unauthorized live transmissions of their performances.

4   From *Théberge v. Galerie d'Art du Petit Champlain inc.*, [2002] 2 S.C.R. 336.

12: Globalization and Scholarly Communication: A Story of Canadian Marginalization

FRITS PANNEKOEK, HELEN CLARKE, and ANDREW WALLER

Introduction

Within the last five years Canada's libraries, archives, and museums, the prime institutions for communicating Canadian identity, have moved aggressively into a digital environment. Five years ago academic libraries subscribed to a few digital databases and full-text journals. Now many of the largest subscribe to over 25,000 digital full-text searchable journals each, and most have at least a half a million full-text searchable digital monographs. Many are also creating their own digital products and are developing digital repositories for faculty research output, although this remains in its infancy. Their motives for doing so are mixed.

While these institutions have embraced the digital environment, they have also exacerbated the accompanying problems. Their failure to resolve these problems will seriously affect scholarly communication and their ability to exercise their responsibility to maintain repositories. In short, academic libraries have contributed to economic concentration in the digital publishing industry and become so enmeshed in international treaties, conventions, and practices, albeit not of their own making, that rather than being instruments for the advancement of the national identity and memory, they have become agents of globalization. As we shall see, despite the rhetoric of free unfettered access and a professed role in preserving intellectual output, they have failed to significantly alter their information purchasing, preservation, and cataloguing practices to maximize the opportunity to develop a national digital information infrastructure. They remain mired in the past, tinkering with the digital world on its periphery, but rarely addressing the core issue – an alternative economic model that will not only allow but facilitate the mobilization of knowledge by society. What we have instead is an information environment in which the best information is sometimes less accessible than it was in print, is more controlled by corporate agendas, and more than ever subject to government regulation. Before investigating the current issues in some detail a more general discussion might be useful.

The current digital environment within the academy took shape almost overnight. Until recently, most Canadian academic libraries neither planned their response, nor were involved in the creation or capitalization of new information products. That was left to visionaries in the private sector. Two companies that developed economic models to recoup capital investments and generate handsome profits for their shareholders were Thomson Gale and Elsevier. Elsevier has a long history of owning, publishing, and/or managing thousands of the most prestigious scholarly journals. By carefully mapping the transition from print to online, by offering outstanding product, and by exploiting aggressive pricing, Elsevier has become the *bête noire* of the academic world. Their annual price increases threatened the very viability of even the largest libraries in the 1990s (Jones 2002). In order to keep the best journals, university libraries cancelled thousands of other titles during this period (Bergstrom and Bergstrom 2001). For smaller specialized Canadian journal publishers, most of which were in the social sciences and humanities and were for the most part ignorant of what was happening, this meant falling subscriptions and marginalization. Chances of being renewed by financially strapped academic libraries anywhere were uncertain. Canadian academic book publishers, whose print runs were often under one thousand, were also squeezed as more and more academic libraries had to make choices between scientific and international digital journals and small-run national information products.

Following these changes was the advent of the "big deal." The major science and medical publishers offered university library consortia literally thousands of digital journals at heavily discounted prices, provided they bought the entire collection and they bought them in digital form. Libraries were eager to move to this model not only because of the increased number of titles it offered, but also because of the enthusiastic acceptance of electronic journals by researchers.

To finance this, Canada's academic libraries successfully applied to the Canadian Foundation for Innovation, the major federal government science research foundation, for $20 million (of a $50 million project) to support the acquisition of digital scientific journals for sixty-four of their number. The balance of the monies came from provincial sources. While on the surface it may appear a reasonable strategy to reduce costs, after four years of support many libraries will need to pick up the full cost of these journals. Science and medical faculty have enjoyed the new acquisitions, and further pressure to continue these subscriptions in an environment of continual cost-cutting will further erode already fragile Canadian scholarly book and journal publishers, which are generally based in the social sciences and humanities. Simply put, many libraries will more likely cut the weakened social science and humanities products than the science products required by the competitive science units on their campuses. Smaller Canadian social science and humanities journals are of little interest to major journal aggregators who have been purchasing the majority of reputable science journals, or contracting to represent them. There is no doubt these small publishers will be increasingly marginalized.

However, the blame for the problems facing Canadian social science and humanities book and journal publishers cannot be laid entirely at the feet of the academic library community. These publishers have failed to pay attention to the new digital technologies and the new market place, preferring the modest profits derived from Social Science and Humanities Federation grants, which unintentionally discourage online no-charge journals. For example, a no-charge digital journal was recently denied support because it did not have a demonstrable subscription base, although it certainly had a very strong online readership and excellent citation rating. As well, Canada's small academic publishing industry has also been occupied in surviving the Chapters/Indigo fiasco, which destroyed their bottom lines (Toller 2000).

Academic libraries, driven by the cost of scholarly communication rather than the new opportunities for learning and exchanging ideas offered by digital environments, have supported international attempts to mitigate costs by supporting various open access initiatives, such as the Budapest Open Access Initiative,[1] the Scholarly Publishing and Academic Resources Coalition (SPARC – the initiative of the Association of Research Libraries, an American assemblage of the research libraries with fourteen Canadian members, meant to foster less costly counter-journals), and BioMed Central, an open access publisher that generates its revenues through page charges to authors or their institutions.[2] Canadian academic libraries are enthusiastic supporters of international endeavours to cut subscription costs, but they have yet to explore digital environments which might evidence Canadian leadership in scholarly communication and knowledge mobilization.

Where Canadian scholarly presses can directly influence Canadian journal production and behaviour they tend to see the future in international and economic terms and not in terms of national need or the transformation of communication. For example, the University of Toronto Press has allied its journals with the American aggregator Project Muse at Johns Hopkins rather than contributing to a national collaborative that would have seen a collection of large and small journals creating a truly national product.[3] As well, many Canadian presses, including the University of Calgary Press, have shaped relationships with American-based NetLibrary.

This means that smaller Canadian journals that would benefit from association with more significant journals in a Canadian aggregator package now have to find different solutions, perhaps aggregating with American "disciplinary" packages. For example, there might be North American history, communications, political science, or literature packages. Another option will be to join third-party generalized aggregators. However, the dominant journals will be American with their larger markets, and the aggregation will be subject to American law and regulation.

There has been active discussion amongst Canadian librarians, the Canadian Association of Learned Journals, and most recently the Social Sciences and Humanities Research Council of Canada, of the need for an information infrastructure that will encourage scholarly communication directly relevant to Canadian social, political, cultural, and economic issues through a digital environment. The hoped-for outcome was the mobilization of research-based knowledge to inform regional and national decisions.

While that discussion was leading edge several years ago, Canada's failure to mobilize this interest has led to frustration and further marginalization. The research environment in Canada is increasingly dependent on access to digital information hosted and controlled in Europe and the United States. Despite this, Canadian researchers and information professionals show little concern for developing national platforms for hosting, archiving, and disseminating information. Indeed, in the 2005 Canadian Foundation for Innovation grant cycle, Synergies, a multi-university project led by the University of Montreal and the University of Calgary involving over twenty universities as well as the Canadian Association of Learned Journals, that would have seen the transformation of Canadian scholarly discourse in the social sciences and humanities from print to online, was considered not essential to Canada's research infrastructure. It has been re-submitted in 2006 amid hopeful signs that there has been a change of perspective. Instead, except for French-language journals being disseminated through *Erudit*, the innovative and visionary French-language project in Quebec, Canadian journals are moving to being part of the suites of journals assembled by American aggregators (Boismenu and Beaudry 2004). It is interesting to note that the French government has taken the Synergies proposal and is using it as a model for a similar French project. The loss of the leading journals in Canada to American aggregators, and their likely omission from any Canadian national aggregation, means it will be all the more difficult for smaller Canadian journals to flourish in a digitally aggregated environment.

On the surface, this reliance on a foreign information infrastructure would appear to have served Canadians quite well. The Canadian National Site Licensing Project (CNSLP) saw 64 research libraries across Canada invest $50 million for access to 750 full-text journals and indexing sources, and most Canadian researchers now have access to a robust collection of information resources. However, none of these funds were used to build a local infrastructure or archive for disseminating this information. Instead, access is based on publisher-owned servers in the United States and Europe. While this means that funds were used to buy the greatest amount of information content possible, it also means that Canada will have no way to assure long-term access to this information. Since it has so committed resources to acquisition of foreign material, there is little left to support a discourse based on national interests.

Why a Canadian Information and Scholarly Communication Infrastructure?

We must have a national information and scholarly communication infrastructure for three key reasons. First, Canadian social science and humanities research will otherwise be marginalized and not inform our national decisions. Second, not owning the means of distribution of information puts Canada at the mercy of other national agendas. Third, it makes Canada a peripheral player in the new initiatives on knowledge mobilization and scholarly communication.

Canada's general approach – leasing rather than owning information and the means of distribution – has created an incredibly fragile information and scholarly communication environment. CNSLP developed a ground-breaking national licence, one that is widely used in Canada as a litmus test for what information sellers are expected to deliver. This licence includes rights to access information paid for during the subscription period, even if the subscription should later cease. Since that licence was developed, this has become a standard element in most licences between libraries and commercial suppliers. However, with the ironic exception of the University of Toronto, which is increasingly tying itself to the American marketplace, there is little evidence that universities are concerned about this dependence on external non-Canadian sites for this long-term access.

If Canada can maximize access to resources by relying on the infrastructure of other countries, rather than investing in its own system of hosting, archiving, and distributing, then why is this not a wise use of scarce public funds? After all, this information doesn't represent national heritage or security; it is the product of work done by scholars internationally, including Canadian scholars, and most commercial publishers have developed means to securely archive their products.

The need for a national infrastructure to support hosting, archiving, and communication of commercial scholarly information arises from an information environment that has deeply changed from 1996 when CNSLP was first envisioned, a time when the "serials crisis" was the most high-profile challenge facing academic libraries. The serials crisis saw the erosion of library journal collections because of the runaway inflation in subscription prices.

This serials crisis remains with us but in a radically changed environment, with aggregator packages that offer increased title content for far less than equivalent print subscriptions, but which libraries have funded through cancelling print and losing the archival access they represented. The move to electronic information sources means that the current environment is distinguished by a dependence on electronic means for finding and sharing information, the primacy of licensed over owned information resources, and the evolution of the ability to create personal electronic spaces for scholars. Scholars at every university now have an extremely high expectation that they should be able to access to all digital resources and that they should have the ability to share information with colleagues (De Rosa et al. 2003).

Relying on licensed resources hosted in other countries threatens long-term preservation of access and memory for Canadian researchers. Scholars depend on stability in information resources equivalent to that provided by a library's print collection. Academic libraries are committed to preserving the scientific, cultural, and intellectual memory of society (Thomas 2002). Yet relying on commercial publishers for long-term access to information is problematic. Most commercial academic publishers will ultimately be challenged by problems ranging from financial failure to changes in national policy.

Another risk inherent in a dependence on non-Canadian commercial scholarly vendors is the compromised ability of Canadian scientists to share information with colleagues abroad. Unfettered communication is critical to modern research and is a significant factor in allowing national and institutional partnerships to flow across borders. Canadian universities establish productive partnerships with institutions in other countries, including exchange of resources and researchers. However, there is evidence that our dependence on licensed access to information under the control of other nations and commercial interests will limit our ability to develop partnerships and maximize those already established. Recent international events have demonstrated how quickly national policies with respect to information exchange can change.

Another particularly troublesome development is the evolution of digital rights management tools. These tools have the potential to trace the use of digital information, including articles and books by individuals, regardless of location. Individual or institutional access can be removed without warning. This means that, unless licences stipulate otherwise, Canadian institutions cannot offer Canadians the basic protection or guidance offered by Canadian law. Most certainly this weakens the autonomy of the national debate on the balance between the benefits of copyright ownership and the public good of free exchange of information.

How serious the limits on scholarly communication may become as dependence on technology grows is illustrated by examining commercial products that allow individuals to remotely store reading lists, notes, and tables of contents. For example, Furl, a free software program hosted in the United States, allows users to store links to web resources. As well, most commercial information services now provide alerting services tied to the individual users. Customization abilities are extending to the information discovery tools – catalogues, linking software, meta-searching applications – that libraries provide their users. The impact of this is that user privacy and confidentiality cannot be protected under a single set of agreed standards, in this case Canadian law. Foreign laws, such as the U.S. Patriot Act, can be used to retrieve information on Canadian citizens working in Canada. Canadian communication amongst academics flowing through American servers is at risk under the Patriot Act.

Together these developments mean that not only are the original sources of information such as electronic journals and texts no longer controlled by the institutions who lease them, but also that the work and communications of individual researchers are open to interference from other nations and commercial entities. These reflections are not hypothetical.

Scholarly Communication with Embargoed Countries

On September 30, 2003, the United States Treasury Department's Office of Foreign Assets Control (OFAC)[4] issued a ruling that required American publishers to seek a licence in order to edit and publish material from authors in

countries under interdict.[5] Even collaboration with these authors required a
licence. The work of scholars from embargoed nations could only be published without a licence if no substantial enhancement had occurred. This
meant that a journal publisher could accept and publish an article from a
researcher in an embargoed country, but it could not be refereed or edited,
since that would be adding value. In essence, given the blind peer-reviewing
practices of scholarly journals, little research from "banned" states could
appear in U.S.-based scholarly journals, which make up the bulk of the journal literature. The same situation held true for monograph publishers.

This violated the basic tenets of open scholarly communication. After considerable pressure, particularly from academic libraries, a number of American publishers took action to have the OFAC regulations revoked. The Institute of Electrical and Electronics Engineers (IEEE), which, based on OFAC
regulations, had informed members in Cuba, Iran, Libya, and Sudan in January 2002 that they would not be able to take advantage of any member benefits
and services, save for print journal subscriptions,[6] appealed to OFAC on October 6, 2003, to exempt the peer-review process and style and copy editing.
In a letter sent to IEEE on April 2, 2004,[7] OFAC did exempt peer review and
style and copy editing, provided that these activities did not result in "substan-
tive or artistic alterations or enhancements"[8] of manuscripts. The ban on collaboration with researchers in proscribed countries (North Korea, Cuba, Iran,
Libya, for example) remained. When the Canadian Association of Research
Libraries sought to file a protest, their counterpart in the United States, the
Association of Research Libraries, of which at least fourteen Canadian libraries are members, declined to allow Canadian intervention, arguing that they
would be a sufficiently effective representative. The Canadian Association
acquiesced, although they may not have had any choice.

Others took up the fight. On September 27, 2004, a coalition of the American Publisher Professional and Scholarly Publishing Division (AAP/PSP), the
Association of American University Presses (AAUP), PEN American Center,
and Arcade Publishing filed suit against OFAC asking the United States federal court to strike down the OFAC regulations.[9]

Then something somewhat unexpected occurred; the OFAC position
changed, although only partially. On December 15, 2004, OFAC issued a new
ruling which allowed "U.S. persons to freely engage in most ordinary publishing activities with persons in Cuba, Iran and Sudan."[10] The details of the
ruling indicated that most aspects of the academic publishing enterprise, including collaboration, were now permitted. The decision to make this change
was apparently based on the feeling that earlier rulings were being seen as
discouraging the expression of dissent in these countries. Many restrictions

still remained in place, however, such as contact with the governments of the embargoed nations and travel to these countries.

It is worth noting that the OFAC regulations are interpretations of U.S. legislation. Two pieces of legislation passed by Congress, the Berman Amendment (1989) and the Free Trade in Ideas Amendment (1994), state that "informational materials" are specifically excluded from any trade sanctions.[11] The OFAC regulations are simply very narrow interpretations of these amendments. This demonstrates the risks of relying on other jurisdictions for access to information resources, especially when the rules governing this access are subject to debate and multiple interpretations within those jurisdictions. The impact of the OFAC rules and interpretations on Canadian researchers are not obscure. Even with the December 2004 change, the situation could always swing in the reverse at some point in the future. Academics at Canadian universities who work cooperatively with counterparts in countries under United States interdiction might well find that the results of their research cannot be published by American or by American-owned publishers, even if the publisher is located in or has offices in Canada.

Information to Embargoed Countries

As alluded to earlier, the flipside to the OFAC regulations involves the provision of information licensed by Canadian universities to their programs in proscribed countries. This emerged as an issue in 2003 and, so far, has been mostly faced by schools with medical and engineering programs.

In the fall of 2003, the American Medical Association (AMA), publisher of the highly regarded *Journal of the American Medical Association* (JAMA) and the several other top-level scholarly health science journals, sent a new site licence to subscribers of the AMA's online journal content. Subscribers were supposed to sign and return the new licence as part of the renewal for the 2004 subscription year. The new AMA site licence included a startling new clause:

[The] Licensee agrees that it shall not make the Licensed Materials available in such countries as advised in writing by AMA where such availability may be prohibited by U.S. law ...[12]

This section had serious implications for non-U.S. subscribers. Essentially, even if someone is an authorized user of the licensed content (faculty, staff, and students of the licensee institution), if they are resident in a nation under American embargo, once notice is given from the AMA, they should not be granted access to the AMA journal content.

From a Canadian perspective, the problems were serious. Many Canadian universities have established distance education programs and other cooperative ventures in countries that fall under or might fall under U.S. embargo. Many Canadian academics have colleagues in these countries and teach and conduct research in these nations. Obviously, if a Canadian institution signed a licence with this clause, they could be legally bound, at least by American law, to refuse to provide content. Adherence to American law might violate other agreements a Canadian university signed with foreign universities or with the Canadian federal government agencies, which might require Canada to manage both a scholarly communication process or access to scholarly information. The U.S. control of scholarly communications has become so pervasive and insidious that it may well limit Canadian foreign policy initiatives as well as the international work of its universities.

Some university libraries have attempted to remove the contentious clause from the AMA site licence. Although AMA staff has been helpful in changing other sections in the licence, they have steadfastly refused to remove the clause in question. It is not clear whether the AMA restriction is a self-imposed one, or one imposed by U.S. authorities. It is very likely that the American Medical Association has included the restriction based on legal advice. What would have happened if Elsevier Science had been headquartered in the United States and was subject to the Patriot Act rather than in the more liberal Netherlands?

The situation involving the restriction of the provision of licensed information to embargoed countries has continued. The 2005 renewal of the AMA e-journal package was accompanied by yet another revision of the AMA site licence. Changes from the 2003 version were minimal but the contentious clause remains intact. In addition, similar clauses and wording have begun appearing in other licences. At the less blatant end, many American publishers of electronic content are now incorporating a "catch-all" clause in the "force majeure" sections of their licences, which note "government restrictions" as something for which they will not be responsible (along with natural disaster, war, etc.). At the other end of the spectrum, the 2005 version of the licence for SPIE Digital Library, a full-text collection of technical reports and journals published by the Society of Photo-Optical Instrumentation Engineers (SPIE), included this very straightforward clause:

SPIE shall not be required to distribute, and Client shall not redistribute, the licensed material or any article therein to a country to which export is prohibited by U.S. law or regulation.[13]

The Patriot Act

Even more insidious than the control of collaboration, communication, and publishing is the enhanced ability of American law enforcement agencies under the Patriot Act[14] to retrieve private and personal information held on American servers regardless of its national origin. A situation could arise where personal information about Canadians, such as the search histories of Canadian university faculty and students in a particular database, is taken by American authorities despite Canadian objections and without our knowledge. It is also entirely possible that, if these records were seized, Canadian institutions would no longer have access to their records on deposit in American servers. Should offending Canadians enter the United States they might find themselves subject to prosecution and persecution.

Canadian institutions could deal with such a scenario by local loading of database content. The majority of online databases are produced by American publishers, loaded on computers in the United States, and accessed at distance by Canadian subscribers. Mirror sites sometimes exist, but these are often not located in Canada. Local loading would ensure that Canadian-connected data and associated patron use information did not reside in the United States. However, the practice is not yet widely considered other than in British Columbia. There, the Information and Privacy Commissioner, David Loukidelis, initiated a major study of the implications of the Patriot Act on outsourcing by the British Columbia government.[15] He received over five hundred submissions, a number of which were from library associations. He agreed that, if British Columbia contracted with an American company for goods and services of any kind, that data on British Columbians might well be inappropriately housed on American servers. This would expose British Columbians to an invasion of their privacy by a foreign power. However, rather than preventing government contracts with American companies, he determined that changes to the province's privacy legislation would offer sufficient protection. Personal information would have to be housed on Canadian servers and be subject to Canadian law. The amendments to British Columbia's privacy legislation as a result of the report are complex, but the end result will be that in that province Canadian information will have to be located on servers in Canada. To give teeth to the amendments, the Commissioner recommended a fine of $1 million for violation. It will be interesting to determine whether the Canadian federal government and the other provinces will follow suit.

In part, Ontario has done so. In Canadian academic circles, the most well-known local loading initiative is the Scholar's Portal in Ontario. A primary purpose of this project is to ensure that the licensed information will be available in the future. A project of the Ontario Council of University Libraries (OCUL), funded by the provincial government, the Scholar's Portal was established in 2002 and was designed to provide a consistent interface to the suite of electronic journals licensed by OCUL member libraries. These journals are locally loaded at the University of Toronto, retaining the journal content and all the related data (usage statistics, search histories, etc.) in a Canadian setting, providing a "north of the border" solution.[16]

Lack of a National Debate

While Canadian libraries and universities have an ongoing national dialogue concerning the importance of preserving Canada's digital heritage, a discussion of the risks in depending on commercial and other nations for scholarly communication and its preservation has not had a public forum. The Canadian National Site Licensing Project (CNSLP) illustrates the point. CNSLP argued passionately for the importance of access to information in creating a competitive Canadian research community. But it remains removed from any debate on long-term access. In its most recent incarnation as the Canadian Research Knowledge Network (CRKN), it still views the primary problem to be solved as access, not preservation or the freedom and rights of individual researchers.[17] As a key licensing agency, it might be in a position to marshal support, but like the Canadian Association of Research Libraries it failed to do so.

The Canadian Council of Prairie and University Libraries (COPPUL), a consortium made up primarily of western Canadian libraries, has embarked on an ambitious project to independently develop a technological infrastructure that would fully support users' interaction with digital commercial resources. This project, called reSearcher, is planned, like a number of its American counterparts, to include a link resolver to link from databases to full-text resources, an interlibrary loan system, a citation manager for storing and organizing citations for individual users, and a cross-database searching tool.[18] However, it remains silent on the question of archiving, stability, and the threats to open scholarly discourse. While it offers at least one tool for helping individual users manage information, nowhere does it discuss how this might provide users more stability and privacy than competing non-Canadian tools.

The Canadian Institute for Scientific and Technical Information (CISTI), which serves as Canada's de facto national science library, provides researchers with reasonably priced, rapid access to a world-class collection of science journals and conference proceedings. Many university libraries depend on

CISTI for access to expensive or specialized titles that they cannot afford. In its strategic plan, CISTI acknowledges this role; however, the nature of this role or how it can be achieved is not elaborated.[19] CISTI's parent organization, the National Research Council, publishes a number of journals itself and signs a significant number of licences, but it has been silent on issues emerging from the Patriot Act. In summary, there has been no national debate or even acknowledgment of this problem.

International Discussion

A review of the 2003 bibliography on preservation of digital resources, compiled by Kathleen Shearer for the Canadian Association of Research Libraries, provides little evidence that other countries are more advanced in discussions of national preservation strategies for commercial information (Shearer 2003).[20] A major breakthrough has been the agreement between Elsevier and the Royal Dutch Library. Elsevier has agreed to keep a copy of its retrospective digital collections in escrow in the royal library, although it remains at the moment a "dark" archive available only to authorized subscribers.

The United Kingdom is something of an exception. The Joint Information Services Committee (JISC) of the United Kingdom provides a central group for planning and implementing a shared information infrastructure. In its 2002 strategy document,[21] JISC recognized the importance of preserving commercial and institutionally created digital information: "The needs of researchers, students, staff and institutions will often require ongoing availability and confidence in the future accessibility of these materials."[22] The strategy included a recommendation for the development of a national repository of e-journals.

NESTOR, a German national preservation project for digital resources was founded in 2003. While still very much in a start-up phase, it seems to cross over from the standard national interest in heritage materials into commercial products. It is actively investigating issues for the preservation of electronic journals and the impact digital rights management and copyright law could have on a preservation program (Dobratz and Neuroth 2004).

Other discussions of archiving electronic resources consistently make two points: that commercial publishers are unreliable archives and that archiving requires deep resources, often at a national level. Taken together, these observations reinforce the importance of developing national information infrastructures that include commercial products in their planning.

As an international issue, digital rights management has received some attention as libraries try to understand the implication of the new technology.

Intellectual property rights are becoming subject to international trade laws, specifically the World Trade Organization. This may lead to the domination of the economic concerns of richer nations over the social benefit of information exchange. Digital Rights Management systems are a technology that may enable commercial or national controls that are in contradiction to local needs and laws (May 2003).

Laura J. Murray, in "Protecting Ourselves to Death: Canada, Copyright, and the Internet," reinforces this view (Murray 2004). In discussing the rhetoric that surrounds Canadian discussions of copyright, she argues that Canadians often conflate the protection of copyright holders with protecting national culture. In her criticism, Murray describes the fair use doctrine as it is applied in Canada and how this differs from the application in other jurisdictions, namely the United States. She demonstrates that copyright is not only an international issue of property, it is also a reflection of cultural views and norms as they evolve through consensus in national debate. Much the same could be said of norms of privacy and confidentiality of information. Digital rights management systems have great potential to subvert the autonomy of this debate, imposing externally derived controls that override national laws or even international conventions. Canada and Canadians must control both the hosting and use of content to protect citizens and resources from external control.

Further Implications

On the surface, the impact of the above discussions on Canada's other memory institutions and publishers would seem to be minimal. Except for the occasional Canadian publisher, archives' and museums' information offerings are rarely part of international aggregator packages. Yet the same issues of marginalization, preservation, ownership, and control apply, although perhaps in a more subtle and insidious way.

Canadian digital information generated by its archives and museums is free. It is housed for the most part on Canadian servers. However, the fact that it is free makes it often virtually inaccessible and inconsistently indexed by university libraries. The fact is that academic information found in commercial aggregator packages is treated more seriously by academic libraries than free information generated by its memory institutions. Academic libraries may well argue for open access and for the liberation of scholarly discourse, but their own indexing and preservation habits testify to a more schizophrenic behaviour. This has meant that some key Canadian cultural information is not included in the material validated by the library acquisition process.

While this may not matter where there is an incredible density of cultural material, it does matter where cultural memory is fragile. It also suggests that open access outside aggregator packages or information outside the commercial framework is not yet an accepted form of scholarly communication. What is free would appear to be of less value. Rich archival collections of primary materials are critical to research, to the questioning of decisions, and to a healthy ever-inquiring community. While American, British, and European collections are aggressively present in pay-for-view digital environments, like those of Alexander Street Press, Canadian materials are not generally present in these packages except as add-ons and are not easily identifiable on the Web. This means that free information informed by Canadian content is marginalized.

There are several reasons for this. First while Canadian academic libraries purchase information, they rarely harvest free information and include it in their primary access points – catalogues. This means, for example, in Canadian universities, products like "Our Roots," "Our Future Our Past," and "Early Canadiana On-line" are not obviously accessible to students. Free full-text Canadian materials available through leading Canadian archives like the National Library and Archives Canada are also not consistently identified. Libraries and archives argue for free, open, and unfettered access, but unless there is an exchange of money, it would appear that access is not taken as seriously. While academic librarians and archivists might well rail at "Google," often it is a reliable guide for free national information.

Examining access to four key Canadian primary source and archival databases at the three largest Canadian university libraries, the University of Alberta, the University of British Columbia, and the University of Toronto, is instructive. "Early Canadiana On Line," "Our Roots/Nos Racines," "The Alberta Heritage Digitization Project," also known as "Our Future Our Past," and the *Indian Affairs Annual Reports* produced by the Library and Archives of Canada were searched on the library catalogues of these institutions. "Early Canadiana On Line" was selected both because it has the support of the library community and because it is a pay-for-view as well as free site. "The Alberta Heritage Digitization Project" was selected because it is a regional primary and secondary source site built on solid academic principles of peer review, but free of charge. "Our Roots/Nos Racines," the pre-eminent local history site in Canada, reflected a cross-national bilingual product developed under a university press and an academic library and is available at no charge.

The *Indian Affairs Annual Reports* reflect a key free searchable database for both Canadian and Aboriginal studies.

A Google search for "Canadian local history" immediately brings up "Our Roots/Nos Racines" as number one. Remote access to the University of Alberta's library catalogue indicates its availability, but no access without authentication is allowed. Searching the same product through The Alberta Library, a consolidated catalogue of all post-secondary and public libraries in Alberta, including the University Alberta, again suggests only one location in Alberta – the University of Alberta – but direct click-through access is allowed. The University of British Columbia library had no apparent reference to "Our Roots" in its catalogue.

The University of Toronto catalogue is of particular interest because it is transparent in what it catalogues.[23] It identifies products that the university subscribes to, but not those that are free, other than through indexes generated by American librarians or their institutions – in which Canada is rarely identified. "Our Roots" could not be retrieved using the general catalogue search or their general electronic resources search tool. While it can be found through intermediary sites, few students and faculty and fewer non-academic Canadians would have the information literacy skills to make this retrieval.

The case of "The Alberta Heritage Digitization Project/Our Future Our Past," which has approximately 500,000 pages of text, is equally instructive. An imprint of the University of Calgary Press, it is not identified in the University of Alberta library catalogue. It can be retrieved in The Alberta Library Catalogue with a holding identified in the Short Grass public library system. It is no surprise that it is not identified at the University of Toronto, the fourth ranking library in North America, since the Canadian West is hardly relevant in eastern Canada. What is interesting is that the terms "Alberta and history" confined to e-resources did return licensed western Canadian titles published by western Canadian university presses that make digital product available through the American-based netLibrary. To be licensed to the University of Toronto is to be aggregated by an American information corporation.

The conclusions might be that, if academic products are not pay for view or are not part of wider aggregated digital collections, they are marginalized. Aggregated free digital resources rarely emerge in Canadian academic library catalogues. It should be no surprise, however, that toll-gated digital collections can be accessed through university library catalogues with considerable ease. "Early Canadiana On Line," or ECO, is always clearly indexed both in the library catalogues as well as separately in their digital resource listings. The collection is available online for free, although with less functionality. None of the catalogues link to the "free version" – all link to the toll-gated version. Even The Alberta Library, which provides some links to digital data that is free, links to the toll-gated version. Perhaps toll-gated products provide greater service and stability. But more likely, the toll-gated product follows existing identification, purchasing, and cataloguing flows within academic libraries. Harvesting and preservation systems are yet poorly developed within academic libraries, and little thought has been given to the need for systems review. A cynic might conclude that academic libraries are primarily serving as cash aggregators for commercial publishers.

A final e-collection that was examined was Library and Archives Canada's *Annual Indian Affairs Reports*. These were selected because they are government documents, which in the past have generally been free. However, while the print versions are available at all academic libraries, the electronic references were not readily accessible. At the University of Toronto Libraries, they were not linked, although they were at the University of Alberta libraries and at those of the University of British Columbia. The point is not to be critical of the information-seeking behaviours of researchers, students, and citizens, but rather to observe the inconsistency of academic archives and libraries in their support of scholarly communication.

While the above proves little other than government documents online and purchased information are more likely to be catalogued, the implications for Canadian journals who want to pursue an open access model must be carefully considered. So must the implications for the movement to find new structures for scholarly discourse that might or might not replace the journal. Currently the scholarly communication food chain includes scholar/creator, publisher, referees, and buyers (one of which might be a library). The new digital medium allows the creator/scholar to determine whether the publisher, the referee, or the buyer/memory institution adds value. Academic libraries argue that they have a role to play in the facilitation of the new scholarly discourse. But the vendor/librarian relationship rather than the scholar/librarian relationship remains the key one. Academic librarians still prefer to be masters of the "toll gate."

This suggests that, without a fundamental shift in the internal operations of libraries, academic library activities to facilitate scholarly communication will likely be limited. Many academic libraries, for example, have adopted digital repositories to house faculty scholarly production, many using DSpace software from the Massachusetts Institute of Technology. However, libraries have complained that take-up by faculty has been limited.[24] Without full integration into a single search engine, which incorporates all information types, DSpace will be a marginal scholarly communication strategy. It will remain a marginally accessible "add on." Should Goggle integrate DSpace, there might well begin to be traction. But if DSpace is protected behind individual university library authentication processes, the only impact will be to tease – not to create access.

If part of the failure of open digital communication lies with academic libraries and their librarians and administrators who are unwilling to live up to the promises of their rhetoric, responsibility for the floundering of the open access movement for scholarly communication lies with scholars themselves. Most recently, in a discussion in the Budapest Open Access Initiative forum, several scholars debated the impact of self-published literature and where digital objects would best be housed. The consensus by some was that they would be best housed at the departmental level within universities. While some argued that this would minimize impact of the research, it was equally argued that the "invisible" college would know where to find what it needed. The option of the university library or university archives facilitating and housing this kind of discourse did not immediately come to their minds.

This was curious given the connection of the Budapest Open Access Initiative with the Directory of Open Access Journals (DOAJ). DOAJ aims to create a comprehensive directory of open access journals searchable at the article level. The initiative originated at the First Nordic Conference on Scholarly Communication at Lund (http://www.lub.lu.se/ncsc2002), funded by SPARC and the Open Society Initiative in Budapest. This is possibly one of the most positive steps in the creation of open discourse within the context of tradition. Because the journals are aggregated and available with professional indexing standards, Canadian academic libraries are including the journals in their catalogues. However, at the moment there are only about a dozen Canadian journals amongst the 1,362 journals (only 334 are searchable at the article level) and most of these are in the medical fields.[25] Will this initiative housed at Lund University gain traction? Will it stall? Will Canadian journals drift to European aggregation? If the Nordic universities deposit the collection at OCLC, will it too eventually fall under the Patriot Act?

The open source initiative appears to be sufficiently distributed and supported by smaller national scholarly activity that it will survive. But how many journals are still based on inflexible government support systems like that offered by the Social Sciences and Humanities Research Council, which demand paid subscriptions rather than readership? Can Canadian systems for scholarly communication change?

Conclusion

The digital world offered incredible opportunity for open communication that could ignore international and disciplinary boundaries. The initiatives in the digital world by Canada's memory institutions, however, have not been driven by the opportunities offered by the new technologies; rather their innovations have initially been driven almost entirely by serials pricing issues. This myopic perspective means that innovation has only happened as a reaction to journal price increases. If anything, the division amongst memory institutions and fragmentation within the scholarly communication community (really the academy as a whole) has increased. The failure lies squarely with the academic libraries and their failure to identify the elements of the problem, their failure to look at their own systemic dysfunctions, and in the end their failure in exercising appropriate leadership. Academic libraries have argued that they are the bulwarks of intellectual freedom and that they are the keepers and the access providers for intellectual memory. In Canada, their behaviour has not evidenced that role. Their pleas to the Canadian Foundation for Innovation to acquire international toll-gated products were successful, but their support for a profound transformation of scholarly communication remains tempered. CFI sees it as an interesting but not a critical issue that could have been argued as eligible for their emergency funding.

Their relations with the Canadian journals and publishing community remain tangential. While they are the primary consumers of Canadian scholarship, they have done little to understand or to nurture Canadian scholarly communication. They have failed to engage the Canadian scholarly community and its journal community, choosing rather to support American academic library initiatives to fight the international aggregators. But in so doing they ignored the crisis in their own backyard. Canadian publishers were going bankrupt as Canadian and American libraries were focusing on the Elsevier-generated crisis. Licences were being signed with few complaints about the impacts for Canadian intellectual freedom. Free intellectually sound products are not being indexed to ensure uniform access.

If the academic libraries are failing as agents of change in an increasingly complex information communication environment, it is because they lack the national conviction and will to develop their own independent leadership within the international context. How can it be otherwise when over half of the members of Canada's leading academic library association, the Canadian Association of Research Libraries, are also members of the Association of Research Libraries, a conservative organization of leading American large academic institutions who are members of a system that preserves (whether intentionally or not) American hegemony over scholarly communication? They will tamper at the edges but will be very slow to change traditional practice and assumptions. The glacial pace of change could leave the senior academic libraries marginalized – it is up to the younger and more nimble to be the leaders of tomorrow.

Select Bibliography

Bergstrom, Carl T., and Theodore C. Bergstrom. 2001. "The Economics of Journal Publishing." http://octavia.zoology.washington.edu/publishing/intro.html.

Boismenu, Gerard, and Guylaine Beaudry. 2004. *Scholarly Journals in the New Digital World*. Trans. Maureen Ranson. Calgary: University of Calgary Press.

De Rosa, Cathy, Lorcan Dempsey, and Alane Wilson. 2003. *2003 Environmental Scan: Pattern Recognition*. Online Computer Library Center Inc. Dublin, Ohio, http://www.oclc.org/membership/escan/toc.htm.

Divis, Dee Ann. 2004. "PoliSci Journals Torque Library budgets" *UPI*, http://www.upi.com/view.cfm?StoryID=20040811-085949-8276r.

Dobratz, Susanne, and Heike Neuroth. 2004. "Nestor: Network of Expertise in Long-Term Storage of Digital Resources – a Digital Preservation Initiative for Germany." *D-Lib Magazine*. 10 April, http://www.dlib.org/dlib/april04/dobratz/04dobratz.htmlGeorge.

George, Lee Anne, ed. 2003. *Library Patron Privacy Kit* SPEC 278. Washington: Association of Research Libraries.

Howell, Robert. 1998. *Data Base Protection and Canadian Laws*. Ottawa: Industry Canada.

Johnson, David, ed. 1998. *Smart Communities Report on the Panel on Smart Communities*. Ottawa: The Panel on Smart Communities.

Jones, Wayne, ed. 2002. *E-Serials Publisher, Libraries, Users, and Standards*. New York: Haworth Information Press.

May, Christopher. 2003. "Digital Rights Management and the Breakdown of Social Norms." *First Monday* 8(11): http://www.firstmonday.org/issues/issue8_11/may/index.html.

Murray, Laura J. 2004. "Protecting Ourselves to Death: Canada, Copyright, and the Internet." *First Monday* 9(10): http://www.firstmonday.org/issues/issue9_10/murray/index.html

Shearer, Kathleen. 2003. *Preservation of Digital Resources: Selected and Annotated reading list*. CARL/ARBC Backgrounders Series, Canadian Association of Research Libraries, http://tinyurl.com/kfjnz.

Thomas, Sarah. 2002. "From Double Fold to Double Bind." *Journal of Academic Librarianship* 28(3): 104–8.

Toller, Carol. 2000. "CBA plans to fight Pegasus in Ottawa: parliamentary committee will examine wholesaling venture". *Quill & Quire*. 66(1) (January): 4.

White, John, ed. n.d. *Intellectual Property in the Age of Universal Access*. The First Society in Computing.

Notes

1   Open Access Initiative, http://www.soros.org/openaccess/.

2   BioMed Central: The Open Access Publisher, http://www.biomedcentral.com/.

3   Note some of the key University of Toronto journals at http://muse.jhu.edu/
    journals/index.html.

4   OFAC "administers and enforces economic and trade sanctions based on US
    foreign policy and national security goals against targeted foreign countries,
    terrorists, international narcotics traffickers, and those engaged in activities
    related to the proliferation of weapons of mass destruction."
    www.treas.gov/offices/enforcement/ofac/ (accessed 20 October 2004).

5   OFAC ruling 031002-FACRL-IA-11. http://www.treas.gov/offices/enforcement/
    ofac/rulings/ia100203.pdf (accessed 20 October 2004).

6   http://www.ieee.org/portal/site/mainsite/menuitem.818c0c39e85ef176fb2
    275875bac26c8/index.jsp?&pName=corp_level1&path=about&file=ofac.
    xml&xsl=generic.xsl (accessed 20 October 2004).

7   OFAC ruling 040405-FACRL-IA-15. http://www.treas.gov/offices/enforcement/
    ofac/rulings/ia040504.pdf (accessed 20 October 2004).

8   Ibid.

9   See http://www.aaupnet.org/ofac/ and http://www.aaupnet.org/ofac/release.
    html (both accessed 20 October 2004).

10 http://www.treasury.gov/press/releases/js2152.htm (accessed 22 March 2005).
    This is the press release for the new ruling. The new ruling in full can
    be accessed at http://www.treasury.gov/press/releases/reports/
    office%20foreign.pdf.

11 There is a good timeline incorporating the Berman Amendment and the
    Free Trade in Ideas Amendment at http://aaupnet.org/ofac/background.html.

12 AMA site licence, 2003.

13 SPIE site licence, 2005.

14 Uniting and Strengthening America by Providing Appropriate Tools
    Required to Intercept and Obstruct Terrorism (USA Patriot Act) of 2001
    (Public Law 107-56, 115 STAT.272, H.R 3162).

15 http://www.oipcbc.org/index.htm for a full text of the report and subsequent
    legislation.

16 Ontario Scholars Portal at http://library.queensu.ca/libguides/databases/
    scholarsportal.htm.

17 Savoir: monthly communiqué for members and stakeholders. Vol. 1 (October
    2004). http://www.cnslp.ca/wiki-files/savoir/October2004.pdf.

18 About reSearcher products. Canadian Council of Prairie and Pacific Univer-
    sity Libraries. http://www.theresearcher.ca/product_about.html.

19 Bridging the innovation gap: strategic plan 2000 to 2005. Canadian Institute
    for Scientific and Technical Information. 4 September 2003.
    http://cisti-icist.nrc-cnrc.gc.ca/about_cisti/stratplan_e.shtml.

20 Kathleen Shearer, Preservation of Digital Resources: Selected and Annotated
    reading list CARL/ARBC Backgrounders Series, Canadian Association of
    Research Libaries. http://www.carl-abrc.ca/projects/preservation/
    2003Backgrounder.PDF.

21   A continual access and digital preservation strategy for the Joint Information
     Systems Committee (JISC) 2002–2005. Joint Information Systems
     Committee. Neil Beagrie, 10 January 2002. http://www.jisc.ac.uk/
     index.cfm?name=pres_continuing.

22   Ibid., A4.

23   http://link.library.utoronto.ca/MyUTL/guides/index.cfm?guide=iqs.

24   http://dspace.org/news/dspace-news.html.

25   Directory of Open Access Journals at http://www.doaj.org/.

13: Broadband at the Margins: Challenges to Supernet Deployment in Rural and Remote Albertan Communities

DAVID MITCHELL

As far as media goes, a great deal has changed in the way that we as Canadians communicate over the course of the past two decades. If we look back say to the early 1980s, using Paul Audley's (1983) assessment of Canada's communications and cultural industries, we get a very different sense of what the landscape looked like at the time – and what many nationalists felt ought to be done. Audley's text echoed a common view that the health of these industries was compromised by American domination at every turn but also by an underdevelopment of these industries coupled with a lack of political will. Fortunately, this bleak diagnosis was accompanied by a full array of solutions, mostly in the form of federal policy interventions including: funding for production; access to distribution and exhibition; income tax incentives; restrictions on foreign investment, etc. Together this diagnosis and prognosis for Canada's communications and culture industries were accepted as received wisdom.

But few observers at the time were able to guess at the shape and the extent of changes to come. Over the next two decades we saw the emergence of such trends as: free trade in the North American marketplace; the deregulation and opening up of competition in telecommunications; the (digitally enabled) convergence of broadcasting, cultural industries, and telecommunications;

the explosive growth of the public Internet; and the eventual success of Canadian film and video products in both domestic and export markets.

These factors together are changing the nature of how we in Canada and elsewhere use media to communicate. Reflecting on the past we recall that twenty years ago, as individuals we used telephone services to talk with one another, telecommunications services were mostly only used by large corporations to exchange information, and together we sat as a mass audience in front of TV sets, choosing between the limited news, sports, and entertainment programs that the few large networks deemed worthy business cases to push our way. Today, we take it for granted that all three of these activities can be supported over a variety of convergent modes: cable, telephone, and consumer Internet. But the more relevant observation is that as individuals and groups we are beginning to use these new media in different ways. We still talk with one another using phones, but increasingly we are gravitating towards Internet-mediated transmission (voice-over IP) as telecommunications becomes transformed from a historically scarce to an increasingly abundant (and thereby cheap) resource. These days, information services are no longer the province of mostly large corporations, but they are used by all sizes of providers and users. And while critics continue to bewail the great array of prepackaged content that is being pushed at us over the Web, the users' experience bears more resemblance to the earlier experience of searching for information in a public library than that of sitting before a television screen in the era of big networks. Perhaps more importantly, the new modes permit much higher levels of interactive communication in real time. Today, broadband networks are beginning to support efficient and cheap videoconferencing platforms[1] that make communication over the Web more like a natural conversation between people, replete with the full range of audio and visual complements that were missing in either text-mediated or telephone-mediated modes.

This said, some observers, such as Vincent Mosco and Robert Babe, continue to insist that there is nothing fundamentally new about the changes we are witnessing today and that we should continue to wield the critical weapons of the past with steady conviction. I would agree that this habit of mind will help us to recognize familiar patterns of politics and economics that we have seen before, but I would also counter that this singleness of mind may blindside us from appreciating the emergence of genuinely new trends.

In what follows, I will try to bear both of these perspectives in mind as I describe how an entire province in Canada is being propelled into a networked future.

The Alberta SuperNet

An experiment is currently taking place in the province of Alberta which will have national and international significance for many years to come. This is the construction of the Alberta SuperNet – a broadband network that will connect 429, or 95 per cent, of the communities within the province. In late September 2005, this network was officially lit up to provide communities a variety of business- and social-services-related applications through a combination of Internet and dedicated telecommunications modes.

The construction of the SuperNet will be of interest to other provinces and territories in Canada, and to other countries beyond Canada, for various reasons. For one, the Government of Alberta has developed a very interesting business case for constructing the network as a public-sector/private-sector partnership. For another, the government has demonstrated how quickly an initiative of this scope can be moved on when a governing body wields sufficient political will.

Now that the build has been completed, the roll-out of SuperNet services will be of interest for some years to come. On the one hand, the provincial government has constructed a fixed rate for telecommunications services irrespective of location. In addition, many constituencies will want to know whether the SuperNet-delivered services present a cost-effective alternative to the way similar services are already made available.

At this time, we can suggest with considerable assurance that this broadband network will positively enhance the way that social/information services are deployed in many communities across the province. The government also hopes that the SuperNet will have positive economic development impacts in many communities, but it is too early as yet to project whether and to what extent this may transpire. Notwithstanding the best intentions of the provincial government, there will be communities within the province that will not be able to secure the full benefits of the network.

In what follows, I will report on the Alberta SuperNet from a number of perspectives, including:

- What the federal context is for utilizing broadband technology and services as a tool of community development;
- What the provincial government is hoping to accomplish in the areas of social and economic development with the SuperNet;
- Why the Alberta experiment can be characterized as precedent-setting;

- Why the SuperNet phenomenon looks so interesting to a number of social science and humanities researchers in western Canada (i.e., Alberta SuperNet Research Alliance);
- What we as researchers have learned through public consultation with rural and remote communities across the province regarding their concerns and expectations about the SuperNet;
- What barriers some communities face that will make it difficult or impossible for them to secure the full benefits of the deployment of broadband services in the near future.

Media and Community Development in Canada

The notion of using technological means to develop Canada as a nation – economically, socially, culturally – is as old as the country itself. As Robert Babe (2000) has pointed out, originally this strategy involved the construction of transportation infrastructure, particularly railways; later, it shifted to communications technology, particularly broadcasting, where it entailed a combination of content provision and extension of service. References to using information technology as a nation-builder date from the 1970s and are usually tied to industrial development policy.

In the early 1990s the phenomenon of convergence in information and communications technologies and services created a new environment for political discourse: Canada as a knowledge-based economy and society – made possible by high-speed broadband networks. This vision became a widespread topic of discussion within the media, universities, the private sector, and government and non-governmental institutions.[2] During this time, the government set up the Information Highway Advisory Council (IHAC) to advise on a national strategy for developing Canada as a networked society. Through a series of reports, the committee suggested that the government should implement policies and programs to develop Canada's capacity in three areas: *connection* (broadband network infrastructure); *content* (digitized and Internet-mediated content); and *community* (networked development) programs. In response to these recommendations, the federal government has taken action mostly in the area of *connection*, providing resources in combination with the private sector to construct a series of nation-wide commercial and research information superhighways. In contrast, initiatives for developing *community* did not get much practical support until the late 1990s.

The first notable stress on using new media for purposes of community development appeared in 1998 when John Manley, then minister of Industry, rolled out his *Connecting Canadians Strategy*. One of the pillars of this strategy involved support for the creation of twelve "smart communities." The idea here was to invest large funds ($5 million per community) to build a series of high-profile demonstration projects across the country. It was hoped that these projects would stimulate further development in their respective regions.

In addition to the *Smart Communities* initiative, another program of support, called the *Community Access Program*, was implemented to help small rural and remote communities acquire basic Internet access and facilities. The funds made available through this program were quite limited and usually only provided for minimal equipment and a basic dial-up service located at a community centre. While this program has helped some small communities to get started with Internet use, it also magnified the digital divide problem (i.e., network access, equipment, technical training and support, etc.) that exists between these communities and the larger towns and cities in the south of Canada.

Partly in response to the digital divide problem, the National Broadband Task Force was established in 2000 to consider a new vision for Canada as a broadband-enabled nation. The task force noted that at earlier points in its history Canada had been transformed by various technologies: railway transportation, mechanization, and broadcasting. The task force concluded that the extension of broadband networks (and applications) held considerable promise for the development of Canadian communities, particularly those in underserved areas. The committee felt that providing broadband access to rural and remote communities had the potential to improve the quality of life in many areas: education, information, security, culture, and health. Based on this view, the main recommendation of the task force was that all Canadian communities should be provided with basic broadband connectivity by 2004, where basic broadband is taken to mean a minimum of 1.5 Mbps symmetrical connectivity.

Thus while the task force on broadband was able to present a far-reaching vision of the nation connected and enabled by the new technology – and a target date for landing this vision – there was no follow-through by the federal government. Brian Tobin, then minister of Industry Canada, failed in his bid to prioritize this initiative over and against Paul Martin's (Minister of Finance at the time) policies of deficit control and debt reduction. Two years later, when the government did at last release funds for programs in this area, they were effectively only for pilot demonstrations.[3]

The SuperNet as a Precedent-Setting Case

While the task force's vision of connecting all Canadian communities with broadband by 2004 did not happen, a provincial version of this initiative is taking place within Alberta. And, while it is true that the extension of high-speed telecommunications networks seems to be almost commonplace in developed nations these days, the Alberta case is a precedent-setting one in many ways.

THE SHEER GEOGRAPHIC SCALE AND THE OUTREACH OF THE PROJECT

There are many broadband connectivity initiatives currently in place or underway around the world, but most of these are confined to wiring single cities (e.g., Chicago), or connecting cities (e.g., Malaysia), or extending connectivity to under-served communities within a fairly restricted geographical domain (e.g., New Brunswick). One quick look at the map of Alberta should settle this first point: the province is vast in territory, and the network that is being built is highly comprehensive – connecting virtually every town and hamlet within its vast boundaries.

THE SPEED AT WHICH THE NETWORK IS BEING CONSTRUCTED

Given the scale and comprehensiveness of the SuperNet, it is fair to say that the project has advanced from the concept to the implementation stage in a very short time. The original notion of the SuperNet emerged out of discussions within the Alberta Science and Research Authority (c. 1999–2000). It decreed by fiat that there would be a provincial broadband network built (c. 2001) and moved quickly in 2002 to settle contracts for the build (mostly Bell West)[4] and the eventual management of the network (Axia SuperNet) in place. The lessons here are that the government in power was able to move as quickly as it did. It accomplished this, first, because it had such an overwhelming majority of seats in the legislature; and second, because the province had the ready capital at its disposal to proceed.

THE BUSINESS CASE FOR THE CONSTRUCTION OF THE NETWORK

The provincial government developed a very interesting business case for how the SuperNet was to be constructed. When the original concept was floated to build a comprehensive optical network for the province, the project was sold as a way of providing a more efficient way of handling the flow of its government information services across the province, which at that point were costing roughly $70 million/year. Beyond providing a more efficient way of handling information services related to government programs as well as social service applications in such areas as health and education, it was also hoped that the proposed network might have community economic development potential. But how was this to be achieved?

Since the government had recently privatized Alberta Government Telephones to become a private-sector player (Telus), it hardly wanted to revert to a public model for telecommunications ownership. At the same time, it desired a more competitive environment for telecommunications than Telus was providing as the provincial incumbent. But how much opportunity for competitive services would there be for a fully provincial broadband network?

Accordingly, the government asked the telcos to calculate: if each of you were to carry the costs of building a province-wide network by yourself, how many communities do you think have viable business cases that would justify connecting them to the network? In other words, how many communities have sufficiently robust economies such that private firms would want to step forward to compete over the private delivery of Internet and related telecommunications services? Originally, the answer was very few – less than thirty. So the government rephrased the question to become: if the provincial government were to cover about two-thirds of the costs of constructing the network, how many communities would you estimate might then be able to support competition for the delivery of Internet and related telecommunications services? This time, it was suggested that there might potentially be hundreds of communities in this position.

In retrospect, it is easy to understand how the government could easily have gone it alone, especially in light of recently having paid off the remainder of its debt. But the government, it would appear, did not want to reverse its general direction in the area of infrastructure (e.g., gas, electricity). Wherever possible it held that infrastructural services should be privatized, deregulated, and opened to as much competition as their respective markets could bear.

THE BUSINESS CASE FOR OPERATING THE NETWORK
Quite early on, the government made two significant decisions concerning how the network would be operated, once the build was completed. First, it did not award the network operation contract to the telco firm constructing the network – Bell West. More importantly, it awarded the contract to a small firm – Axia SuperNet (originally Axia Netmedia) that had no prior experience in telecommunications. We can only surmise that the decision here to choose a third-party player was oriented by the desire to keep the operations of the network as open as possible to competition.

Second, the government insisted that the basic rates for carrying telecommunications services (calculated on a megabit/month basis) would be the

same across the province. This contradicts common telecommunications bill-
ing practices. Typically, rates for telecommunications are lowest in the larger
cities and towns and more expensive in the hinterland. These prices are fac-
tored by the volume of telecommunications services that are being carried
and by the costs of construction and maintenance.

It is interesting to note that, in both of the above business cases – the build
and the operations – the government did not choose to follow a competitive market model. Left to its own logic, no telecommunications firm would
see the point of building a broadband network beyond those communities in
which it could actually project business cases. So the government stepped up
to the plate in covering the major costs of constructing the network, and as
major investor, it was also able to insist that the rates would be set at the same
level province-wide. The government's interest here was to create a system
that would strategically improve the chances for small communities – specifically, to improve the chances for businesses to prosper and for high quality
services to be deployed.

But why was the government so intent on providing better social and economic opportunities for the rural and remote communities? Now a cynic
might claim that the Progressive Conservative government's altruistic moves
here were only self-serving inasmuch as its electoral strength was based in
the rural ridings. But this charge would not undermine the larger social fact
that many of the rural and remote communities are seeing their populations
steadily shrinking. Sometimes the drivers here are chiefly economic: land-
based industries such as agriculture and forestry have become increasingly
mechanized and increasingly sensitive to international market disputes related
to prices and health issues. But there are social drivers as well. Small communities offer fairly limited leisure activities, limited post-secondary educational
and training services, and health services. And yet, many of the people we
have spoken to in our travels around the province as part of our SSHRC-INE
study have indicated to us that, if the above factors were ameliorated, they
would prefer to go on living in their communities. For these people, the quality of life that they enjoy is unrivalled – the sense of community is paramount,
the beauty of the natural environment is largely unspoiled, and the more
human pace of life is something they would not trade with city dwellers.

Researching the Social and Economic Impacts of the Supernet

When the SuperNet project was first announced in 2001, a number of academics attached to the Centre for Information and Communication within
the Van Horne Institute met with the Alberta Ministry of Innovation and

Science to inquire whether there would be opportunities for social and economic research. We suggested that the project could benefit by research projects that evaluated such things as: residential and business needs for certain
services and the prices that could be borne by users. We were told at that time
that the government's chief priority was to settle the construction contracts
so that the right-of-ways could be negotiated and construction could begin.
Representatives present stated that no social scientific research had been carried out to date but that research inquiries of the sort we had described could
potentially be relevant at some later date.

The opportunity to carry out human scientific (i.e., jointly social scientific
and humanities) research on the SuperNet project came quite unexpect-
edly from another source in 2002 when the Social Sciences and Humanities
Research Council of Canada (SSHRC) announced a new program of major
research grants, entitled The Initiative on the New Economy. This was a
$200 million envelope that Industry Canada had given to SSHRC that was
targeted at research on the new (electronically mediated) economy in Canada
that could forward ideas that would be relevant to federal policy planning in
the areas of both social and economic development. In response, our original
Van Horne team expanded itself into a larger interdisciplinary consortium
of fourteen researchers drawn from four western universities (i.e., Calgary,
Alberta, Athabasca, and Simon Fraser). We developed a proposal to study
the SuperNet from a number of theoretical and methodological perspectives – organized within eight sub-projects that were coordinated via a central
(administrative) team.[5]

Our proposal was awarded funding ($900,000 over three years) and began
operations in the spring of 2003. In awarding the project, there was some concern on SSHRC's part (and perhaps also Industry Canada's) that the project
might be misinterpreted by the provincial government in Alberta as a kind of
federal audit of one of its infrastructure programs. And indeed, the project
was treated with some suspicion within Alberta Innovation and Science for
the first year or so.

Public Consultation: Talking with Albertans about the SuperNet

One of the first initiatives that the central team undertook was to select a
sample of ten or more communities across the province that could be accessed
by any of the sub-projects for their research. Some of the sub-projects chose to
base some or all of their research in these sample communities, while other
sub-projects chose to work with their own sets. Throughout the summer and
fall of 2003, the public consultation team carried out exploratory visits with a

good number of communities throughout the province to gauge interest. For those communities that expressed clear interest in becoming involved in our project, the public consultation team organized town hall meetings.[6] These meetings were open to the public and, wherever possible, were connected to other researchers within the alliance via IP-based videoconferencing. While some research team members voiced skepticism in advance of going out to the communities, much of this dissipated as the research group in general began to appreciate the value of community contact. Why did the Alliance bother with public consultation? Several reasons can be given here:

PUBLIC CONSULTATION PROCESS ALIGNS WITH THE PROJECT'S GOAL OF INFORMING POLICY IN THIS AREA

To the extent that the project has any overarching theoretical/methodological approach, it would be that of Constructive Technology Assessment (CTA) (see Rip et al. 1995). This is an approach that was developed in the Netherlands over the past decade concerning technology development. In short, CTA insists that it is beneficial to include as many players as possible in the planning and the implementation stages associated with any new technology that is of national strategic significance.

PUBLIC CONSULTATION IS A TWO-WAY STREET

We wanted to enter into public consultation for two reasons. First, because we are committed to making the results of research openly available to the citizenry of Canada. Second, because we honestly believe that talking with individuals and groups from outside the academy will help us learn things that we would otherwise not learn. Both of these reasons align with SSHRC's concept of *knowledge mobilization*[7] within its new *transformation agenda*. They emphasize,

If Canadians are to see, understand and value what ... [human sciences] do, what they contribute, then researchers, when they define their questions, must listen to the concerns of their fellow citizens. Researchers must also use new and different ways to share what they learn. This "two-way street" is a central requirement for enabling thoughtful public discussion, enhancing appreciation of cultural richness, and maintaining a democratic, civil society.[8]

IT IS HISTORICALLY INTERESTING TO STUDY NOVEL TECHNOLOGIES BEFORE THEY ARE IMPLEMENTED

Every day we are flooded with new products and services coming onto the market. Very few of these are truly innovative. Fewer still are innovative in ways that have implications beyond their immediate scope. Looking over the historical record of the past few centuries, we can only identify a handful of technological innovations that significantly transformed society in a wide variety of ways. Some of the most striking examples of these transformative technologies come from the field of communication and information technologies and include such things as: the printing press, the telegraph, the telephone, radio, television, computers, and the Internet. In almost all of these cases, with the exception perhaps of the Internet itself, these technologies were brought into widespread social use before any systematic studies were undertaken. Thus, insights into what designers thought their innovations would do – as compared to what users thought the new technologies might accomplish – were never gathered. This primary stage of information gathering is important because historical studies of technological innovation has taught us that regularly the uses that designers imagine their innovations to accomplish have little or no relationship to how they are eventually taken up in social use. History abounds with such examples: no one anticipated in the mid-fifteenth century that the printing press would accomplish anything more than providing an efficient way to copy the Bible; no one guessed that it would play fundamental roles in the Protestant Reformation and the rise of industrial nations. Likewise, when the telephone was invented in the latter decades of the nineteenth century, Western Union never guessed that the new technology posed any competitive threat to its monopoly over long-distance communication. In historical cases such as these, we can only appreciate with the benefit of long hindsight how an innovation of this sort would settle into its eventual social context of use. But in the meantime, we have lost much of the texture of uncertainty and speculation that surrounded its original inception.

In our view, broadband technology (when it is implemented on a comprehensive basis) may conceivably join this class of transformative technologies. This is because broadband connectivity demonstrates a kind of threshold condition for the convergence of information and communications technologies. Despite the fact that we have heard much about convergence over the past decade – it has not been possible for end users to access highly interactive applications in real time. The Internet without broadband connectivity is an environment constrained largely to downloading content and exchanging messages in a handful of numerical modes and natural (text-mediated) languages. In contrast, broadband networks (which include both the commercial Internet and dedicated telecommunications services) enable users to access deep and complex database systems and to immerse themselves in interactive environments that are simply not possible under current dial-up (56 to 64 kbps) and high-speed (500 kbps to 2 Mbps) conditions.

Accordingly, we felt that the expansion of broadband technology out into the hinterland presented a rich opportunity for social research. Rather than waiting to study the so-called effects or impacts of this technology after it has landed in use – and found its eventual social shape – we believed that it would be valuable to collect perceptions about the technology before it was implemented.

What We Have Learned from Public Consultation with Communities

The public consultation process has involved the following steps:[9]

- Initial meetings with town councils to assess possible interest (spring/summer 2003)
- Town hall meetings in thirteen communities (summer/fall 2003)
- First symposium on the SuperNet (University of Calgary: February 17, 2004)
- Baseline surveys: residential and business[10]
- Organizing a major conference: *SuperNet Opportunities* (Telus Convention Centre, Calgary: June 20–22, 2006).[11]

In what follows I will concentrate on what we learned in the course of the town hall meetings. Much of what we learned about the possible impacts of the SuperNet was echoed in subsequent research activities: in the First Symposium on the SuperNet, in the baseline surveys, and in the discussions that have emerged in our online forums.

In the summer and fall of 2003 we carried out a series of town hall meetings in thirteen communities across the province. In selecting the communities to be visited, we started out by bracketing out the two large cities (Calgary and Edmonton) inasmuch as the network was explicitly designed to enhance rural and remote communities. We subdivided this latter set into the following ideal types:

- bedroom communities near a major city (Morinville),
- towns on major transportation routes – with the sense that citizens might just as easily drive for business and economic services rather than access them online (Canmore, Vegreville),
- rural towns off of major transportation routes, where the above option is not so readily available (Athabasca, Oyen, Drumheller, Pincher Creek, Vulcan),

- truly remote communities (Grande Cache), and
- Aboriginal communities (Sturgeon Lake, Kikino Metis, Red Crow College).

When we visited these communities, our team typically received the same opening set of responses. Despite the fact that we introduced ourselves as a group of federally funded researchers, often times the audience held on to the perception that we were part of a provincially orchestrated information campaign. Accordingly, the first barrage of questions and concerns voiced were always the same: "When will the SuperNet actually be lit up in our community? And how much is it going to cost?" In all of these cases our research team would defer these questions to representatives of our partner organizations – particularly Don Tinordi of Axia – who had a better sense of where the build schedule was at and what the costs of lighting up the network and monthly fees would entail.

Later, we would move on to more general considerations regarding what the network might do for a community. Very early on in our town hall visits, it became clear to us that the provincial government had not carried out any perceptible public information campaign in these communities. Beyond reading a few snippets in newspapers or on the broadcast media, most individuals we spoke with had practically no knowledge of what the network was or what it might mean for their communities. Most had heard that the province was building some kind of fancy high-speed network, which was supposed to improve the deployment of social services and perhaps also the local economy. But most citizens had no sense of:

- how the network would be connected (i.e., by fibre or microwave) to their community,
- which social service organizations would be connected (e.g., government office, community school, health clinic, library) and at what cost,
- how the network services would be extended, if at all, across their community (e.g. cable, DSL, wireless) and again at what cost, and
- what kinds of applications would actually become available.

Following the above tech talk sessions in each of our town halls, we tried to move the discussion away from what the technology is to what it might do. Here we tried to engage each community audience with respect to how it saw itself as a community – both socially and economically – and how it would define its distinctive needs and aspirations.

Communities would begin by talking about their local industries, and perhaps the historical heritage of the town. Invariably, the talk would turn to the reasons why they preferred to live in their respective communities – for the beauty of the natural environment and for the relaxed pace of life. Out of this discussion would usually arise the sentiment that many residents, if they were given the right conditions, would prefer to stay on in their town. But often these towns did not have the right mix of economic and social opportunities to retain their own residents.

In fact, most admitted that external forces mitigated against this option to choose freely. In many towns we were told that the populations were shrinking. In general, we heard that the young migrated from small towns into the cities in pursuit of better post-secondary educational opportunities and career choices, while the elderly often left town in pursuit of better health care services. We were not surprised to hear that people were leaving town in search of economic opportunity in those communities that had subsistence economies. But we were surprised when we heard this issue mentioned in communities that had fairly vibrant economies. For example, in Drumheller, we heard that a good number of job postings (with salaries well above minimum wage) typically went unfilled. The problem was that many of the young people left the town in search of more opportunities (jobs and social life) in the larger cities and jobs were left vacant as a result.

Social Services Applications

In general, our description of potential social services (e.g., health, education, disaster and emergency, and libraries) was greeted with guarded optimism. Our team was well versed in the kinds of applications each of these social services would like to make available over the proposed network. For example, when we demonstrated how our portable IP-based videoconferencing technology (using ViaVideo units over H.323 transmission protocol) made it possible for us to include researchers from afar in these events, many of the participants agreed that this kind of technology had considerable potential for connecting groups across distance for the purposes of K-12 and post-secondary education and for governance. Participants also appreciated the likelihood that the SuperNet could support telehealth services – such as the ability to access databases in a secure fashion, as well as the capacity to carry out ultrasonic inspections that could be relayed for expert analysis within large city clinics and hospitals. In addition, participants in various rural and remote communities expressed their hope that, if the SuperNet were successful in enhancing social services within their communities, this factor might encourage the young to stay longer – and perhaps also the old to stay on in retirement.

While some individuals worried that the new technology might exacerbate social dislocation, the majority felt that the services involved would enhance quality of life opportunities within their community.

Business Applications

But we were less ready to project futures for business applications – this despite the fact that two of our sub-project teams were exploring these very issues. On the one hand, the discrete choice team was surveying the costs that residential and business users would be willing to pay for enhanced network-delivered services. On the other hand, the virtual industries clusters team was trying to determine whether the SuperNet would make it possible for some clusters to emerge outside the major cities.

At this time, it is very difficult to forecast whether and to what extent the network will positively enhance economic development in rural and remote communities. Why is this?

For one, there is very little literature available on this issue. Much of the studies regarding the impact of broadband on rural economic development has been associated with telework; that is, work based in the cities that is either being taken home by regular employees or outsourced to workers in the hinterland (e.g., Symons 2000).

For another, Industry Canada claims that small to medium enterprises (SMEs) in Canada are very low adopters of online business applications.

SME adoption of advanced e-business models and practices lags seriously behind adoption by larger firms. While many SMEs are using basic applications such as e-mail and non-transactional Web sites, they lag in the use of advanced e-business applications such as e-procurement, supply chain management, accounting and finance management and human resource management. This is despite the substantial cost saving and profit-enhancing potential of these applications.

Research by the Canadian e-Business Initiative (CeBI) through its *Net Impact* work identifies the reasons that Canadian firms, particularly SMEs, have been slow to adopt advanced e-business models and practices. One possibility is that most applications are designed for large-scale enterprises and are not adapted to the needs of smaller firms. Another is that many businesses lack the skills and resources needed to identify and apply e-business solutions.[12]

Broadband at the Margins: Barriers to Broadband-Mediated Community Development

Our consultations with communities enabled us to achieve a strong grasp on the various barriers that threatened the success of the SuperNet initiative.

ACCESS BARRIERS

Based on discussions with Innovation and Science and information available on their website,[13] we learned that communities would be connected to the SuperNet as follows:

- The network would be connected to a community via fibre (80%) or by microwave means (20%).
- The network would be connected to a single Point of Presence (POP) in each community, which could be lit up at a cost of about $4,000.
- Each POP would then be connected to a number of standard community organizations within the boundaries of that municipality, including: community school, library, health clinic, and government office. Costs for monthly services here would be about $150/Mgbs.
- The POP could be extended by an Internet service provider to distribute services at costs to residents or businesses via various means (e.g., cable, DSL, wireless). ISPs could be of various types: private firms, publicly owned by the town, or co-operatives.

When this general information was made available, typically by a representative of Axia or Bell West, discussion went in different directions, dependent upon the type of community we were visiting.

Extension of Service Barriers for Communities with Viable Economies

In those communities with viable economies, audiences often wondered about ISP options for extending the signal within their community. Most of these communities already had cable systems in place that offered a combination of television and Internet services; in contrast, very few had Digitized Subscriber Line (DSL) services. Most communities were satisfied that the incumbent cable operator would be able to extend the Internet and dedicated telecommunications services associated with the SuperNet at reasonable cost. In contrast, in Grande Cache, which was being serviced by a cable firm at a distance – some of the audience members wondered whether it might make more sense to develop a home-grown firm or co-op to undertake the extension of these new services within their town. They felt that it made sense for the local community to maintain control over cost of services and any plans to extend the system.[14]

One of the most striking things we learned regarding the extension of SuperNet services in rural and remote Alberta was brought to our attention in our town hall meeting in Pincher Creek. One of the attendees, James Van Leeuwen, pointed out that the provincial government plan to provide Super-Net connectivity only to municipalities (with at least a community school) was fundamentally flawed in those regions where the major industries were land-based. He argued that the town of Pincher Creek served mostly as a service centre for land-based industries such as ranching and farming, which were carried out in the surrounding territory. Both of these industries were becoming subject to globalization economic trends and were sensitive to forces well beyond their provincial and national borders. James pointed out that making a living in these industries today requires access to the most sophisticated and up-to-date information regarding climate, pesticides, animal inoculation, international prices, quotas, and so forth. In other words, these industries require the best kinds of enhanced information and communications business services that the SuperNet could offer.

But these industries, specifically the people on the farms and ranches outside the municipal boundaries of the regional service centres, found themselves outside the pale of viable extension of service. Small ISPs could find viable business cases for competing in a local municipal market – by cable or wireless means – but there was little likelihood that homes and businesses that were distributed far out on the land could be connected in a way that would return on the infrastructural investment.

It was not clear to us whether this was a blind spot in the original provincial design for the network or just a simple recognition that limits would have to be put on the costs of subsidizing the build. But, to the extent that economic development is one of the chief rationales for the network, some thought will need to be taken to address this shortfall.

Application Service Provision Barriers

While it was regularly unclear whether and to what extent the SuperNet would enhance economic development in rural and remote communities, there was generally a high level of expectation that the network held considerable promise to improve an array of social services.

Some of this optimism was grounded in the practices of social services organizations (e.g., schools, clinics, libraries) that were already planning to move some of their information-related functions over to SuperNet-mediated applications as soon as they became available. In these cases, umbrella groups – school boards, health regional boards, The Alberta Library – already had a strong sense of what the new online applications looked like and what the training and support issues amounted to.

But a good deal of the wave of rising expectation for social services that we encountered in communities we visited seemed to be more grounded on faith alone. A good example was the excitement over real-time applications – particularly Internet Protocol (IP) mediated videoconferencing. In many cases, when we used our portable technology (ViaVideos over H.323) to connect to distant researchers, this was the first time that community members had ever seen this technology. Despite the fact that the quality was fairly low-grade and subject to crashes, most participants felt confident that the technical problems were largely incidental and would naturally be fixed in the course of things as they were encountered. For the majority, the promise of how the technology might eventually function far outweighed the poor technical performance of the present. In fact, the frequently lively discussions that ensued quickly overrode any technical limitations we may have encountered. This view bears resemblance to the high adoption rate of cellular phones in areas where technical quality remains fairly low: the increased functionality over other modes much outweighs the poor quality of service.

Some audience participants had heard or read about the use of videoconferencing in educational experiments across the province – particularly in Fort Vermilion and in Red Deer. The majority were excited about the potential of this technology: for expert teachers to teach over long distances; and for students at a distance to work together interactively. For most people we spoke with, their expectation was not simply that two communities could be connected on a point-to-point basis but that any number of communities could be connected within a large region. For this hope to be realized, though, an entirely different level of technical challenges would need to be addressed. Conferencing between two communities in real time is a relatively simple matter, but conferencing between more than two sites requires multi-site capability, which can only be provided by network bridges or by multicast transmission capability. Both of these options are relatively expensive and require a fair level of technical support. This is not to suggest that solutions here are not possible, but rather that a good deal of partnership needs to be developed between communities and organizations within regions to cooperatively come up with the resources to meet this higher level of expectation.

Here, as in other instances, public expectation regarding the promise of an application regularly outstrips technical and/or economic feasibility.

Extension of Service Barriers for Communities with Subsistence Economies: The Case of Aboriginal Communities

The differences here are those of both scale and kind. Communities with subsistence economies include the very small towns and hamlets distributed around the province, which are barely hanging on. Virtually all Aboriginal (i.e., First Nations and Metis) are of this category – with the exception of the lucky few that enjoy resource royalties. In what follows I will focus on the conditions in the majority of Aboriginal communities.

In the spring of 2003, we applied for seed money from the Industry Canada Broadband for Rural and Remote Development (BRAND) program. This program was set up to encourage a number of pilot projects across the country that would provide useful models for broadband deployment. The BRAND program was set up to find ways to get communities connected to broadband networks. To this end, the federal government would provide 50 per cent of the costs of constructing the capital infrastructure to make this happen – for such things as bringing in fibre lines or constructing satellite, microwave, or wireless plants. The BRAND program was not set up to enable further extension of Internet service within communities already enjoying broadband connectivity. This criterion placed virtually all communities within Alberta at a clear disadvantage. The provincial government had solved the first problem; now would the federal government be willing to solve the equally important second issue – that is, further extension of service? In our letter of interest (LOI), we made it patently clear that we would pursue answers to the second question – extension of services within Treaty-8 Alberta communities. When we were funded, we proceeded directly upon this course.

During the fall of 2003 we were led to believe by both federal and provincial spokespersons that the reserves would not receive the same level of connectivity as the other communities within the province. We were told that the POPs would be situated at the edge of each reserve since these lands were inside federal, rather than provincial, jurisdiction. It was not clear at that time how the POPs were to be connected (as with all other communities) with the various social services (i.e., community school, clinic, band council office) within each community, as was the standard provincial expectation. Beyond this, there did not appear to be any discussions underway concerning how the SuperNet services might be distributed to households across each of these First Nations communities.

Throughout the fall of 2003, I, along with two graduate research assistants (Sharon Mah and Yvonne Pratt) travelled extensively throughout Treaty-8 Alberta to look into the options for extending SuperNet connectivity within the many villages of northern Alberta.[15]

Very early on, we came to recognize that there was no chance of enticing a firm to come into these communities to provide Internet service. There was simply no business case that could be made that would return the costs of construction, never mind subsequent maintenance of the sub-network. There is almost no likelihood that the town (or band) council will be able to take up this initiative on its own. By definition, the SuperNet will be connected to every town and hamlet in the province that has at least a community school. In many of the reserves that we visited, the "town centre" amounted to a few public buildings (i.e., community school, band council office, health clinic) within sight of each other. The centre also included a handful of residences, but usually the majority of homes were spread out in pockets deep within the bush or prairie. This geographic distribution presents a serious challenge to the potential of broadband networking – if only for the purposes of enhancing social services.

In many of the communities we learned through meetings with members of the band council (and in some cases with some elders present) that they were hoping that broadband networking might help them solve their most pressing social problems – education and health – and also facilitate more efficient governance. In each of the three areas that we visited, First Nations representatives felt that enhanced information and communications technologies might play positive roles for their communities, although they described themselves as just starting out.[16]

Governance in these communities involves the coordination of political action within a local community and across a larger constituency. But it also involves the design and coordination of social (and, where possible, economic) development programs. However, coordinating the planning and administration of programs is challenged at every turn by the remoteness of these communities. Small communities within reserves are often at a considerable distance from the other communities that lie within their council territory. Further, the nine councils that comprise Treaty-8 Alberta are likewise spatially removed from each other, making group meetings very difficult to organize and exceedingly expensive in terms of travel costs. Transportation within northern Alberta – and we might add remote and northern Canada, in general – is never easy. In the winter the ice roads can be fairly stable but treacherous nonetheless. But, at times, the weather can make travelling impossible. In the summer the weather is generally mild, but this warmer weather tends to make many of the roads impassable when they pass through areas of muskeg. Communications technologies provide considerable promise to overcome these barriers of distance. In fact, band councils were generally very excited about the prospects of using IP-videoconferencing technologies for meeting purposes. Talking with each other and using their native languages if they wished over this technology would not only overcome the barrier of spatial distance, it would also reduce the long hours and the risks required to drive between communities. With this technology in place, more time could be spent on the issues at hand rather than the effort of getting together.

Health services also looked forward to better coordination and planning between their various regional centres, through the use of enhanced communications technologies. The health care providers and patients alike looked forward to gaining access to sophisticated databases that were specific to the treatment of those health problems that were prevalent in their community, including: diabetes, tuberculosis, and side effects from drug and alcohol abuse. Treatment for various emergency procedures could also be improved with ultrasonic diagnostic equipment connected to hospitals in the main cities, which could give ready access to technical expertise and skilled professionals at the click of a mouse.

We spent a good deal of our time visiting the schools within these communities. Some of them were fairly new – products of recent INAC investment – and some were even well stocked with computer equipment. Others were much smaller in size, required renovation and operated with little or no computer support systems. But whether old or new, the schools were clearly the pride of their communities. They functioned literally as community schools – in the daytime for the purposes of K-12 schooling, and in the evenings as a place for adult education and training as well as for sport and cultural events.

In most communities we learned that the attrition rates were very high at the secondary level such that few students achieved high school graduation. We also learned that most of the teachers had to be brought in from outside and from predominantly white communities since very few Aboriginal people hold teaching credentials.[17] Many communities hoped that their schools would slowly begin to graduate more students, that some of these students could be persuaded to go on to college and university, and that some of these students might return to their communities as teachers and as health workers. A number of teachers and administrators that we spoke with also expressed hope that the new educational and leisure services associated with the Super-Net might help play a role in keeping students motivated to stay on longer in school. But is this a well-founded hope?

When we visited these schools, none of them had anything better than dial-up connectivity to the Internet; some had no connectivity. Thus, while a school might be well-equipped with a computer lab, there was no way that students could access the Web in an optimal manner – that is, with sufficient bandwidth to download software upgrades. Eventually, this barrier should be overcome when the POPs are lit up in these communities. But this will not solve a larger problem: the process of a child's education outside the school. Traditionally, a child's education has not been confined to what happens within school walls within daytime hours. Much educational work in the form of homework takes place in after-school hours in the home environment. Internet connectivity can play basic roles in supporting the way individuals learn on their own, as well as how they work together in groups. But this only occurs where Internet-related services are fully distributed across a community region or where users are given reasonable access to services outside normal school hours. Otherwise, the restricted access may prove to be just one more insurmountable obstacle for those who are already struggling with achieving their educational goals.

What are we to do here in the face of these vicious circles that reproduce dependence in these communities? Are there policy alternatives that might instead cultivate independence? In Alberta we understood that the provincial government's investment in the infrastructure extended only as far as connecting community schools, clinics, and so on within municipal boundaries. This in itself is a significant investment in community development. But no funds would be invested to further subsidize the extension of signal across a municipality, or a region, or Aboriginal reserve lands.

Will federal government initiatives be able to mitigate the blind spots in the provincial plan of support for Aboriginal communities? As noted in the prior discussion, under the terms of reference for the BRAND program, Industry Canada would provide 50 per cent of capital infrastructure costs only for constructing broadband connectivity. We recognized quite early on that this target was simply not attainable in virtually all of the Aboriginal communities we visited.

Realizing that we had reached an impasse, we organized a meeting of senior federal and provincial representatives associated with network infrastructure and social service delivery in Aboriginal communities. These included representatives in the areas of:

- broadband deployment (Industry Canada, AB Innovation and Science),
- health (Health Canada, AB Health and Wellness),

- Aboriginal affairs (Indian and Northern Affairs Canada, AB Aboriginal Affairs), and
- First Nations (Treaty 8)

This meeting took place on November 14, 2003, in Edmonton. The attendees present were joined by Ottawa officials via teleconference. At this gathering, we began by outlining some of the above challenges that small Aboriginal communities faced in getting connected at all – or having such minimum connectivity extended across their respective territories – and what this meant for the successful delivery of social services. We also pointed out the chasm that lay between where the SuperNet program left off and where the federal BRAND program began.

We closed with a call for action, if only a willingness for the respective federal and provincial agencies to work together to find more optimal solutions to the problems that we described. In some cases, we suggested solutions that would involve overcoming jurisdictional conflicts, or redundancies in program services, or blind spots in each of their programs. In general, we argued that more efficiencies would result from deploying a coordinated approach for social service provisions in these communities, rather than relying on a host of federal and provincial agencies expending resources independently. We further made the case that the barriers to deploying broadband technology and services in First Nations communities shared commonalities with many small rural and remote communities across Canada, as was expressed in our BRAND proposal:

For rural, remote, northern and First Nations' communities, a sustainable business case based on economic considerations alone is difficult to define and the deployment of a broadband infrastructure for these communities may depend on the initial phase and perhaps even in the long run on government subsidies. The business model, therefore, in addition to assessing the economic viability of broadband infrastructure, needs to address and incorporate the social benefits, values and needs and the opportunity costs of not having affordable access. Modeling studies to evaluate how the First Nations use and further define what they want from broadband technology to support social development in the areas of culture, education, business, and health will result in a "sustainable technology model" for these small First Nations communities by articulating both social and economic impacts and benefits of the ongoing use of this technology.

Justification, based on social benefits and values, for a sustainable broadband infrastructure in rural, remote, northern and First Nations communities, therefore, requires the concerted collaboration of all stakeholders, nationally, provincially and locally, without whose involvement a successful business plan would be difficult to achieve.[18]

While some of the official representatives expressed interest in working together as a general team, the majority expressed resistance. INAC officials, in particular, suggested that they were already working on draft programs in this area and viewed any suggestions coming from the academy as meddling. We were told that there were closed negotiations underway between the federal and provincial counterparts that were working to extend SuperNet connection from the POPs not only to the schools but also to other public offices within each reserve. This in itself was comforting news. But no one expressed interest in pursuing the problem of extending connectivity beyond these central points. In other words, there would be no point in pursuing the social service enhancement case if there was no underlying viable business case. It came as no surprise, then, that BRAND funds were eventually awarded only to those Aboriginal communities that were already economically robust.

Conclusion

In retrospect, the process of public consultation that we have undertaken with rural and remote communities across Alberta and with Aboriginal communities in particular has been instructive. As participants in this process, we have learned first-hand about the various barriers that impede the full deployment of broadband services within small rural and remote communities. For one, there are *technical barriers*, involving such things as lack of connectivity, insufficient extension of signal, and quality of service. There are also *jurisdictional barriers* associated with the deployment of social services by different levels of government. There are also *economic barriers* related to the costs of acquiring and maintaining equipment and applications. In addition, there is a manifold of what might be called *socio-cultural barriers* associated with such things as the knowledge and skills of end users, trust in the technology, and the fit of the technology in the surrounding culture.

These days, it is commonplace to insist that the socio-cultural barriers will be the more intractable ones to overcome. This claim sounds right, but it tends to underestimate the complexity of solving the other barriers to development. For example, it is regularly remarked that solutions to merely technical problems are invariably the easiest ones to realize. The difficulty, though, is that effective solutions in principle only get implemented when there is a heavy wave of economic and/or political will. Indeed, the policy literature is replete with good technical solutions that have never been implemented. The recommendations of the *Report of the National Task Force on Broadband* are a good case in point. In other words, while it is relatively easy to categorize barriers to social and economic development, it is not so easy to implement coordinated solutions. Even viable solutions to technical barriers are not likely to be realized without additional support from political, economic, and social-cultural domains of action.

At the end of the day, if policy makers do not take the full compass of barriers to development into account, even the best-intentioned policies for using new media to improve the social and economic opportunities for small rural and remote communities may end up reproducing the inequities they were designed to address.

Bibliography

Audley, Paul. 1983. *Canada's Cultural Industries: Broadcasting, Publishing, Records and Film.* Toronto: James Lorimer; in association with the Canadian Institute for Economic Policy.

Babe, Robert E. 2000. *Canadian Communication Thought: Ten Foundational Writers.* Toronto: University of Toronto Press.

Rip, Arie, Thomas J. Misa, and Johan Schot. 1995. *Managing Technology in Society: The Approach of Constructive Technology Assessment.* London: Pinter.

Symons, Frank Stewart. 2000. Telework and Bandwidth. *Canadian Journal of Communication* 25(4): 553–64.

Notes

1 For example, *Access Grid,* one of the new open source platforms, should no longer be described as videoconferencing – it is fully multimedia and interactive in character.

2 The main documents are:
  • 1993/95: Reports of the Information Highway Advisory Council (IHAC);
  • 1998: *Report on New Media* (Canadian Radio, Television and Telecommunications Commission, CRTC);
  • 1999: The Connecting Canadian Strategy (Industry Canada);
  • 2001: Report of the National Broadband Task Force.

3 These include: Broadband for Rural and Northern Development (BRAND) program; and the National Satellite Initiative (NSI).

4 The original construction date of July 1, 2004, was too optimistic and was scaled back quite early on to December 31, 2004. Subsequently, this target was revised to the actual completion date of September 30, 2005.

5   The eight sub-projects include: *Public consultation*: David Mitchell, Janice Dickin (Calgary); *Discrete choice*: Stuart McFadyen, Adam Finn (Alberta); *Virtual industries clusters*: Cooper Langford (Calgary); Richard Field, Doug Cummings (Alberta); *Telehealth*: Penny Jennett (Calgary); *Distance education*: Terry Anderson (Athabasca); *Disaster and emergencies management*: Peter Anderson (Simon Fraser); *Libraries and information services*: Frits Pannekoek (Calgary), Marco Adria (Alberta); *Community sensemaking*: Maria Bakardjieva (Calgary), Robert Gephart (Alberta).

6   Transcripts of the various town hall meetings are available on the project's website http://SuperNet.ucalgary.ca under "communities."

7   In the fall of 2005, SSHRC sponsored a national symposium entitled *Knowledge Mobilization for the Human Sciences* (Banff: September 30–October 4, 2005). See: http://km.ucalgary.ca.

8   Social Sciences and Humanities Research Council of Canada (SSHRC), *From Granting Council to Knowledge Council* (SSHRC, 2004, p. 12).

9   See: http://SuperNet.ucalgary.ca.

10   What we had learned in our town hall meetings was echoed in the *residential baseline survey* (fall 2003) and the *business baseline survey* (winter/spring 2004). In both cases we were plagued with very low respondent rates. Individuals and firms were simply not comfortable responding to the phone surveys because they did not feel that they were satisfactorily equipped with the knowledge at hand. If we learned anything from the two baseline survey exercises, it was that the vast majority of Albertans living in rural and remote communities had little or no understanding of what the SuperNet was, or why the government had gone ahead with this initiative.

11   See: http://supernet.ucalgary.ca/opportunities.

12   *The Challenge of Change: Building the 21st Century Economy* (conference background paper for "e-Commerce to e-Economy: Strategies for the 21st Century," Ottawa, 2–28 September 2004. Industry Canada, 7–8).

13   See: http://www.albertaSuperNet.ca.

14   This self-reliant attitude on the part of this community is a reflection of their past pattern of communal problem-solving. For example, when the local coal mine was shut down in the 1980s, the town rallied in front of the provincial legislature to make their concerns known and to seek solutions.

15   Treaty 8 Alberta includes those parts of greater Treaty 8 that lie within Alberta and includes a series of Treaty Councils that are spread out from Edmonton north to the sixtieth parallel. The greater Treaty 8 area includes parts of northwestern B.C., southern N.W.T., and northeastern Saskatchewan.

16   What proved especially surprising in our travels was the case of Tall Cree, one of the most remote communities in our travels, in which a full council meeting was pulled together with only one hour's notice. This community, situated one and one half hour's drive from High Level on a barely negotiable summer road, presented the most receptive and proactive vision for

broadband technology that we encountered. The fact that this community had planned for a videoconferencing set-up some years back was also intriguing. It seemed that the right blend of people with the right attitude could make all the difference, provided the right circumstances were in place.

17   With the rise in both Aboriginal population and those Aboriginals who are currently seeking post-secondary degrees, we may soon see a shift in this trend. (Source: *Aboriginal Peoples' Survey* 2001).

18   David Mitchell, Sharon Mah, Mo Watanabe, and Joanne Weiner, *Treaty 8's First Mile* (Proposal to Industry Canada's Broadband for Rural and Remote Development program, November 20, 2003).

Keywords in Canadian Communication: A Student Afterword

The conference in the course of which this volume took shape benefited significantly from the enthusiastic involvement of several students from the Graduate Program in Communications at the University of Calgary. They designed and organized the sessions, provided comments on the papers and participated in the discussions. They spoke for all students and young scholars who make up the potential audience of this collection. Therefore, we have decided to give them the final word on "how Canadians communicate." We invited them to articulate and reflect on those key concepts that the chapters of this book have highlighted for them in a new and memorable way. What are the pointers that these fledgling researchers take away from the current volume as future reference for their own pursuits in the field of Canadian communication and beyond?

Yvonne Poitras Pratt and Sharon Mah

COMMUNITY

As we examine *how* Canadians communicate at the onset of the twenty-first century, we might also benefit from redefining *what* and, maybe even more importantly, *who* constitutes the realm of communications. In the past, media observers have focused on broadcast models to examine our national state of communications. Yet, as we fast forward into the future, scholars and other interested parties are finding that the more traditional and once dominant forms of media expression, including newspapers, music, radio, books, magazines, and even the television industry, are increasingly being put to task by a myriad of involved citizens and community groups.

As those who study the field of communications become increasingly aware of the limitations of old models to explain new ways of being and communicating, we are compelled to seek out new models to make sense of what is going on. To this end, a number of authors within this second volume of *How Canadians Communicate* embark on a bold venture into explanatory territory. Not too surprisingly, the concept of community transpires as a central constituent of one possible communication model underlying this discussion.

Community, understood as a personal commitment to a shared interest with others, is what Michael Keren identifies as the key missing element in his study of weblogging. Without any real sense of personal commitment between online participants, Keren rightly characterizes the communication between an online author and her respondents as a cursory interaction rather than a lasting effort to build an authentic sense of community.

Marc Raboy and David Taras also acknowledge the inherent power of community within any effective communications endeavour. In fact, their disclosure that an exodus of community support soon followed the shutdown of local CBC stations across the country is highly instructive. It appears that even though the CBC has the potential to represent a cornerstone of Canadian community life, once the local station pulls up its community roots, community support soon withers away. It is not all that surprising that Canadians are reticent to embrace what they cannot see – especially in terms of public support. Surely an active community presence can make all the difference in how Canadians not only see themselves, but also in how they view and support their public broadcaster.

The second volume of *How Canadians Communicate* also speaks to the need to address the place of ethnic minority identity and community as a part of Canada's reality. The construction of self-identity is a dialogical process that involves the community (Taylor 1994). The recognition of an individual's identity is based on his or her primary community, and the larger public sphere. Today, Canada has accepted the responsibility for ensuring the country's media reflect ethnic minority and First Nations identity with the Multiculturalism Act, followed by the Broadcasting Act and the Ethnic Broadcasting Policy, to govern ethnic minority broadcasting.[1] However, despite Canada's efforts to reflect ethnic minority through specialty television, the CRTC's (1999) review of the 1999 Ethnic Broadcasting Policy[2] found that technological access and financial constraints hindered many ethnic minorities from accessing specialty television (Mah 2001, 5). As is often the case, the practicalities in real life had overcome the actual intent of the policies.

The CRTC's review of the 1999 Ethnic Broadcasting Policy demonstrated that ethnic minority communities rigorously wage battles for representation in their ethnospheres and in Canada's dominant media spheres (Mah 2001). These negotiations of rights and privileges and the struggle for good governance require real exchanges of dialogue that are not reflected in the atomized consumption of television. Several contributions to this volume (Bakardjieva, Keren, Mitchell) demonstrate that the new modes of communication proliferating today grant individuals within communities a degree of agency to change, express, and cultivate an adequate representation of their realities through the Internet. Today, the Chinese-Canadian community, for example, uses new communication technologies such as broadband, satellite, and other wireless technologies to connect to multiple communities around the world, creating diverse hybrid identities that are empowered and mobilized in online communities (Qui 1999). The Internet provides a place in which real dialogue is exchanged between citizens of various nations to mobilize resources around a common goal at incredible speeds.[3] The same sort of movement is taking place, albeit at a slower rate, within Canadian Aboriginal communities in what Avison and Meadows (2000) have termed the "Aboriginal public sphere" (3). When communities are actively involved in the communication process, they reflect their own set of unique values, common goals, or needs. However, technology alone will not transcend barriers erected by institutions that limit access or deny rights and privileges. This is particularly true for communities such as First Nations communities, who have been historically neglected in ways that technological solutions alone cannot remedy. Mitchell's comments on the development of broadband technologies in Alberta's SuperNet project reveal that, although policy makers envision a province free of information barriers, the very act of constructing broadband networks, without community consultations, ultimately disconnects the community. The empowerment of communities relies on their ability to shape communication technologies and put them to meaningful use.

PARTICIPATION

The fact that new communication technologies have changed the media landscape in Canada is now irrefutable. What remains the topic of much debate is the changing role of the media consumer who, as Longford suggests, is now blurring the traditional boundaries of media relations by taking an active role in media production. While Hamilton maintains that much of the controversy erupts around issues of ownership in areas such as satellite delivery and music file sharing, users are also growing increasingly aware that an active role in media production affords them certain intellectual property rights. What is less certain is how these new media producers will be represented in national discussions around media issues.

As one proactive response to this query, Bakardjieva explores the possible political significance of researching the everyday practices of diverse users on the Internet. Bakardjieva contends that the very act of participating in research projects can be construed as politically empowering when community members envision the process as an opportunity for their voices to be heard. Moreover, Bakardjieva asserts that researchers have a vital role to play in advancing the interests of citizens by acting as intermediaries between local communities and influential policy makers. This observation is noteworthy within any re-articulation of new media policies.

Similarly, Mitchell writes on the participatory experience of engaging rural and remote Albertans on the topic of broadband connectivity. In adopting an ethos of community consultation in researching the possibilities of the Alberta SuperNet for provincial citizens, Mitchell engaged in a dialogue with a number of local communities. His reason?

We wanted to enter into public consultation for two reasons. First, because we are committed to making the results of research openly available to the citizenry of Canada. Second, because we honestly believe that talking with individuals and groups from outside the academy will help us learn things that we would otherwise not learn. (270)

Without question, as the research strategies of scholars evolve and "mere consumers morph into users and creators through the heady combination of computers, networks, software, knowledge, and increased awareness" (Hamilton, this volume, 219), there will be untold implications for how we communicate as citizens and furthermore as a nation. Recognizing that this transformation is already well underway, several authors in this volume maintain that if Canada is to retain its world-class standing as a leader in new media practices and as a model of multiculturalism, we must also part ways with outdated communication policies. Indeed, enacting communication policies under an assumption of top-down control over broadcast modes has little purchase in a complex and increasingly intertwined world of users and producers (see Goldstein, Schultz, Hamilton, Beaty and Sullivan, and Dornan, in this volume).

Furthermore, with new media applications such as Wikipedia's online file sharing and open source software movements on the rise encouraging collaborative and knowledge-sharing efforts amongst interested players, a clear distinction between media consumers and producer is further complicated. Other interactive technologies such as webcams and videoconferencing also make possible face-to-face and real-time dialogue with users, not only from all parts of the country, but also from around the world. As these traditional restrictions around access, control, distance, and time are lessened by the introduction of new technologies, perhaps it is time that we revisit Innis's notion of knowledge sharing as one possible new way of communicating – in Canada and around the world.

Darren Blakeborough

CHOICE

"Globalization" is a term that is bandied about regularly in both academic and mass media discourses about our rapidly expanding/contracting world. In this second volume of *How Canadians Communicate*, we find the terrain no different. "Globalization" is a term that has different connotations and seemingly possesses various inherent meanings depending on who is invoking it and the context in which it is used. "Globalization" is often used interchangeably with "Americanization" (Schultz), or pointed to as the source of the increased fragmentation in our society (Goldstein), or even as a gateway to access and diversity (Beaty and Sullivan). Other authors in this volume also reflect on notions of choice – be it lack of choice (Dornan), media convergence and technology as a conduit for choice (Longford), or the Internet as a vehicle of lifestyle politics based on choices (Bakardjieva).

We are regularly presented with the argument that the logic of globalization is increased choice – be this a reality for all or not. Choice is often tied to technology, with the idea that new technologies allow for increased choice, and by default, increased consumer participation in an apparently democratizing process. If we construe of democracy as having choices, choices not apparent in other models, then when we choose products as consumers we are participating in the democratic process. Choice is seemingly offered up as democracy. As such, then, the process of globalization is legitimized as democratic. This is a very important point as it links globalization to politics, choice to democracy, or perhaps even more poignantly, choice as democracy. As an apparent product of globalization, choice, in whatever form, still privileges specific populations and people at the expense of others. Rather than serving as a tool for global equality, globalization in this respect simply reinforces disparity, as it also creates and solidifies new inequities.

These increases in choice also seem to be fragmenting society, and this fragmentation is manifest in notions of nation, community, and identity. This is also creating and perpetuating a fragmentation of the media as they strive to fulfill their niche mandates and offer up even more choices for the consumer. So while globalization might presuppose a large homogenous culture, it may just be having the opposite effect as small heterogeneous cells emerge to make sense of their nation, community, and personal identities in this rapidly changing landscape.

This volume of *How Canadians Communicate* remembers that economics plays a large part in this globally, and Canada is no exception. Dornan demonstrates that TV channels are currently licensed in Canada that cannot air due to economic constraints or other restraints that exist. This could put French-speaking Canadians at a disadvantage as English, being the global language of economics, is favoured. Commercial interests also have precedence over public interests. Seemingly lost in the rhetoric, however, is the role of the consumer. Scholars have to be wary of getting trapped looking only at cultural production and forgetting the role of agents and their consumption practices. There are indeed more channels, more music, more books, and more choices than ever before, but what does this truly mean to us?

In Canada, political participation, in the aspect of voter turnout at least, has slowly been declining over the last fifteen years (Statistics Canada 2000). During this same timeframe, our available television universe has exponentially increased to include a myriad of specialty and pay channels available with cable or satellite subscriptions which, as the *Innovation Analysis Bulletin* (Statistics Canada 2004) so readily points out, give Canadian consumers more choices. What is the connection between voter turnout and TV channels? Does this increase in perceived democratic participation through consumer decision making fill the political void that many Canadians are thought to feel? Is there a correlate between decreasing voter turnout and increasing brand and product choice? These are among the questions that we need to start looking closer at as we move deeper into this new century and ask ourselves what the logic of globalization truly means.

Georgina Grosenick

LEGISLATION
In *How Canadians Communicate*, discussions surrounding media, identity, and globalization regularly turn to questions of public policy and legislation.

Primarily at issue is the ability of public policy to preserve Canadian culture and the effectiveness of legislation over evolving and new forms of globalized media.

At the heart of much of Canada's legislation governing media content and ownership is the belief that the culture of Canada can be preserved if not strengthened through maintaining minimal levels of Canadian content and ownership. As an example, the Broadcasting Act states the purpose of Canada's broadcasting system is to: "serve to safeguard, enrich and strengthen the cultural, political, social and economic fabric of Canada" (CRTC 1991). In this Act, the legislated role of broadcasters is to "provide, through its programming, a public service essential to the maintenance and enhancement of national identity and cultural sovereignty" (CRTC 1991). Other public policy initiatives direct media groups to meet minimum Canadian content and ownership requirements. In many cases, they are also required to invest and support Canadian content development.

A common argument that is put forward in support of public policy related to content and ownership is that legislation allows Canadian cultural industries to prosper in the shadow of the larger and more powerful American industries. Without legislation, it is argued, there would be no Canadian media. This argument assumes that, given the chance, American media conglomerates would gobble up Canadian media industries, and then having gained the axes of control, use this power to replace all Canadian or local content with American. Dornan (this volume) argues that the assumption that Canadian ownership equates with Canadian content needs to be reassessed. Less protectionist perspectives on the value of legislation suggest that policy that supports Canadian ownership and content is a reflection of Canada's desire for self-determination and independence from the United States. *How Canadians Communicate* shifts the debate from the purpose of the legislation to its ability to achieve its stated objectives. For many of the authors in this volume the grade assigned is unsatisfactory.

Prescriptive legislation over content can only be effective if development and public access can be limited and enforced. Contemporary circumstances suggest that legislative control in this regard is severely challenged. For example, Straw and Sutherland identify the new modes of distribution and artist development that bypass regulated production and distribution systems. Beaty and Sullivan point out the many challenges faced by the government as a result of the grey market satellite industry. Legislation, these scholars argue, may be out of step with consumption; the content many Canadians are accessing in the current media environment is no longer limited by Canadian content quotas.

The effectiveness of current legislation is further complicated as Canadians integrate new media into their daily communicative practices. Of specific note is the Internet. As many of the authors in this volume have attested, any one country's legislation faces significant challenges when applied to such a global medium. Further, any attempts to control content and ownership are frustrated by the speed at which new applications of the Internet are introduced. Public policy always plays catch-up and proves inadequate to meet the changing needs of the new media. Even if a system of global media governance can be achieved, as Longford points out, whether it would be effective has yet to be seen.

Changing technologies and production and consumption practices weaken Canada's ability to legislate out other cultural influences. To achieve the intended vision of cultural preservation then, one policy option would be to support those cultural industries that do forward this mandate. In the past, this has been achieved through legislating financial support for these groups through direct and indirect government and industry grants and programs. However, as the options and technologies in the media environment become more diverse, the support from public and private sources becomes stretched to the breaking point. Demand on limited government funding increases and the plethora of choice in the new digital environment divides the subscription rates and advertising dollars among more and more players. With uncertain economic stability many media groups, in turn, are unable to honour their commitments to reinvest in Canadian industry as set out under their licence agreements. The net result is that there is less funding available for Canadian program and artist development and ultimately, a reduction in the quantity and quality of Canadian programming. Yet, the legislative path to redress this situation is unclear as, despite the economic challenges facing many Canadian media industries, popular and successful Canadian media content is being produced.

A final argument that is periodically raised surrounding issues of Canadian legislation of content and ownership is that the value of the public policy lies not in the products and programming it generates but in the security of knowing that *Canadian-ness* is being preserved through legislation. Perhaps the most significant challenge facing legislation, if its purpose is to preserve Canadian culture, is defining what is meant by this term. Without a clear understanding of the intent, the effectiveness of the legislation is difficult to assess, and this was one of the findings of the recent study of Canadian broadcasting by the House of Commons Standing Committee on Canadian Heritage (Canada 2004).

Questions of Canadian media, identity, and globalization are also questions of legislation and public policy practices. For legislation governing content and ownership to be effective, it must be responsive to local and global consumption practices and also recognize new and evolving media practices. It must also critically reflect on its mandate and purpose and its ability to achieve those goals in the current social environment.

Bibliography

Avison, S., and M. Meadows. 2000. "Speaking and Hearing: Aboriginal Newspapers and the Public Sphere in Canada." *Canadian Journal of Communication* 25(3), http://www.cjc-online.ca/viewarticle.php?id=586&layout=html.

Canada. House of Commons. Standing Committee on Canadian Heritage. 2003. "Our Cultural Sovereignty. The Second Century of Canadian Broadcasting." Ottawa: Communication Canada Publishing.

CRTC [Canadian Radio-television and Telecommunications Commission.] 1991. Broadcasting Act, www.crtc.gc.ca/eng/LEGAL/BROAD.htm.

——. 1999. Public hearing on third language and ethnic programming, http://www.crtc.gc.ca/eng/PROC_BR/Transcripts/1999/c012999(montreal.html) (accessed 2 January 1999).

Hume, Mark, and Geoffrey York. 2005. "The Day the Net Became a Worldwide Lifeline." *Globe and Mail*, 7 January, A5.

Mah, S. 2001. *Inclusive and Exclusive Spaces: A Look at Ethnic Television in Canada.* Ottawa: Carleton University.

Qui, H. 1999. *From Five Lakes and Four Seas: Online Expatriate Chinese Student Magazines and Community Mobilization.* Carleton University, Ottawa.

Statistics Canada. 2000. Percentage of registered voters who voted in federal elections, 1980–2000, http://www.statcan.ca/english/freepub/89F0123XIE/00002/32.htm (accessed 18 July 2004).

——. 2004. Cable and satellite television, 2002. *Innovation Analysis Bulletin* 6(1): 17, http://www.statcan.ca/cgi-bin/downpub/listpub.cgi?catno=88-003-XIE2004001 (accessed 18 July 2004).

Taylor, C. 1994. *Multiculturalism: Examining the Politics of Recognition.* Princeton, NJ: Princeton University Press.

Notes

1   The Canadian Radio-television and Telecommunications Commission has segregated Aboriginal television and French television programming gover-

nance from ethnic minority television. Aboriginal television and French-language television are currently governed by the Broadcasting Act.

2   The CRTC's review was held in five of Canada's large urban centres: Vancouver, Winnipeg, Toronto, Montreal, and Halifax. Many ethnic minority individuals, organizations, and media groups attended these hearings to comment on the state of ethnic minority broadcasting.

3   The tsunami disaster of December 26, 2004, saw individuals from around the world connect, express their horror, and generously give to relief organizations (Hume and York 2005).

Notes on Contributors

MARIA BAKARDJIEVA is an associate professor in the Faculty of Communication and Culture at the University of Calgary. She is the author of *Internet Society: The Internet in Everyday Life* (Sage, 2005) and co-editor of the first collection of *How Canadians Communicate* (Calgary, 2003). She studies communication media in context, considering the role of users in shaping the related technologies and social practices. Her current projects focus on Internet use in the home and in rural communities.

BART BEATY is an associate professor in the Faculty of Communication and Culture at the University of Calgary. He is the author of *Fredric Wertham and the Critique of Mass Culture* (Mississippi), *Unpopular Culture: Transforming the European Comic Book in the 1990s* (Toronto), and *Canadian Television Today* (Calgary, 2006).

DARREN BLAKEBOROUGH is a PhD student in Communications Studies at the University of Calgary. He earned his master of arts degree at the University of Calgary in 2004 with a thesis that explored representations of aging on television's *The Simpsons*. His current research looks at direct-to-consumer advertising of pharmaceuticals in Canada, addressing both representations and policy with their implications for our nation's aged.

HELEN CLARKE is Head of Collections Services at the University of Calgary Library. She is the current Chair of the Resource Selection Committee of the Lois Hole Campus Alberta Digital Library and has served on the Evaluation Task Group of the Canadian Research Knowledge Network.

CHRISTOPHER DORNAN is an associate professor in the School of Journalism and Communication at Carleton University. His research interests include the Canadian news media and journalism as a cultural form. Currently, he is an Erasmus Mundus fellow at the Danish School of Journalism in Aarhus and at City University, London.

KEN GOLDSTEIN is president of Communications Management Inc., the consulting firm he established in 1975. His professional and research interests include the economics of the mass media, the impact of new technology on the media, and the history of the media in Canada.

GEORGINA GROSENICK is a PhD candidate at the Carleton University School of Journalism and Mass Communication. She completed her MA at the University of Calgary in the Communication and Culture program. Her research seeks insight into the role, relationship, and opportunities available to non-profit volunteer organizations through the mass media and their ability to influence and advocate on public policy issues relevant to their mandates.

SHERYL N. HAMILTON is an associate professor in the School of Journalism and Communication and the Department of Law, and the Canada Research Chair in Communication, Law and Governance at Carleton University. Her research interests include: intellectual property, technology and culture, media and gender, and cultural studies of law.

MICHAEL KEREN is a professor and Canada Research Chair in the Faculty of Communication and Culture and the Department of Political Science at the University of Calgary. His research interests are political theory and political communication. His most recent books include *Zichroni v. State of Israel: The Biography of a Civil Rights Lawyer, The Citizen's Voice: Twentieth Century Politics and Literature,* and *Blogosphere: The New Political Arena.*

STEPHEN KLINE is a professor in the School of Communication at Simon Fraser University, a co-author of *Digital Play* (McGill-Queen's, 2003), *Social Communication in Advertising* (Routledge, 2005) and *Researching Audiences* (Arnold, 2003). His research interests include children's media culture; video gaming, media, and consumer literacy; and advertising design and persuasion in social, political, and consumer advertising messages.

GRAHAM LONGFORD is a post-doctoral research fellow in the Faculty of Information Studies, University of Toronto, and an executive member of the SSHRC-funded Canadian Research Alliance for Community Innovation and Networking (CRACIN). Dr. Longford's research interests include community networking, e-democracy, and theories and practices of digital citizenship, and his work has been published in journals such as *Techne, Polity, Citizenship Studies*, the *Journal of Community Informatics*, and the *Canadian Journal of Communication*, as well as in various edited collections. Dr. Longford's most recent funded research project is the Community Wireless Infrastructure Research Project (CWIRP), which is studying community-based wireless broadband infrastructure provision in Canada.

SHARON MAH is a PhD candidate in Communications Studies at the University of Calgary. She completed her master of arts degree at Carleton University on ethnic television and the Canadian ethnospheres. Currently in her dissertation she is collaborating with First Nations communities from rural and remote Alberta to examine the role of telehealth/telemedicine in health care services as a means of shaping technology design, health care practice, and health care policy.

DAVID MITCHELL is professor and associate dean (Research and Graduate Programs) in the Faculty of Communication and Culture at the University of Calgary. He is also academic director of the Centre for Information and Communication within the Van Horne Institute and lead applicant of the SSHRC-INE Alberta SuperNet Research Alliance project.

FRITS PANNEKOEK is professor of History, and president of Athabasca University. His research interests include Metis history, digital environments, and public policy. His current projects include investigation of information-seeking behaviours in the SuperNet environment, a major Metis digitization project, and a review of public post-secondary education policy.

YVONNE POITRAS PRATT is a PhD student in Communications Studies at the University of Calgary. She earned her master of arts degree at the University of Calgary in 2005. Her applied research at the master's level explored the role of action-oriented approaches to communications development in three Aboriginal communities. Her doctoral work continues to concentrate

on empowering these marginalized communities to take an active role in the
adoption of new media and/or broadband technologies.

MARC RABOY is full professor and Beaverbrook Chair in Ethics, Media, and
Communications in the Department of Art History and Communication
Studies at McGill University. His research focuses on Canadian and global
media policy issues. From 2001 to 2003 he served (with David Taras) as expert
advisor to the House of Commons Standing Committee on Canadian Heritage for its study of Canadian broadcasting. His most recent book (with Nor-
mand Landry) is *Civil Society, Communication and Global Governance: Issues
from the World Summit on the Information Society* (Peter Lang, 2005).

RICHARD SCHULTZ is a James McGill Professor in the Department of Political Science at McGill University. His primary research interests are Canadian political economy and public policy, particularly telecommunications
and broadcasting regulation. He recently served as a researcher for both the
House of Commons and Senate committees undertaking studies of the Canadian broadcasting sector. He is currently writing a book with Hudson Janisch
entitled *Contested Networks: The Political Transformation of Canadian Telecommunications, 1976–1994.*

WILL STRAW is associate professor within the Department of Art History and
Communications Studies at McGill University. His research focuses on the
music industry, tabloid newspapers, and urban culture. He is the author of the
forthcoming *Popular Music: Scenes and Sensibilities* (Duke, 1997).

REBECCA SULLIVAN is an associate professor of Communications at the University of Calgary. She specializes in the area of feminist media and cultural
studies. She is the author of *Visual Habits: Nuns, Feminism and American
Postwar Popular Culture* (Toronto, 2005), and the co-author with Bart Beaty
of *Canadian Television Today* (Calgary, 2006).

RICHARD SUTHERLAND is a PhD candidate in Communications Studies at
McGill. His research is concerned with the Canadian sound recording industry and with cultural policy – the result of a number of years working in the
Canadian recording industry. He currently teaches in the Faculty of Communication and Culture at the University of Calgary.

DAVID TARAS is professor in the Faculty of Communication and Culture and
director of the Alberta Global Forum at the University of Calgary. He served

as an expert advisor to the House of Commons Standing Committee on Canadian Heritage and co-authored most recently *The Last Word: Media Coverage of the Supreme Court of Canada* (UBC, 2006).

ANDREW WALLER is serials librarian at the University of Calgary Library where he oversees the serials collection. His areas of interest include e-journals, journal packages, electronic product licensing, scholarly communication, especially Open Access, and the effects of information-related legislation on libraries and researchers. He regularly speaks and writes on these issues.